Sociability and Society

SOCIABILITY AND SOCIETY

Literature and the Symposium

K. Ludwig Pfeiffer

Stanford University Press
Stanford, California

STANFORD UNIVERSITY PRESS
Stanford, California

English translation © 2023 by the Board of Trustees of the Leland Stanford Junior University. All rights reserved. *Sociability and Society* was originally published in German in 2021 under the title *Das Symposion. Sozialer Zusammenhalt in Geschichte und Literatur* © 2021, Velbrück Wissenschaft.

No part of this book may be reproduced or transmitted in any form or by any means, electronic or mechanical, including photocopying and recording, or in any information storage or retrieval system without the prior written permission of Stanford University Press.

Printed in the United States of America on acid-free, archival-quality paper

ISBN 9781503630987 (Cloth)
ISBN 9781503634848 (Paper)
ISBN 9781503634855 (Ebook)
Library of Congress Control Number 2022022172
CIP data available upon request.

Cover design: Steve Kress
Cover image: Helen Lessore, *Symposium I*, painting, 1974–77, 1680 × 2137 mm, Tate, England. © The Estate of Helen Lessore.
Typeset by Motto Publishing Services in 10/15 Sabon LT

Contents

Acknowledgments vii

Introduction

1

PART 1
Dimensions of the Symposium: Theoretical and Historical

CHAPTER 1
Conceptualizing the Symposium

11

CHAPTER 2
Power and Signs of Power in the Middle Ages

41

CHAPTER 3
Sociability and the Humanities

53

PART 2
Modernization and Social Gatherings

CHAPTER 4
The Splintering of Culture: Reading versus Salon

79

CHAPTER 5
Proust and Nineteenth-Century Salons

96

CHAPTER 6
The Silence of Power: English Clubs, or Oligarchy versus Democracy
105

CHAPTER 7
A Symptomatology of Critical Shifts
116

PART 3
Sympotic Relics: Secrets and Literature

CHAPTER 8
Securing Power and Auxiliary Evidence
157

CHAPTER 9
The Paradigm of Isolation and Its Consequences: Joseph Conrad
182

CHAPTER 10
Beyond the Sympotic:
Aesthetic Productivity and Sociable Bonding in the Detective Novel
200

CHAPTER 11
Consequences and Conclusion(s): The Anthropological-Institutional Trap and the Resurrection of Literature
230

Notes 245
Bibliography 263
Index 277

Acknowledgments

This book owes its existence to various coincidences. It all began with my decision, for no particular reason, to reread (or rather to read thoroughly for the first time) Jacob Burckhardt's history of ancient Greek culture. In this long book, Burckhardt appeared to devote an inordinate amount of attention to the symposium, the drinking ritual in ancient Athens. He saw the symposium as the most important institution for the formation of the Greek spirit and the cohesion of Athens society, an institution both social and sociable in nature. This made me look for texts on sociability. The best I could find was Georg Simmel's theory of sociability, initially developed in his inaugural lecture for the first meeting of the German Sociological Society in 1910 and later part of his *Grundfragen der Soziologie* (Basic questions of sociology [1917]), a text that subsequently went out of print for decades.

I had hardly finished these texts when, some years ago and owing to partly surprising factors (the embarrassing defeat of the German soccer team by 0 to 6 against Spain, among the three worst defeats in the long history of the national soccer team; the fact that butcheries and bakeries went out of business in large numbers; global crises unheard of before with a strong impact on national and local societies, such as the Covid pandemic), fears and complaints were spreading that social cohesion in Germany, and by and large elsewhere too, was in jeopardy. Assuming that crises may always look threatening and perhaps more than challenging for the times in which they occur, was there something like coping devices in the symposium that later social and sociable institutions did not possess or had lost?

Venturing into such fields of inquiry posed daunting risks for me, since I am neither a sociologist nor a classical scholar. On the classical side, though, the contact and exchange with Oswyn Murray (Balliol College, Oxford) was eye-opening. Even so, I had to rely heavily on the evidence provided by my own field, that is to say, literature. I could not have done so without the crucial support of Hans Ulrich Gumbrecht, especially with respect to this Stanford edition, which in some parts differs quite noticeably from the original German edition published by Velbrueck in 2021. Over the years and decades my indebtedness to Gumbrecht ("Sepp") has taken on such enormous dimensions that it is now, as it were, beyond gratitude. At Stanford University Press, I had the additional good luck of encountering a rare combination of professionalism and benevolence in Erica Wetter, to whom I am very grateful indeed. Thanks in this respect are also due to Caroline McKusick and her efficiency. On the European side, I had the good fortune to enjoy, together with encouragement from some German friends and colleagues (Profs. Peter Gendolla, Ralf Schnell, and Klaus Vondung), the intellectual stimulation and sociable hospitality of the Villa Vigoni, the German-Italian Centre for the European Dialogue on Lake Como.

As I am a German scholar, my English needed to be subjected to rigorous scrutiny. I am deeply grateful to Michael Lackey, Distinguished McKnight University Professor at the University of Minnesota, Morris, for having shouldered, in the midst of more than many other obligations, that time-consuming task, in which Phil Mothershaw, Brigitte Pichon Kalau vom Hofe, and Dorian Rudnytsky were also involved; Michael's great act of kindness provides me with an occasion to reminisce about twenty years of collaboration and friendship with great pleasure. Equally pleasurable for me has been the cooperation (if the word is appropriate—it was she who did the work in the spirit and commitment of superb conscientiousness) of Karin Sekora, who, for both the German and the American editions, took meticulous care of the complex task of bringing the text into publishable shape. With regard to the US copyediting side, I simply had no choice but to admire the rare combination of the amount, quality, and precision of work demonstrated by Christine Gever. Gretchen Otto, the production editor, shepherded the book through the production process with sovereign competence. Warm thanks also go to the Stanford team that produced the cover design and to my classmate, namesake, and friend Peter and his daughter who found its source, the picture "Symposium" by Helen Lessore.

Finally, I am very much obliged to my wife, Fumiyo Ido-Pfeiffer, who rose to the challenge of running what we came to call the Pfeiffer secretariat with great efficiency, devotion, and indeed enthusiasm for the cause (perhaps even for the man?).

Kronberg (Germany), April 2022
K. Ludwig Pfeiffer

Sociability and Society

Introduction

ON JUNE 12, 1823, Thomas Jefferson sent, among many other words, the following message to William Johnson:

> The doctrines of Europe were that men in numerous associations cannot be restrained within the limit of order and justice, except by forces physical and moral wielded over them by authorities independent of their will. . . . We (the founders of the new American democracy) believe that man was a rational animal, endowed by nature with rights, and with an innate sense of justice, and that he could be restrained from wrong, and protected in right, by moderate powers.

Aldous Huxley quoted these lines in his *Brave New World Revisited* (1958). And he expanded on them, admitting that Jefferson was partly right but also asserting that he was partly wrong. Huxley maintained that democratic institutions are "devices for reconciling social order with individual freedom," that these devices, given "a fair chance" as "an indispensable prerequisite," might enable human beings to govern themselves. In modern times, the biggest threat against this human self-empowerment must be ascribed to the press and the mass media. It must be ascribed to the trajectory (as Huxley probably would have said were he still alive) from propaganda to fake news or, as he did in fact say, in their being "in the main [concerned] neither with the true nor the false, but with the unreal, the more or less totally irrelevant."[1]

Today the situation is much more complex and unstable. Modern societies, many thinkers hold, absolutely need the mass media; after only one month without the media great nations would dissolve into tribal societies, into tiny heaps of clans and village economies.[2] Correct as that assumption may be, I doubt that many people are worrying about it. In 2020/21, the Covid pandemic, by contrast, appears to have tested and challenged the cohesive stamina, the "resilience," of modern societies in much more threatening and visible ways. It has accelerated my enterprise in this book, although it has not supplied its deeper motivation.

Huxley's *Brave New World* came out in 1931. In this book, we are introduced to a "world state," with the world controller Mustapha Mond at the top and the motto "community, identity, stability." In a new preface in 1946, Huxley claimed that the speed with which the world was approaching the utopian (or rather dystopian) conditions featured in his book was much more rapid than he had assumed back in 1931. In the 1958 book, owing to the combined impact of overpopulation, inflated organization, propaganda, and the arts of selling, brainwashing, and chemical and subconscious persuasion, as well as hypnopedia, modern societies had taken another giant step toward dystopia.

I've written the present volume to demonstrate that it is rather the contrary that is the case. True enough: the *kind* of chemically produced and maintained individual and social stability depicted in *Brave New World* must appear like a nightmare to us. But this is not our situation; instead we are suffering from other forms of instability, from what Anthony Giddens has called "the consequences of modernity." This means that an ever-radicalized "disembedding" or in fact disappearance of most of the institutions of yore has been taking place. Institutions have gone that "in the world we have lost" (Peter Laslett) seemed to guarantee a more or less stable or at least standardized life in which risks (natural disasters, war, illness) were well known. While ruling dynasties might change, there was no talk then of failing states such as we have been used to since the beginning of the 1990s. In general, according to Giddens, "the world in which we live today is a fraught and dangerous one."[3]

The present volume, however, does not aim at a mere illustration of Giddens's thesis. From the vantage point of today, it is not too difficult to see that Jefferson and Huxley are right and wrong in their own ways. We are less troubled by the nightmare of an artificial social stability; rather, we have come to fear forces of disruption and disintegration from all kinds of "associations" (as Jefferson says, incidentally using the currently correct sociological term), small or big; local, regional, national, or international. In this respect, race and racism, for instance, as well as fanaticisms and violence, have become burning issues all over the world. In the Fortieth Anniversary Edition of C. Wright Mills's *The Sociological Imagination* (2000), Todd Gitlin castigated Mills for not having seen that "race has become so salient in American social structure as, at times, to drown out other contending forces."[4]

Our present situation, threatening as it may appear, is sometimes not without its comic aspects: in Germany, serious authors have expressed concerns about the decline of the national soccer team, which was seen as the last bulwark against social agony and anomie, after all the traditional guarantees of cohesion (the church, political parties, trade unions, regional grounding, etc.) had failed to provide even a minimum of social solidarity.

Again, this book is not a sociological treatise, which, to put it mildly, I would be ill qualified to write. Rather, I am using materials and evidence from literary, cultural, and social history for the sake of what at first glance looks like an improbable confrontation: a confrontation of that evidence of failure with the cohesive power that an ancient (Athenian) drinking party—the symposium—has exercised. I do not mean Plato's dialogue of that name but a gathering of fairly high-class Athenian males regularly engaging in drinking rituals embedded in and adorned by a rich array of other exercises in cultural and personal pleasure. The book tries to explore the question of whether there have been, throughout cultural history, institutions capable of deploying similar achievements to those accomplished by the Athenian symposium. Without falling victim to apocalyptic thought, we might assume that an answer of no to that question would not bode well for modern societies. Certainly, to say this right at the beginning, no institution of what is called, by Georg Simmel and others, *sociability* can function as a totally successful antidote or panacea against social division. But the structure and spirit of sociable interaction can do a lot.

Methodologically, I have been inspired, in spite of disowning any sociological responsibility and in the face of Gitlin's criticisms above, by C. Wright Mills. His plea for a sociological imagination is less indebted to and "not at all expressed by sociologists." Rather, he thought, in England for instance, the sociological imagination is well developed in journalism, fiction, drama, poetry, and "above all history." Perhaps, he suggested, the term "human disciplines" would do in order to suggest that "fluidity of boundaries" in which the tensions between private-personal and public-social dimensions are acted out.[5]

In various ways, sociologists have certainly conceptualized relations between these dimensions. Taking George Herbert Mead as an American pioneer in that field, one can only admire the sophistication he brings to bear on the ways in which an individual person grows into a part of the social domain. One might be struck even more, however, when one becomes aware of a sensibility in, let us say, his unofficial writings (collected in the Mead Project's Foundational Documents in Sociological Social Psychology) that goes beyond the conceptual makeup of his official work. Thus, in a speech on the death of a colleague, the labor historian Robert F. Hoxie, in 1916, Mead has the following to say:

> It was because he [Hoxie] felt the forces, the impulses, and the subconscious valuations that lay back of the outer conduct and speech of those in the struggle, that he could comprehend them. He had an emotional realization of the issues that were at stake. And as long as these are essential elements of the social problem, no man for whom these elements do not exist can scientifically state the problem, and they cannot exist for the man who does not feel them. That is, the man who does not bring an equipment of emotional response to the study of a social problem cannot get all that goes to make up that problem. Mr. Hoxie had that rare combination of intellectual acumen, scientific conscience, and emotional response which made him able to make his own, the problem of labor, that central problem of our industrial age.[6]

It does not matter much whether my assertion that Mead's official theory and a more intimate discourse are drifting apart is correct or not. The mere suspicion made me look for a theoretical and indeed sociological framework and a cultural historian of the symposium in whom such a sensibility is quite openly there. The theoretical framework embodying and displaying that sensibility was provided by Georg Simmel. In his opening speech for the first German meeting of professional sociologists and elsewhere, he introduced the crucial distinction between social and society on the one hand, sociable and sociability on the other. The nineteenth-century cultural historian Jacob Burckhardt in his turn was the one who dared to assert that the symposium made for the "happiness of life" (*Lebensglück*) of ancient Athenian society. For similar reasons of conceptual range and emotional transparency, I have placed quite some emphasis on German philosophical anthropology, in which the full range from the biological to the spiritual and social existence of human beings is examined. More on that later.

In any case, the happiness of a relatively exclusive elite of ancient Athenians does not seem to be of great import for us and our woes. Its importance seems to shrink further once we consider the trivialization the word *symposium* has undergone in the course of its history. The joys of drinking, to say nothing of its accompanying pleasures, have mostly given way to somewhat dubious conferences—dubious because of the perks with which, very often, specific groups of people are baited, coupled with the expectation of some reciprocity for the donors. And yet the assumption that an Athens-style symposium has become irrelevant is wrong. It is true that the *Oxford English Dictionary* does not seem to see more than a "transferred sense" at work in this history, but this sober judgment hides a sociocultural dynamics of considerable importance.

The importance is concealed in the seemingly harmless distinction between "social" and "sociable" mentioned above. The Athenian symposium is a sociable ritual; its communicative modes are bathed in an intense corporeality, both literal and metaphorical. It depends on and produces "presence" in the sense developed by Hans Ulrich Gumbrecht.[7] In such contexts, sociability leads to social (and political) repercussions that have turned it into a very important—some would think the most important—event in the ordering of the affairs of the ruling elite and the recruitment of new members in ancient Athens. It is the task of this book to find out whether later history has any analogies to offer in this respect.

The task seems hopeless, the number of possible candidates either well-nigh infinite or zero. Difficulties seem to begin with the fact that the symposium in classical and later Athens was a drinking event. Yet it is impossible to accept that restriction; eating, in most cases, cannot be excluded. Objections on that count are pointless anyway, even in the case of Athens: the Athenians, to be sure, were able to concentrate on drinking because they had eaten before. The symposium can therefore be taken as the "classical" example of a ritualized event for a relatively small group for whom it provided crucial functions of psychosocial bonding. By ritualization I mean a cultural "program" (recitals, games, etc.) in which bonding is strengthened. Here I am not concerned with its history but with its potential transformations over the course of history. The range of plausible transformations depends on sociopolitical frameworks that encourage or impede their emergence, a list of possibilities that could not be drawn up beforehand. Oswyn Murray, the great historian of antiquity, has stated the problem and its opportunities very clearly:

> We should not doubt that the rituals of the bourgeois dinner party, the formal western public or fraternity banquet, the Sunday family lunch,

the English pub or the continental café, the Japanese tea-drinking ceremony, even the negative pole of the Temperance League, have complex relations to the societies that practice them.[8]

In many cases, it will be impossible to decide whether the connection between a sociable event and its social relevance can be established or not. Thus, today the regulations of the Society for the Humanities at Cornell University make the following demands with respect to fellowships: "The nature of this fellowship year is social and communal—Fellows forge connections outside the classroom and the lecture hall by sharing meals following weekly seminars and attending post-lecture receptions and other casual events throughout the year." Here, "communal" is the crucial term, with its implications being that the social relevance and reach of sociability are blurred.

People today may not (and I certainly do not) have sufficient experience to assess the relationship, absent or present, of social and sociable elements in modern digital social media such as Snapchat (where "presence" definitely seems absent but might be recuperated later on) or in festivals such as Burning Man. The latter, lasting up to ten days, has been organized since 1986 with enormous success, as indicated by a tremendously increasing number of participants (from twenty to seventy thousand, thus dwarfing Woodstock). Burning Man aims at nothing less than the squaring of a social-psychological circle: the reconciliation of radical individualism and the strong bonding of communitarianism. For that purpose, a plethora of ritualized and aestheticized events are staged, in which both individual desires and a strengthening of interpersonal ties are supposedly getting their due. Relatedly, one might find modern clubs (in Berlin or Cologne) in which the organized virtuosity of presence and pleasure (dancing and more) has been pushed to new frontiers. Here, however, the social dimension appears to have evaporated in the self-referentiality of pleasure. We will see, however, that there are characteristic "middle-range" examples, such as the French salon, the (traditional) British clubs, or the modern party, in which the rewards of investigation should not be in doubt.

I have tried to minimize the dangers of constituting and selecting a body of evidence by using literature, both cautiously and resolutely, as a source of relevant knowledge. This is evidently risky because it is difficult to determine the literary form(s) of knowledge: "*literature*," as the motto in Peter Ackroyd's *The Plato Papers* has it, "a word of unknown provenance, generally attributed to 'litter' or 'waste.'"[9] Quite a few professors of English literature have argued that eighteenth-century British literature is very interesting in a purely literary sense but appears to be stuck in a position of strange social aloofness, missing out on the crucial realities of the time. Earlier and later, even Shakespeare and Dickens have come under similar fire.

But, on the other hand, the same Dickens has been nominated, by fellow writer (and painter) Wolfgang Hildesheimer, somewhat in the vein of C.≈Wright Mills, for the title of best nineteenth-century sociologist. The German philosopher, sociologist, and anthropologist Arnold Gehlen, who will play an important part in this book, has credited top modern novelists such as Marcel Proust, Thomas Mann, Robert Musil, and others with an acumen and acuity of thought that one would like to see in more professional philosophers. Caught in the midst of such conflicting arguments, I prefer to raise the stakes and propose an even riskier assumption located between the notion of literature as a mirror and the assertion of its autonomy. Literature certainly is not catching, representing, or dealing with something like raw realities. That is why literary theorists have talked about a "vocabulary of reality" (Hermann Broch), a "repertoire" and its referential system" (Wolfgang Iser) or "presupposed situations" (Siegfried J. Schmidt) not depicted but *exploited* for cognitive purposes of some kind.[10] I claim that the sympotic tension between the social and the sociable has accumulated, throughout history, a particularly rich mine of such literary "presuppositions." Literature can interfere with, handle, and transform them. Hidden in such procedures, the problem, hardly dealt with in literary theory, of the representational dignity of the presuppositions looms large. By and large, literature stands in dire need of presuppositions both precise and complex, stable and dynamic, concrete and abstract; only then do we get models of rational and emotional intensity as minimal but open guarantees of reality. Without them literature degenerates into *l'art pour l'art*—the sophisticated croaking of frogs despairing in their swamps (Nietzsche)—or into ideology. Such problems come to a head in the detective novel, which will therefore play a conclusive role in this book: for some, it is the patron saint of triviality; for others, such as Umberto Eco (but indirectly also for Luc Boltanski), it is the last haven of metaphysics.

The makeup of this book is fairly straightforward. After some more remarks in the theoretical and historical vein, a sweeping picture of the Middle Ages will present a first test. Because of the famous otherness of that period, the test is not an easy one. I have therefore used an opportunity in the writings of Jacques Le Goff for a comparison subsequently expanded into the role of the humanities in more general terms, including a longer evaluation of philosophical anthropology. The analysis moves on into the (mainly English and French) eighteenth century with a significant bifurcation into solitary reading and sociable forms of performance. Then the development of the French salon, emphasizing the central importance of the picture drawn by Marcel Proust, shows plenty of evidence that the bells have begun to toll for sympotic forms still deserving that name. In the traditional British club and the international role of the party, the tolling of the bells comes full circle. Processes of sociopolitical modernization cause the scene to change drastically. Sympotic evidence must be laboriously gleaned from psychological pressures such as confession and secrecy. It appears to be drowned in secret societies and socially overbearing forms of (political and other) crime. Ultimately, the detective novel takes over. In conjunction with a final sketch of philosophical anthropology, the detective novel signals the end of socially relevant forms of sociability—and, at the same time, opens up intimations of its renewal under totally different auspices.

PART I

Dimensions of the Symposium
Theoretical and Historical

CHAPTER 1
Conceptualizing the Symposium

JACOB BURKHARDT'S USE of the term "happiness" for the achievement or the function of the symposium in ancient Athens must and can be reformulated.[1] What he means is that the symposium brings about, in the participants, a feeling of inner affinity and solidarity, perhaps even affection. This does not at all exclude aggressive and competitive behavior in ordinary social life (to say nothing about enemies from the outside, of which there were plenty). That such a feeling exists, and then is mostly called sympathy, was asserted, probably for the last time in unambiguous terms, by eighteenth-century philosophical and economic thinkers such as David Hume and Adam Smith. For that period, however, the assumption already looked like an emergency measure mobilized against the inroads of social differentiation. It brought about a sharpening of class distinctions (in England already officially sanctioned by the Clarendon Code, 1661–1665, most of it repealed only in the nineteenth century), of economic pressures such as the beginning of the Industrial Revolution, the persistence of the slave trade, and on an entirely different plane, the delirium threatening an individual consciousness relying only on itself. Philosophers such as Axel Honneth have rephrased problems of community (loosely speaking) in terms of mutual recognition. I do not and cannot decide here to what extent such an approach can live up to theories of envy such as those of René Girard.[2]

Today, in any case, expecting an answer to questions about guarantees of social cohesion would be expecting too much from most people. In the mass media, the search for such guarantees has been pursued for quite some time at a frantic pace. The nation has degenerated into a figment of the imagination (an imagined community, in Benedict Anderson's terminology). The churches are losing members by the thousands. Smaller groups ("associations"), while they may, for instance, promote and produce local *sociable* events, can hardly claim any *social* scope. In Germany, serious newspapers have worried about the threat to social togetherness because during the past few years roughly 30 percent of local bakeries and butcheries have gone out of business.

The feeling that social structures are not enough has even invaded science. Philosophy of science has acknowledged that social and sociable factors may enter scientific work and results. For the Reality Club and the Edge Foundation of John Brockman, such general assertions were not enough. Edge.org brought together pioneers of science and business. A kind of common ground was achieved, for instance, by dinners where the participants could tell stories that highlight the common ground of their professional work. These practices have been compared to the knights of Arthurian legend and accordingly called "Round Tables of the Present." Brockman was promoted to the rank of "social alchemist," in charge of rearranging debating groups and of the common concerns possibly implicit in specialized scientific work.[3] He shut down his "scientific salon,"[4] however, after financial relations with Jeffrey Epstein were made public. We are not concerned here with individual guilt, but the fate of Brockman's Round Table does indicate to what extent efforts toward coherent reconstructions of the social-sociable kind are easily undermined by very problematic, in this case also heavily criminal, interests.

Luckily, this is not case with another high-level and comprehensive effort by eleven universities and research institutes in Germany. In March 2020, this group founded the Research Institute Social Cohesion under the overall control of Constance University. In a critical mood that may not do justice to the enterprise, one might object that the founders did not look closely enough at the *systemic* conditions that have already frequently marred giant research projects in the humanities. Communication in such institutions tends to splinter into an incoherent mass of opinions; their pluralism has very often tended toward nontransparency. It is not the pluralism recommended by the high-level German jurist Thomas Fischer, who has tried to stem the tide of an inflationary urge for social unity:

> This program, under the sign of unidirectionality, has always shown up in silly fairy tales of the unity of above and below, of serving and the duty towards the social whole, and of the many forms of identity. Violence there is not the exception, but its nature. Whoever preaches to the people, from the pulpits of harmony, about the terror of splits and the desire to overcome them in a great totality, may be asked, occasionally, whether she practices the devil's business better than the devil himself.[5]

Fischer's objections to the urge for totality are justified, but they do not touch the symposium of ancient Athens at all. Let me first elaborate on what, in comparison with our situation, the symposium is *not*. Living in the age of globalization, we must pose and repeat the question asked by Niklas Luhmann and others a long time ago. There is no real need to wonder about the impression that the unity of modern nations (which in most cases never existed anyway in any substantial sense) has been falling apart. There are the pressures of mass migration, of global financial transactions, of huge masses of merchandise taking on, in giant container ships, almost terrifying aspects. Finally, there are nontransparent events, happening somewhere and imposing effects everywhere, challenging understanding beyond any boundary. Luhmann's questions, therefore, whether modern societies (however defined or delimited) can have some unity at all do not allow for an unqualified yes. It is unlikely that beyond the confusing mass of social systems there emerges something like a "total social system" of "society." Whether, if it exists, it can be described best by concepts of communication is no longer clear.

In terms more precise than Luhmann's, his colleague Richard Münch has insisted on the necessity and the difficulty of social integration. The strength of integration wielded by modern nation-states has distinctly declined; "reality" has fallen apart into systemic processes of globalization and local or regional, in any case "provincial," forms of life. Societies can no longer be classified into tribal, traditional, and modern forms. Necessary forms of cohesion are not provided by either ideological, economic, or cultural agencies. Münch favors an integration through solidarity, but he does not tell us which sources might be tapped for its sake. Instead, he holds, correctly but somewhat uselessly, that sociological theories of integration are neither sufficient nor without value.[6]

On the occasion of Jürgen Habermas's ninetieth birthday on June 18, 2019, we were reminded of his slim but important volume on problems of legitimation in late capitalism.[7] For our purposes here, his examination of universal aspects of social systems is not important; the challenge of the book resides in its analysis of the logic of development in worldviews (extension of the secular domain, increasing autonomy, shift from tribal-particularistic to both universalistic and individualistic orientations, increasing reflexivity of faith).[8] It is mainly these factors that tax the steering capacities of modern societies to the utmost. Unfortunately, Habermas's analysis remains chained to the somewhat idealistic level of learning processes open to the criterion of truth and to increasing but somewhat vague insights both theoretical and practical. The investigation keeps a prudent distance from factual developments such as the handling of crises.[9] Empirical mechanisms remain shrouded in mystery.

Burckhardt's nineteenth-century job with the symposium, it would appear, was somewhat easier. He would talk without hesitation about the unity of "the Greek nation," stabilized above all by language and heroic myths.[10] Apart from cultural games and competitive but amicable performances, apart from physical proximity and interaction, participants could talk to each other about any kind of problem, including very intimate ones. The symposium turned into the best medium for the formation of the Greek "spirit," surpassing even the *agora* and its intensity of debate. In this fragmentary way, sociability was transformed into social and political relevance. There was no need for totalizing approaches and strategies, for globally valid results. The Athens symposium preserved its privileged position because, in the absence of sweeping claims, it managed and exemplified *informally* both bothersome questions of self-recruitment and the transition from a smaller sympotic-sociable group to social relevance within a much larger society. This is very different from what Habermas considers the fundamental question for modern societies: the continuing existence of a mode of socialization depending on the criterion of truth.[11] Habermas privileges the question whether the social system can produce its unity through the overlapping identity formation of its socialized individuals;[12] whereas ancient Athens preferred physical proximity and elastic debate, an issue that Habermas does not discuss. Clearly, with such questions, one is pushed into pathetic theories of individuality and its disappearance with which even Habermas does not feel comfortable. "Discussions of the splendor and misery of the bourgeois subject turn sour easily" because, after Hegel, it has become difficult to access the history of consciousness.[13]

On the other hand, physical proximity is also an unsatisfactory term. Yet the communicative-interactive positioning of the body belongs to the feeling of existence we are talking about here. This means that an assessment of the social-sociable binding strength will have to go beyond a notion of the personal defined in merely sociological or psychological terms. Consequently, I venture into a short digression here in order to exploit the body therapy theory of Moshé Feldenkrais.[14] This theory seems compatible with Gumbrecht's category of presence, with present-day neurobiology, and with Simmel's move from society into sociability. In doing so, we should not concern ourselves with Feldenkrais's opinion, seemingly contradicting my use of Burckhardt, that life has little or nothing to do with happiness—that is, with inner states of being happy. If that is meant as a denial in principle, I would deny that denial in my turn.

If that denial claims specific reasons, however, I might go along with it. Feldenkrais concedes that our civilization makes extremely crass and difficult demands in regard to our social adjustment and conformity. Therefore, we easily run into trouble when trying to perform all kinds of movement-based actions, especially sexual ones. A basic thesis of Feldenkrais, similar to Simmel's switch from the matter to the form of action (to which we will come in a moment), would indeed maintain that the manner of performing an action is more important than the content.[15] Good performance paired with easy execution entails the relaxation and serenity of the mind and the harmony of body tension and emotion. Thus a positive attitude of the body will result in fast, fluid, and effortless action, an action incompatible with an excessive tension of the muscles and violent emotions.[16] In such a case, creative thought reinforces a connection with older brain structures.[17] The ordinary norms and practices of a society, on the other hand, will usually evoke external or alien motivations, throttling performance even in the case of routinized action.

In the symposium, the ease of talk and interaction does not rule out intensity. I strongly suspect that this could be called an aftereffect of the situation in the *Iliad*, diminished in but not eliminated from the *Odyssey*, in which individual action and movement do not result from conscious will and intention: rather, it is a god, goddess, or demon who, the person thinks, is telling him what to do.[18]

Now, we cannot expect that the symposium would habitually produce literal applications or transformations or illustrations of Feldenkraisian theorems. But if we look at Murray for the sake of comparison or perhaps confirmation, we find the same idea, attributed to the ancient Greeks, of a bodily based cheerfulness (*euphrosyne*). *Euphrosyne* suggests, very strongly it would appear, a cheerful self-experience on a physical or physiological basis of easily, smoothly, and well-done body movements. Up to the end of the classical age this experience is interpreted as a parallelism of spiritual and bodily pleasure. Aristotle's conception of human beings as *polis*-animals is valid only if we can presuppose an bioethical theory that grants us the possibility that all human potentials can indeed be brought to full fruition.[19] According to this framework the symposium attains the rank of a core form of sociability even if many later, Hellenistic forms may deviate from it.

Feldenkrais is not directly interested in pleasure. But a pleasurable sensation may take hold of us if social risks are minimized or if action is conspicuous by its performative excellence or virtuosity. A possible action is really at our disposal in case we like to do it and can do it easily. Ritualization is a means to facilitate a well-formed and well-executed action. We may assume that this was the case for the symposium. A strongly willed urge to reach the goal without the preparation of physical ability as quickly as possible can produce the frustrating opposite.[20] If this happened in the symposium, the offender would be met with derisive laughter. The symposium did not, however, or only rarely or in a late stage, adopt a Dionysiac, ecstatic model of behavior that has flooded parts of society throughout history. Nor did the symposium tolerate intoxication—a decent man had to be able to walk home without help. In Aldous Huxley's theory of a human need for self-transcendence, upward (religion, often music), sideways (some cause), and downward (*The Devils of Loudun*, 1952), intoxication is described as well-nigh universal (Huxley, slightly misquoting A. E. Housman, says that "beer does more than Milton can to justify God's ways to man" [*Devils of Loudun*, 315]). But it is a self-transcendence of the "downward" kind. The symposium, by contrast, does not fit neatly into Huxley's typology. If squeezed into it, it would come close to the horizontal, the sideways form of self-transcendence that, for Huxley himself, must accommodate a multifarious collection of commitments from trivial or precious hobbies to research in physics, from running a business to composing music. For Huxley, horizontal self-transcendence, although in itself mostly good, must be made even better by an upward, that is, a spiritual tendency. The symposium, with its elements of ritual and of the various arts, holds the potential for that.[21]

Generally, ancient Greek models of human nature are characterized by a side by side of different, often heterogeneous or even, from a modern perspective, contradictory qualities. The coexistence of reason and madness provides perhaps the best example. Burckhardt has evoked the aggressive ("agonistic") and competitive quality of both interior interaction and foreign politics in very eloquent terms.[22] His invocation of happiness as an experience of social cohesion is, if anything, even more frequent and eloquent. I have selected the symposium as that institution in which happiness is experienced as an occasional, bodily grounded communicative state by which social cohesion is tacitly established. This is the core thesis of this book. Its core question follows in a relatively direct way: Can we identify, for later societies, institutional analogies of this crucial element in the upper, politically prominent parts of a population?

Even if we want to look only for the beginning of an answer, a few more obstacles must be cleared out of the theoretical way. I take it that systems sociologists are right in asserting that there is no communication outside the communication system of a society. But what kind of system, what kind of society are we talking about? Apparently, both system and society can vary a great deal. This, again, would justify the assumption that if systems (of whatever kind) have to produce the elements they consist of as units or unities themselves, any basic common structure of the system is out of the question. We cannot decompose systems in order to discover ultimate substantial elements.[23] Even so, societies, however shaky the foundations, produce and reproduce themselves as social systems (223). They use language, media spreading information true or false, and "symbolically generated media" (a term coined by Niklas Luhmann, who names truth, love, property, money, power, and law, as well as perhaps basic values and a few more today, as candidates). This type of medium generalizes complex, often nontransparent matters and thus enables us to handle them in a kind of symbolic shorthand (222).

Clearly, language and the different types of media can only create units, to say nothing of unities, in precarious and provisional forms. The world surrounding a system (and we have to assume that such worlds exist) is not just an imaginary opposite number. But each system, if only because it removes itself from its environment, projects a different environment. A system perceiving what it takes to be its environment cannot see this environment as an operationally capable entity (249). It perceives itself as surrounded by an intractably complex mass that it cannot handle with its own tools. With respect to other people: Who dares, given the separation and individualization of their bodies and their consciousness, given the limited resources of their own memories and of their field of vision, to maintain that imagining the relevant contexts would suffice, against all odds, to understand them? (217). Society, Luhmann has stated peremptorily, can never make communication about anything and everything possible (249); even less can it enable us to fabricate consensus (237). Any word spoken or written down provokes one or several countermeanings pretty quickly (218).

Thus, the "happiness" in the symposium does not spring from understanding others and finding a consensus with them. But how then should one level out obvious discrepancies in character and complexity? How can one prevent them from creating havoc in interaction? By simply respecting the other person? Luhmann, for one, has seen precisely that this kind of ethos erodes very quickly in complex societies. Still, we go on defining discrepancies in moral terms, thereby following the example of a standard procedure in eighteenth-century novels; at the same time, codes for intimate relations are increasingly privatized and psychologized. Approaching social cohesion in such ways, then, is courting disaster (320–321).

Finally, failure looms large when we project such problems onto what is called world society today. National societies, to be sure, continue to exist, but they most certainly do not exist as closed, self-sufficient systems. This means that the gap between interaction and society can in no way be bridged anymore. No form of interaction can represent society. Accordingly, it has also become much more difficult to establish an upper class or a "good society" because any status reached can immediately be disputed. The effort, recommended by some, to renew social barriers, traditional status security, and the like by an appeal to institutions hallowed by age or so-called good sense does not work anymore.[24] It probably did not work in ancient Athens either: although there definitely was a ruling upper class that managed the symposium, the rules for admission and recruitment of new members and social ascent were anything but clear. Arnold Gehlen's recommendation, issued like an order without alternative, that individuals, whether high or low, should allow themselves to be "consumed" by institutions (state, family, economic and legal powers), in order to make up for their own weakness, will not work anymore. It fails because in most cases the legitimacy of many of these institutions is itself cast in doubt once charismatic authority, in Max Weber's sense, has lost its appeal.[25]

It appears, then, that we are confronted by a first provisional and uncomfortable conclusion. Society channels the opportunities for individual interaction, but it is itself the result of interaction. For systems theory, this double conditioning makes sociocultural evolution possible. But the decisive aspect of social evolution, in contrast to the biological one, consists in an immense increase in speed,[26] in an accelerated mass production. Instead of an inflation, to which societies are often helplessly exposed, we would need the filter of an ecology of interaction—a filter such as the symposium provided for classical Athens. In general, an ecology of interaction would find its place in the tension between two types of reality. One type is made up of elements the reality of which is only rarely called into doubt: classes or similar groupings, everyday processes without which we could hardly do, regularities on various levels. While there may be changes in these elements, of course, we would be sorely challenged if they occurred all the time. The other type of reality is the dynamic one, often called cultural, in which change is desirable, even necessary. Changes cannot always be profound (in which case we would speak of revolutions); they need not and should not shake the foundations of existence all the time. But some variation, creating the impression of novelty, is desirable if life, apart from sameness, is also meant to be interesting. Let us designate an important area within the first type *society*, and a crucial one in the second *sociability*.

Society and Sociability

However one may define society and sociability, there will always be frictions and tensions of some kind between the two. They cannot be neatly kept apart; they will always overlap in some ways. This does not mean, however, that there are always relations that deserve this name. The overlaps can be constructive, in which case the term "relations" would be apt, or they can be neutral or negative—that is, without relations to speak of. Occasionally society, in the form of authoritarian political power, can more or less crush sociability; or sociable groups may expand into political interest groups of no small influence. In the latter case, oligarchies can arise; their power, in present-day "democracies," is commonly underestimated.

In many cases, individual behavioral options are and have always been limited. We can seek and find groups whose activities chime in with our inclinations, although such luck is often spoiled by dominating egocentrics. Assuming dominating attitudes, claiming or pretending to be right or rather luring people into adopting such attitudes, can be called the operating principle of modern social media, whose raison d'être consists in giving people the feeling that their opinions count. But unless these opinions accumulate in the mass movement known as a "shitstorm," the opposite is the case. One may give up on such groups, instead exploiting the offerings of industries of self-referential pleasure in which contact with other people is superficial or merely pleasant while it lasts. The lengths to which behavior can go are not necessarily predetermined, however: getting into closer contact may be pleasant, but it is also risky. The picture has been painted, whether realistically or not, by many films: for example, Woody Allen's *Midnight in Paris* (2011), where Gertrude Stein tries to revive true sociable mutuality in her Paris salon. She fails because most of the characters, including Stein herself, are chained to the habit of confusing individualistic greed with models of mutuality. It is amusing to see Ernest Hemingway, of all people, give a most impressive speech on the mutuality of love. Older critics have opined that, in modern media generally, only forms of secondhand experience are available, so it is hard to say where and how we might find offers of experience that are both individually rewarding and socially significant. The title of this book, accordingly, functions as an abbreviation: it points to the difficult search for individually satisfactory forms of experience and action that stay in touch with transpersonal, systemic, and social realities.

The search appears to be so difficult, in fact, that the sociologist Stefan Bertschi, having discovered little evidence that sociology has even begun to tackle what he dubs the double stylization of behavior or the in-between of individual and society, has called it the blind spot of sociology. As far as I can judge, he himself has largely refrained from embarking on that search.[27] He discusses Georg Simmel's theory, refers to Simmel's short book on basic questions of sociology (subtitled "Individual and Society"), but neglects its third chapter on sociability almost completely. While Simmel may not have solved the problem, he offers alluring perspectives that might defuse the dilemma. Simmel adopts the strategy of making the concept of sociability emerge as it were by necessity from his analysis of society. It is symptomatic in that respect that Luhmann, too, although he sometimes uses Simmel concepts as building blocks for systems theory, does not take up Simmel's suggestions concerning sociability. Some of these concepts, such as tact, sophisticated conversation, culture as the competence to select and talk about possible topics that Luhmann thinks important in order to structure the domain of interaction, would evidently fall under Simmel's higher-order concept of sociability. (Incidentally, this is a concept that Burckhardt had already used in connection with his happiness theme [774].) It would certainly be wrong to say that Luhmann has written a sociology of society, while Simmel has privileged a sociology of sociability. But Simmel's priorities were on clear display when he opened the first meeting of professional German sociologists in 1910 in Frankfurt am Main with a talk on sociability. In Luhmann, the concept serves only for the analysis of suitable or improper topics for conversation, which, again, appears to have been a problem only for seventeenth- and eighteenth-century European salons.

Simmel, by contrast, has reserved a crucial function for his concept. It comes into play with the transformation of everyday practices (in the sense of the first reality mentioned above)—that is, the "directly concrete places of all historical reality"—into independent energies and forms. Simmel is driven by the basic social dynamics through which practical necessities, the "matter/materials of socialization" (49), are deprived of their practical service and elevated into playful and aesthetic forms with a value of their own. In the midst of society, a turn of the axis in the stuff of life's necessities takes place. In the redefinition of these materials, the "certainty of life-forms" by virtue of their dogmatic social materiality is transformed into higher aesthetic and existential values (51).

An aside is necessary here. Simmel's transformation of everyday practices into values of their own appears to be immediately relevant for literary theory as outlined in the Introduction. Sociability in Simmel's sense harbors an important literary potential in that it "preforms" material suitable then for literary treatment. This is because the transformation combines suggestions of reality with possible changes and alternatives. Literature can deploy methods to unite precision, such as the precision of metaphor, with complexity. Thinking along such lines would also help to explain breaks or opposed tendencies in literary production. What appear as breaks in the continuity of literary history are the variations of distance in the relations between society and sociability and the seeming autonomy of the economic-technological development revolution.

Although Simmel's concept of "a playful version of socialization" (*Spielform der Vergesellschaftung*, 53; German original in italics) may look somewhat unhistorical, his claims are far-reaching. Real "society," society proper, he asserts, consists in living with, for, and against each other; in this way material or individual contents are formed and promoted. "And now these forms gain a life of their own, they are freed from all their roots and practiced purely for their own sake and for the sake of the charm which they exude in this liberation. This is precisely the appearance of sociability" (52). People may form groups because of special necessities and interests in economic associations or blood brotherhoods, in cult associations, or in robber gangs. But beyond their special contents and obligations, these forms of socialization are accompanied "by a feeling of satisfaction . . . for the value of coming together as such, by an urgent drive towards this form of existence." This drive toward sociability removes the process of socialization from the "realities of social life and turns it into a value and into happiness" (52)! The greater the perfection of a merely formal relation to reality comes to be, the better will be "a symbolically playful abundance of life and a significance" for "deeper human being," a significance that the superficial person seeks to find only in the concrete contents (53).

It seems possible that Peter Sloterdijk had something like Simmel's sociability in mind (without using the concept) when he wrote certain parts of his monumental trilogy *Spheres*. Its first part insists on the priority of a couple-type of relation independent both of special individual myths and of the elusive totality of society. The third part (*Foams*), by contrast, draws up an inventory of a presubjective and preobjective continuum of relations—that is, forms that are possible only in the mode of sociability, not within the domains of crude social power. For the pluralistic "spherology" of *Foams*, life is enacted in a plurality of spaces. Its contours emerge in loose contacts of cells touching each other; their foam-like combination is as flexible as it is fragile. Examples can be found in the agriculture of lots, in the stack architecture of apartments, and in air-conditioned hothouses, mobile-home settlements, and space capsules.

There is little to nothing to be objected to in that. But if one does not want to tacitly give up the notion of happiness and its relatives (abundance of life, pleasure, etc.), then a critic will quickly become aware of a conspicuous conceptual gap, both in Sloterdijk and, in retrospect, in Simmel. The latter describes the transformation of heavy social materials and deeply rooted 'individual' peculiarities into aesthetically playful forms of interaction; he does *not* describe the institutions in which this transformation takes place or could be tested. Sloterdijk's spherology, with its list of essential dimensions of the "anthroposphere," in its turn, does not sketch a profile that would show the forms and degrees of satisfaction ("happiness") that the different foams are capable of delivering. Quite apart from the fact that the formation of and bonds between couples are not enough in psychosocial respects, that they collide all too easily with official forms such as marriage, one would like to know whether, in the framework of the nine topoi or dimensions, phonotope, thermotope, uterotope, and erototope, for instance, are supposed to be of equal value. All four offer attractions: the phonotope people living together and listening to each other, the thermotope as a matrix of experiences of comfort, the uterotope the widening of the mothering zone with the feeling of belonging and a shared existential aura, the erototope as the place of primary erotic energies of transferral, etc. But all of them also display clear deficits, some mentioned by Sloterdijk himself, others easy to nail down (the erototope. for example, and its transformation into a field of jealousy under stress).[28] Institutions of sociability, however, should open up possibilities of satisfactory, desirable or pleasurable, and certainly stress-reduced experience if forms of cohesion are supposed to be welcome. The problem does not disappear even if the notion of happiness might not be available or appear naïve in the face of present-day standards of sophistication.

In *The Symposion*, the classicist Oswyn Murray tends to avoid the notion of happiness and has chosen the concept of pleasure instead.[29] But he has to confess that his treatment later (in the fifth part of the book) is only very tentative, since philosophically and historically helpful studies of pleasure are not really available.[30] Almost any activity today can be transformed into pleasure or be proclaimed as such. Yet conservatives can still maintain that such transformations are often made the victims of a consumerist manipulation or, worse, like the mask of a death wish.[31] Situating pleasure would need a counterpart: a coherent version of a political history of customs.[32]

In what follows, I hope to show that we do not have to leave the connotational sphere of happiness and pleasure if we cannot define these concepts precisely. It would also suffice to have a political history of customs in a very rough form only. I suspect (see also Chapter 7) that forms of pleasure have parted company with the history of custom and social questions of power: they have been reduced to self-referential technologies.

In that respect, the validity of Simmel's perfection of the merely formal sociable relation to a social reality in which the individual probes her own depth becomes doubtful too. The weight of social norms and materials does not simply disappear but rather asserts itself in smaller or bigger residues. Accordingly, my topic must be read also in a redefined form: How does a society assure itself of its cohesion in the manifold, dynamic, and centrifugal forms of its sociable institutions? Or is it still enough if "society" creates artificial stress for its members in order to push and force them into some kind of obedience to the norms?

The Symposium as Paradigm

It would be pointless to carp at Burckhardt's and Simmel's talk about happiness and the abundance of life. Consistent conceptual criticism would be ill chosen, if merely because not all forms of ancient symposia (e.g., Spartan *syssition*) can be characterized that way. The tension between society and sociability hides matters of existential import that also seem to be absorbed by social structures no longer transparent. We have to get used to the problem in shapes in which its conceptual makeup is exposed to contradictory demands. In Simmel, the practices of sociability are supposed to touch deep personal and existential layers but have also to be able to swerve into more superficial and playful forms; thus, they keep open the road back into society. Simmel himself calls that "a very strange sociological structure" (*Grundfragen der Soziologie*, 54).[33] Real interests of social profit in the service of wealth, social position, prestige, and merit may impose themselves. In such cases, individual particularities cannot be granted much space. In contexts of sociability, too, these particularities may have to be cut down. "Individual impulsivity," attractions of all kinds, "personal eccentricities and self-aggrandizement," "most intimate elements of life, of character, of mood, of fate" must be kept under control (54–55).[34] Therein lies the special quality of *tact* as the self-regulation of the individual in two directions. (Luhmann has taken this up—see *Social Systems*, 413–414.) Tact keeps the aggressiveness of both personal and social claims at bay; in return, it opens up a scope in which the chances of both an alluring re-intimization and a necessary social distance are put at interactive disposal. As elementary and elaborate examples, Simmel has named feminine coquetry, social games (in a double sense), and conversation (59–64).[35]

The double direction of concepts used below or beyond their usual meaning has haunted and is still haunting disciplines such as sociology too. The early but classic version of the topic "community and society" (*Gemeinschaft und Gesellschaft*) in the work of Ferdinand Tönnies, for instance, was much more complicated than one would normally imagine.[36] Tönnies denies ever having presented his two basic forms of social organization as independent types of their own: "I do not know any state of culture in which the elements of community and the elements of society did not exist simultaneously, that is in a mixed form, and where they were not strongly associated with mutual hostilities" (269). Moreover, in an evolutionary perspective, the concept of society designates "the law-like normal decline" of all communities (107). The order of community receives its legitimacy from traditions and customs; modern society follows a progressive individualism. This individualism is committed to the fight for equal rights but easily degenerates into a violent, economically oriented individualism. An "individualistic capitalism" looms large (218). Finally, Tönnies looks at communities as a series of real forms (family, village, town) but at societies as a "pure object of thought" that tries to become real. In the beginning, society is embodied by the city, in which the exchange of goods comes to dominate (103). A partial return to forms of community always seems possible. In Germany, it has happened with the social policies of Bismarck, albeit, what with compulsory school attendance, military service, and insurance, in a deficient and, with Nazi fascism, fraudulent form (214). In a final turn of the conceptual screw, Tönnies builds a theory of the will into his construction—there is supposed to be a will of essence for communities and a will of choice for societies (108, 112, 244). The role of this psychological dimension is dubious, not in the least because Tönnies perceives signs of the coming world society at the same time.

The distinction between community and society does not correspond precisely to the one between sociability and society. Tönnies's approach does not focus on the quality of interaction. We cannot even assume that the situation of the individual in economically driven societies is more uncomfortable than in communities relying on well-practiced roles and traditions. Parts of modern comparative sociology, quite by contrast, appear to have rehabilitated Burckhardt's talk about and Simmel's reference to happiness in groups, however individually distributed, by elevating individual well-being into an important factor of social cohesion.[37] We do not have to worry about the methodological question whether the category of individual happiness and well-being can be handled like criteria of just income, social security, democratic rights, or even religion.[38] Literary scholars might be skeptical in this regard because literature, although designed, it would seem, for explorations of the emotions has more and more tended to emphasize their ambiguities and elusiveness. The third section of Chapter 10 will have more to say on that.

At this point, we can at least claim, with the help of Tönnies and comparative sociology, that there is an increasing amount of evidence to suggest that the ancient symposium can be understood and further exploited as an impulse-like and stimulating institutional complex. We may fall prey to a myth if, like Paul Ludwig Landsberg, we praise the extraordinary intensity and emotional range with which people felt their membership in the *polis*. According to Landsberg, the symposium brought about an acquaintance of all free citizens with each other, thus creating a peculiar way of making life public.[39] To repeat: It will not be possible to draw up an inventory of conceptually and empirically identical successors. We must be satisfied with finding a group of typical institutions linked by family similarities in Wittgenstein's sense. We must treat them as typical cultural symptoms pointing back to a fictive origin in the symposium. The horizon of thought in which, after the lead provided by Burckhardt and Simmel, the discussion ought to be conducted has mainly been opened up by an interdisciplinary dynamic. This dynamic, more than any other complex approach, has forged analytical instruments out of disciplines ranging from philosophy and anthropology via linguistics, sociology, and social psychology to biology (and often in fact anatomy and zoology). This is German philosophical anthropology. This enterprise owes its emergence to the catastrophic history of Germany in the twentieth century, a history in which not only did the question of the human makeup arise with unprecedented urgency but also the analysis of group formation had to go beyond its concentration on masses (these, of course, remained hugely important) and approach behavior in smaller groups. Arnold Gehlen, one of the main representatives of this school of thought (representative also because of his own problematic behavior during the Nazi period), has repeatedly stated the central purpose of philosophical anthropology: to make us aware of the pluralistic, indeed the anarchic, bent in human behavior; of the fluidity of drives and the power of fantasy and imagination; of the stupendous, contradictory abundance of customs. Helmuth Plessner, in some sense Gehlen's antipode (Plessner called Gehlen "a rogue" after World War II because of the latter's behavior during the Nazi period), already felt driven in 1924, very early in the school's existence, to establish boundaries—that is, a specific group orientation in interaction. We have to learn techniques with which human beings can come close without hitting each other, with which they can leave without hurting each other. Consequently, we have to accept the artificiality of social (and sociable) forms in order to acquire a relaxed self-confidence of behavior so sorely missing in German culture.[40] At a much later stage, when the group orientation seemed dormant, Dieter Claessens, who must be considered a member of the school, published one of the very first introductions to groups and group clusters. Generally, because of chaotic change and insecurity all around, the time of the Weimar Republic can be called the era of behavioral doctrines. Perhaps Helmut Lethen's book on behavioral doctrines of coldness, on experiments of life between the wars (*Verhaltenslehren der Kälte. Lebensversuche zwischen den Kriegen* [1994]), itself a kind of late offshoot of philosophical anthropology, has become its best chronicler. There will be further discussion of this in the second section of Chapter 3.

From the vantage point of this short introduction to philosophical anthropology (which will be enlarged upon later) we can further advance the evaluation of the symposium in ancient Athens. Above all, it is easier to understand the side-by-side existence of group formation and aggression that is not really explained by Burckhardt. The achievement of the symposium takes on additional significance because other energies working toward effects of unity—apart from language and heroic myth—were hardly available. This assertion applies also to the *agora*, the second important locus of conversation in the culture of Athens.[41] Without conversation about the *agora* and in the symposium, Burckhardt has categorically maintained, the development of the spirit in ancient Greece is less conceivable than for any other people. The effect is felt in Aristotle, for whom the sense of community turns into the most important political category; the implementation of this sense is best achieved in an organizational form such as the symposium.[42] In view of the comments on philosophical anthropology just made, we can also understand Murray's astonishment that nobody has wondered about the fact that more texts on the symposium have been transmitted into later times than on any other matter.[43]

The Greek *polis* understood itself as a community of free men, not as a class society in our sense. Metics—permanent foreign residents without the rights of citizens—and slaves did not count; they were not citizens. Whether they counted as human beings at all "is a question not debated."[44] On the other hand, to repeat: Athens does not represent a class society in our sense. Even early periods show little evidence of feudal conditions, some vague references to the existence of a nobility notwithstanding. The role of relatives, too, seems to have been of minor importance.[45] Other forms of social organization such as phratries (associations of family groups) and *hetaereias* (formations based on friendship) are hard to define in any precise sense.[46] Since there were also distinctions between the free citizens (such as *aristoi*, the best, not to be confused with a rank, class, or station in the medieval or modern sense), which, however, did not harden into rigid demarcations, it is the *elastic* qualities of sympotic elements on all levels (participants, performative genres, forms of playful *agon*) that come to the forefront. Agonistic performances, discussions, recitals of texts and songs and of politicizing and philosophical dialogues, riddles, and parodies are all welcome. Problems can be discussed in both serious and playful moods. Such discussions are controlled by an all-embracing politeness and tact that are held to be a gift of the gods.[47] The range of participants spans from "celebrities" down to persons not invited (but coming, for instance, in the wake of somebody invited) and parasites.[48] Again in some contrast to recent studies, and general politeness notwithstanding, Burckhardt also emphasizes the scope available for both intimacy and distance in physical as well as intellectual respects. Nowhere in the world and never in world history has a drinking party been a "vessel of the spirit" to such an extent.[49] This did not inhibit but rather encouraged a striking openness, naturalness, and impartiality in talks about and indeed confessions of conditions and situations in life. The communicative potential of the symposium could ascend into the heights of speculation or descend into mystical depths, with the suggestion that the mysteries of life could be touched upon only in the symposium. Seeing it from this angle, perhaps Plato's enterprise of a sublime speculation on love in the *Symposium* becomes more easily understandable.[50] Murray also claims that, apart from religious poetry, the largest part of ancient Greek poetry was composed for one symposium or another. He is also convinced that for the most part the iconography of Greek vase paintings owes its inspiration and motifs to the symposium.[51]

The course of the symposium was ordered by many rules, including such seemingly small issues as to whether the goblet has to move clockwise or counterclockwise. More important, the symposiarch had to make sure that the effects of alcohol did not provoke violence; as I mentioned above, the respectable man had to be able to walk home unaided. Yet no one could prevent occasional violence, especially if violent moods, particularly those caused by political strife that had been brewing awhile, were imported into the symposium and exploded there with unforeseeable consequences.[52] Granting this, Murray still thinks that the autonomy of the symposium was not damaged by such incidents. The rules were stronger and more explicit than those of everyday life, and behavior was better kept under control through its higher degree of ritualization. Murray gives examples such as the rhythm of dancing and drinking, bodily positions, musical and lyrical genres.[53]

Group Size and Power

Simmel has derived sociability from the "coarser" structures of society. This might create the impression that the cohesion of society could be founded by sociability per se, emanating, as it were, out of the rich reserves of its communicative-interactive potential. This impression, if entertained, however, would be wrong. Forms of power and of law, together with a more or less definite territory, a language, symbols, and their affective charges will normally provide a framework that allows the identification of a sociopolitical entity. Power will be invested in people who are able to stylize the elements just named in such a way that they can be grasped as the representation of a higher being. This is, of course, not meant to compete with Max Weber's well-known allocation of the power to rule (rational, traditional, charismatic). Ancient Greece never represented or constituted a state. In early periods, men were made into kings who were visibly able to promote the vital interests of the "people" in some way. They were swept aside by transitional power groups that, for want of a better term, were vaguely seen as an aristocracy;[54] further transitions changed this highly unstable form into temporary and no less unstable oligarchies. All these forms can be roughly identified but were also threatened by additional criteria, such as the distinction between freemen and slaves; tyrants in particular were subject to the adage that it is easier to win than to stay in power.[55] In what was called democracy, the distribution of power, much like today, was much more complicated. There were laws, and there were interest groups; there were sycophants, showmen, and scandalmongers, "social pestilence" Burckhardt calls them, who also as they do today enjoyed a lot of social recognition. Consequently, we face the task of assessing the relative ranges of social power and sociability. In attempting this, we have to treat them both as entities unto themselves and as nexuses of interlocking streams of power. Results in this complex field would amount to an index of the conditions in which a society finds itself.

Recent research has already made efforts to track down such complications. Their full appreciation is hampered by contradictions incurred by those who try to prove that the symposium of the fifth century BC was the exclusive affair of an "aristocracy." Marek Wecowski, for instance, describes the symposium as an aristocratic event in principle but in a culturally encoded form, only to add in the following sentence that this aristocracy is not precisely to be defined. He knows a "strict élite" of the best, the good, and the noble but does not hesitate to water down its identification in subsequent analyses. Ultimately a result emerges that is worth quoting:

> Put briefly, I would define the archaic and early classical symposion as a hub or focal point of the mechanisms of natural selection for the Greek aristocracy. Understood in these terms, the symposion was about dynamically defining the aristocracy, deciding who was and was not to be counted, and providing those admitted with a perfect forum to confirm, display, and negotiate their aristocratic status. It was the ultimate

setting for achieving social recognition by those aspiring to the status of the *aristoi*.[56]

Another definition moves toward self-rebuttal even more clearly: "In the briefest terms possible, I would call the symposion a 'transgressive feast' because of its inner dynamics and its fleeting hierarchies, which consciously ignore the external rankings of the community."[57]

In this view, the dynamics of self-recruitment is decisive, because it presupposes a considerable openness of a selection that Wecowski also calls natural. Then, under this condition, it is suddenly possible to speak of "a wider privileged élite" as opposed to the narrow one postulated in the beginning. Now access is decided by social and ideological conditions. Since wealth and riches can be interpreted as gifts and favors of the gods, changes in these criteria can lead to changes of status. Labels of ill-defined status also stick to those who are not invited but who must be accepted for some reason or another. The strongest pressure to accept them comes from invited free citizens who act, as it were, as their guarantors; the uninvited ones must indemnify regular guests with comic performances.[58] In later periods as well as in Roman times, these people will be called "parasites." Systems theory, especially in the way practiced by Michel Serres, has newly discovered and highlighted the important role parasites play in seemingly very different contexts such as media, conflicts, scientific and scholarly schools, and as advisors. The usual terms used by regular members of a symposium among themselves (e.g., *philoi hetairoi*, "dear friends," or also only *sympotai*) do not identify class and status in very reliable ways; it is only the free citizens who can be defined clearly, that is, legally.

The relevant contexts from which candidates for membership would come certainly included the social and political power that could be ascribed to them. In such cases, power and culture became interrelated in ways not identical with Simmel's account of the origin of sociability but also not completely alien to it. This book is devoted to finding analogous models of interrelationship or separation of social and sociable domains in order to get somewhat closer to questions of social cohesion. With the symposium, we have a paradigmatically successful model. It is also successful because it transforms "politics in action" into the more sophisticated and indirect model of "politics through cultural performance."[59] In other cases, the socially binding power of the sociable symposium can extend into the military domain. The paradigm here would be the Spartan *syssition*. This was the smallest unit of Spartan public life and, at the same time, the foundation of the social order. The interrelationship between military and civil life may have been particularly tight here, because the *syssition* likely originated in tent communities in the field.

On the other hand, cultural performance can also gain independence and distance itself from political involvement. Cultural performance in the symposium may thus turn into a driving force, for instance in the literary productivity that I have claimed in the Introduction. Classical philology has coined the term "symposium literature" for the many forms these products have taken. For literary theory, this diversity is quite significant, because the texts cannot be reduced to a common denominator (such as fiction or fictionality in modern literary theory). Between political function and literary independence, we could locate symposia with an educational purpose, a use of the symposium granted even by the satirist Aristophanes in the *Wasps*.

So far, though, I have not dared to approach perhaps the toughest problem both for the symposium and for social cohesion in general: group size. Even modern social psychology, for which the size of groups should be a central concern, has neglected to deal with it at any length. It is interesting that Aristotle should have given some thought to the matter, although his use of it seems rather limited. In order to safeguard the self-sufficiency of the state, he thinks the number of citizens must be large enough but not too vast. More to the point: In order to assess the real vitality of a group, Dieter Claessens has said, we have to form a notion of the fullness of its possible relations. In most cases, however, there are too many of them. If a group contains more than twelve members, subgroups can organize themselves very easily; whenever this is possible, it is tempting to do so.[60] And once this happens, the direction of activities in a group can change drastically. In the perspective of psychohistory, Peter Sloterdijk has said in his turn, the deepest and most far-reaching caesura in social evolution occurs when the empathy still possible in groups with up to one hundred members meets with emptiness once it is supposedly extended to bigger groups. Heterogeneous macro groups will then have to be kept at bay through propaganda, dynastic hypnosis, and other dubious maneuvers such as the exploitation of religious feelings.

Sloterdijk does not give away the secret as to where the knowledge about the deepest caesura in social evolution comes from. There certainly must be a big difference not only in numbers but also in quality between a group of twelve that would warrant investigation for Claessens and a group of 100. The dynamics with a group of 500, the number that has supplied the limit for Irenäus Eibl-Eibesfeldt, an excellent behavioral and evolutionary biologist, should be totally different and unpredictable. "If a community grows beyond that number," he says, "then it needs guidance, leadership and special social techniques in order to make sure of social cohesion."[61] The crucial fact here is whether group members can still know each other sufficiently or not. Further significant thresholds could be built into this construction (e.g., 150, 2,500): if there are more than 150 people among whom interaction takes place, necessary information will no longer reach all of them without ritualized and formalized channels.

In his article on the symposium for the *Oxford Classical Dictionary*, Oswyn Murray assumes a standard size for the drinking group of between fourteen and thirty. I fervently pray he is right, for this would corroborate my theses in this book quite considerably. If we further assume (as an exception to Wikipedia) that between 250,000 and 300,000 inhabitants lived in the Athens of the fourth and fifth centuries BC, among them 100,000 slaves and 60,000 free citizens—that is, 60,000 participants in political life and symposia—then the number of symposia ought to have been sufficiently high to both stabilize and keep open matters of relation and concerted action and to provide the necessary elasticity for the self-recruitment of the elites. The symposium must have enjoyed, we will say, the advantage of small numbers valued highly by Max Weber, that is to say, the chances of the ruling minority's being able to communicate quickly with each other and to apply subtle and cultivated measures for the preservation of power.[62] The symposium offers a core figure for cultural and political processes of diffusion—that is, a balancing less of differences in concentration, as in chemistry, but rather of differences in communication. Evidently, optimizing group numbers depends on the purpose of the group, in its sociability being more or less embedded in social power structures and their conditions of communication.

The preceding two paragraphs present abstract versions of the problem. Even so, with their help we should be in a better position to sketch variants of simple models of symposia and their equivalents. They will allow us afterward to tackle more complicated analogies. In spite of Burckhardt's terminologically unusual point of departure with the notion of the "happiness of life" (*Lebensglück*) in a full society, and in spite of unusually bold philosophical demands to which the symposium is exposed in Plato's text of that title, the classical symposium in Athens can be accepted as a relatively simple case. Whatever empirical complications and conflicts there may have been—the interrelations of basic power structures, demographic conditions (number of citizens), group size and possibilities of interaction and debate in the home country of political talk, the delight in playfully agonistic conversation, as Nietzsche put it[63]—in principle all of these can even today be imagined with relative ease. Certainly there were intoxicating and nonmandatory additions; "luxurious things" may have become rampant.[64] But on the whole we can again follow Burckhardt: "The course of the symposium is simple."[65]

Sympotic conditions in earlier, tribally structured periods appear to have been even simpler than in the times of the *poleis*. This thesis would seem to apply even when these periods follow classical antiquity rather than preceding it. Aaron J. Gurewitsch has painted a very clear picture of the function of banquets (eating and drinking) among the Germanic tribes during the migration and the early Middle Ages. He follows Tacitus, who reported that the Teutons spent their time in feasts when they did not go to war. They consumed war booty as far as possible and, if possible, in demonstrative fashion and in public. Such events took place during banquets where as many people as possible were present. The booty did not merely serve as food—it was the most important means for the leader to unite followers into a collective and maintain his authority.[66]

And yet, the connection between interactive groups and society at large (especially national societies later on) will remain an open wound in the investigations that follow. Should we, for instance, include table talk? And if so, since there is also a scholarly edition, would Hitler's table talks serve as an example? The hope is that my choice of examples is a significant and symptomatic one. For the moment, let me just add an example that shows how complex the situation can be even in relatively early times. There is the *Deipnosophistae* (Banquet of scholars) by Athenaios of Naucratis, who lived around the turn of the second/third century AD. The book poses as a "report" on a symposium that lasted for several days. During the symposium the guests talked about any conceivable topic discussed by well-educated people, ranging from cookery books to the seduction of royal mistresses, all of them discussed in a relaxed, slightly distanced mood remote from any form of pedantry.[67] Because of the wealth of "information" that it contains, well-known classical scholars have called it one of the most important books of antiquity. Even so, it is difficult to find an intention in this semifictive, unrealistically exaggerated report and to see any purpose in the event. The report may mean to be a self-presentation of the educational sophistication of a social and sociable elite; it may intend a comparative picture of Roman and Greek levels of culture and imply a claim concerning the equality of their rank—the host was Publius Livius Larensi(u)s (who died after 192), who, as director of the imperial central cash desk and *pontifex minor*, was a well-known public figure in Rome.

Analytical economy, however, demands that the ambition of the following investigation be directed more precisely toward the comparability of sociable groups and their potential to promote—or to impede—solidarity and trust in the midst of the centrifugal pressures of modern societies. The self-irony in this ponderous formulation should be taken as a hint that, even in the case of comparable groups, exact results are only rarely to be expected. My text is not a "raid on the inarticulate" in T. S. Eliot's sense but a "raid on approximations." The effort should be worthwhile.

Deceptive Continuities

Sympotic structures and potentials may disappear abruptly. Their cultural and aesthetic elements may survive and indeed be interpreted by later times as cultural continuity and tradition. But their sociable practice and social repercussions can easily be destroyed under new political conditions. Two forms of association existing in antiquity and in some loose form also in later periods—the Platonic Academy (also condensed into the contrast Plato vs. Aristotle) and the Roman banquet—help to illustrate the sudden otherness of cultural and social binding energies under the guise of a pseudocontinuity of names and ideas.

In his lecture and debate on the Platonic Academy, the famous German classical scholar Otto Seel has declared the academy to be a symbol of scholarly existence in which forms of disciplinary communication and forms of life are united. He has tried to prove the real continuity of these institutions until the closure of the academy in the sixth century and its reanimation in fifteenth-century Florence and elsewhere. Seel did not really explore the possibility that in spite of the longevity of the academy (roughly from 387 BC to 529 AD), its founding idea might have signaled not the beginning of a coalition of knowledge and life but rather its end.[68] But he knew that the mere fact of the shift of place for the academy to a garden lot beyond the city limits would have to signify a "wall between school and life," a wall not at all known, for instance, in the philosophizing of Socrates. For a short time, Seel finds himself close to Landsberg, for whom a Greek philosopher, in a true community of life, originally belonged to his city. Not surprisingly, Landsberg's prime example is also Socrates, who would rather die than leave his city. The city presents itself as a more or less obligatory community to the individual. Plato's Academy, however, creates a community that stylizes itself into the community of a cult. We do not reliably know how to evaluate the fact that Plato, as the free citizen that he probably was, founded a philosophical school outside the city limits, whereas Aristotle, the metic, "had to suffer political pressure and suspicion all the time and was forced to lead an unquiet life."[69] But certainly we can suppose that such factors in combination with the separation of the academy from the totality of the *polis*—in short, the differences in the type of isolation[70]— produced not only remarkable differences in the style of thought of the two but also a different positioning with respect to sociopolitical and sociable institutions. The Platonic Academy develops into a first model for the *organization* of intellectual work, a feature that may have helped to mitigate older aspects such as its cult status and to prevent a fall into dogmatism. It could not exclude the intrusion of risky and old-fashioned religious ways of thinking. Under Xenocrates (leader of the academy from 339 to 314 BC), for instance, progressive ideas such as the protection of animals but also superstitious elements such as belief in devils, angels, witches, and ghosts made their entrance into the academy.

As soon as Seel alludes to differences between Socrates and Plato, he starts to play them down, thus blurring the break in tradition that in fact occurred. Socrates, he says, not only spent his philosophical and vital energies in the streets but, together with an inner circle of friends, implemented first approaches toward the formation of a school. Strangely oscillating between philosophical and sociological perspectives (as he does not say but should have said), he resharpens distinctions again by mentioning "certain peculiarities of a purely personal kind" in Plato, to which he ascribes paramount importance. He links aristocratic traits in Plato with his tendency to fill his writings with proofs that really prove nothing. Plato is supposed to have known this himself and in this way to have initiated his ultimate distancing from the written word and even from spoken language. Consequently, an irrational and revelatory supreme authority makes its way into his doctrines. That authority, in its turn, creates the necessity of an existential community of followers, a community of experience of teachers and learners.[71] In such a community of experience, the ideal of teaching and learning becomes a reality lasting to the present day. The probability that such a community would build up a polemical opposition against the *polis* does not enter Seel's picture.

In fact, quite the contrary. Without mentioning the word, Seel implies a rapprochement between academy and symposium. Thirty years later it also takes place with Hermann Schmitz, a German philosopher and classical scholar with considerable polemical powers. We should not, the latter says, imagine the academy to have been a mere association for eating and satisfying the demands of a cult. Nor should we conceive of it as a school, in which Plato, like Hegel, held lectures committed to writing by his students. Rather, the academy must be seen as a political and philosophical club in which Plato played the presenter. Plato did not dominate the discussion like a monarch dominating his household but maneuvered like the head of a government who has to accommodate conflicting opinions. There must have existed, Schmitz concludes, a very liberal climate of discussion.

This may have been the case, or it may not. The rapprochement is treacherous. Landsberg insists, with good reason, on a "sociologically completely new form" for the academy, a form that converts a Socratic "community of memory" into a sectarian "community of education and redemption."[72] He relies on Nietzsche, for whom all Greek philosophers after Plato were founders of sects (28). For Plato himself, Landsberg asserts, the aristocratic, stern, and Doric-conservative sect of the Pythagoreans furnished the guiding imagery (31). Here we do not need more detailed characterizations of the sects of that time: in any case, a special doctrine must be part of them, in Plato's case a theology that separated him from Athens in terms of ideas, and also sociologically, a doctrine of redemption that did not want to improve but to do away with the world (59). Aristocratic doctrine took the place of aristocratic birth (85).

We might, however, be easily deceived by the simplicity of the formulation. We simply have to look at a comparison with Aristotle, who was pushed into a certain social distance from the *polis* by origin (he was a metic), through the founding of his lyceum, and by other matters. Like Plato, Aristotle had written a text called *The Symposium* (also going by the titles *Convivium* and, less plausible, *On Being Drunk*). Thematically, both texts could hardly be further apart from each other. Plato is only marginally interested in the sociable institution. Participants, to put it cautiously, give speeches on eroticism and the possibility of using and transcending it for the higher, indeed the highest, refinement of the soul. Aristotle's fragment details the behavioral norms that must be respected when visiting the symposium.[73]

The Symposium is perhaps not typical of Plato's writings, but it points to a general discrepancy between the two philosophers. This discrepancy extends from their personal relations into cognitive style and interests; it can be observed in their respective positions in the older academy. While the symposium as a sociable institution is not in question, it can serve as a vanishing point toward which the differences are oriented. The seventeen-year-old Aristotle entered the academy when Plato was absent on a two-year stay in Sicily. Hellmut Flashar, an expert in the field, is convinced that Aristotle, early on, had defined his position with respect to Plato and other academicians and then marked it in sharper and sharper terms. Rumors of an unpleasant kind, concerning their personal relations, were disseminated (230).

A philosophically constructive relation in terms of concepts and ideas can always be established between the two. This is true even if the view that Aristotle developed from a follower of the Platonic doctrine of ideas into a designer of speculative sketches and from there into an empiricist remote from Plato cannot be defended anymore (179–180[74]). In order to gain relevant materials for understanding the symposium, I would like to emphasize the role of the cognitive-conceptual dimension. Some modern interpretations of Aristotle have described this direction as a "rehabilitation" of his "practical philosophy." More precisely, it has been characterized as the return of politics that, in the course of time, had emigrated from philosophy (Flashar, *Die Philosophie der Antike*, 183). There is no denying the fact that both Plato and Aristotle opted for the priority of theoretical life (see the complex arguments in Flashar, 342). But one cannot erase the important difference that Plato thinks of politics from the perspective of ethics, whereas Aristotle treats ethics and politics in two separate texts. In Plato, ethics and politics become well-nigh identical because the order and structure of human beings and the state are grounded in the order of being itself (336). Reasoning on such a basis is very different from Aristotle because empirical problems lose their importance. One should not be surprised, therefore, to see Plato's *Politeia* frequently called a utopian text and classified as the beginning of that genre. Consequently, Landsberg's approach in the sociology of knowledge gains a particular urgency (see below).

Aristotle, to be sure, incurs problems of his own, having to do not with his reasoning as such but with the relative strength of his arguments. He mobilizes empirical evidence in support of the need for justice in politics—so far, so good. But the strength of the argument is not enough: it does not help much to draw attention to the ambiguities in language and the different situations in which people see justice done or not (340). But when Aristotle, in the *Nicomachean Ethics* and in *Politica*, extols a form of friendship and networks of friendship that go beyond the personal relations in the household (the household being, properly speaking, the group with the most basic reality claim), there yawns an empirical gap. The gap is also visible when he declares these forms of friendship to be "the source of cohesion in the *poleis*" (338). The gap is there, moreover, when this friendship is supposed to ensure the unanimity of opinion. How can friendship be made the basis of political interests? How should friendship guarantee unanimity of opinion? There may be some private friendships that can live up to this task, but most would need an *institution* in which they are produced, not presupposed, in which they emerge through communication and interaction. The symposium was such an institution for ancient Athens.

In other words, Plato has pushed the *Politeia*, together with the *Symposium*, into idealistic utopian fields and almost completely neglected the social achievements of the symposium especially. Aristotle ventures forth into empirical fields in his ethical and political doctrines but is far from doing justice to their extent. He lacks a concept such as the symposium or analogous descriptive concepts with which he could catch the group dynamics and the forces operative in the state. Aristotle has written a text on the symposium and knows its rules, but he does not care very much about what the symposium *means* as an institution. In this connection, it does not matter that because Aristotle wrote his *Politica* at different times, it might lack unity.

In this book I am ignoring Roman matters almost completely, which needs some apology. The Romans were committed to an ambitious program of culturally emulating the Greeks (*aemulatio*); in many cases their achievements equaled those of the Greeks. Yet the gnawing suspicion kept haunting them and especially others that they could not really interiorize, for instance, the Greek artistic essence. Even the *Oxford Classical Dictionary* denounces Roman aesthetic achievements as being decorated with mere "trappings" (s.v. "Rome [history]"). From its beginning, others have said, Roman history was subject to military priorities. We may legitimately wonder if such relentlessly pursued priorities were imposed anywhere else in the world on an advanced civilization like the one that Rome had quickly become. Within Rome, the cultural tension with respect to Greece was doubled by the conflict between *plebs* and patricians. That conflict was more or less deflated, with the parties coming to an arrangement by negotiating the distribution of power within a complex structure of offices. We have to take it for granted, says the *Oxford Classical Dictionary*, that the extension of Roman rule, after the subjection of the Italian territories, would be carried beyond their boundaries. The empire was born. Seel formulates it more mildly but says the same thing: the Romans were the people of organization, of earthly institutional order. The Greeks were busy cultivating humane commitments such as the spirit supposedly penetrating the technical and organizational worlds. They ruined themselves by not paying sufficient attention to and indeed despising state institutions.[75]

Both Greek and Roman civilization, like most other civilizations, spent their aggressive energies in permanent wars. But the Greeks, with the exception perhaps of the Spartans, were never as successful as the Romans in developing a military professionalism capable of creating an empire.[76] We do not have to activate a great deal of imagination in order to understand that an empire of roughly 5,000,000 square kilometers, populated by heterogeneous masses of people numbering about 55,000,000 in the second century AD[77] did not have much use for the Greek symposium. (Just to complete the comparison: as of 2022, Italy measures 302,068 square kilometers, with a population of 60,286,829 inhabitants [estimates according to UN data as presented on the web] distributed in a very different pattern of settlement, including a large number of big cities. The probability that there will be sympotic structures even if they take mafiotic forms is very high.) Roman banquets, with an emphasis on eating and allowing women to attend, degenerated easily into the boastful self-presentation of the badly educated nouveau riche. The prototype for the nouveau riche shows up as Trimalchio in the most famous but also most notorious of Roman banquets and their texts, here the *Cena Trimalchionis* in the *Satyrica* of Petronius. In the first section of his article "Convivium" for the *Oxford Classical Dictionary*, Oswyn Murray has described this degeneration and change of function in very lenient terms as a re-embedding of sympotic elements in a "hierarchy of honor" and in "social and family structures." These were structures from which the Greek symposium had liberated itself. In any case, from the outset F. Scott Fitzgerald, who originally wanted to use the title *Trimalchio* for his novel *The Great Gatsby*, presented the main character as well as his parties in the twilight of a dubious model (see the second section of Chapter 7). It is, on the other hand, not really a paradox that in the Roman environment literature was easily marginalized. That marginalization created the mental space for the flourishing of particularly subtle combinations of self-conscious fiction and object-oriented thought. The renewal of classical philology has responded to such stimuli with impressive results.[78]

CHAPTER 2

Power and Signs of Power in the Middle Ages

THE ASSUMPTION APPEARS PLAUSIBLE that simple couplings of power after the fashion of the Teutons have meanwhile died out. Yet, although the assumption is wrong, we must take into account increased complications in general and, in particular, complications with socially or politically, as well as sometimes culturally, leading figures. Positions of leadership vary tremendously, from presidents of the US or French kind—that is, with a strong and comprehensive equipment of power—down to the "influente" type in Mexico or the trivialities of today's influencers. This variance makes more difficult the interpretation of those signs that are meant to stage, to visualize, and to stylize positions of power. Such difficulties blur the range and circumference of effective power, a blurring that, of course, is often intended. In the Middle Ages, the role and position of universities, for instance, are couched in an ineradicable ambivalence. In general, one must say, following Huizinga, that if signs are clear, they are one-sided and polemical; they are then signs of group egoism and programmatic ideologies.

Starting in the twelfth century, the growth of the universities changes the picture. Forms of intellectualization and, in their wake, forms of distancing slide themselves between the bearers of power and the possibilities of demonstrating their power in clearly perceptible ways. Forms exercising distance are capable of undermining or destroying, at least of calling into question, the arrogance of power, but they are also capable of producing new sympotic forms. This happens mainly in the thirteenth century, which Jacques Le Goff has consequently dubbed the century of the universities.[1] An almost parallel development gets under way, with a shorter span of life, knighthood, and the age of chivalry on the one hand and the long-term institutions of universities and cities on the other. Taken together, all of these contribute to the emergence of analogous and partly overlapping, partly opposed, sympotic profiles. The impression of being sealed off from the rest of the world has tempted the late Middle Ages, as it were, to look at both knighthood and university as equals—that is, to proclaim both institutions as pillars and preservers of the human and divine order. As if to confirm this idea, in 1533 the French king François I tells the doctors of the university that they are knights too.[2]

There are between sixty and seventy universities in the world more than five hundred years old; aside from church institutions, one rarely finds such staying power. We would know that the chances for university survival are or were on the whole much higher than those of knighthood, even if history had not told us so in such a clear form. Whatever François I might have said, knighthood and the university certainly embody radically different forces of cohesion. Knighthood came gradually into existence during the multifaceted but ideological fusion of "soldiers" (*miletes*) with "horsemen," who ultimately turned into aristocratic vassals. Around 1100, the terms *ritter*, *herre*, and *fürste*[3] appear to be interchangeable in German-speaking countries. Courtly ideology was generally adopted by the European aristocratic knighthood.

But that ideology was suspended, as it were, in thin air. In the context of permanent, often violent power politics of the higher lords, it was never securely in place. The aristocracy, on all levels, was fighting with itself because it was caught in never-ending conflicts of interest and prestige. (In Germany, this situation slowed down and restricted the use of power even by king or emperor as long as these, since the second half of the thirteenth century, were elected by the secular and spiritual electors.) The fight of the aristocracy against itself started in the family with the uninterrupted revolts of sons against their fathers who lived too long.[4] For Huizinga, blood feud is the essential motive dominating actions and destinies of dynasties and countries. Presumably, it was not only the English court that appeared to many to be a hell of hate; special feuds in which the only intelligible motive seems to be envy of the property of others are pursued everywhere.[5] Changing distributions of power in Germany raised the question where the center of the empire might be located, or more radically, whether there was a center at all. Some would see the diets in that role because these were also social events, places where news was exchanged and where one could measure one's own strength and the resources of others. During diets, those making the decisions entered into formal negotiations with one another, but much more important, could also meet informally; there were opportunities to renew old bonds and forge new alliances.[6] But inevitably this also made for an insecurity concerning the "reality" of power distribution.

Everybody had to cope with a certain fluidity of conditions much more conspicuous than in the centralized monarchies of France and England. The competition between monarchy and the so-called parliament (very different, of course, from today's institutions) or between monarchy and the Estates-General in its turn took on a dynamics of its own that came to fruition later.

The harder a ruler had to fight in order to secure his power, the more he would try to demonstrate that power through signs. Representing a superior and luxurious lifestyle was less a matter of actually possessing the means for it and mainly a problem of convincing others through the symbolic power of signs. Since one could not go to war all the time, if merely for reasons of cost, conflicts of power and prestige were also conducted in forms of self-stylization, among which sympotic elements played a crucial role. Power must be seen and therefore required signs symbolizing it. Such symbolizing was particularly evident in acts and rituals of extravagance: the ruler was strong to the extent that he could afford much and offer it to others. This mechanism has been well known in modern times as well since the end of the nineteenth century, when Thorstein Veblen presented his concept of conspicuous consumption—that is, ways of exhibiting one's wealth practiced by the moneyed aristocracy, not the hereditary nobility. Early European behavioral forms made themselves felt in the building of residences in the twelfth and thirteenth centuries. Before that, kings and princes moved around in their territories, exploiting the hospitality of their subjects. In terms of techniques of power, this was a difficult and awkward situation, which Shakespeare dramatized in mythic and archetypal terms in his *King Lear*. It was above all later French kings (or Japanese shoguns, to jump into an entirely different area momentarily) who proved that a residence could be made into a center of power by forcing the aristocracy to live there at least part of the time and thereby relegating them to a hierarchy of subjection.

In terms of a logic of representation, residence formation is followed by the formation of a court and a court society. A court administration is needed for practical and financial reasons, and priests officiating at court do what they always do. But how does the princely household—that is, court "society" properly speaking, kill time? Evidently, we are dealing here with a parasitic institution. Yet medievalists such as Joachim Bumke have invested them with central functions. Bumke, for one, holds that court festivals were immensely important to the extent that everyday reality was banished from the notion of court(ly) culture. It is above all literature that is responsible for painting a picture in which festivals and feasts were the normal form of aristocratic life.[7] In a literal sense, this was certainly not the case, but if everyday life must, in point of fact, do largely without festivals, it stands in dire need of stylization. The experience of stylizations (sympotic rituals of eating and drinking together with festivities) can be so intense that its "reality" overwrites everyday miseries. In terms of phenomenological sociology, it may arrogate to itself the character of a paramount reality. This is what Otto Borst implies (even if he does not put it quite that way) when he says that it was only festivals and play (also in the sense of games) that led the way out of everyday *tristesse*. It is symptomatic that while the sympotic core activities of eating and drinking are still in place, their festive extensions, especially games such as tournaments or, as we will see, literary stylizations, may come to the forefront in order to make up for a life that seems much more unsatisfactory and disorderly than everyday life in ancient Athens.[8] That is why most cultural historians have painted dismal pictures of the barbaric conditions in medieval castles. That is also why the arsenal of media producing what the German Middle Ages called *vreude* (pleasure) was comparatively diversified. Walther von der Vogelweide praises his colleague, the older Reinmar, for having increased the "vreude" of all of courtly society. Music and dance were important. Likewise, however, forms of "poeticizing" and "intellectualizing" took on increasing importance in using the suggestiveness of words (and thoughts couched, of course, in words) for more sophisticated reality effects.[9] Many aristocrats studied at universities; for them, it was not only practical intellectual competence that counted for their intellectual self-image but also knowledge of French literature, which was considered a marker of superior achievement. Around 1200, the self-image of German aristocrats is noticeably charged with German epic literature.[10]

It is essential to be aware that when speaking of the "knowledge" of literature, no mere knowledge of literary history is meant. Rather, in extending their vocabulary and syntax by literary means, these aristocrats widened their grip on experience and realities that the texts preproduced for them and that otherwise might have remained inaccessible. Quite some time ago, Rolf Sprandel emphasized the function of literature as a help and mediator for the "self-representation" of aristocratic groups. In that sense, literature changes into a real sympotic element that, as we will see, will have great difficulties maintaining itself later on. Literature is for reading, but it is not only, perhaps not even primarily, for reading. It was Sprandel, too, who pointed out, early on (and with the help of Simmel, of whom he may not have been aware), that the widening of real experience by texts came together with fluid transitions in the play(ful) side of social reality, with festivals, dance, hunting with falcons, and tournaments. It was a matter of seeing one's own life in meaningful terms, of a vitally intensifying management of strength and energies, purposes for which songs, for example, might have been of great use.[11]

In due course and still within the Middle Ages, this performative drift of texts is threatened by the transformation of literature into a material for reading and nothing else. This "reduction" impinges with particular force on the role and modes of work of the epic poet. The epic court poet is supposed to enhance the splendor of the court, but, in the logic of such transformations, including competition, comes to spend much more time on the composition of his texts than on their presentation. With that an important part of the sympotic spectrum is gone. In this sense, Bumke has traced the career of Heinrich von Veldeke and his hopping from court to court.[12] Bumke assumes that the composition of an epic poem of some ten thousand to twenty thousand verses would, as a rule, have taken several years, during which he would not really be available for performative and festive occasions.

Therefore, and in spite of the importance of epic poetry or rather narratives for aristocratic images of the self, Bumke's and Sprandel's focus comes to be directed more strongly on "lyric" poetry. It is true that we do not know how long it took writers of epic to present their work, but they do talk a lot about the possibility of reading their texts. Moreover, the epic manuscripts of the thirteenth century became bigger and more expensive because of illustrations ("illuminations"). Also, very often several works would be collected in one manuscript.[13] It seems fairly evident that, under these circumstances, such texts encouraged reading or being looked at in spaces removed from performance. There is a new division of labor: the performative gap that had opened up with the developments just mentioned will be closed by purely performative (musical, acrobatic, magic) genres.[14]

It is also highly significant that the recital of "lyric" poetry concentrates on two genres closely related to each other. In Germany, this is the *Minnesang*; in southern France, the love poetry of the troubadours. In terms of motifs, then, the aristocratic sympotic practice hitches up with the ancient symposium. The *Minnesang*, an art for the nobility, presupposes a courtly sociability; in this framework it treats, directly or indirectly, a central problem of this class—namely, the relation between love and marriage. With marriage, it is also questions of power that are in question. For the troubadours, the negotiation of the risks of marriage is even more intense than in *Minnesang*: the troubadour poetry operates on the basis of an erotic social life that is both old as well as new, both understandable and customary as well as surprising. The erotic life was predicated on extramarital and adulterous sexual relations.[15] Poetry uses a language that explores both the somewhat distant ramifications as well as the more intimate complications of this situation. As we shall see, this double direction will be a central feature of sympotic events. Sprandel has treated this double direction in a perhaps somewhat cavalier fashion: "Poetry did not remain in the artificial world of literary permanence but received the full force of physical life. It had functions in this life. It wanted to be heard, wanted to have effects, as deep as possible."[16] Huizinga formulates the idea like a poet himself: "It is not faithfulness which transforms knighthood into the beautiful form of life *kat' exochen*. Nor could the immediate roots of the lust of fighting have elevated knighthood into that form if women's love had not been the burning embers which donated the warmth of life to this complex of feeling and idea."[17]

For Huizinga, the erotic motif has penetrated medieval sport above all. In order to be culture, he goes on to say, eroticism must find a style that keeps it within bounds; he calls it the epithalamian style or apparatus. Before, it had been part of the sacred marriage rites; now it is used to season the life of love in general, with its indecencies, obscene allusions, and ambiguities rampant at all times for suitable and improper occasions.[18] In the transition from the first (1235) to the second (1275) *Roman de la Rose*, literature has set up the account of these changes.

There are certainly many reasons for the downfall of knighthood and chivalry. A very concrete, technological factor would be the development of firearms, which the knights could not profit from, unlike their adversaries, emperors, kings, and cities. An important role should also be granted to the internecine narcissism of knights fighting knights, which destroys the binding power, high in principle but overtaxing a relatively young social system—that is, the system of *law* and its leading institutions—and depriving it of its efficiency. In the Holy Roman Empire of the German nation, there were two supreme courts: the Reichskammergericht, which took care of affairs of the estates of the empire, and the Reichshofrat, which functioned rather as a body of advisors for the emperor. This structure seemed reasonable in theory, but in practice it failed. In principle, the supreme courts exercised the function of stabilizing the empire: to the emperor, to the estates of the empire, and to subjects they imparted the feeling "that they belonged to a living community of law."[19] Step by step, however, this function was undermined and in the end destroyed by the type and number of quarrels. The effect of religious conflicts was devastating and provoked a split in the legal structure. "None of the adversaries questioned the religious peace openly. But each kept armies of legal representatives who, in endless and hairsplitting interpretations, tried to get the best for their own side."[20] Gotthard diagnoses "a disastrous break of communication." For the present study, this can be seen as one piece of evidence that social communication and sociable communication are drifting apart. Legal discourse loses its elasticity and consequently its meaningful contact with other forms of language. The accumulation of dogmatic interpretation produces chaos. In terms of a philosophy of law, the empire is gliding into a permanent constitutional crisis: Since, if only for financial reasons, one cannot go to war for each quarrel, the appeal to one of the two supreme courts appears to have been the action that is taken. The courts, in their turn, are flooded with lawsuits; accordingly, their bureaucratic management regularly breaks down.

I have mentioned this development of the legal system both because it is one element in the history of declining knighthood but also, more important, because the self-referential closure of legal discourse draws attention to an analogous trend in knightly life-forms themselves. The sympotic dimension (especially festivals or parts of these), a central feature of the semiotics of power, is chained to a vicious circle of overreaching itself. The signs of power, which it is supposed to represent, can fulfill their task only if they can be seen as outdoing the competition. Knighthood (also) declined because the costs of symbolic and sympotic self-representation were spiraling out of control. Festivals come to be staged as an autonomous sign of power. A disproportion between factual status and real power, on the one hand, and symbolic efforts, on the other, becomes endemic. Symbolic and sympotic efforts, as Huizinga puts it, are driven by an imagination that has become threadbare.[21] To determine what is going on, we could also use Huizinga's verdict that there was an excessive extension of the visual coupled with an atrophy of ("realistic") thought in the late Middle Ages.[22] (Symbolic) climax and (real) crash are very close to each other. In his great book on life-forms in the Middle Ages, Arno Borst is more concerned with the description of catastrophes, with consideration of those killed during festivals and the ruinous costs of the latter, than with the festivals themselves. Nobody could draw attention to the fact that they were ruining themselves with their spending behavior.[23] The lack of binding or merely regulatory power manifested by social institutions with sociable parts and effects, evoked by Borst in strong terms, must have been even more aggravating. Family and local groups will normally provide greater portions of permanence and peace than a single life fending for its own. Working together in the immediate environment, a family may enlarge its scope; if it is successful, more and more people will flock into its orbit. But family circles are too concrete and restricted to satisfy a desirable openness to the world. With an increasing number of people in a family, relations will likely become strained; frequently, companions at home become enemies.

For larger groups, Borst thinks, no prototype of sociability existed anyway. One type, tending toward cooperatives on a voluntary basis, might have succeeded in creating stable life-forms. But that type also tended to develop, like religious orders, exclusive circles open only to an elite, or they adopted characteristics of charitable brotherhoods, with only a very limited range of efficiency. Whether in historical or social terms, their range was small. For nonmembers, their existence was in any case of dubious value, since they could embody norms of behavior only among the small circle of leaders. They were confronted and had to deal with an amorphous mass of people: the rabble, the rank and file, subjects and underlings of all kinds, laypeople, and God's own followers. Claims and realities of integration diverged wildly.[24] We could also say there was a lot of sociability, but in contrast to ancient Athens, there was no overlapping of social, to say nothing of political, institutions and isolated sociable routines or events.

I would like to extract one more bit of inspiration from the rich mines of Borst's *Lebensformen im Mittelalter* (Forms of life in the Middle Ages) that connects my argument with an earlier theme. In this case, however, I intend to turn Borst's thesis around in order to gain plausibility. For a while, the thesis that *scholarship* isolates its practitioners far more from history and society than literature looks convincing;[25] Abelard, for example, is said to have had that painful experience. Moreover, Borst maintains, medieval universities resembled machines, because teaching, its methods and themes, was pedantically prescribed. He is astonished that such a human machine could have functioned for so long and tries to explain this by assuming that the factor of time played its role in the shape of timetables, not in the form of generational conflicts—that the university represented a "specialized community" that did not have to take care of the particularities of families, estates, ranks, and nations.[26] For me, the knowledge produced in universities is of greater importance. Knowledge is power not only in Francis Bacon's relatively straightforward sense but involves power as a mostly abstract disposable mass of thought. Under ordinary circumstances, it collides only rarely with social, political, or even religious institutions, although such collisions, too many in the eyes of the adherents of knowledge, have certainly occurred. There is, for instance, the twofold condemnation of 219 theses that, the bishop of Paris alleged in 1270 and 1277, were taught in the most important university of Christendom. This "authoritarian intervention into scholarly and scientific development" (Kurt Flasch) was nonetheless unable to slow down or stop the thrusts of rationality in the twelfth century: after 1200, the scholarly world learned about Aristotle's texts on the philosophy of nature; in 1255, the statutes of the Paris faculty demanded what had been forbidden before: the exegesis of the writings of Aristotle in general. Flasch regards this as a shift of world-historical importance.[27] In any case, such collisions are rare. In the future, the significance of knowledge will rather be that it poses a threat—that of judging social and political power together with everyday mentality at any time; that universities have to act on that threat rarely happens.

Thus, I am not contradicting Borst but changing his emphasis so that the picture of the Middle Ages fits much better into my overall theme. The relation between knowledge and power often resembles a stalemate. Knowledge immunizes the universities to a large extent against the arrogance of power. In many cases, the representatives of power do not even understand the danger knowledge may have in store for them. Consequently, universities can build up a scope, fairly protected against external ignorance, in which they can establish and stabilize knowledge internally. We can recognize agents of stabilization in the methodical quality of research and, almost of equal importance, in sociable activities with a considerable portion of sympotic elements. Quite a few university colleges, among them several from Oxford and Cambridge, have become famous both for their scholarly and scientific excellence and for their embodiment of life-forms without which that excellence would hardly be possible. In many cases, they were able to preserve a reputation to that effect well up to the present.

Arno Borst was certainly justified in comparing medieval academic work to a machine. But it is unlikely that medieval academic work would have totally lacked those special qualities that Dorothy L. Sayers attributed to a (not only fictitious) Oxford College in her novel *Gaudy Night* (1935), qualities both attractive and problematic. I am breaking chronology not least because the continuity of academic existence, though certainly limited, has not completely vanished. An anticipatory glance at a serious twentieth-century novel with a detective-story structure can illuminate the attraction, however problematic, of collegiate sympotic institutions. Sayers highlights, first of all, "the remarkable solidarity and public spirit" displayed by an Oxford Women's College "as a body" in the face of criminal challenges. The college is seen from the perspective of John Donne as a "paradise" and as "*Horti conclusi,* . . . *Gardens that are walled in.*"[28] Intellectually and psychosocially, a college can boast of a unique existence, where students, but especially also teachers, can learn what they really want and are able to do. For teachers in particular, but not exclusively, writing good prose turns into an emotional, indeed visceral, excitement "over-riding other possible tendencies and desires" (124), because, in the sense of inner commitment and conviction, one knows that one is right (169–170). "To be true to one's calling, whatever follies one might commit in one's emotional life, that was the way to spiritual peace" (31). True enough: this may be just a dream even for those who hold that faith, a dream stubbornly thwarted by the realities of life and by unmitigated "psychological oddities" (73). And, certainly, writing good scholarly prose must be an activity pursued in what in nineteenth century Germany was called "solitude and freedom." But even Wilhelm von Humboldt, to whom we owe this phrase, went on immediately to say that human achievement was, to a fair degree, also a matter of comprehensive cooperation (see also the first section of Chapter 3).[29] In the novel, scholarly activity is embedded in (sometimes playfully) agonistic conversation and a daily series of rituals that have to be seen as a sequence of events framed by eating and drinking.

In countries such as Germany, in which the college structure has not imposed itself, its place is occupied by other combinations of scholarly and sympotic aspects. Here we have to name the faculty, in the sense of an institution uniting related disciplines rather than of individual members. Otto Seel has credited faculties, perhaps in a vein too idealistic and optimistic and yet perhaps essentially correct, with the strength of lasting through the centuries, of being elastic and so full of life as to adapt themselves to all the changes of a spiritual and scientific kind. What is more, faculties have regained the position of spiritual leadership that they had lost, irreducible to relics of times long past, in this way remaining a heroic element in the history and organization of spiritual life.[30]

Yet there is no denying that the scholarly-scientific achievements (or rather the pressure to be able to claim them) and the sympotic rituals can destroy lives. Sayers's Women's College is exposed to attacks of violence, whose origin is traced back to a forger, a lecturer in the college, together with the discovery of the forgeries by a woman lecturer also in the college. The forger, deprived of any and all career opportunities, committed suicide; his widow, reduced to a life of misery and working as an unknown servant in the college, perpetrates the attacks in revenge. When arrested, she delivers a barrage of reproaches against the college. One cannot easily ignore the direction her criticisms against the work and form of life of the college are taking, even if, in point of fact, they are incorrect: "There's nothing in your books about life and marriage and children, is there? Nothing about desperate people—or love—or hate or anything human" (*Gaudy Night*, 427; for academic self-criticism, see also 191, 220).[31] Although, literally, the attacks are untrue, they are only pushed aside and not refuted (429–430).[32] The attractions of academic life described above, including an affective or even sensual satisfaction accompanying academic achievements, cannot be reconciled with serious doubts that a consistent, supposedly superior total conception of life can be conceived, practiced, or imposed. Any satisfactory combination of professional and sympotic elements must largely be paid for by others who do not have the means to afford it for themselves.

Furthermore, the history of European universities seems to demand the admission that any new project will go far beyond its original goals: the fear of discovering consistency deficits will provoke both exaggeration of the conception and frantic countermeasures. This is owing to the assumption, abundantly manifest in Europe, that improvements can be made by revising and refining original concepts. While this assumption is not wrong, it has resulted in what Arnold Gehlen has called the Platonizing conceptual realism of European scholars.[33] One could create a long list of other "miscarriages" of academic promise. In the Middle Ages, university practices soon called forth the genre of university satire, which has firmly established itself as part of the talk about universities down to the present day. As soon as, for instance, the University of Paris became an identifiable institution, complaints about a loose curriculum, about the conversion of what is here called sympotic elements into what appeared as a boundless joie de vivre, began to run wild.³⁴ Le Goff, who proclaimed the thirteenth century as the century of universities, feels compelled to lament their provinciality—that is, their national and regional limitations in the fourteenth and fifteenth centuries: "The intellectual world cultivates its conformity with political stereotypes."³⁵ Real humanism is no longer taught in the universities but in the elite institution that will ultimately be transformed into the Collège de France. Aristotelian philosophy became part of the regular academic program. Once this had happened, people began to criticize its one-sidedness: it turns out that Aristotelian ethics had adopted the dubious function of codifying the norms of a wealthy, healthy, and married landowner with theoretical inclinations. The ideal life seemed to have been invented for an intellectual aristocracy; Aristotle leaves no doubt that children, women, sick people, and slaves would never reach the goals of this ideal.³⁶ The thrusts of rationality with which Flasch had mainly credited the universities could not completely shake off the irrationality of the world.

Finally, the breach between science, teaching, and life, much lamented especially in the twentieth century, had already begun to show up in the late Middle Ages.³⁷ The legacy of the medieval university for its modern successors consists very strongly in the contrast between joyful science and its opposite, about which Nietzsche, but not only Nietzsche, had come to be so very concerned. In the twentieth century, Nietzsche's diagnosis shook the humanities to its foundations. The absence of joy in the activities of science and scholarship has created so much trouble for some of its representatives that parody has seemed to offer the only alternative.

CHAPTER 3
Sociability and the Humanities

THIS CHAPTER ELABORATES on the idea, already hinted at several times, that the humanities might have turned into a model of sociable life with enormous social significance. From the nineteenth century onward (some would regard this as the real beginning of their history), their social and cultural significance has been invoked at regular intervals. Correlatively less and less has been said about their sociable side, which still played a crucial role for the late eighteenth and early nineteenth centuries in Europe.

Collecting Evidence

Apart from the split between the ideal of a joyful science and the reality of a joyless one, the history of science (in the comprehensive "German" sense) has documented another discrepancy, which raised its head in the nineteenth century, albeit to some extent as early as the seventeenth (when, to be sure, humanities in our sense did not exist)—namely, the widening gap between the natural sciences and the humanities. The humanities, a loose group of disciplines, enjoys, or rather suffers from, an assortment of different names in different countries, a variability indicative of their varying status in different cultures. Although I cannot go into the reasons for this here, the break is foreshadowed in the seventeenth century, accelerates partly in the eighteenth century, and hardens in the nineteenth century into the notorious two cultures deplored later by C. P. Snow. The philosophy of science has helped to moderate that split, having ascertained that it is not only the humanities but also the natural sciences that need to come to terms with problems of understanding. Formulating concepts can be a very difficult task in the sciences too.

Histories of scientific and scholarly thought have, however, been plagued for a while by another asymmetry, which has reanimated the opposition between the two fields. Alfred North Whitehead identifies three driving forces behind the natural sciences: first, the methodological generalization of the concept of rationality that in the Middle Ages was invested in the concept of God; second, the technological wave in the Renaissance; and third, the advances in mathematics.[1] Clearly, the humanities can claim only the generalized type of rationality. In spite of analogous conditions, the methodological grip on objects of investigation in the natural sciences reveals a (self-)assurance sorely lacking in the humanities, where such assurance degenerates readily into dogmatic opinion. The reason why natural scientists might also be able, as many people have noted (Paul Feyerabend, Paul Valéry, et al.), to live the joyous side of their work with fewer inhibitions may lie hidden in the self-assurance of approach.

It also follows that natural scientists are more obliged to and "disciplined" by their methodological standards. And it is doubtful in what sense one could attribute a "methodology" to the humanities at all. It is not for nothing that the title of a famous and important work for the humanities and their hermeneutics, Hans-Georg Gadamer's *Truth and Method*, implies an opposition. It does not mean that method is a precondition of truth. Looking for them, one can find similar assertions, especially by prestigious representatives of the humanities. Theodor Adorno states categorically that methodological "cleanliness," general control, consensus of scholars, documentation, and even the logical consistency of argument do not open the way to the spirit the humanities are looking for. For him, the methodological net that the humanities have thrown over their objects is more like a fetish. Long before Adorno and Gadamer, the philosopher Nicolai Hartmann (to whom we shall return) had written a comprehensive work on spiritual existence and the humanities, *Das Problem des geistigen Seins. Untersuchungen zur Grundlegung der Geschichtsphilosophie und der Geisteswissenschaften* (1933), culminating, with respect to the latter, in the somewhat meager conclusion that the strength of the humanities does not lie in knowledge about procedures but exclusively in a masterful style of handling some method; the method itself is a secondary affair of later reflection pursued by epigones. Hartmann thought that fruitful work in research might well be achieved without an explicit methodology.[2]

I have not referred to Adorno's, Gadamer's, and Hartmann's skeptical ideas concerning method in order to disparage the humanities. I do not take these remarks primarily as criticism but rather as indirect questions as to where else a focus of "humanistic" activities could lie. In looking at their history and some seminal texts, however, it may dawn upon us that a reorganization of the relation between scholarship and the sympotic dimension might not be the worst of possible reformatory ideas. It is clear that method cannot simply be replaced by sympotic orientation, but in any case, the voices that would like to liberate the humanities in order to take over other tasks beyond scholarship do not fall silent.

Wherein might these tasks consist? There is a suspicious emotional charge in the proposal to reinvent the spirit in order to escape from the lack of it that, some say, has come to haunt today's universities. This charge is no less suspicious if the concept of the spirit is opened up in order to welcome human desires of a more sensual kind as well. It is probably true that, by and large, the "de-eroticized" organization of research today has kicked the emotional and affective needs out of the universities. We are not really told what such suggestions are meant to amount to. Once upon a time, when theorists had already spoken about the vital needs of human beings engaged in the humanities, the signs were ominous. The philosopher Erich Rothacker, hardly known today but of considerable influence in his own time, did not shrink from clarity: he said the humanities were serving as an ideological protection of open flanks in the framework of fights in life and thought. Even more clearly, such theorizing unmasked itself as a product of the heyday of fairly crude but disastrous ideologies of the 1920s and 1930s.[3] At the end of the twentieth century, some humanities (including law) practitioners have tired of the constant demands for usefulness; they look at the humanities as a luxury embellishing situations of sociability.[4]

It was, however, difficult to see what kind of sociability they had in mind. With some effort one could perceive that they were targeting a special commitment of researchers in order to do justice to the richness of life depicted or evoked in their objects and their embodiment of a highly cultured form of life. Embedded in such contexts, the humanities turned into a luxury that a society might or might not afford.

Within my network of arguments, I could claim that the humanities might have advanced into a central sociable *and* socially valuable position. They seemed to be able to combine the possibility of sympotic events with advanced intellectuality. In one of their main object domains of research, namely literature, vital areas of human life were explored. That exploration of the vital values of life could easily be extended to painting, especially portraits, which Hegel in his *Aesthetics* had already reactivated as representatives of a vitally suggestive liveliness. Here we see a relatively strong historical logic at work: In the eighteenth century, important perspectives for a theory of sociable existence in a highly educated society began their unfortunately short-lived career. These perspectives were not only compatible with Simmel's sociology of sociability but indeed anticipated it.

In a long and important essay dating back into another era, Norbert Altenhofer has done justice above all to the role of Friedrich Schleiermacher. In contrast to his theory of hermeneutics, Schleiermacher, in his theory of sociable behavior, does not restrict himself to object domains such as philology and literature. Rather, his views encompass the full relation of the free play of individual powers with a comprehensive aesthetic range. Certainly, we must not expect a total congruence of Simmel's positions and those adopted by Schleiermacher. But like Simmel, Schleiermacher emphasizes the inevitability with which the distancing of everyday professional and private life tends to take place in the face of their exhaustion and lack of attraction.

> All educated persons demand a free form of sociability uninhibited by any external purpose. It is one of their first and noblest needs. Whoever is thrown back and forth between domestic burdens and the business affairs of civil society will approach the higher goals of human existence slowly—the more so the more faithfully he repeats that way. Professional work banishes the activity of the spirit to a tight circle. However noble and respectable it may be, it always ties the person's effect on and way of looking at it to one point of view. Thus, the highest and most complicated standpoint, like the simplest and lowest point of view, will produce one-sidedness and limitation. Domestic life brings us into contact only with a few people and these are always the same: the highest demands of morality in this domain will soon be familiar to an attentive mind, and its harvest of the manifold opinions of mankind and its activities will decrease to the extent that everything is legally acceptable and the moral economy has been perfected.

This is Schleiermacher's diagnosis. He draws the consequences immediately and in a very clear form:

> Consequently, there must be a state which completes the other two [domestic life and business], which enables individuals to have their sphere intersected by the sphere of others in ways as diverse as possible, and where their limits open up perspectives into other and foreign worlds so that all the phenomena of mankind will gradually become known to them. In this way, they will, as it were, become friends with even the

most foreign minds and conditions and can look upon them as neighbors. This task is solved through the free intercourse of reasonable people.[5]

Schleiermacher goes on to say that the free intercourse between well-educated and self-educating people will open up the "intellectual world" for them. But he does not and cannot maintain this limitation to the intellectual world. The opening of the intellectual world is directly followed by the "free play" of human powers that people can continue to "develop in a harmonious manner," following nothing but the laws which they have made for themselves (180). The main medium of this ongoing development is art—that is, the playful occupation of individuals with themselves in contrast to the constraints imposed by business (181). This "self-manifestation of individuality" does not primarily refer to art in a narrow sense; rather, individuals turn into artists themselves by leaving traces of themselves in all their works. Their manifestations are invitations and pleas to fellow human beings for recognition. They open up their personality by appeals to the consciousness of the species (181).

We do not have to decide what, if any, consistency Schleiermacher's project can claim; his main point, reminding us of Simmel, is well taken. In Altenhofer's words: "The artistic character of sociable behavior will remain underdeveloped or be reduced to the extent in which the manifestation of individuality is subordinated to conformity with convention or to the restriction to the lowest common denominator" (185).

To a considerable extent, it is the humanities that has to examine and cultivate preferential and well-defined forms of artistic-sociable behavior. In Schleiermacher's case, these forms definitely included rituals of eating and drinking. He was a regular member of several intellectual associations and for some years chairperson of the Gesetzlosen Gesellschaft zu Berlin (Society of the Lawless [or, of the Informal Ones]); he frequented literary salons and exchanged addresses of wine merchants with Hegel, with whom he normally quarreled a lot, not least for philosophical reasons, even foiling Hegel's acceptance by the Berlin Academy of Sciences. Their mutual antipathy also had to do with religion: for Hegel, Schleiermacher, himself a high-ranking court preacher, professor of theology, and much more, did not take religious service seriously enough. Schleiermacher, indeed, viewed service as an art too, as well as attaching a much greater importance to conversation in the practice of philosophy than Hegel would countenance.[6] In his "literary" hermeneutics, the literary or other character of texts, apart from the knowledge of textual and genre traditions, had also to be determined to some extent in talking about it. Again, Schleiermacher moved back and forth here in the "boundary area of sociable and aesthetic activity."[7] Jürgen Kaube offers an interesting final judgment: Schleiermacher was attracted, he says, by whatever could be seen as an expression of spontaneity, "even the riots of the fraternities" over which he quarreled with Hegel again.[8]

Many of the texts that we have come, in Schleiermacher's way or another, to call literary have themselves surveyed this boundary area. One would assume that the disciplines broadly called literary scholarship and devoted to the elucidation of such texts would not neglect it either or fall back behind the investigative level of their objects. Doing this, we could perhaps get a clearer idea of what Klaus Heinrich, quoted above, might have meant by a phrase such as "the vital subject," whose embodiments he could not find anymore in the universities, and what Schleiermacher had in mind when he looked for the boundary areas in which the self-manifestation of individuality would often take place. The lessons taught by modern art in that respect would, however, have been in vain if we failed to see that such themes cannot be treated today without irony and a deflation of emotional investments; yet even this has largely already occurred in so-called literature itself. Heimito von Doderer, for instance, in whose texts the sympotic element has advanced so far as to include the subtleties of coffee-brewing, has the young historian Stangeler complain about the humanities sections of modern universities, which leave no space for coming to terms with those forces of the mind troubling the full human being: "The contact reaches, in expert fashion, as far as to the collar button, and the classical philologist is an engineer in the same way as the historian for the modern period."[9] We could find similar passages, combined perhaps with analysis, in Robert Musil's *The Man without Qualities* and others. We could also call to the stand an impartial witness such as Eberhard Lämmert, a former professor of German and president of the Free University of Berlin: "The professors, too, are only responsible for one screw of the left front wheel. Understandably, in the process, professors of history become as stupid as workers for Ford, and, if you look at the product, our students as well as our Ford cars are unsafe at any speed." Confronted with such irony, we may be permitted to reintroduce some residual sentiment: admitting that special competence in the workplace is necessary, people in the humanities need, above all, "the ability to respond to the questions, wishes, troubles of people in very different situations." The humanities must promote "unprofessional" [!] thought on general problems of life.[10]

Calling for unprofessional thought in times in which professionalisms seem to claim priority in all respects, Lämmert is running quite a few risks. It would perhaps be more cautious and more precise to speak of semiprofessionalism here. Helping students to tackle problems of life, one cannot really proceed without more or less accepted relevant knowledge, be it theoretical or practical. Selecting that material and mastering it could be seen as the professional part; applying it to and interpreting it for individual cases could be regarded as the creative side. The humanities might present themselves in semiprofessional shape because they cannot assert themselves by virtue of their disciplinary strength of research and reflection; they depend on imports, especially in terms of theory. Literary scholarship, for instance, would not progress very far if it did not exploit philosophical, psychological, sociological, and other results. However, they can and must rely on their own creativity when it comes to the question of how to reconcile that mass of material with the needs of the individual case at hand. The body of knowledge imported is transformed into playfully, creatively handled materials, with any luck producing that absolute intellectual excitement the elements and sociable contexts of which Dorothy Sayers tried to fathom in *Gaudy Night*.

In the process, let us hope, the college context would assume essential elements of a sympotic model. Its time comes—or should I say, ought to have come with the twentieth century—because the mounting pressure, in Schleiermacher's sense, of one-sided, stressful, and certainly professional business activities must be counteracted. In Great Britain, the college teacher, accordingly, tries to position themselves between the amateurism of the nineteenth-century "man of letters" and the professionalized manager-type scholar or scientist who has taken over in the late twentieth century. In Germany, the situation is less transparent, because the high claims for the *Gelehrte* (embracing both scholar and scientist) made by and in the wake of Fichte have spread a generalized philosophical prestige across the professoriate. Likewise, the concept of the intellectual has taken on rather different connotations in the United States, Great Britain, France, and Germany.

Most of the variants that have been envisaged for the universities are suffering from a deficit that hinders or prevents their practically and structurally efficient implementation. In Europe, these projects result from and are hemmed in by financial, administrative, and legal—in sum, governmental—handicaps while also being embellished by fashionable ideas about what a university should look like. Between the handicaps and the ideas, however, falls the shadow. Universities turn into the victims of their own as well as alien constraints. The paradigm for this, comic in its rigidity, was set up by the philosopher J. G. Fichte; realistic conceptions, on the other hand, including strong sympotic elements such as those proposed by Wilhelm von Humboldt, have been blocked by governmental authoritarianism. In terms of teaching practice, Fichte awards priority to the dialogical form in a "true academy" and thus keeps alive sympotic possibilities in the face of the incontestable success of book culture, but he destroys these himself by sacrificing them to a strange mixture of arbitrary criteria.[11] Scientific and scholarly disciplines are rigidly classified; students are rigorously disciplined; regular students and professors must wear uniforms that no one else may wear.[12] Fichte seems to remind us of sympotic orientations when he demands a communal household (102) or would like to look at the regulars as a family whole (109), but his family of professors and students looks very much like a pocket edition of the authoritarian Big Brother state in Orwell's *1984* ("They are constantly questioned and observed as to the development of their mind"[13]). Individual behavior is judged by the family; punishment, though not intended as deterrence, may be practiced as segregation and banishment (109).

Humboldt's conception (like Schleiermacher's, incidentally) is couched in terms that are much more elastic. Its only drawback is that—in contrast to what Germans and even German experts think—it never did become a reality in Germany itself. The foundation of US elite institutions, starting with Johns Hopkins University, came much closer to what Humboldt had in mind. This is true especially for financing as suggested in Humboldt's "Antrag auf Errichtung der Universität Berlin Juli 1809" (Application to establish the University of Berlin July 1809): "For the benefit and purpose of the university it would be best if the university and the institutes connected with it received their annual income through the [initial] donation of agricultural estates."[14] The universities would derive their income from the profitable management of the estates.

Humboldt's elasticity (and, one might say, his antiauthoritarianism) becomes even more apparent in regard to the university as a form of life. Certainly, Humboldt did write the famous and indeed notorious words on "solitude and freedom" as prerequisites of academic work. But immediately after having named these as "main principles," Humboldt narrows down their meaning drastically and almost changes them into their contrary:

But since spiritual-intellectual work flourishes only as cooperation, not only in the sense of one making up for what the other does not possess but rather in the sense that successful work by the one should kindle enthusiasm in the other and make visible the general and original power which in the single person shines forth only in individual and derived form, thus the inner organization of these institutions must bring forth an uninterrupted form of cooperation revitalizing itself all the time without constraints and intention.[15]

Humboldt's nonchalance in demanding, in the capital of Prussian authoritarianism, a certain autonomy for both intellectual conceptions and organizational structures is remarkable indeed. That authoritarianism has been well portrayed in Klaus Vieweg's biography of Hegel, who himself was severely criticized for his (alleged) authoritarianism.[16] It is, by contrast, the elasticity of interaction and a corresponding style of thought that guarantees cohesion, a more than regional scientific solidarity, and an intellectual creativity; the state, in other words, must know that it cannot preordain what is called academic excellence today. This applies with particular force to scientific and scholarly activities in their "liveliest and strongest vitality."[17] Rather, the state must help to eradicate any one-sidedness in the higher institutions of learning (276). Top performances need few and simple organizational rules, but these must interfere at a deeper level than usual (277). Then the way toward achievement is simple and secure, because it coincides with the cultivation of all human faculties (278). The closeness to Schleiermacher's theory of sociable behavior is obvious. For Humboldt, a plurality of scientifically as well as interactively promising institutions (social and private associations—members need not belong exclusively to one or the other) should correspond to elastic organizational forms of academia (281). In the case of academies that represent the highest sanctuaries of the academic intellect, the state should not be allowed to interfere at all (281).

I suppose one would be justified in calling Schleiermacher's and Humboldt's conceptions realistic. They might look idealistic or naïve because in Germany, for instance, given the overall realities of politics and mentality, serious efforts at implementation were not really made. If, with respect to the political system after World War II, authoritarian state interventionism has not increased, it has not decreased either. Dimensions of the sympotic certainly do exist, but they tend to be hidden or cut off from intellectual work.

It is of course possible, even probable, that financial constraints, imagined or real, and the impact of globalization have meanwhile leveled out many differences between national university systems. Globalization has tremendously increased pressures toward the comparability of universities and the rankings that follow from it. A mere glance at Great Britain should make us aware that complaints about the essential quality of academic work have invaded that country of traditions too. One could, in contrast to Sayers's *Gaudy Night*, read contemporary satiric university novels and take seriously, despite their age, books such as Bill Readings's *The University in Ruins* (1997), tracing the ruination from rationality to culture (in the context of the nation-state) and from there to the quantification techniques imposed on or embraced by universities as transnational corporations. We could also follow A. H. Halsey and the ramifications of the distinction between "professionism" and professionalism. A degree of professionalism is necessary in almost any activity today; the totalization of narrow professionism, by contrast, is nefarious. Halsey, one of the last great British sociologists with, as one obituary had it, the experience of real life, quoted for instance Max Weber's typology of academic teachers (the charismatic teacher, the "cultivated man," and the expert) but found to his dismay that the cultivated person hardly exists anymore. Certainly the old type of the professor as gentleman cannot be resuscitated. That many older rules regulating life in a university, such as the celibacy rules, especially in Oxford, have been dropped is a good thing. On the other hand, as late as 1930 the US university "expert" Abraham Flexner, founder of the Princeton Institute for Advanced Study and author of the well-known book *Universities: American, English, German* (1930), did not hesitate to praise the universities of Oxford and Cambridge because their professors "can without effort or sacrifice be host to a Minister of State, a great scientist or a philosopher."[18] The cultivated persons—that is, those who are, despite the odds, still there—should act as a bulwark against professionism and, worse still, "proletarianization" (124) and present themselves as "exemplars of learning for the rising generation" (170). Incidentally, one of the old tenets concerning the cultivated person was the demand "that the table be as lavishly provided as the library" (171).

De facto, it is the experts who rule supreme. They do so on the grounds that the nature of modern science demands their services, that universities must cultivate them, if merely for reasons of international prestige, reputation, and visibility. They work toward highly organized, methodologically as well as bureaucratically standardized research projects. Since the sciences, as Habermas for one has known for many years, have thrown their nets over everyday life and terrorized people via the media with dire forecasts should their knowledge not be heeded, the experts must step in as bridge-builders between research projects ever more arcane and an ignorant public. Halsey, backed by empirical evidence, has already noted changes in the atmosphere of the senior common rooms, an atmosphere impersonal, fragmented, busy and at the same time apathetic. Senior common rooms came to look more like "a high-tech factory boardroom" than an "academic club room" (4, 36, 170). Professionism, in its turn, seems to carry the stigma of nonproductivity, lack of inspiration and creativity; therefore, understandably, "senior common room morale is low" (124). The concepts used in the opinions quoted by Halsey are often annoyingly vague, but we cannot doubt that an expression such as "the cultural failure of the universities" (46) does indeed mark problems of the university relevant here. If in the past a university capable of some combination of cultured interaction, sociable enjoyment, and scientific achievement was still visible, for Halsey the future of this institution is "bleak" because its ambition concentrates exclusively on "market solutions." (269).

The Spirit of the Humanities and Philosophical Anthropology

Halsey's book, its pessimistic conclusion notwithstanding, does not spell the impossibility of sympotic amalgamations for the humanities. Late eighteenth- and early nineteenth-century conceptions (Schleiermacher, W. von Humboldt) had in fact prepared blueprints—in Humboldt's case, of almost global impact—for a spirited coexistence between academic work and life. During the nineteenth century, however, the humanities were run over by two developments to which a famous saying often attributed to Ralph Waldo Emerson could have been applied: the plan was noble, but the details melancholy. One detail consisted in the pressure of the sciences on the humanities to prove their scientific character. This provided an impulse for the foundational activities of Wilhelm Dilthey. As we have seen at the beginning of the previous chapter, these activities were not only unnecessary, but in their misleading emphasis on the duality between understanding and explanation they prepared the way, unintentionally to be sure, for a misuse of a more serious kind. The humanities, donning the armor of the varieties of the philosophy of science, did not pay sufficient attention to the ideologies that infiltrated them in spite or rather because of and together with the armor. These ideologies were particularly powerful because they served to ennoble the nation-state—in retrograde Germany (the belated nation, according to Plessner and others) a matter of particular urgency.

And there was a third element making the humanities vulnerable, to which Heinz Schlaffer has drawn our attention: The bookish learning invested in philology and in most cases rather remote and alien cultural matters did not bode well for the treatment of the poetic word, which began as enthusiastic song and ended as dry writing. From its inception, the pedantries of philology met with mockery, since they seemed to consist only in the interpretations of interpretations and in books about books. The feeling had already emerged in Shakespearean characters, who, like Hamlet and Troilus, complained about "words, words, mere words" ("no matter from the heart"). The expansion of the sciences and of scholarship demanded adaptation to scientific standards and erased essential elements of aesthetic experience. Certainly, the humanities and especially philology had to position their objects of investigation at a distance in order to see them better. But Schlaffer is surely right to be struck by the fact that self-descriptions of philology never talk about aesthetic enjoyment and appear to remain untouched by the development of eighteenth-century aesthetics. The suspicion that there was neither a need nor the capability for it is hard to ward off.[19]

For a less incomplete picture, further examinations of Dilthey and philosophical anthropology would seem appropriate. Schlaffer's diagnosis does not, we might object, apply to the great achievements in the humanities of the nineteenth century. The so-called foundation of the humanities by Dilthey does not take place against the background of a retreat into an otherworldly silence of textual interpretation or philological strange objects lost somewhere in history. Rather, Dilthey invokes action as the real destiny of human beings.[20] In order to elaborate plausible models of action, one needs the evidence worked out by all the "sciences" dealing with human beings, with society, and with the state.[21] There was, it must be said at the outset, a big obstacle to such an endeavor: the sciences could not be fused into a coherent whole anymore. In any case, however, a practical orientation appears to dominate in volumes 18 and 19 of the *Gesammelte Schriften*, which contain preliminary work and sketches from the years 1860 to 1890. But in volume 5, devoted to the "intellectual-artistic-spiritual world" (*geistige Welt*), the practical bent is superseded, in barely noticeable form, by worlds not only free from action but rather opposed to it. Instead, Dilthey speaks quite emphatically about the happiness provided by work in the humanities:

> Our actions presuppose that we understand other persons everywhere. A large part of our happiness springs from feeling our way into the soul of others. Philological and historical scholarship is based on the assumption that understanding individual or singular matters and states of mind can be brought to objectivity. Historical consciousness is built on that. Modern people thus can make the whole past of humanity present to themselves. They can look beyond all the barriers of their own time into past cultures. They absorb their power and enjoy their magic: a great increase of happiness comes to them from that.[22]

Unfortunately, the use of a vocabulary of happiness by Burckhardt and Dilthey is treacherous. In Burckhardt, happiness results from all kinds of communicative and performative acts of people finding themselves in bodily presence with each other. Materials used for communication and performance may include texts insofar as they can in fact be performed. We cannot decide when and to what extent a culture strongly marked by symposia or perhaps similar institutions can handle written, later printed, texts. It is equally impossible to decide whether the symposium and writing or print largely exclude each other. But it is clear that, for Dilthey, the happiness of the present depends on the texts of the past. Therefore, one would like to know which cognitive and psychological modalities are necessary in order to produce happiness and magic in the experience of reading. We do not have to doubt the possibility, but probability might suggest that the infinite number of possibilities of action "of all humanity" that one might meet in reading would favor skepticism in regard to the likelihood of action. For Simmel, quite in contrast to Dilthey, the tragedy of culture consists precisely in the mass of cultural products, particularly texts, which can be absorbed and digested only very selectively.

Sixty years later, Arnold Gehlen demonstrated, applying a slight conceptual shift, how easily Dilthey's construction may crumble. In his Habilitationsschrift, *Wirklicher und unwirklicher Geist* (1931), he objects to Dilthey's "hermeneutic" foundation of the humanities on the grounds that it presupposes a "spiritual essence of reality." That the absolute was spirit was evident for Hegel, and it was the basic experience of the mystics. "But who dares to say today that he or she has understood that?"[23] In a conceptual move in which we see the first storm clouds of philosophical anthropology, Gehlen does not simply write off the spirit: he circumvents the apparent opposition "real"/"unreal" by a successive order of *degrees of being* that in their turn are projected onto a *logic of situations*. The content of reality in a situation or person increases to the degree that more and more sides and aspects of a person and situation can be liberated from their mere potential and transformed into actuality. "Any transitory or permanent restraint or repression of a talent or passion, of a drive or interest or of merely a thought, *de-realizes* the person together with his or her objects" (153). In Gehlen's construction, even the possibility of happiness is entitled to a comeback: degrees of happiness and being merge into each other. And there is only one kind of happiness: "the happiness of unconditional existence" (154). By contrast, melancholy is characteristic of lower degrees of being. Demoniac degrees assert themselves if someone has an idea about a world and assumes that they stand alone against it—a world, they think, not given but more powerful than they are (154–155, esp. para. 3).

Literature, indeed, can easily produce such an impression; contemporary psychological thrillers seem to have subscribed to corresponding narrative techniques. In any case, in his time Gehlen, starting out from a logic of situations, was still able to imagine analogies and successors of the symposium. The "only adequate object of human beings is the *other human being*, and it is in the relations of people to each other that being in its essential forms becomes reality" (159). Unfortunately, the states of being available to human beings change with history, and prospects for most kinds or relations are not very good. Whether we can hope for more for family or other elementary forms of relation remains an open question (160). Gehlen's view of historical degrees of being does not necessarily shift the probability of higher degrees into the dynamics of "extra-human objects" (161). But with the criterion of "wholeness" (161) and the example of love (160) he offers aspects difficult to put into practice or to generalize about.

Keeping the promise to give back to humanity forms of being adequate for full flourishing has led to the point of despair that has haunted so-called philosophical anthropology, mainly in the first half of the twentieth century in Germany. I must come back to this anthropology because it is anything but a provincial enterprise. I introduced it in the third section of Chapter 1 in order to show how historical circumstances—namely, the effect of World War I in Germany—may have produced modes of thought that go far beyond their historical occasion. The breakdown of overblown imperial ambitions set loose the search for forms of behavior more conducive to the improvement of human potentials. First, it is true that the search is directed, according to the philosophical and anthropological claim, toward a new and much more comprehensive as well as subtler picture of evolutionary human equipment. For that purpose, analyses are based on a much broader array of disciplines, from philosophy down to biology and anatomy, taking, for instance, neoteny—that is, the implications of slowed-down human development—into account. Second, there is a shift (not a complete one, of course) from individual to group behavioral aspects. Third, there is an emphasis on tensions rather than on the relative smoothness with which human socialization has often been described.

As to the second point, the most important book by Arnold Gehlen is in fact concerned with the single person (*Der Mensch. Seine Natur und seine Stellung in der Welt* [Man: His nature and place in the world]; see also Max Scheler's *Die Stellung des Menschen im Kosmos* [The human place in the cosmos]). The focus on crucial problems of experience and group behavior is, however, distinctly sharper in books such as *Urmensch und Spätkultur* (Early humans and late culture), *Moral und Hypermoral* (Morality and hypermorality), and *Die Seele im technischen Zeitalter. Sozialpsychologische Probleme in der industriellen Gesellschaft* (Man in the age of technology: Sociopsychological problems in industrial society). The last book especially may be taken to have indicated that Gehlen's main concern is with social psychology, a term not really generally accepted and therefore avoided by philosophical anthropologists. It is also striking that an early text by Helmuth Plessner (*Grenzen der Gemeinschaft* [Limits of community]) was written shortly after he had come to Cologne and, as it were, "invented" philosophical anthropology with Scheler. (For a short characterization of the book, see the third section of Chapter 1.) Plessner's point, important for my general argument, is that the limits of community, in regard to totalitarian programs, for instance, also imply limits of individualism. We cannot exhibit our raw individuality and impose it with all its peculiarities on others; we must come close to others without hurting them, and we must be able to distance ourselves from others without offending them. One could call this a general version of behavioral demands for the sympotic type of community too. Finally, and most strikingly of all, Nicolai Hartmann, a philosopher more of the traditional type, has cast his notions of spirit into a distinctly social frame; his problem of spiritual being will be discussed at some length below.

So much, in the way of introductory hints, for the third point—that is, that there is an emphasis on tensions rather than on the relative smoothness with which human socialization has often been described. Philosophical anthropology, as far as it is relevant here, could then functionally and perhaps somewhat paradoxically be seen as a series of subtle variations taking care as a stopgap, as it were, of an ill-defined field often but not satisfactorily called social psychology. Its main representatives—Max Scheler (1874–1928), Helmuth Plessner (1892–1985), and Arnold Gehlen (1904–1976), all of them philosophers, sociologists, and more—have taken the differentiation of disciplines and fields of research and the pluralization of knowledge seriously but not at their face value. Rather, they treat them as indicators of problems to be reformulated in their perspectives of philosophical anthropology. Thus Scheler may appear as a Catholic philosopher, as the founder of the sociology of knowledge in Germany, and as a phenomenologist of the emotional a priori. It would be pointless to try to present the repertory of thought of this group, but it is profitable to test parts of this repertory in order to see to what extent they can throw new light on the complex of the symposium and its transformations. The implications of philosophical anthropology have an immediate effect on the options open for the humanities.

The birth of philosophical anthropology can be dated precisely, as taking place immediately after the end of World War I. In 1919, Scheler and Plessner met at the newly founded University of Cologne. Some years later, in 1925, they were joined by Nicolai Hartmann, who, however, cannot be readily included, owing to his immense but traditional philosophical range. His central relevance for philosophical anthropology is, nonetheless, amply warranted by Plessner's long review of his *The Problem of Spiritual Being* (1933).

Philosophical anthropology has experienced several cycles of success and neglect. After 1970 it appeared to be marginalized, yet on September 5, 2017, in an interview with Joachim Fischer, the author of a standard work on philosophical anthropology, Peter Sloterdijk described himself as belonging to the second contingent of representatives for a philosophical anthropology. In his opinion, philosophical anthropology has always functioned and will function again as a "reserve of reflection" (*Reflexionsreserve*) for times when the dominating modes of thought such as the technological one today have exhausted their persuasive power. Its function as a reservoir for neglected or avant-garde modes of thought is evident precisely with Scheler, who dares, in a move perhaps bolder than that of Freud, to import concepts such as sublimation and libido into philosophy. Scheler's move is also more complex than Freud's, because for him, "preexisting dispositions of an intellectual kind" should not be left out; libido invests them with additional energies but does not necessarily subjugate them.[24] At the other end of the spectrum, as mentioned above, Plessner explores the limits of community, but with them those of individualism as well. Existence needs forms (and formats, we would add today) that can be really lived. For a community held together by common practical interests (*Sachgemeinschaft*) as well as a community of love (*Liebesgemeinschaft*), Plessner insists emphatically on a certain degree of artificiality or "masks," on a style of life that can combine distance, reserve, ceremonial skill, and the hygiene of tact with compliance, a feeling for the whole, and love.[25] Yet regarding the organization of interactively suitable forms and formats, it is the same Plessner who organizes the reform of rigid and pompous academic conference habits. For the Third German Congress of Philosophy, held in Bremen in 1950, he introduces a series of so-called symposia (!), which break up the mechanical scheme of lecture and discussion and in which professional philosophers as well as the public at large are supposed to engage in "creative talks."[26] This looks like a step in the direction of the old symposium under very different conditions. That such steps could be taken in more radical forms was suggested (unfortunately not until fifty years later) by the brain researcher Wolf Singer, who strongly recommended a revision of the relation between verbal and nonverbal (visual, musical, movement-oriented) dimensions in situations such as conferences, where new knowledge was supposed to be harvested. The inertia of academic procedures seems to have prevented Singer as well as others from pursuing this track.[27]

Let us continue, then, with the short discussion of the early Gehlen. The situation of the spirit that is looking for a form in which to assert its own reality and does not want to be diluted into mere fantasies is hardly encouraging: "The state in which I find myself is one of dissatisfaction" (Gehlen, *Wirklicher und unwirklicher Geist*, 139). It is a dissatisfaction with sensations of superficiality; disgust with what can be known and done; experiences of partiality, hopeless repetitions, and marred infinity; and nostalgia without an idea as to how its object can be won and a state of being ultimately reached (139). Dissatisfaction may intensify and turn into black melancholy or apathy, into certainty that there is or should be a true reality, into the deep and inner despair, evident in the faces of so many human beings, that we haven't lived the potentialities of the true reality in us (140).

Gehlen takes great pains to show that, in spite of the odds, we can get hold of this reality by grasping it in the form of "the reality of a passionate situation" in a relationship with the other (204). A situation does not become real through knowledge; "we get to know ourselves only through our actions, and whoever wants to wait until they have come to an end with their reflections would do so in vain" (142). Nor will a person who, like Scheler, falls prey to their fantasies gain anything. Hypostatizing one's fantasies means that the progress of a situation becoming real has been prematurely and arbitrarily stopped (149). The modes in which fantasies (or, we might add, the imagination) appear do not automatically end in states of unreality; they circle endlessly around the point where reality and spirit might meet (150). Falling back on the concept of spirit, however, makes the argument more difficult again. Gehlen assumes that the objects handled by the great philosophies of the past were realities clearly delineated and understandable by their authors (concepts such as idea, will, *extensio et cogitatio*, *deus sive natura*, absolute spirit). These, he asserts, "were no general concepts, without object inductively extracted, but *experiences*" (160; italics in original). They cannot really be thought anymore; at best, as for Karl Jaspers in his psychology of worldviews, they can be psychologically deciphered (136). Generally, the names of the highest things (universe, essence, soul, reason, love) have degenerated into cheap vocabulary (137).

Clearly, Gehlen has scored some strong points. Also clearly, he has weakened their potential validity by a certain reticence concerning the nature of the passionate situation. Since he does not say anything about desirable or optimal group size, we have to assume that he only has a two-person situation in mind. Such situations may be as passionate as they are liable to disturbances. We might put the blame for such an insistence on indeterminacy on the existentialist cast of his early work. No matter in what way a person may try to push through the thicket of existentialist sentiment, the odds of the humanities, born of the interaction of historical and psychological interests, ascending to the stars that illuminate human aspirations or descending into the depths and turning home whence we came, are slim. In the products of the humanities, one will certainly meet great achievements with which such experiences are possible. But as a rule, Gehlen's own criticism of Dilthey and the humanities in general proves stronger. Dilthey, who, as we have seen, ascribed to the humanities the courage and strength to shape the present by understanding the past and other cultures, is told that he has become the victim of an "extraordinary deception of evidence," a deception that is particularly surprising because in any case belief in the power of understanding was close to extinction in Dilthey's time (342). By and large, Dilthey's "practical-utopian reasoning" has therefore been abandoned by the humanities. The leftovers are dismal: "What remains, is the strange spectacle of an ever ready, indifferent, totally inconsequential and vague ability to understand. This ability exhibits and spreads out, before our eyes, the flood of historical and psychological textual materials in ways neither pleasing nor painful to anybody" (343). Understanding the other person makes sense only if it helps to clear up our own problems, thus leading us to ourselves. The rest is a futile playing around, without any reality, of an unemployed and distracted mind. Such a mind is always old; Hegel (who when young was already called "old man"), Savigny, Schleiermacher, and Humboldt were, it is said, never young (343, 344).

Gehlen's last remark is almost certainly wrong, but that is of little importance here. What is more important is that he finds, after all, something useful in the midst of the disadvantages of historical and literary understanding. He does not apply his verdict to anecdotal history because it can show real human greatness. Similarly, an interest in tradition(s) and, more surprising, his acceptance of romantic-idealist versions of history lighten up an otherwise drab picture. The latter is welcome because it creates the sense of a deep and artistic significance out of an unfulfilled higher conception of life (344–347). But Gehlen never retracted his general verdict (although it was clear to him that later readers would call his text an existentialist one). It would be his later book *Urmensch und Spätkultur* (Early humans and late culture), in which he heaped criticism with a certain gusto (ignorance of the world, surrogate for life) on Dilthey and the humanities in general.[28] That the humanities are not fit to impose themselves as a sympotic analogue is, for Gehlen, less due to the fact that they cannot take care of the priority of action (a constant worry with him) or win a sufficient amount of respect for the status of an institution (a later key concept); rather, they suffer from an inability to condense their activities into a logic of situations in which at least the promise of higher states of being looms large.

Again, there is another side to this. Given historical change, we may doubt that talk about degrees of being must be the final word. One must indeed say against Gehlen that his approach in his Habilitationsschrift is overly existentialist; that in the later doctrine concerning the central value of institutions a gap has opened up between institutions and the individuals who are supposed to let themselves be consumed by them. It is the job of institutions to free the mind from the constant demand for trivial decisions in everyday life. But Gehlen does not liberate the mind. Quite to the contrary: a person must now follow what institutions seem to command. Moreover, it is unclear whether smaller groups and their possibly attractive processes of communication might not and should not escape the dictates of larger social institutions. It is also unclear because Gehlen's occasional lists of institutions are quite disparate: state, family, economic, and legal "powers"; exchanging letters with various persons counts as an institution as well.[29] The idea that institutions might themselves be subject to historical decay and would often need reform or something more drastic has apparently not entered his mind.

There is no doubt, nonetheless, that Gehlen has demonstrated the powers of analysis of philosophical anthropology and therefore presented a penetrating picture of the woes of the humanities. There would be little sense in going through the highly variegated writings of Max Scheler, that "chameleon of philosophy," in order to get a second opinion.[30] A book title such as *Von der Ganzheit des Menschen* (On the wholeness of human beings) would lead us to expect great revelations and probably disappoint us; Scheler's sociology of knowledge will accordingly grant us more-relativistic insights. Gehlen has stated that all later writings of quality on philosophical anthropology depend on Scheler's short book on the place of human beings in the cosmos (*Die Stellung des Menschen im Kosmos* [1928]), "and thus it will remain"; yet he has severely criticized what he thinks are sloppy propositions on the highest things.

Moreover, because it targets the humanities directly, it will be more instructive to tackle Nicolai Hartmann's thorough and challenging picture of the relations between a philosophy of the "spirit" and the disciplines of the "spirit"—that is, the humanities. Hartmann's terminology looks deceptively conservative, but his implications are not.[31] To date, this book reaches farthest in connecting older philosophies (such as Hegel's) with possibilities and motivations for sympotic analogies in the humanities. Above all, he has rearranged Hegel's concepts of the subjective and the objective spirit in such a way that there need be no limits to sympotic groups "in principle" (190). But groups can neither be dissolved into single persons nor be detached from them (265).

With Hartmann, Hegel's subjective spirit turns into the "personal spirit" (45–174). The personal spirit looks like a more empirical version than its predecessor. Yet it does not work as a new guiding concept if we take it as our empirical self, because our "individuality proper" is accessible even to ourselves only with great difficulty; we are not sufficiently transparent even for our own perception. What we call knowledge of human beings is nothing but the routine of categorizing for practical purposes that we can improve at any time (45–174).

The individual person possesses a mind of their own. But individuals can neither claim a world of their own nor position themselves as the other side of a putative common world (99). Hard intellectual work intensifies isolation and impoverishes the life of the body, which ultimately may break down. For Hartmann, it is a simple fact that there is a kind of vital degeneration in the educated classes using mainly their minds for work (106). The high cultural level of historically leading peoples must be paid for dearly. Educated people tend to forget that immediate behavior in certain situations is more natural than Descartes's *cogito*, that "emotional experience" precedes the "experience of intellectual knowledge" (127, 137).

Hartmann's redefinition of the personal spirit remains open. In a first comparison with the objective spirit, they appear to be of equal importance. It is, however, precisely the objective spirit—the only term taken over from Hegel—in which a revolutionary break with Hegel's conception, clothed in harmless garb, is hidden. "The objective spirit is no product, no result; it is nothing that could be ascribed to a creative subject as its source. We cannot construe it on the basis of class, blood, drive, economic-political conditions, nation or people, or landscape. Whatever it may cover like a vault is not enough to explain it. Basically, the complete book is centered around this idea."[32] There is, it is true, a sphere of spiritual-intellectual mutuality, a shared life of the spirit that spans across the individuals, connects them with each other, and carries them on (176). Indeed, more can be said: people are nothing without an objective environment into which they keep expanding (178). Hartmann's main example is supplied by the sciences (including scholarship? probably). No scientist can incorporate all the materials of their discipline; specialized research projects may run parallel to and lose sight of each other. Such accidents, however, cannot touch the unity of science (262). Statesmen, too, do not carry around all of political life in their heads, yet here "a unified totality of the objective spirit" shows in more tangible form than elsewhere (265). In the different spheres, then, we can discover an awareness of the (an?) objective spirit. But this awareness does not amount to a higher common consciousness beyond the sum of individual forms of consciousness; we find it in ourselves, in the individual person. Sharpened into a seeming paradox, this means that there is no adequate consciousness of the objective spirit (311).

But there are institutions in which the impression of a self-representation of the spirit can "materialize" more easily than in others. Hartmann adheres emphatically to the conviction that each shape of an institution for the living common spirit must have a unique fit with historical circumstances. The uniqueness of the living common spirit and the singularity of historical situations seem to condemn the spirit to an extremely transitory and irretrievable life (281). A specific form of that life takes place only as an analogy with a few common characteristics (282). It is unclear why Hartmann should have formulated such harsh conditions for both the life of the spirit and the analogies of historical conditions; the probability for successors roughly in the lineage of the symposium is consequently very low. It comes as no surprise that Hartmann's examples for the living common spirit are couched in fairly vague and overly general terms: a city, a class, a worker's group, a political party may possess that spirit (190). The spirit is not inherited; a person acquires it by growing into it, for instance, by virtue of the treasures of language (217–218). The contents of the spirit may also migrate from person to person. The risks involved in Hartmann's theorem of uniqueness are evident in his belief that he can easily identify false forms of the spirit ("genuine and fake," 338). He enumerates: mass suggestion, conventional morality, so-called majorities and public opinion, greed for the sensational, artificially imposed lifestyle, habitual self-deception, small talk and similar forms, "babble," and so on (338–366). There is no way in which conceptual or empirical controls for these forms can be squeezed into their analysis.

Hartmann takes a final risk, interesting and dangerous at the same time. For him (and this is very reasonable), the analysis of those volatile forms of the objective spirit (or rather the analysis of concepts) is handed over to the humanities, especially to the departments of literature (188). Indeed, one might have expected that Hartmann would leave this task exclusively to the disciplines mentioned, because the spirit brings forth products that, once they exist, belong to the "objectified spirit." This is the spirit responsible for "real creations" that remain unalterable (works of art, systems of thought, paintings, etc. [406, 451]). For its ongoing existence, the objectified spirit, like the objective spirit, depends on human feedback (423), on recognition (in a double sense), on a conscious openness and welcome (427, 478) by the personal spirit. Masterpieces of art and literature can often celebrate their resurrection in different periods. This means, however, that the recording of the content of the work of art itself can only be a relative one (496), which in turn means that the "Being-for-us" (452) of the objectified spirit may meet an "adequately" receiving spirit (463) much more easily than in the case of the highly unstable dynamics between the personal and the objective spirit, where there is no work to act as a stabilizing agent. It is also easy to imagine that a training in descriptive, analytical, and interpretational competence can take place in better ways when we have go-betweens (one might even say, institutions) such as recorded works that can act as inspirations as well as controls.

Still greater importance must be attached to the fact that Hartmann has tried to prioritize the objective spirit. As we have seen, he was not fully successful in this enterprise, but his problem of spiritual being, culminating in the status of the objective spirit, illustrates the necessity of a transition from theories of the subject to those of a lively commonality more than any other conception. We could also say that the development of theories of the subject must entail theories of commonality and its institutions; the symposium in ancient Athens is offered as the first historical example. Hartmann's book also corroborates the assumption that a structural history of such institutions of commonality can only consist in selective "analogies of certain features" (282). Within the field of experience, in which empirical forms of the spirit move "in a variety of appearances" (73) other options, unless wildly speculative, are hardly available. In Plessner's (slightly vague) terms: In the framework of philosophical anthropology, spirit can be made transparent only in its forms of experience (74); the question whether the spirit can acquire a profile of its own, whether it can protect itself against media degeneration and emerge as a sympotically valid energy, remains open. Consequently, the present volume must track down modes of experience in their contexts and institutions. The following chapters are intended to offer a selective history of experience and institutions, both characterized methodologically (if the word is not too ponderous here) in relatively loose ways.

PART 2

Modernization and Social Gatherings

CHAPTER 4

The Splintering of Culture
Reading versus Salon

THE EUROPEAN HUMANITIES and their early forms in the eighteenth century came into being for various reasons. Let me sum that up in a terminology of my own but moving into philosophical anthropology once more. One set of reasons, as Chapter 3 has endeavored to show, has to do with forms of emotional alienation in which areas of life seemed to diverge from their earlier familiar forms and were thrown into situations where their emotions did not seem to fit. Long novels were written in the eighteenth century to renegotiate the widening distance between the emotions of individual experience and the social meaning of life situations. The topic has been impressively expanded and reassembled by a second-generation philosophical anthropologist (and, again, sociologist, etc.) in terms of tensions between "concrete" and "abstract" evolutionary and social dimensions—namely, Dieter Claessens and his book (for which greater recognition has long been overdue) *Das Konkrete und das Abstrakte. Soziologische Skizzen zur Anthropologie* (The concrete and the abstract: Sociological sketches on anthropology [1980]). Small wonder that Claessens, as mentioned in Chapter 1, also worked on the role of group and group size, or that I mention here the surprising repercussions of the problem that have surfaced in law with respect to jury size, decision rules (including unanimous decisions), communication, and interaction within juries.[1]

A lack of concreteness, in the sense of a defective familiarity of important areas of life (among them business with partners and competitors), haunted a group of people growing into their roles in the midst of new combinations of risk and success. Around 1700, Friedrich Tenbruck said in his seminal and succinct study "Fragments Concerning Civil/Bourgeois Culture," the "citizen" comes into existence. Citizens did not represent a new rank, class, or estate but rather embodied a new type that had to adapt, among other things, to a relative centralization of government and to aristocracies losing power but often remaining behavioral role models, albeit without a meaningful function.[2] This transsociological, economically oriented, but still inhomogeneous group was forced to decide about courses of action, often crucial economic ones, and had to do so without much help from the older role models to be found in the aristocracy or in the teachings of the church and normative social behavior. New groups of writers showed up, offering conduct books, educational treatises, spiritual autobiographies, and last but not least, novels that could be read as conduct books. Quantities of these were enormous, since new and obviously restricted forms of freedom had to be reconciled with new social duties. It takes time and inner strength to learn how to perform new duties, and learning is more difficult because conduct books of whatever kind cannot shake off a certain abstract character. They cannot anticipate all contingencies; experiences and moral recommendations do not apply to everybody. A secondary need for behavioral models with a higher sensitivity to potential complexities in emotion, thought, and action and their interrelations drove the production of novels to unknown heights, since novels can simulate the handling of all kinds of surprises simply by creating fictive situations. For the minds of, say, eighteenth-century people not used to such uses of fiction, this must have been of considerable importance.

Philosophically, the problem was well known, but the narrative and representational powers of philosophy were limited. Simplifying drastically, just look at David Hume's lament that, although being an author active in the department of "literature" (which for him included philosophy), his philosophical books did not sell at all. The fictive simulation of behavioral models in the novel was supported by socially real, to some extent even sociable, institutions—that is, places for role-training such as salons, clubs, and coffeehouses, or on a different level, newspapers and essays. Understandably, even the joint impact of all of these could not anticipate the occasional loss of control in behavior. The eighteenth century had to digest economic risks in unprecedented forms. Bankruptcies on a large scale have become a field of special investigation in economic history; in domestic drama they reappear in moralized form as an effort to stem the tide of ruinous gambling (George Lillo, *The London Merchant* [1731], Edward Moore, *The Gamester* [1753]). The Swiss writer Claude Cueni has written a novel about the Scottish mathematician, gambler, financial adventurer, and for some, serious and highly modern economist John Law (1671–1729).[3] As director of the Banque Générale and *contrôleur général des finances* he was probably the most powerful man in France for a while. With Law, financial markets already appear extraordinary and even weird to such an extent that Joseph Vogl's image of the specter (*The Specter of Capital*)—that is, in Claessen's sense, the extremely abstract, intangible character of advanced financial transactions—is amply justified.

If we transfer this picture to the context of society and sociability, it obviously produces situations in which the coordination of projecting and judging possibilities of action has become much harder. On the one hand, tendencies of professionalization carry internal blueprints of decision-making. To follow them may help, although in the case of disappointment, the situation will be worse than before. On the other hand, neither option is of much use for those who would like—or who are forced—to choose the profession of writer. They must choose either forms of self-abasement and humiliation in the old system of patronage or the blackmail-like business of market-driven "hack writing." In any case, the eighteenth-century writer, to say nothing of the hack writer as the author of printed literature for the masses, could not pose as a divinely inspired seer any longer. Thomas Carlyle described that role in the nineteenth century, albeit with the intention of relegating it to the distant past when men of letters, such as Dante and Shakespeare, were still called poets. Although books are among the most wonderful things human beings have invented, they stand little chance against the machine-like mechanization of the world of which they are themselves the product. To dig in other sources for a hallowing of the writer's role is tantamount, at best, to borrowing authority.

Goethe may be the proverbial great exception here; Dr. Samuel Johnson, the greatest name in the writing business in mid-eighteenth-century England, is not. On the contrary: we have arrived at the situation, only seemingly paradoxical, that the greatest English writer of his time, a writer active in all genres, not only literary ones, chose the profession of writer only as the last possibility for his making a living. His (honorary) doctorate (in law!) is emblematic of a situation unheard of in earlier times: it was awarded to him even though his chief merit with respect to legal studies was his "collaboration" in the writing (i.e., partly the forging) of legal lectures for his friend Sir Robert Chambers, successor to the great Sir William Blackstone. Chambers suffered from writer's block, possibly because of the crushing weight of his predecessor, and could not always fulfill his contractual lecturing duties; if asked and willing, Johnson, who could write on anything, would jump in.[4] Paul Fussell has described Johnson's point of departure before he embarked on a career of universal literary man, of a man for all seasons of writing, in inimitable terms:

He was to become a writer by default and by accident, prevented by poverty and ugliness from aspiring to any other life. He finally had to find a profession in which his shocking person could be concealed from his audience. . . . Johnson's entry into Grub Street was distinctly a last resort, undertaken only after every other means of earning a living had blown up in his face.[5]

I will return to Johnson shortly. But in order to prepare for that, let me first correct a wrong impression that I may have left with respect to Schleiermacher. On the one hand, in his *Essay on a Theory of Sociable Behavior*, he saw the need for sociability in the human makeup. On the other hand, he was immersed in a society that was taking giant steps toward a "literary" culture—that is, a culture for which reading was turning into the main source of education in the shape of the famous or rather notorious *Bildung*. Schleiermacher, in his *Hermeneutics and Criticism* (1838), tries to do justice to the textual turn of culture by elaborating criteria for the correct understanding of texts. The tension, in Schleiermacher and many other writers, between a culture of reading, of getting to know enough about culture(s) by reading about them, and a culture of performance and interaction (or presence, in Gumbrecht's sense), a tension strongly felt in Germany but not absent from other cultures to various degrees as well, has never been amicably and adequately resolved.[6] Schleiermacher is one of its more interesting exemplars.

To a considerable extent, the erosion of socially relevant sociability is negotiated and made up for in the imaginative attractions depicted by novels. The opposition against narrative fictions does not easily die out. Resistance is finally broken in the nineteenth century, when theorists and practitioners could take the liberty of speaking of the "sacred office" of novel writing or of calling novels forms of art.[7] In a few cases, such as the reading tours of Dickens, the novel succeeds in inserting itself retroactively into the older performative-interactive culture.

Even so, the reading experience, lively as it may be on its own terms, can hardly claim a more than solitary communicative value. It is hard to communicate that experience to others; reports tend to be impressionistic or dogmatic. Older standards of the rhetorical and poetological kind may help with a more communicative analysis but very often do not apply to the relative formlessness of novels. Yet there is no doubt that novels have established themselves as big players on the literary scene because they do convey both a sense and fragments of a meaning of life in the face of its disappearance in economic and social risks. The combination of an apparent empirical abundance with hints for behavioral orientation is appealing.

The protestations of authenticity, however, the semblance—if not of empirical reference—of empirical import of some kind, however complex and indirect, cannot completely shake off suspicions of unreality and irrelevant fiction. One can forget about it as long as one is engrossed in reading. But the protestations sound hollow to those who think they know so-called real life. If, as we have seen, anything said or written can be said or written differently, the novel, in the course of its history, must exploit this possibility to the utmost. In the end, we can enjoy and admire Joyce's *Ulysses* for its perfection in handling styles, but we might also deplore that there is no matter from the heart and that nothing remains for the heart.

In any case, some such contrast marks the cultural situation of the eighteenth century. For Dr. Johnson in England or Hegel in Germany, reading novels may be useful for young people who have to form images of life without having digested the necessary amount of real-life experience. Dr. Johnson has salted that attitude with the assertion of never having read such a book (or any book, for that matter, except perhaps travel reports and other factually oriented texts) to the end and of not understanding how one could do that. Such assertions may involve jealousy in regard to successful novel writers, but the problem is there.[8]

We can indeed add an additional twist to this idea. Many eighteenth-century novels are conspicuous by their excessive length and/or by the impression of artificial constructedness that they convey. Such criteria may be arbitrary, but if an author such as Samuel Richardson takes roughly fifteen hundred pages to portray the life and death of a nineteen-year-old young lady (in *Clarissa, or, The History of a Young Lady* [1747–1748]), if the process of dying takes about two hundred pages, then we are not confronted with a question of length only. It is the very notion of understanding such a text that is in question, or rather does not make sense anymore. Such a mass of text does not allow us to distinguish between the subtleness and sophistication of what is represented, on the one hand, and its redundancy, on the other. Yet without doubt this is a great novel. Another novel by Richardson, *Pamela, or, Virtue Rewarded*, of about nine hundred pages, has been always criticized for the dubiously construed moral—or rather, immoral—motivations of the main character. Even Fielding might come under fire, as the single-mindedness of his comic perspective (the novel as "comic epic in prose") does not seem to be totally appropriate for the multifaceted nature of life. Furthermore, there are quite a few readers who have ventured to assert that their own lives are more interesting than the lives of the characters in novels that they are reading. Defoe's strategy in *Robinson Crusoe* to claim factuality and authenticity in the beginning and then correct the obvious defects of such assertions later in the sequels does not appear so convincing to skeptics.

Certainly, reasons galore can be found to justify the ways of authors to men and more especially to women. But it is common knowledge that, up to the end of the nineteenth century, the novel did not generally satisfy readers aesthetically or in terms of a philosophy of life, if that heavy expression be allowed. At that point, its adaptability and flexibility outweighed misgivings and scruples. Still, one could ponder the question as to what the very different spans of life granted to aesthetic forms might imply. And one could also ask why many experienced authors including Dr. Johnson in England, Denis Diderot in France, and Jean Paul in Germany either stayed away from novel writing or wrote against the textual logic of the "genre" they were themselves practicing. In Johnson's case we might be dealing with an author whose disillusionment with life appears to have doubled through the illusionary nature of fiction ("No man is pleased with his present state"; Arnold Gehlen seems to have copied him: "The state in which I find myself is one of dissatisfaction"[9]). Dr. Johnson made his livelihood by writing and publishing an enormous number of texts in a classical mode, grasping this opportunity, as Fussell has said, only after all other options had blown up in his face. Then he threw himself fully into the fray, tackling, as it were, any textual possibility: satires, a tragedy, essays, biographies, literary criticism, philosophical tales, invented—that is, forged—parliamentary speeches and reports on parliamentary debates, legal texts (see above), and finally, the great dictionary of the English language. (As Lipking correctly assumes,[10] *Rasselas*, often called a novel, should rather be called the opposite of a novel, if such a thing exists.)

If one describes the middle years of the eighteenth century in England as the "Age of Johnson," this would normally mean "the absolute dominance of one author to an extent hardly met with at any other time."[11] We should not forget, however, that this is an author who despises the dominant literary genre of his day. Moreover, the relations and distances between the different forms of prose, novels, essays, letters, biographical works, historical narratives, and so forth are much more complicated than we would normally allow when speaking of literary history. Rousseau, for one—and following him, several decades of readers—read Defoe's *Robinson Crusoe* as a philosophical tale. "We would do well," Bernhard Fabian has said, "to follow him there."[12]

Johnson gained his dominant cultural position not merely as a writer but, more significantly, through the forms of sociability he cultivated. In later years, encouraged by the painter Sir Joshua Reynolds, he founded the Literary Club, which became famous later on, with Oliver Goldsmith and Edmund Burke, among others, as co-founding members; according to the internet, the club was in existence at least until 1969. More to the systematic point to be made in this book, however, is that twelve members were considered the best number for purposes of sociability, even though membership rose considerably beyond that limit, at a certain point reaching thirty-five.

It has been said that the club was composed of the best intellects of the time and consequently that Johnson found himself at the center of its intellectual life.[13] But he extended his sociable activities far beyond this circle, for which Robert DeMaria has coined the perfectly fitting term "social expansiveness."[14] In addition to other clubs, this expansive tendency included the Thrales, the family of a beer-brewing company, as well as gatherings in pubs such as the King's Inn, which must be specially mentioned because the participants were reminded, according to Johnson's biographer, Sir John Hawkins (*The Life of Samuel Johnson* [1787]), of the Greek symposium, and in particular by Johnson's role as a born symposiarch, communicative virtuoso, and director. Part of that reputation is certainly due to mythologizing tendencies in James Boswell's biography (*The Life of Samuel Johnson, L.L.D.* [1791]), which turned Johnson into a "Herculean figure" and his life into a "fairy tale."[15] But I balk at DeMaria's assertion that Johnson's "most important legacy is his writing." Since there was nothing else for Johnson to leave, the assertion is of course trivially true, and it is also trivially true because DeMaria goes on to interpret this sentence as meaning that now Johnson is "responsible for the production of many more pages per year than he ever was as a living writer."[16] But it is problematic and misleading in that it takes for granted a cultural shift toward a status enhancement of "literature" in general, an enhancement that can be imputed to Johnson himself only with hesitation. Johnson's own definitions in his *Dictionary of the English Language* (1755), in the semantic field of "literature and poetry," are conventional: *literature* is defined as "learning; skill in letters"; *novel* is not listed; *author* and *writer* are narrowly hedged in (*author* is reduced to the etymological *auctor*, while *writer* is limited to one who practices the art of writing); and *fiction* shows up as poetic fiction—that is, the invention of poets (those who write in measured language)—as invention pure and simple or as a downright lie.

The profound skepticism of great writers—that is, those who have been acknowledged as such—in regard to the dominant textual forces of their time extends to Jean Paul in Germany and Denis Diderot in France; more examples could easily be found. In most cases, resisting novel writing or writing novels undermining their own textual drive amounts to a preference for communicative forms with sympotic dimensions. Jean Paul, for one, is remembered as a novelist whose texts seem to demand enormous amounts of exegesis and commentary. Not only did he write them with an attitude of mental reservation, but he harbors a more fundamental objection against his own craft that has to do with its intellectual level. He rejects the novels of his time "because German novelists and poets" obviously do not possess or display sufficient knowledge of human beings. They reveal what he calls a *Menschenunkunde* (ignorance of human beings). They do not know the things and ways of the world, nor do they know people. He shares the opinion of G. C. Lichtenberg that the characters in these novels are good, meaning sugary products of a pastry shop that melt pleasantly on the tongue. Jean Paul quotes La Bruyère, for whom long narrations are the sign of a weak mind; by contrast, he prefers situations with a high amount of dramatic narrative and intellectual complexity, where wit and erudition are coupled like two birds flying back and forth across the table.

This is supposed to be the case, with a vengeance, in one of Jean Paul's strangest texts, known as "Jean Paul's Letters and Impending CV." Constant witticisms, knowledge of all kinds, and permanent reflections are likely to stifle anyone's interest in a fictive or fictitious action. Some action takes place, of course, but it cannot compete, in terms of quality and intellectual level, with such witticisms, knowledge, and reflections. When Jean Paul complained about the difficulties of inventing a good story to the writer Johann Wilhelm von Archenholz, the latter answered that such invention could not be difficult for a man (such as Jean Paul) who had mastered the art, much more difficult, of being witty and entertaining on a high level.[17] Jean Paul did indeed enjoy a reputation for advanced sociability, which was successfully put to the test during his visit to Weimar,[18] but that reputation remained in doubt because his reputation as a difficult writer preceded him. His texts fascinated those who read them, but they also nourished the belief that a difficult writer must be a difficult person as well. Consequently, Jean Paul began and ended as a maverick writer who enjoyed a substantial number of sociable episodes.

Given the evidence presented so far, to be corroborated later by the example of Diderot, the following hypothesis appears to be emerging. A great deal of older literature as well as its authors, especially of the poetic and dramatic type, is bound up to some extent with group situations. From the group poetry of the ancient Greeks via collaboration in the context of drama and group constellations of the dramatis personae to eighteenth-century literary coteries, group relations and their standards, while not exclusive, are conspicuous. With the eighteenth century, the "business" of writing, especially novel writing as well as characters in novels ("heroes" and "heroines"), tends toward some kind of individualization. (The most glaring representative in that respect might be Julien Sorel in Stendhal's *Le rouge et le noir*.) For the eighteenth century, Johnson's case, by contrast, is fairly anomalous yet to a considerable extent also typical: an extremely individualistic person who in fact invites or provokes psychoanalytical interpretations (a price to be paid for belonging to his times), keeps aloof from the novel, but also engages in an enormous amount of sympotic activities and writing in either classical or nonliterary genres. In comparison to the Greek situation, however, a different type of change demands attention. The Club, chaired for a while by Johnson, was certainly the sympotic gathering of an elite, but this elite was too heterogeneous in its composition and could not distinguish itself in social or political commitments. In Athens, the symposium served both private sociability and its relation to sociopolitical power; in Johnson's London, it is a symptom and document of a split between culture and social power. Johnson's communicative virtuosity must—unfortunately, I am tempted to say—be regarded therefore rather as the self-staging of a "literary dictator"[19] whose histrionic abilities were well known. In this regard, Lawrence Lipking has understandably wondered: "What is the source of Johnson's power? . . . From one point of view, his authority looks like a mystery or mystification; no academy stands behind him, no law or police force. When he appeals to the common reader, moreover, he calls a witness he has himself invented. Does anything solid back this imposing façade? Only a text, retreating into more texts."[20]

That Johnson has exaggerated and indeed falsified his individualistic stance cannot detract from his more general significance. Modern research has played down the cultural import of his famous letter to Lord Chesterfield, maintaining that the age of patronage had passed anyway and made way for a textual market system. There were relics, of course, of the old system, and Johnson himself accepted a government pension a few years after the Chesterfield incident.[21] But such details, while telling, are side issues; of systematic importance is another matter already alluded to. In classical Athens, more or less the same people were involved in sociability and the handling of political power. It was a question of the communicative distribution *between* sociability and power. In eighteenth-century London, Johnson was the undisputed opinion leader *within* narrow circles of sociability—even if, as in the case of the Literary Club (aka The Club), it was ennobled by a national elite of some kind. The range and reach of sociability differed widely in both cases. We could say that London sociability became concretistic and abstract at the same time: it turned concretistic because it was enacted in very small circles, while it became abstract because it loosened the bond with sociopolitical power.

It is hardly a coincidence that the reorganization of the English political system in the eighteenth century—that is, its transformation into cabinet politics—produced forms of a secluded sociability of its own, albeit a sociability from which the shadows of corruption cannot be removed. Political history has adduced characteristics such as back-room diplomacy, confusion and anarchy in party politics, election and office patronage, the nontransparent roles of "friends," court intrigues, bribery and the manipulation of elections, and special-interest cliques of managers. All of these and more undermined official steps toward democracy.[22]

At this point we should turn back and make use of the pioneering work of Jürgen Habermas on the structural transformation of the public sphere, which—small wonder—has also concentrated on England. While his analyses have largely remained valid, especially insofar as they have focused upon the unstable and polemical authority of authors, the separation of sociability, and the march of politics into self-referentiality, they should be framed in a somewhat different way. After the foundation of the Bank of England in 1694/95, after the expiration of the Licensing Act in 1695 (i.e., after the repeal of parts of censorship), after the formation of cabinet governments combined with budget problems and their capitalist control, a debating public establishes itself in coffeehouses, in newspapers, and on the streets. Writers such as Daniel Defoe are instrumental in adding impulses toward social reform to its profile. Habermas thinks that there is also a peculiar connection between literature and politics in such authors as Pope, Gay, Arbuthnot, and Swift.

Regarding Defoe, we might be struck by the fact that he was not simply hired by Robert Harley (a great patron of the arts, especially writers, often called "Prime Minister" before that title became official with Robert Walpole), a man of various high offices (also accused of high treason but acquitted). Rather, Defoe made a living as a secret agent for the government and as a pamphleteer for Harley. He worked first on behalf of the interests of Harley's Tories; then, after their fall in 1714, went over to the Whigs. Apart from being a novelist, then, Defoe was also a "free" journalist in a sense unknown (or too well known) to our own age—not quite the picture of Defoe that Habermas cherishes.

In an analogical fashion, coffeehouses and clubs of various kinds (though not the ones dealt with in Chapter 6) may have been seen as hotbeds of political unrest, but it does not follow that they should be credited with political influence. Their situation was very different from that of the French salon in the eighteenth century and the writings produced there. Habermas himself quotes Robespierre, who celebrated the *Encyclopédie* as the introductory chapter to the French Revolution. It is unclear why Habermas insists on asserting that the French bourgeoisie, insofar as they were interested in political debate, could *not* institutionalize their critical impulses efficiently, since the opposite seems to be true.[23] For Habermas, the number of agencies and associations encouraging and producing political awareness and commitment was increasing in England. The political system was forced to reckon with authors, coffeehouses, clubs, journals, newspapers, and finally public opinion. Habermas sees a consistent expansion from individuals to sociable associations and from there to social media, a judgment that is formally correct but neglects the "quality" of political commitment. The picture painted by the famous historian G. M. Trevelyan, is a somber one: the greatness of England in the eighteenth century must be judged by looking at single persons, not at public institutions. According to Trevelyan, corruption ran wild, especially during the ministries of Walpole and of the first and second Pitt. The Industrial Revolution imposed itself on a loosely organized aristocracy that did not realize that the bell was tolling for them. Just as this revolution was making reforms in the institutions of the state more urgent than ever, nothing happened that would stem or direct the flood of drastic economic change.[24] Trevelyan's judgment may be too harsh: with respect especially to the first Pitt, the judgment of the German historian of

England Kurt Kluxen is more lenient (for Kluxen, see Chapter 6). On the other hand, Pitt's reputation of being "incorruptible" may also have been due to the management of his self-image in the new media, which evidently were important in the process of political opinion building. But this importance is more debatable than Habermas has bargained for.[25]

The case of Denis Diderot in France resembles that of Dr. Johnson yet deviates from it in fundamental ways. As far as narrative literature is concerned, Johnson tried to shield himself against the invasion of fiction(ality) by emphasizing facts (however problematic in principle). As Lipking says correctly in regard to *Rasselas*, he also appealed to (human) truth and morality.[26] Although such criteria are certainly not to be taken at their face value, Johnson's attitude and power of persuasion may have made them acceptable. Diderot's approach is much more radical and modern. He stages a virtuoso game with perspectives, motives, opinions, and fragments that seems to deprive texts such as *Jacques le fataliste et son maître* and *Le neveu de Rameau* of any intelligible narrative core. For Hegel, who was fascinated, challenged, and repelled by such techniques (which may have touched something in him that he did not care to acknowledge), Rameau's nephew embodies the age of *Bildung*. Strictly speaking, this is the ideal of individual education and formation to which many German thinkers ascribed a fundamental value for full human development (see also the first section of Chapter 3). While Hegel was, in principle, among these thinkers, with Diderot he seems to have become aware of the shakiness of the concept. He had to acknowledge the ease with which it turned into a mass of barely related materials of knowledge, early forms of what T. S. Eliot would call, in the famous phrase from *The Waste Land*, a heap of broken images, or what Georg Simmel would see as an embodiment of the tragedy of culture. In the very place where Hegel is concerned with the pure form of *Bildung*, he becomes aware of its convertibility, a prime example of the way in which dialectical thought changes concepts and with them things, sometimes into their opposite and at least into something different. The dream of a harmonious and full development of human beings is transformed into the nightmare of thought playing with itself, dissolving and tearing apart its own materials. In that sense, Rameau's nephew represents *Bildung* in the form of a spirit alienated from itself. If Humboldt, Schleiermacher, and others extolled the splendor of the concept of *Bildung*, Hegel, confronted with Rameau's nephew, faced its misery. Hegel quotes a passage from *Le neveu de Rameau* and takes on that "mad musician" who amasses about "thirty arias, Italian, French, tragic, comic, of all kinds" and mixes them up with each other. And he complains about the "shamelessness" and "fraud" of which "the complete reversal of all concepts" is guilty.[27] Evidently, Hegel was concerned; perhaps, we may surmise, he did not hide his anxiety completely. Perhaps that is why he was not so concerned about consistency, because the threatening reversal of concepts could also be taken as a form of his own cherished dialectics. In his afterword to the *Phenomenology*, indeed, Georg Lukács did not hesitate to impose the burden of a historically real dialectics on Hegel. The "perpetuum mobile of opposed concepts merging into each other" was no mere game but an early form of a dialectics going on in the real history of alienation. This thesis is not implausible, but it also appears as a one-sided "leftist" interpretation of Diderot's text. Diderot practices this merging with such matter-of-factness, insistence, and frequency that Gumbrecht's view seems the more plausible one: Diderot anticipates the full amount of that consciousness of contingency that has become an almost natural element—namely, the assumption of the general contingency of the world, of the twentieth-century mind of intellectuals.[28]

Whether we opt for one reading or the other, Diderot's narrative texts, including seemingly more conventional ones, do not fit into the framework of orientations for a better life offered by most other eighteenth-century novels. Compared especially to radical levels of "pluralistic" thought in Diderot, many of these novels fall victim to the suspicion their authors tried to avoid: they appear as misleading idealizations, as pedagogical inventions committed to arbitrariness but not at all to contingency. In some of his narrative works, Diderot removes the mask from this veiled arbitrariness by pushing it to the extreme of nonsense.

On the other hand, as in Dr. Johnson's case, his inventiveness comes into its own in a richness of observations and arguments in genres of the most variegated kind: philosophical essays, plays, criticism of art and literature, and last but not least, more than three thousand articles, out of roughly seventy-two thousand, for the *Encyclopédie*.[29] The *Encyclopédie* was a gigantic enterprise. To a great extent it owed its success to the sociability of small groups organized and managed by Diderot. Diderot was not Fontenelle, who spent the last fifty years of his sociable activities (starting each day around noon, for about eighty years in all out of a life lasting one hundred years); Diderot joined French salon culture at a relatively late age.[30]

But as soon as he participated and became a very active member, his situation took a very different turn from Johnson's. His style of communicative practice in fairly small groups took effect like an insidious poison. His wit and the enormous range of his knowledge, fascinating and endlessly stimulating precisely because of its absence of a system; his gift of concrete observation; and even the organizational constraints of the *Encyclopédie* pushed him almost automatically into changing forms of intellectual, affective, and culinary sociability. Larger groups, for instance, met in the salon of baron d'Holbach, small ones in the Hôtel du Panier Fleuri near the Palais Royal. Other venues were available. Group sociability was productive, sooner or later having effects in various domains of life even if it did not explicitly and directly proceed on an Enlightenment ticket. The most significant result of delayed productivity asserted itself in the shift toward a technological worldview that had its often-tacit origins in the articles and illustrations broadly related to the *arts mécaniques*, to which Gumbrecht has repeatedly drawn attention. The extent of their epistemological and, in a wide sense, political consequences is probably not sufficiently appreciated even today. In comparison to these articles, those devoted to conventional or even innovative political topics and concepts such as "Droit naturel," "Pouvoir," "Représentants," or "Souverains" look fairly pale.

More than in most cases, it is impossible to reduce Diderot to a formula. In critical writings on Diderot, words such as "contrasts" and "oppositions"—irreducible ones into the bargain—appear to dominate the scene; synthesis seems impossible. There is an emotional—indeed, sentimental—side to Diderot that comes to the fore in plays, in some narratives, and especially also in the "Éloge de Richardson." With the narrative texts, one has also to keep in mind that most of them were not published during Diderot's lifetime—that they may have been written for close friends only. The strange fate of the manuscript and copies of *Le neveu de Rameau*, with Goethe in the middle, is well known. With the Richardson text, Diderot interfered in a debate about the English author. Voltaire condemned Richardson's novels as nonsense. Given Diderot's intellectual level in most of his texts, it is hard to take his assertions concerning the profound reality and truth of Richardson's characters literally. For my own part, I find it impossible to ignore the strength of the purely intellectual dimension in all of Diderot's texts, with the exception perhaps of the plays. Consequently, *Le neveu de Rameau* and *Jacques le fataliste et son maître*, those "anti-romans par excellence" (Henri Bénac, editor of the *Œuvres romanesques*), continue to provide the dominant perspective.[31]

Johnson, then, more or less ignores the novel; Diderot, through the medium of his own narrative writings, makes fun of it. (Let us leave open the status of the fairly unique outbreak of enthusiasm in Richardson's case.) In both cases, handling a historical need of consciousness for making sense of life in such rough ways, both authors point to and embody a split in "bourgeois" culture. Still, their answers to and positions within that split are different. While both switch to other genres and reactivate sociability, with Johnson sociability is undermined and overwhelmed by overbearing forms of self-presentation. Diderot works in contexts of sociability too, but he uses forms of knowledge in a both personalized and seemingly objective way—that is, in most cases without taking sides. Moreover, sociability in eighteenth-century French salons seems better suited for a limited public distribution of knowledge than English coffeehouses or pubs. These aspects would argue for a more moderate version of the split in the French case, which would diminish further if one could take the plays and the "Éloge de Richardson" seriously as documents of a culturally significant "réalisme pathétique."[32]

Here, however, the role of the French salons must take center stage. That Diderot's sociable practice did not amount to or end in the monumental dogmatism of an author but lead into a historical movement to which we are still indebted is due, to a considerable extent, to the crucial role of French salons and their importance for cultural politics. After the symposium in classical Athens, we encounter here the second well-defined and impressive example of the communicative cohesion of a group, with in this case even national significance. French literature registers and displays the psychological consequences following in its wake.

The salons come into being following the decline of the political power of the aristocracy. Politically neutralized in the early seventeenth century, the aristocracy shifts and assumes hegemonic power in the cultural domain, a development that can be precisely dated as beginning with the salon of the marquise de Rambouillet in 1610.[33] A well-known process in psychocultural history takes its course and repeats itself: a social group tries to compensate for the loss of political power by proclaiming itself an embodiment of the most valuable human qualities. The cultural sociologist Clemens Albrecht has accordingly and repeatedly drawn attention to the aristocratic rejection of professionalization (49, 64, 68–70). The marquise claimed the ability, right from the beginning, to elevate any topic to its significance for humanity at large (34); Mlle de Lespinasse enjoyed the reputation of "validating the 'esprit' of the others" (39). In such ways, the salon became attractive to the "bourgeoisie" as well, whose members were admitted if they submitted to the rules of conversation and behavior. Albrecht holds that, with only few exceptions, all the great names of seventeenth- and eighteenth-century French culture are thoroughly marked by salon culture.

There are enormous consequences to this concentration on culture and human as well as sociable qualities. First, its repertory of norms and expectations is fixed and identified in the ideal of the "honnête homme" together with features such as "galanterie, politesse, bienséance, urbanité" (49). Second, it engenders a reflexivity and self-reference of cultural thematizations allowing and indeed demanding a constant intensification and "improvement" of themes together with a high formality of salon culture (43–44). A certain artificiality would seem to be unavoidable, and boredom could perhaps not be avoided completely. According to Albrecht, three main areas of conversation are supposed to inject variation into reflexivity and ward off boredom: norms of language, psychology of the salon, and cultural criticism. Aphoristic moralizing in the way of the great French *moralistes* turns into the medium of a specific mode of thought in French salon culture in which the themes are tamed and collected (49–53). The necessity of reverting to texts, written or oral, takes up and enlarges upon the need for texts felt by medieval knighthood and its "courtoisie." Without epic or lyric texts, *courtoisie*, the central aristocratic value in the Middle Ages, could not have been made intelligible; knights would have become fools (45). In similar ways, the salons appropriated moralistic discourse in order to stylize their topics and enhance their intelligibility and significance.

In due time, salon culture is exposed to a dynamics of its own. By starting the engine of self-observation, its main medium—namely, moralistic discourse—also comes to target the claims of representing humanity in its true and natural forms put forward by others. In this way, any conceivable claim is slowly but inevitably crushed. The salons try to remedy that situation by exchanging naturalness in its alleged highest form for progress. This step transforms the *querelle des Anciens et des Modernes* into the dynamics of progress, which, along with the Enlightenment, is more amenable to empirical proof (see 55–57). Moreover, salon culture can, in this way, maintain its autonomy for a longer period of time and at the same time serve the purposes of enlightenment, since enlightenment is not primarily

meant for specialists but is supposed to advance general human progress
(68–70). With his *Discours de la méthode,* thus the salon story goes, Descartes did not write a scholarly treatise, a *traité,* but a text close to conversation and narrative; he reinforced this tendency in the *Méditations* and the *Passions de l'âme.* The *Discours* is read enthusiastically in the very year of its publication in the Hôtel de Rambouillet (82–83). In the later eighteenth century, the salon extends its communicative and public range, after having incorporated scientific developments, into the political domain; the most famous salon, understandably, will then be a "bourgeois" one, the salon of Mme Roland.

In the long run, of course, the diverging philosophical, scientific, and political trends cannot be unified into encodings of a general human nature. The conflict between Jansenism and Jesuits—that is, between an individualized worry about salvation and the necessity of a common belief as a prerequisite even for salon culture—is resolved, for the last time, in favor of the Jesuits (95). Likewise, the Enlightenment *philosophes* are still successful in stylizing themselves into a fairly homogeneous group of heirs to French classicism. The *moralistes* keep on thriving in the eighteenth century because they use a language that is aesthetically flexible and undogmatic, a language aware of science but not determined by it. But it is, of all people, sociable Diderot who, hidden behind as well as in the fog of the older salon culture, sets out, hardly noticed, on his way to a different world. His reports on visits, by himself and other Enlightenment colleagues, to the ateliers of craftsmen are replete with hints that their style of work no longer conforms to a unified taste (see 95). It turns out that the craftsman must be an artist, too, that his work deploys a new logic of materials and shapes that demand visions in their own way. The technological world that will rule the nineteenth and twentieth centuries will enforce alliances as well as competition between the techniques of the craftsman and the technology of the machine. Diderot is also modern in the sense that he perceives the intricate but constructive-creative paths that Francis D. Klingender, for one, has so splendidly illustrated in his own classic work, *Art and the Industrial Revolution* (1947).

CHAPTER 5
Proust and Nineteenth-Century Salons

IN THE COURSE of the late eighteenth century, then, and with the shattering impact of the French Revolution, the salons could not preserve their status as the scene of representative culture with its privileged but generally intelligible discourse. Fontenelle had been able to chat about the astronomical knowledge of his time with educated ladies (*Entretiens sur la pluralité des mondes* [1686]). But he fell from grace when, toward the end of his long life, he defended the physics of Descartes against Newton. The step from Descartes to Newton did not only signal an exchange of doctrine; it implied a change, that is, a reduction in general intelligibility, because the aphoristic-moralistic and similar types of discourse could no longer do justice to the specializing tendencies of modern science—a problem that, if anything, has grown worse in modern times, coming to haunt the salons of both the aristocracy and the bourgeoisie in the nineteenth century. All of them competed for members with prestige and money; thus their political competition, which had become obvious after the Revolution, diminished, reduced to a competition for social prestige.

In the hundreds of pages of his *À la recherche du temps perdu* devoted to conversation and interaction in, as well as analysis of, Paris salons, Marcel Proust has probably offered the most precise insights, thereby carrying on the tradition, preserved from the earlier nineteenth century and asserted by writers as different as C. Wright Mills and Wolfgang Hildesheimer, that select novelists were the best sociologists for the period from Balzac to Zola. It would seem, however, that in concentrating on microsociological matters such as conversation and interaction, Proust distorted the larger historical dynamics of the period. Toward the end of this of this long but always intriguing work his narrator is, perhaps understandably, more interested in the aging of people than in the obsolescence of social structures. The "évolution de la société"[1] is occasionally cut down to a kaleidoscope of interchangeable elements and kept going in this same way, as exemplified in the Dreyfus affair (1894–1906). If there had been a war against Germany during this time, then the kaleidoscope would have turned differently. The situation of the Jews would not have deteriorated, because French society would have recognized and acknowledged their patriotism; instead, the Dreyfus affair inflamed anti-Semitism. In any case, the affair is important because it belongs among the few political events that arouse emotions in Proust's salons; not even World War I is capable of triggering more than a slight amount of concern in the salon people or the narrator. What is called "the people" does not really show up in Proust's text. The deaths of millions of unknown people "nous chatouille à peine et presque moins désagréablement qu'un courant d'air" (3:772; hardly tickles us and almost less unpleasantly than a breeze). The narrator pleases himself with a comparison between war and boxing: insofar as "de géants assemblages" (giant units) are at stake in war, this quarrel ("querelle") impresses us more by its "formes immenses et magnifiques" (immense and magnificent forms) than the movements of millions of waves that lift the ocean. A greater beauty emanates from mass war than from the conflict of two people (3:771). The "expériences de sociologie amusante" (experiments in amusing sociology) performed by Charles Swann turn out cruder still, if also far less harmful. Swann does not merely accept existing society, although this society may be the reason for tragic failure, but also amuses himself by rearranging persons and groups by transferring people to groups to which they do not belong. This is, as he knows, like replacing clove by cayenne pepper in a gravy (1:520–521). The internal and external loss of contact with history, frequently described by Arnold Gehlen, for instance, could hardly be demonstrated more efficiently.

By contrast, Proust's observation of interaction and dialogue in the salons uncovers the idling of a loquacious conversation machine with almost microscopic precision. It is an idling that deprives the institution of the salon of its historical relevance, a loss that is facilitated by the internal constraints of salon communication. Interaction and communication in upper-class salons thrive on the general possibility for everybody to say something. This internal pseudodemocratic rule requires a honing down of provocative or highly idiosyncratic contributions, but it need not result in completely inconsequential small talk or merely animated but historically irrelevant storytelling.[2] Ulrich Schulz-Buschhaus has shown how the neutralization of or taboo against risky conversational content can still be used as an active ingredient in the criticism of the commonplace phraseology of "idées reçues." In the frequently extended conversations during the many matinées, dinners, and soirées, we can witness, at least, how the narrative organization of contributions confirms their real lack of social function. A history of salon conversation would be able to prove that clichés in Flaubert were indeed mere clichés but were charged with energies that advanced the action.[3] In Proust, however, self-referential elements enter and permeate salon conversation, a self-reference that is not interested in topics and problems anymore. Speakers and listeners are not interested in what someone says but in how they perform the utterance of irrelevance—an early example, together with a negative answer, to Stanley Cavell's question "Must we mean what we say?"

Historical "content" thus shrinks to a minimum. From this minimum, however, Proust extracts a maximum of psychological consequences. In the absence of reliable knowledge on the sociable and even the social qualifications of potential members, all salons, from the high bourgeoisie to the high aristocracy, focus on qualities that, precisely because they cannot be verified, can be claimed in any invented amount. Status and estate (or class) are only external frames for rough and provisional estimates. For the upper-bourgeois salon of the Verdurins, and not only for them, the required qualities of the *copains* (companions) consist above all in the pseudomoral value of fidelity (the *copains* are also *fidèles* [faithful]), a quality that can be defined only negatively: whoever visits other salons or keeps up relations with "boring" people (*ennuyeux*) is out (see Proust, *Recherche*, 1:188–190). Moreover, as already noted, Mme Verdurin judges conversational contributions according to their rhetorical-performative level, not according to the information conveyed. Those guests who have to rely on the interest their special (e.g., professional) discourses may arouse take the risk of losing themselves in a positivistic plethora of details difficult to distinguish from caricature. The Sorbonne professor Brichot, for instance, spreads out his arcane etymological knowledge over several pages without inhibition; he saves himself only by jumping, without any transition, to the death of a friend, the favorite pianist of Mme Verdurin, for whom sponsoring musicians is important (2:888–894). The physician Cottard, in his turn, seems to feel obliged to present meaningful contributions but has trouble distinguishing between emptiness and irony; in order to be on the safe side, he ends his speeches with a smile, hoping to keep them open in both directions (1:200–201, 214). The archivist Saniette tries in vain to please the Verdurin *copains* with hints concerning the definition of intelligence in Fénelon or the pen name of George Sand; as an *ennuyeux* he is ridiculed so brutally by the comte de Forcheville that Swann feels pity for him (1:260–261).

Swann, who seems to abandon the Verdurin personality test for more substantial qualities, will be Forcheville's next victim. Swann affirms that Mme Verdurin possesses magnanimity, nobleness of heart, and sublimity of soul ("magnanimité," "noblesse de cœur," "hauteur de l'âme"), the latter to be claimed only with a corresponding equal sublimity of thought ("hauteur égale de pensée"). He even speaks of her profound understanding of the arts ("profonde intelligence des arts," 1:249). But as it turns out, he concedes such sublime qualities to her only because she has opened possibilities of contact with Odette de Crécy, whom he desires. Later, Swann is socially cut off because he competes for Odette with Forcheville, who belongs, more than Swann, to the *fidèles* of the Verdurin salon. His judgment now changes into its opposite: he does not want to be sullied with the jokes of a Verdurin ("être éclaboussé," with a series of other strong insults, 1:287–289). The narrator himself comments on her sarcastically: twice widowed, she moved up and married the ruined duc de Duras, thus becoming a duchess and later even a princesse de Guermantes. The narrator compares that ascent with a theatrical role and adds his contempt for the prince, who also may have been ruined as a result of the German defeat in World War I. Because of his marriage, the prince has to tolerate the title of "un faux Guermantes, un escroc" (3:955; a false Guermantes, a crook). For the rest, the narrator complains about the mixture of social classes, which in his view allows many people to show up in circles to which they simply do not belong (3:957–958).

In genuine aristocratic salons, restrictions of admission and rules of communication resemble those that are valid for the bourgeois type such as the Verdurins. People who fulfill the crucial expectations of prestige and embody the increase of prestige flowing from a guest to the owner of a salon may turn into guests. Aristocratic managers of salons, however, will have at their disposal additional resources and the ability to discern losses or gains to prestige. Plus, their training is normally also more advanced in the art of polite and subtle hypocrisy, on the one hand, in brutal behavior, on the other, or in an inextricable mixture of both. We hear that the duc de Guermantes was a clever manager of everything that touched the good functioning of his salon ("compère à toute épreuve en ce qui touchait le bon fonctionnement de son salon" [2:453; an accomplice in any test concerning the smooth functioning of his salon]). The duke demonstrates, in exemplary fashion, his competence in a conversation with the princesse de Parme, whom he wants to tell clearly that the marquise de Souvré cannot be invited anymore (2:453-454). He also employs it, in the form of relaxed bonhomie, in a talk with the narrator, to whom he shows his pictures by the painter Elstir and lets him know that, had he been aware of the narrator's wish, it would have been easy to arrange a meeting between him and the painter in the salon Guermantes (2:418-423).

Such abilities explain the ease with which the myth of a paradigmatic or ideal "esprit des Guermantes" could have arisen (e.g., 2:460-461). This myth has a sort of real basis insofar as the Guermantes can justifiably claim the immediately perceptible delicate quality of their social life and the impressive subtlety of their conversation (2:460; "délicatesse de vie sociale" and "finesse de conversation"; see, on the same page: "si mince cela fût-il, quelque chose de réel" [tiny as though it was, it was something real]).

The feature that decisively guarantees top position in the ducal salon, however, is a criterion hovering between sociological concreteness and imaginary evanescence. First of all, we must take it for granted that a successful salon is backed by a generally luxurious lifestyle. This is the prerequisite for aspiring in and with the salon to the highest summits of "mondanité" (being part of the smart set). But if this is the chief reward, it collides with the defining feature of "modernité," which manifests itself as the professionalization of many domains, especially, of course, the professional domains of life, a central characteristic of social evolution in modern times. *Mondanité* and *modernité*, higher worldliness and modernity, have come to contradict each other. The most important guests in the ducal salon, as the narrator tries to formulate in a rather laborious way, can legitimately boast of the greatest talent: they could have had splendid careers in all kinds of professional directions but preferred life in the "coterie." A physician and a painter who visited the salon were therefore treated as men of the world even though they were not entirely respected as such by their professional colleagues. For a diplomat, a similar fate was in store. His preference for the salon had branded him as a reactionary and prevented a great career: "The type of distinguished men who formed the basis of the salon Guermantes was the one of people who had voluntarily renounced (or believed they had) the rest, all that was incompatible with the Guermantes spirit, with the politeness of the Guermantes, with that undefinable charm hated by all those who were different" (2:458, 459).

Claiming a certain reality for aristocratic myths does not invalidate the thesis, proffered above, that rules of admission and communication in both aristocratic and bourgeois salons resembled each other, but it is undermined to some extent by a more deep-seated opposition. Ordinary historical thought has described this opposition, on the whole correctly, as shifts in the distribution of power between these "classes." Yet this historical development hides an evolutionary social process of similar range. Mme Verdurin tries to stem the tide of professional discourses because they reduce or destroy the chances for mutual culture-based understanding. In spite of her resistance, however, specialized discourses are inexorably on the march. Their perspectives are bathed in heterogeneity; they do not project any intelligible structure of society, to say nothing of the world. Mme Verdurin does not understand these perspectives and is, of course, even less able to see life steadily and see it whole (as one might say, adapting a phrase of Matthew Arnold's in his poem "To a Friend"). Since she neither understands professionalized discourse nor is capable of producing a more than particularistic view, she gives up on content- or information-oriented communication altogether. Paltry relics survive in her interest in rumors about the "petites affaires" of important guests (1:227), but for the rest, communication as performance carries her day.

The salon Guermantes, prime example of an aristocratic one, eliminates personal and social particulars for different reasons. For the aristocracy, the corporate state continues to be a natural given. It conjures up an *esprit* defined mainly by *mondanité*—that is, in principle, a suggestive, polite, and witty, intelligent, and sensitive style of communication that polishes off personal and social peculiarities in favor of a higher but vague human ideal. As a consequence, the realities of historical and social dynamics, with few exceptions, cannot be talked about in either the Verdurin or the Guermantes type of salon. In her own salon, the marquise de Villeparisis, aunt of the Duke and Duchess of Guermantes, does not respect these tacit arrangements; it follows that her salon suffers relegation as a second- or even third-class venue. The narrator tries hard to find reasons for this "worldly humiliation" (2:121) or "déclassement" (2:184). A first explanation has to do with trivial affairs and scandals of a remote past (2:184–185). This explanation is so unsatisfactory, however, that he switches over to its opposite. Now he seems to remember that, in Balbec, he was struck by her lack of understanding for the genius of certain artists. This lack does not indicate a narrow sensibility, he thinks, but must rather be seen as the result of "veritable artistic qualities" of her own, qualities that tend to exercise "a morbid influence" on good society (2:185). A third explanation has to do with an excess of intelligence in the marquise incompatible with polite conversation. Such an intelligence threatens to destroy the picture of the world and the ways of action cherished by the less intelligent (2:185). Still other observations suggest the probability that high intelligence tends to prevent rather than promote interaction (2:186), an idea that will come up again at the end of the present volume when chances for a symposium in the head will be gauged. The disturbance of communication by high intelligence can also take place, as we have seen with the salon of Mme Verdurin, by professional discourses accessible only to specialists. In the salon of the marquise, it is a historian of the Fronde who assumes that function. His remarks, apart from always occurring at the wrong time, are incomprehensible to the other guests (2:200, 214–215, 226–227).

In the hierarchy of salons, the institution run by the princesse de Guermantes enjoys the highest prestige; nowhere else can one meet such a large number of people to be addressed as "Your Highness." Yet even this salon is plagued by problems analogous to those of the others. The princess's salon boasts a unique feature of its own: an unusual seating plan. Small subgroups are organized so that they can, but do not have to, turn their backs on each other. For the princess as manager, this feature opens up additional possibilities of observation; she can also multiply contacts between the groups (2:635). Yet we must ask, To what avail? This also increases the risk of hurting the sensitive feelings of the high-ranking guests, in order to minimize which the princess trivializes the communicative occasions. She calls out, for instance, "Mme de Villemur, M. Detaille, in his capacity as a great painter, is just admiring your neck" (2:635). The princess would not have been able to control the situation if Mme de Villemur had not slowed down the speed of communicative acts and redirected them to the remark that she does not know the painter but does know his paintings. Much more often, however, the communicative surplus value of the seating plan gets lost in "formulae betraying stupidity" (3:1226; see also 2:659–660). Following Simmel's rule, individual peculiarities should not be talked about, and in most cases the guests and manager of the salon accept such neutralization and superficiality of the conversation. Inevitably, however, people think about what cannot be said openly; thus an uninhibited conjectural activity is set in motion, with everybody exposed to the tacit judgment of everybody else. The discourse type of modern professionalism is in any case not allowed. This ban, noticeable in other salons as well, appears to be enforced with special strictness in the salon of the princess. A famous doctor ("le professeur E...."), who has treated and cured her husband and is therefore invited to a soirée, has the feeling of being lost like a child and so clings to the narrator in order to have at least one interlocutor (2:640–641). Yet this conversational effort soon fails as well because the doctor can "translate" his knowledge into trivial truisms only.

What then happens to the claim of cultural supremacy still brought forward by the high aristocracy? It is suffering from an advanced hollowing out, which is, of course, not always immediately visible. Developments shattering the balance of cultural prestige are not inevitable but possible at any moment. Looking at the salon of Mme Verdurin, the narrator paraphrases such developments as "timid evolution" "towards the world" or as "latent worldliness" (2:870). The editors of *Recherche* add a description of the worldly rise of her salon (3:1276; see also 3:235–237). First of all, the Verdurins take advantage of the increasing cultural prestige of music, from which their protégé, Vinteuil, in particular, profits. The second development may also be due simply to a change of generation, but it enjoys the dubious reputation of a stricter logic and calculability. The editors' description targets the occasional attractiveness of political ideologies (nationalists, Dreyfusards and anti-Dreyfusards, monarchists, republicans, radicals, socialists, anarchists, etc.) for conversation in the salon. The reasons, however, why one or the other may become attractive change quickly; enemies turn into friends and vice versa. The fact that the Verdurins are Dreyfusards puts them at a disadvantage for a while; later, it is the other way around. Finally, generational change may explain everything or nothing.

Introducing politics into the salons, then, does not make much of a change. *Mondanité* remains the highest value; *modernité* does not have a real chance. Modernity, if it had entered the salons, would not have done away with the plurality of possible orientations but would instead have made them more transparent—would have shown reasons, or the absence of them, for one option or another. In Proust's representation of indifferent, exchangeable political fictions, a significant historical and sociological assumption looms large: That part of "la France bourgeoise" that has become rich in the course of the nineteenth century has merged with the most powerful two hundred, largely aristocratic families, especially insofar as their lifestyle is concerned.[4] The closeness of aristocratic and bourgeois groups, together with a well-functioning central administration,[5] may have achieved a sufficient cohesion of French society. Proust's image of political movements without real commitments is compatible with the politological assumption that the chaos of parties and particularly of the names of parties keeps dissolving into contrasts. These must be broadly, if somewhat vaguely, described as orientations of the left or right side of the political spectrum.[6] In spite of their heated rhetoric and blown-up conflicts, they do not endanger a basic cohesion—especially insofar as that cohesion is anchored in the administrative elite.

Does anything follow from the combination of Proust's lengthy descriptions and a few assumptions of a more empirical kind? It would appear, after all, that the historical achievement of the salons in the eighteenth century, their potential for mediating between public (cultural, scientific, and political) and private, between intellectual and affective domains, has come to be systematically hedged in by difficulties—or rather, the potential of these salons for not allowing these domains to harden into oppositions has come to an end. Politics does not offer any way out. The enumeration of political positions looks like a series of unstable fictions at best. The self-encapsulation and the competition for prestige of the salons is also liable to mar the chances of there being private communication. If culture can also be described, according to an older definition by Luhmann, as a reservoir of topics one can talk about, then it shrinks to a tautological minimalism that the salons must tap all the time in order to reassure themselves about their ranking and prestige.[7] In regard to the role of the salons as they are depicted by Proust, contours of a history of loss are visible. Societies may be stabilized by relations between different, sociologically identifiable groups, but these relations are better if sweetened by affective reinforcements and not embittered by the lack of them. If the exercise of power becomes heavy-handed, oppressive, or arbitrary, if the reputation—that cornerstone of power (Robert Greene)—of those holding power is damaged, or if, on the other side, political commitments are losing their meaning and can hardly be debated, then social cohesion is loosening. Various aspects of such developments are going on in the salons and in the way in which Proust describes them. That his picture may strike us as relatively harmless may be due, among other things, to the restabilization of France in the outcome and aftermath (Treaty of Versailles) of World War I. Today, however, the problem has reared its head again, in the question of the continuity and stability of the United Kingdom, with which we will be concerned in the next chapter.[8]

CHAPTER 6

The Silence of Power
English Clubs, or Oligarchy versus Democracy

AT THIS POINT I must insert a chapter that offers both an instructive contrast to the salons and a highly topical yet also long-term stable communicative element in the morass of reasoning, beginning in 2019, for or against Great Britain's (more precisely, England's) staying in or opting out of the European Union (so-called Brexit). After the Platonic Academy the English club presents another variant, this time in sociological, not philosophical, terms, of institutions producing some kind of commonality yet at the same time perpetuating the segregation of classes.

England has been called the motherland of modern democracy. Dietrich Schwanitz, in particular, has intoned the eulogy for English party democracy, for parliamentarism and the parliamentary government machinery, including the constitutional theory that accompanies it. Nevertheless, England is supposed to have taken over the role of an avant-garde in the universal process of modernization. Closely related to this role, Schwanitz has asserted, we find the pioneering merits that England has acquired concerning the civil religion of the Enlightenment, with an emphasis on human rights and political commitment, and in Habermasian fashion, concerning the forms of public communication in the press, in moral weekly journals, and in reform campaigns, as well as a host of other things.[1]

These merits can hardly be denied. Even so, the political maneuvering of Boris Johnson, elected prime minister on July 24, 2019, as well as the circumstances accompanying this election could have reminded people with a sense of history that the parliamentary machinery does not count for much more than a formalism of often very old practices and procedures with a massively restricted "democratic" range. The members of the Conservative Party who *could* have elected Johnson amount to about 0.35 percent of the English electorate; the number of those who *actually elected* him did not go beyond 0.2 percent of the electorate. In the face of England's esteem for democratic procedures and forms, a counterimage of oligarchy emerges. Such a suspicion must be pursued: it is possible that democratic forms and an oligarchic handling of power, although far apart, are not incompatible with each other. Once more, the catchword "English class society" does the rounds.

It is a catchword indeed, but a catchword that allows its implications to be pulled into broad daylight. It emphasizes the relative firmness of the symbolisms of a society that is a class society but a class society with fairly acceptable elastic structures. Both elements are clearly visible in the trivial transformation of young "revolutionaries" such as rock musicians or critical scholars into mature members of the lower aristocracy and pillars of society. The symbolisms keep alive the idea(l) of a commonwealth with a sociologically ill-defined leadership converging regularly in gentlemanly qualities. Many of these symbolisms can be found in Shakespeare in particularly suggestive phrases. Like many politicians before him, Johnson exploits Shakespeare's suggestively simple but also simply suggestive images having to do with England as an earthly paradise: "This royal throne of kings, this scep'tred isle, / This earth of majesty, this seat of Mars, / This other Eden, demi-paradise."[2] We are dealing with poeticized elastic social structures, especially between the rich or meritorious upper middle class and the lower aristocracy, originally introduced by James I as a way of raising money but also controlling their number by making the title noninheritable. Such structures allow for status change; they can also absorb the real socioeconomic dynamics of society. Historical and sociological writings in England, from Thomas Babington Macaulay to David Cannadine, from Anthony Sampson to Anthony Giddens (a typical case of someone of modest origins with a splendid academic career crowned by a knighthood), have gone into this at some length.

Let me quote from Macaulay writing in the middle of the nineteenth century. He is mainly responsible for the "Whig interpretation" of English history, a school that believes they can trace the ways of England toward ever-increasing democratic conditions. At the same time, it insists on the "conservative" character of English "revolutions." England is different "because we had a preserving revolution in the seventeenth century [and because] we have not had a destroying revolution in the nineteenth."[3] One can find similar arguments in Edmund Burke's late eighteenth-century criticism of the French Revolution, for instance. Burke demanded respect for the long and slow growth of traditions, which he played off against the breathless implementation of abstract programs. British historians such as Asa Briggs (1921–2016) know that reversals of fortune do also happen at "the peak of the social pyramid." But the nobility and gentry profited even from the Civil War and the period of the Interregnum, between 1649, with the execution of Charles I, and 1660, with the return of Charles II; the "landed interest," Briggs says, was "secure and well-established."[4] J. H. Plumb (1911–2001), also a very well-known historian with origins in a worker's family and knighted like Asa Briggs), has insisted in even stronger terms on the central significance, both symbolical and in terms of real power, of the landed interest. For Plumb, the so-called Glorious Revolution (1688), which successfully invited William of Orange to come to England in order to become its king, did not promote democratic but rather oligarchic tendencies. After the revolution, the nobility and influential "gentlemen" quickly reoccupied the positions they had held before the revolution: "They were never to be dislodged again."[5] Social competition shifted into the representational ambition of showing off in the high and low nobility. Only the rich could afford election campaigns; for Plumb, this is the most important factor in the development toward oligarchy.[6] Robert Walpole extended such tendencies into a system in which "control of the House of Lords and manipulation of the House of Commons" grow into the crucial mechanisms of oligarchic rule.[7] Walpole's achievement consisted mainly in giving "not only individuals but classes of men their political identity in the pyramid of authority. And that pyramid . . . lasted for centuries." Plumb's summary must be quoted in full:

[The Whig party] fused the interests of the aristocracy, high finance, and executive government, a process extended by Walpole to embrace the bulk of the landed gentry. By doing so he put the noblemen and gentlemen back at the heart of English political society. This was to be of tremendous importance for England's future development. The seventeenth century had witnessed the beginnings and partial success of a bourgeois revolution that came near to changing the institutions of government. In this, however, it never succeeded. The Revolution of 1688 and all that followed were retrogressive from the point of view of the emergence of the middle class into political power. Socially and economically they continued to thrive, but not politically. The power of the land and of commerce fused to create a paradise for gentlemen, for the aristocracy of birth; it thus became much easier for England to adopt an imperial authority, to rule alien people, and to train its ruling class for that purpose, rather than to adjust its institutions and its social system to the needs of an industrial society.[8]

Later in this book, when we will deal with the detective novel, the fact will be important that Arthur Conan Doyle, for instance, in his Sherlock Holmes stories, describes imperial Great Britain as a state under the rule of law that derives its legitimacy from a compromise between the Crown and Parliament, a Parliament, however, dominated by the great aristocratic families.[9] In his description of an oligarchic stabilization of England following the Glorious Revolution, Plumb has pointed out that right in the beginning the "Bill of Rights which in the first flush of the Revolution promised to be a comprehensive constitutional document" degenerated quickly into "a string of condemnations of James II's actions, followed by a number of hopeful generalizations about the way in which executive power should be used in the future."[10] Plumb is talking about a recurring feature of English (and certainly not only *English*) political history. It could be called and stigmatized as the discrepancy between the official symbolic and the factual-cum-ideological power-political significance of central documents in this history. There is no mystery about the fate of the first and most famous document in this history, the Magna Carta Libertatum (1215), in which this discrepancy asserted itself. The Magna Carta does not record the first democratic stirrings in England. Again, a well-taken quote by a noted historian, here Kurt Kluxen, will set the record straight: "Of course, the general guiding thoughts of the coronation oath, such as keeping the peace, respecting law and property and a fair trial for everyone, had to step back behind the immediate needs of the moment. Out of 63 articles in the document more than half were concerned with feudal complaints."[11] But even those decisions that went beyond feudal law and regulated matters of nonfeudal interest "served feudal interests indirectly like the protection of the peasants. The protection was introduced because the peasants belonged to the feudal estates and because their economic destruction would have damaged the interests of the Lords." Kluxen describes the further history of this document as a "process of reinterpretation" in the course of which the Magna Carta was elevated into the cornerstone of English constitutional law. In this way the Magna Carta came to attain the mythic status of a permanent value in the rule of law.[12]

Such processes of reinterpretation can be and perhaps must be performed secretly. Only in those cases where legitimation is at stake but difficult to prove may an effort in explicitness be better. An example could be supplied by the way in which Antony Easthope has approached John Locke's *Essay Concerning Human Understanding* (1700). In his introductory "Epistle,"

Locke maintains that he is presenting philosophy in a way that might make it fit for use in "well-bred Company and polite Conversation." He proffers the even bolder idea that the *Essay* could be seen as the joint product of the conversations of five or six friends of equal rank who met regularly at Locke's place. Locke perhaps could not have foreseen that twentieth-century scholars would view this as the description of a class product—namely, as Easthope thinks, of the gentry. Occasionally, however, class consciousness may shatter the picture of a well-bred company: Locke betrays a considerable lack of feeling and indeed of problem-related thought when he says that "the greater part of Mankind" are "given up to Labour" so that "their whole Time and Pains is laid out, to still the Croaking of their own Bellies, or the cries of their Children."[13] I readily admit that the textual situation in Locke's *Two Treatises on Government* (1689) looks more complicated; the textual history is confusing. The first treatise can be more or less ignored, because it is busy with a refutation of what, by and large, is already refuted or overtaken by history—the divine right of kings in one or another version. The second treatise does take on central topics but makes understanding rather difficult by plunging them into somewhat strange ambivalences: it appears, for instance, that slavery and wars of conquest are legitimate. Locke seems to favor representative government but thinks it can be practiced in monarchies and oligarchies. Whether the middle class can really turn into a support for the order of the state (E. von Aster) or whether Locke's doctrine of the state must serve as an apologetic veil, and whether the rule of a sovereign needs humanitarian glossing over that can be further developed into a theoretical liberalism (F. Borkenau) —these are questions that cannot be discussed here.[14]

In any case, we need take only one small additional step, which has to do with the role of literature, especially in the eighteenth century, to amass a collection of factors with which we can tackle a characteristic (non)symptotic configuration in England. In the second half of that century, the Industrial Revolution began to exert an unholy impact, producing human misery on a large scale and, "initiated by Britain," with an intensity unknown in most other European countries, ultimately assuming a gigantic shape as "the most important event in world history, at any rate since the invention of agriculture and cities."[15] Combing the pages of English literature for some descriptive help, we may be surprised that we find almost none. Literature, which we like to look upon as a psychosocial system of early warnings, barely takes note of what critical historians have been so much concerned with; extremely sophisticated in literary terms, it exhibits itself in "strange social remoteness."[16] Fabian tends to grant that both literature and politics reduce their distance from socioeconomic disasters in the nineteenth century, once they can scarcely be overlooked, but even this is a moot point. Christian Enzensberger is not the only one who has diagnosed the continuation and indeed the hardening of an attitude that psychoanalysis would call repression, an attitude that Enzensberger ascribes particularly to the poetry of Tennyson and Swinburne.[17] This attitude is comprehensible only if we presuppose a general acceptance of a symbolically embellished socioeconomic system. Enzensberger has extended his analyses to drama and the novel, and has tried, for instance, to muster proof of such a refusal of reality in Shakespeare's *The Merchant of Venice* and in Dickens's *Oliver Twist*. The novel in particular, though, would seem to disprove Enzensberger's thesis, because Dickens spreads out social woes in gory detail and because the nineteenth century is shaken by social unrest and revolt. George Orwell and Arnold Kettle, among others, are convinced that Dickens attacked English institutions with a wildness unequaled ever since. While Enzensberger takes note, he remains unimpressed;[18] for him, the crucial fact in the nineteenth-century configuration is that—even after the Reform Bill and after violent class conflicts—five out of six workers did not satisfy property requirements and therefore were not allowed to vote, or in *Oliver Twist*, did not show up at all. For Enzensberger, Orwell makes use of a gratuitous formula when he argues that Dickens criticized the existing order but did not want to overthrow it, that his radicalism, though vague, is always there.[19] Orwell concedes that the abuses denounced by Dickens can in no way be justified or excused. For Enzensberger, the main problem— that is, capitalist exploitation and its consequences—is not even mentioned by Dickens.[20] In fact, for Enzensberger, Dickens blocks possible changes because improvement is personalized into sentimental morality and cannot be conceived as structural intervention in the "system."

For the argument to be developed here it does not matter whether my quotes from Enzensberger do or do not commit me to his theoretical position; they are not meant to signal adherence to something like a mirror theory of literature. Some of their implications, however, cannot be ignored. It appears as a structurally crucial fact in Dickens's novels that an indeterminate number of problematic realities simply fade away and that characters, even if introduced only in some systemic or professional capacity, are nailed down to a personalized pathology and hardly examined as members of an institution that they in fact represent. The problems of institutions such as the law, the police, schools, the workhouse, and so on are more or less reduced to personal defects.

The historical and literary materials adduced in this chapter so far are intended to illustrate the latent efficiency of a very selective and indeed idealizing political picture and its usefulness for oligarchic exploitation. This argument is essential for an assessment of an almost paradoxical sympotic institution. The English club—that is, among a huge variety, about thirty to forty exclusive and expensive clubs for members mainly of the upper classes—can be described as a paradoxical institution because it perpetuates forms of social segregation and yet, seen in the historical-literary context sketched above, can also be classified as a sympotic instrument of social cohesion.[21] The paradox could be resolved by explaining that the clubs are specially reserved spaces for strengthening upper-class cohesion and exporting it into formally democratic institutions. By tendency, then, institutions acclaimed for their democratic achievements are undermined and made subservient to upper-class domination.

The English clubs are storehouses of institutionalized knowledge about a predefined group of people and their fitness for good society and rule. They are places where one can make sure of relevant knowledge simply by checking the membership and following a few rules for communication. Such rules are necessary (and laid out in the statutes) because the laws and forms of upper-class self-recruitment are not totally conclusive. As mentioned above, dynamic transitions are taking place between the upper middle class and the lower aristocracy, for which reason a homogeneity of interests and investments in solidarity cannot be treated as mere givens.

Production of the institutional and communicative prerequisites of oligarchic rule cannot be left to education in elite schools such as Eton or elite universities such as the proverbial Oxford and Cambridge, either: the range of cohesive strength of schools and universities is not enough. One needs loose conglomerations with a minimum of group specificity—that is, where membership conditions are more or less clear but not too tight—whose members can be assumed, tacitly and with hardly any risk, to be members of the group. When visiting or staying at the club, even a member with very problematic qualities and dangerous secrets would have no reason to fear exposure. Members are encouraged not to think or speculate about other members; in contrast to the petty bourgeois criticism of neighbors, for instance, no member of a club can arrogate to himself sufficient knowledge to talk about, let alone judge, another member. There is, then, a need for forms and institutions of self-organization that promote cohesion without discussing or problematizing the ways in which such cohesion is produced. It is important, a German expert on England has said, to belong to a good club; what you do there is less important—with one exception: "In most cases, a visitor is welcomed by a dignified silence."[22]

In a slightly parodistic way, the novelist Dorothy L. Sayers has described the efforts of an institution called the Bellona Club to impose the tacit self-closure of a power elite in the face of a murder that is not called a "murder" but deflated to a "disturbance" or "unpleasantness." For the club, murder does not provoke moral, legal, or criminological questions: it is an "intolerable nuisance" because the investigations of detectives disturb habitual processes and thus cause physical and mental unrest. In this case, the effort at self-closure is not quite successful, thanks in part to an unorthodox member of the elite, Lord Peter Wimsey, who does not obey the rules. He has become a part-time private detective who, to make matters worse, can rely on the leading detective of Scotland Yard. Yet even so, the rules remain largely valid. The first sentences of the novel compare the silence in the club to the silence in an undertaker's establishment or a mortuary; the largely silent members are compared to dead bodies. Any conversations that occur must be conducted in low tones or by whispering: "Immured by books and silence, confidential conversation could be carried on with all the privacy of the confessional." Whatever the emotional state of the members may be, they are expected to exhibit a well-practiced self-neutralization. Even Wimsey, whose "soul," according to his uncle, might have suffered traumatic war experiences, uses an emotionally smoothed-out language that might best be characterized by the word "bland." In rare cases, he may play self-ironically with the emotional self-neutralization expected by the club in order to vaguely suggest a need for not taking that neutralization too seriously: "I must be getting emotional in my old age."[23] The solution of the murder case, for which Wimsey is largely responsible, confirms the aristocratic ideology of social and emotional self-defense. The club suggests successfully to the murderer, a physician, that he should eliminate himself, for reasons that are self-evident and communicated with the polite but unfeeling words, "As a doctor, you will perhaps prefer to make your own arrangements."[24] By killing himself, the doctor would create less of a stir than a murder trial, although even the suicide is interpreted as another "unpleasantness" for the club.[25]

Nothing should prevent us from using the older term "discretion" for the club techniques of communicative management culminating in communicative refusal. Its upper-class irony or cynicism, though, might get lost. Other features, more or less shown or hidden, are suggested by comparisons with the yellow press and with parties, in regard to which Hubert Treiber has performed instructive work.[26] He reports that the effort to set up an exclusive club after the English model in Zurich failed because the English prohibition against doing business in the club or talking about it could not be implemented. Generally, Treiber thinks that the club is the most discreet and safest social mechanism for the production and maintenance of group homogeneity.

Compared to the club, the communicative and thematic limitations of coffeehouses as well as of French salons are also more visible. Treiber's thesis entails the presupposition, of course, that, with respect to such criteria, silence can in fact be very productive. In the coffeehouses, by contrast, the relative openness of social status and thematizations is less productive than one might expect, as that openness has a tendency to produce a considerable amount of noise. Consequently, coffeehouses often went out of business, their premises then being used as venues for all kinds of clubs with specified and therefore communicatively unifying goals. It is doubtful, therefore, to what extent they can really be regarded, in a Habermasian vein, as places for the formation of political awareness and debate. Coffeehouses ultimately found their grotesque parody but also parallel image in the "freak-circus" of free speech in the Speakers' Corner in Hyde Park, established by a vote of Parliament (!) in 1872. They were occasionally called "penny universities" and made England appear abroad as a model democracy,[27] although this was merely illusionary wordplay. In the French salons, on the other hand, where communication in the form of discussion of culturally or politically defined topics was still allowed, thematic exhaustion and the aging of themes or their dogmatic treatment became their hallmark. In the salons of the French high aristocracy, this type of communication was banned, but the empty formalism of talk could not be maintained for very long.

It is difficult to avoid such schematic ways of criticism. The problem is visible even in Richard Sennett's instructive and far-reaching characterization of the transition from the conditions of sociability in the coffeehouses to those of the club. The point of departure for his model, easily overlooked, is based on the communicative overlaps between the theatrical stage and the coffeehouse. Up to the mid-eighteenth century, the cognitive dispositions of perception were not geared to the theater as a production of mere illusion; rather, they were employed in its realization of the power of expression of real life that transcended the limits of class. The coffeehouse in its turn could enjoy the fiction that social distinctions did not really exist. Almost paradoxically, these distinctions reemerged in the wake of capitalism. As we have already noted, capitalism does not favor democratic developments but enables the nouveaux riches of the bourgeoisie to hang on to aristocratic forms of life. The visible part of this consists above all in the promenade with carriage and stroll, and the club. Public interaction, however, shrinks. In the nineteenth century, the department store will complete this shrinkage: a lot of people spend time in public, but they gather around the merchandise, not around other people.[28]

In principle, the club offers opportunities for private talk. In point of fact, however, it must defend itself against the dangers inherent in such communicative modes, dangers threatening the salon as well as the coffeehouse in their own specific ways (see above): the wear and tear of themes or, complementarily, a loss of control in quarrels and polemics. English clubs for the upper classes therefore try to cut down on the freedom of speech. Silence is prescribed under certain circumstances; discretion is mandatory under all circumstances. Members bound up with each other in mutual silence have turned into the object of satire in many novels. Around the mid-nineteenth century, Sennett thinks (this time without giving reasons), people visited the club in order to spend their time there undisturbed; even in the smaller clubs of the city silence had become obligatory.[29]

Since all club members have gone through a selective procedure of acceptance, they can largely rely on solidarity and cohesion with other members. There is no need to check their credentials. Silence means tacit acceptance; once granted, acceptance can be extended even into the murkier regions of human behavior. Since one never knows enough about other people, one cannot judge them. In contrast to the bourgeoisie, petty or grand, envy is not a category of major importance. The rules of admission safeguard communicative demands; they lay down conditions that may sound democratic but, once one looks at them closely, are replete with exclusionary terms. Thus, the book of statutes of the Whig Club, founded in 1784, restricts membership right on its exterior front page to "gentlemen" who solemnly pledge themselves to support the constitution of this country, according to "the Principles Established at the Glorious Revolution." If one has read J. H. Plumb on the meaning and import of that revolution (see above), then one does not have to be told what that pledge implies.

The validity of social barriers does not have to be proclaimed in such clear albeit slightly veiled terms. A more indirect way of drawing attention to them is practiced, for instance, by the Oxford and Cambridge Club (originally founded in 1821; pressure by the two universities opened the club to women in 1997). Candidates need two supporters belonging to one of the universities, called Proposer and Seconder, which means that they circulate and are circulated automatically within further groups of solidarity and common attitudes. Solidarity may well begin with rules and standards of clothing.[30] More details and information on standards of admission and practices of the admissions committee are not given; those who need to know will know. A careful dosage of information will prevent the wrong kind from leaking out.

Things may change. If the pressure of public opinion does not suffice, perhaps financial ones will. Changes in admission strategies for financial reasons seem to have belonged to the behavioral repertory of clubs early on. With the Whig Club, for instance, the increasing speed and size of recruitment in groups of fifty and then a hundred is striking.[31]

CHAPTER 7
A Symptomatology of Critical Shifts

THE PRECEDING INVESTIGATION is certainly not meant as a "criticism" (or "critique") of damnable peculiarities in the English or British political system. It should remind us, though, that institutions and procedures formally suitable for democratic purposes can also serve other interests. Connections between forms and interests are highly contingent; many people (including Hitler) have admired the British for their forms, ignoring the uses to which they were put.

In terms of sociability, the English club illustrates a boundary case with strong functional, though not formal, affinities with the old symposium. The in-group takes itself for granted; it does not have to, in fact it should not, rehearse its solidarity performatively. (With their libraries, the clubs have indeed assimilated elements of the reading culture.) The clubs cultivate community and sociability but do so within the narrowed-down boundaries of a pregiven solidarity. In comparison with the symposium, the priority of exclusiveness is emphasized. Meanwhile, from the late twentieth century onward, exclusiveness has also become partly invisibilized or at least deemphasized because the risks of visibility have increased. In England, not only the royal family have had that experience more often than they bargained for. In many associations, clubs of various kinds or otherwise, a degree of invisibilization is achieved by visibly publicized humanitarian commitments. Special interests, particularly with respect to international or global business, are certainly not neglected. These interests create forms of competitive solidarity of their own that absorb parts of the cohesive potential of countries and/or nations; the helplessness of the latter trying to recuperate energies of cohesion is often pathetic. Among other reasons, that is also why a relatively short-lived institution such as the *banquet*—that is, huge public banquets with hundreds and occasionally thousands of participants who hardly know each other—has disappeared completely.[1] In France, these banquets took over some of the rhetorical-political functions such as political speeches in public as long as large public meetings were prohibited.² In any case, the usefulness of the politicizing banquet may be doubted. The giant banquet, Sennett has said, was the symbol of a society that clung to the public sphere as an important domain of experience even though it had already hollowed out the social dimension of the public sphere completely.³ If anything, this has become worse: productive political "realities" are enacted far away from a politicizing public condemned to overorganizing deceptive surrogates in talk shows; we must be glad if these surrogates can still be distinguished from alehouse politics.

In these respects, the picture of the salons drawn in the preceding chapters also belongs to the excessive offers of deceptive appearances in modern life and media. The contrast between eighteenth-century salons sketched with Diderot's help and those of the nineteenth century inspired by Proust is suspect because it appears to be merely a history of loss. While such losses may occur, in historical processes we also have to expect substantial changes, which must be called recombinations and forms of repositioning historical materials. Thus, in Habermas's book on the structural change of the public sphere, the concepts of "mutual infiltration" (*Verschränkung*) of the public and private domain and of "polarization" (*Polarisierung*) of social and intimate areas supply the main ingredients of chapters 16 and 17. The concept or image of mutual infiltration, or crossing over, appears to pay a toll to repositionings; the notion of polarization injects dynamic force into the contrast. According to Habermas, toward the close of the nineteenth century the public sphere and the private domain are crossing over into each other's original territory. At the same time, the polarization of the social and intimate spheres seems to take place. Although this thesis may seem to be a contradiction, it is not. Rather, Habermas explores the manifold dimensions of both the public and private domains and the heterogeneous directions of meaning they have meanwhile adopted. The salon as one of the eighteenth-century forms of both limited public and limited private dimensions is one of the more remarkable victims of the new dynamics; it gradually leaves the historical stage, an event important enough for Habermas to mention.⁴ Even so, he condenses private-personal (not intimate) matters and public affairs (not, however, their impersonal variety of economic and political ones) into the concept of sociability once more. In his turn, Sennett has shown that, starting with the nineteenth century, we have to expect difficulties in defining the private (personal? individual?) domain.⁵

What one can say is that in terms of communication theory, sociability is largely blocked or reduced to small units, because the aristocratic salon, self-referentially turning round and round in an increasingly vicious circle, cannot handle this situation. Instead, it opposes it with empty formulas, conjuring up, in the French case as depicted by Proust, the thin veils of *mondanité*. Bourgeois salons, which cannot ignore the proliferation of technical discourses but are unable to understand and make them communicatively available, do not fare much better.

It so happens that Habermas, too, in spite of his conceptual precautions, occasionally slides into a conventional history of cultural loss. In such cases, his complaints are barely borne out by his own historical research. They are transformed into nostalgic cultural criticism, according to which the family loses its function as a literary "resonance area," leading to the obsolescence of the bourgeois salon. Habermas quotes the famous German Anglicist L. L. Schücking, who mourns the dying out of gentlemen's societies and associations, the dissolution of groups of regulars, the desertion of clubs, and the fading of the notion of social obligations. Some replacements, to be sure, have been found, but whatever energies may feed them, in spite of their regional and national variety, they all cultivate abstinence from literary and political reasoning. Reasonable and entertaining conversation is doomed to extinction if it has not already become extinct. In former times, people had to pay for concerts, for the theater, museum, and reading materials—not, however, for talking about them. Today, conversation is brought under talk-show control or taken over as an item on the program of stars for which, somewhere, one has to pay; the market for cultural goods is incorporated into the leisure market. In terms of social psychology, it is a tranquilizer replacing action and progressively being deprived of an active role in the press and in culture.[6] Real privacy—solitary reading, for instance, as a prerequisite for later sociable discussions—"makes room for the fetish of a commonality *per se.*" Neighborliness is imposed: we are obliged to do things together with other people. "Even watching TV together with other people can turn us into good human beings."[7]

I take this to be a joke of the partly serious kind, made by W. H. White, whom Habermas quotes in the context of his theses concerning the "organization man." There is also a serious core in Habermas's fears that modern urbanism is secretly destroying the sphere of familial intimacy. Yet his narrative is far too straight and unambiguous. We may leave open whether the production of crucial cultural works comes to obey sales strategies only in the period of consumer culture or if the laws of the market penetrate into the very substance of the works.[8] I am afraid, though, that we could say such things about Shakespeare, as well as about many novelists officially belonging to high culture—even about the idealistic Friedrich Schiller.[9] Habermas argues historically in more precise and analytically more productive ways when he takes his image of crossing over literally. He has a strong point when he says that a "repoliticized social sphere" has arisen out of the publicly relevant private domain, a sphere in which state and social institutions were welded together into a functional context for which such criteria as public and private no longer count.[10] This development has become conspicuous in collective contracts in the world of labor and in public interventions into private property. It is true that families have become more and more private and that the world of work and organization has become more and more public,[11] even if one wonders how this thesis fits together with the one about neighborhood TV and with the ways in which the welfare state has pulled the regulation of important family affairs into its orbit.

Clearly, since the European late nineteenth century, each of the concepts "public" and "private" must be interpreted in two different, often opposed, ways. On the one hand, the welfare state interferes, with no apparent limit, in what were thought to be private affairs. On the other hand, that interference takes away part of the burden of organizing such bureaucratically difficult matters all the time on one's own. Ideally, therefore, the individual or small intimate groups enjoy more freedom to take care of what privately—that is, individually or for the preferences of small groups—is really important. It is with these small groups especially that Habermas does not feel at ease: he describes them as narrowed-down intimate groups that produce the mere appearance of intensified privacy. The family in particular may shrink easily into a "community of consumers."[12] There are, then, semantic as well as practical shifts, in the context of which even Helmut Schelsky's seemingly simple but in reality complex assertion—according to which the split between private and public has sharpened—can find its place;[13] it does not follow, however, that, for example, after the end of World War I all connections between private and public were cut. Again, though, it may be true that the omnipresent media systems of modern societies have monopolized the fabrication of those images with which we "imagine" politics more or less completely, meaning that a de facto lack of relation and a state of ignorance have come to invade individuals precisely when their favorite topics seem to demand their commitment. Where private excitement is redirected toward the image supply of the media, erroneous opinions are pervasive; they are like a flickering will o' the wisp.

I have chosen this metaphor quite intentionally, because it refers back to a French novella, *Le feu follet* (1931), and even more so to its author, Pierre Drieu la Rochelle (1893–1945)—that is to say, to a period in European history where the clash between highly serious political problems, individual commitments, and media interference came to a first climax and demanded the victimization of at least one element of the trio. In this case, it is the person who suffers, because the cut between media and politics is still also felt as a cut between politics as an existential concern and "mere" professional politics. Drieu la Rochelle tries to follow the models of relatedness (symposium) and commitment (the revolutionary salons), to which he adds a third model, the dandy. But he ends up with the absolute counterimage to all of that—namely, suicide. In the absence of relatedness and commitments, the life of Drieu la Rochelle tots up the bill that one has to pay if one wants to bring politics back into one's life: it is only fascism, including indeed Nazi fascism (for a while), that seems to offer the compatibility of sociability and commitment to politics. It is like the dream of a union of fascists in Europe dedicated to keeping the hegemony of New York and Moscow at bay. The fascist turn, which included support for the German occupation of France, demonstrates how strange had become commitments that were supposed to stop the arbitrariness and, in its wake, the media dependence of politics. Where they fail—and they fail quickly—suicide must complete the nihilistic circle.

Proust's narrative tendency concerning the salon and Habermas's more general perspectives do not seriously threaten or imply dangers for the cohesion of nationally organized societies. Both, however, announce an increased urgency to rethink the *organization* of private and public dimensions of life. As we have seen with Habermas, modern societies are confronted with an increasing and often confusing mixture of both domains, but including the necessity to practice the flexible setup of boundaries. Covid-19 has become an unpleasant example of how radical such a rethinking, here in regard to basic human rights, can and must suddenly become.

Since the late nineteenth century, the institutions of the nation-state in which, among others, such a rethinking must take place have reacted to the need for national identification with the professionalization of national propaganda. In France, this task was rather easy because the country has been used to techniques of national self-aggrandizement (*grande nation*) for a long time. It can also rely, more than many other countries, on a kind of ideological stability of conflicts. This is also true, however, for periodic bouts of frustration (*morosité*). In England, insular self-interpretation, awareness of the empire even if disappeared, the prestige of certain institutions (elite schools and "Oxbridge"), and the splendor of ritual take care of a good part of national stabilization. (Foreigners may not be able to fathom the efficient role of the defunct empire and would profit, for instance, from reading the interview with an Oxford historian, Danny Dorling, in *Der Spiegel*, no. 23, June 1, 2019, 84–86.)[14] In Germany and Italy, centrifugal and regional egoism may endanger the national organization, but with both countries gaining nationhood only in the second half of the nineteenth century, the youth of the nation, allied with old myths that often date far back into the Middle Ages, still produce a sufficient amount of energy. Such energies want to preserve what has been achieved or even, sometimes with brutal force, to go beyond these achievements. All of this must be seen in conjunction with the destructive force of a generalized nationalism in that period, the conflicts arising from which led more or less directly into World War I and destroyed nations and societies. If we believe Christopher Clark, this catastrophe was due to generalized nationalism, not to specific pressures in specific countries.[15]

We need not discuss here the manifold levels and associations on and in which the formation of political will takes place. Their range stretches from local groups, whether representing some political party or independent "free citizens," on up to their parliamentary and governmental representatives. In such associations, the fragmentation of both political and sociable life becomes emblematic. They are not in any way related to the symposium type—that is, an association both creative and recreative, and, above all, not devoted to an emphasis on narrow exclusiveness, whether of party adherence or of class. Since they have become a fairly drab, often fanaticized part of modern politics, one would hesitate to ascribe any psychosocially valuable function to them.

So far this chapter has mainly been concerned with looking for breaks and cracks in the exclusiveness of the English club and, outside its internal mechanisms of subdued sociability, with the ensuing shifts in the private and public dimensions of society at large. Exclusiveness, together with restricted or, better still, restrained forms of sociability, appears to be the price one has to pay for stability. Shifts in the private and public dimensions will continue, carrying with them changing levels of sociability; in the sympotic perspective, this means that we need not worry anymore about reformulations of that difference and its play. It is more important to see how, against a background of predominantly and flexibly public domains, forms and degrees of *intimate* and *distanced* interaction can be structurally and psychologically organized. Regulating behavior in the salon of the eighteenth century would have to use and follow, let us say, the polite fictions that Hans Vaihinger, in his *Philosophy of As If*, holds to be of philosophical importance. But such fictions cannot be preserved in identical shape throughout history. With the nineteenth century and well into the twentieth, they were superseded by demands for sincerity and authenticity. Since social life would and could not follow these demands easily, it was denounced as mendacious. Lionel Trilling, in his *Sincerity and Authenticity* (1972), triggered an enormous amount of debate, culminating perhaps in the book-length question as to whether one can live without lies.[16]

Sociability, in any case, presupposes some scope for talk and behavior in which these may approach either sincerity or lying. For all his love of paradox, Oscar Wilde had a serious point when he wrote about the unfinished condition of nature, including the human condition, which needed "art," that is, some procedure that could be called lying, in order to show its full potential (*The Decay of Lying*). A narrow version of sincerity will not do, because for reasons of semantics and conditions of communication, everything that can be said can be said and understood differently. Our primary need does not consist in resolving the tension between sincerity and lying but in shaping a communicative process capable of exploring the space between intimacy and banality, between existential touch and social distance.

During the first half of the twentieth century, the *party*—that is, the social, not the political, party—established itself as the paradigmatic form for handling this need. Peter Sloterdijk's aphorism alludes to the historical motivation for that form in perhaps a slightly narrow way: "The utopian left had the dream to make life easier, easy to the point of weightlessness. They wanted the big party, now and forever."[17] I suppose it was not just the Left but larger parts of society that wanted to escape from the dead end of an alternative between sincerity and lying. That is why the picture in literature, too, cannot be tied to a political opposition; in formal literary terms, the wider issue is indicated by the fact that the schemes of interminable salon conversation are more or less superseded by shorter and more flexible forms (poetry, drama, scenes in novels, musical pieces).

The situation is still more complicated. In the party, shifts between more intimate and more distanced forms of communication can be explored. Its presence on the literary scene is stronger than the impact of the club on literature because literature can explore the shifts between intimate and distanced forms of communication much better and can connect them to tensions between the inner life and the outward behavior of party guests. In texts in which clubs play an important role, the inner life of characters does not normally assume great complexity. (Evelyn Waugh's *Decline and Fall* [1928] and *Brideshead Revisited* [1945] are not really exceptions because the students' clubs are far too rowdy for that.) Since the party is concerned with communicative shifts, its relation to both the inner world of characters and external social realities can become highly problematic. This is the case, with a vengeance, in A. S. Byatt's important novel (important for various reasons) *The Virgin in the Garden* (1978). All of the third part of this novel and not only chapter 39 ("Party in the Pantheon") may be said to deploy the forces of party-like events in which the fates of several people are acted out.

In spite of Byatt's novel and the other English texts to be discussed, we may doubt that the party has fully unfolded its historical role and potential for measuring the range between intimate and distanced forms of communication at the place of its origin (England). Reading Elias Canetti's *Party in the Blitz*, a book written partly from a sociological point of view combined with a history of mentalities, as well as a book filled with resentment, one gets the impression that the party was invented by the English class society in order to deceive people with images of the niceness of life.[18] Behind that niceness the rule of icy distance in that society demonstrates its full power. Canetti spends quite some narrative energy convincing readers that the decision not to accept the crowds of outsiders has always and already been taken, and to suggest in subtle and indirect terms that the outsiders are stigmatized as such anyway. Many literary texts, such as Virginia Woolf's *Mrs. Dalloway* (1925), try to avoid the risks in such procedures: the guest list is fixed beforehand; the selection is taken for granted and turns into a problem only if the presence of a particularly valuable guest (such as the prime minister in Woolf) is still in doubt.

Canetti's representational tendencies have been hotly disputed, and indeed one cannot take them at their face value. As a subtler example of early and insecure steps in the coordinates of a psychosocial territory between intimate and distanced communicative forms (including but not overemphasizing class), we may take the poem of an author whom Canetti hated with particular intensity, also because he took that author's behavioral skills as an especially perfidious form of emotional coldness and rejection of others.

As a born US-American who took British citizenship in 1927 when he was thirty-nine years old, T. S. Eliot knew Canetti's problems with English class society at least as well as Canetti himself. Eliot's own problem may not have been class so much as overadaptation to the new host country ("classicist in literature, royalist in politics, and anglo-catholic in religion," according to his own announcement), which extended as far as the adoption of an English accent and an almost indisputable anti-Semitism.

Eliot's Alfred J. Prufrock and the image of the party delineated in the poem ("The Love Song of J. Alfred Prufrock" [1915], "Prufrock" in short) may be considered to be the English-American part in the poetic introduction to modernity. Formally, this relatively long poem takes up, at least indirectly, the mainly nineteenth-century genre of the dramatic monologue, in which a speaker articulates their view of a problem in front of a listener who may not say a word themselves. The dramatic monologue, a less popular genre probably because of its complexities, takes into account the increasing need for self-observation; fearing unwelcome revelations about themselves, however, self-observers do not often plunge into the depths of personality. In Browning and Tennyson, however, this need, often treated in cavalier fashion in society at large as well as in many other literary genres, is driven to sometimes astounding depths—or heights. Since a listener is at least implied, the monologue preserves some communicative relics, even if these do not help in the search for truth but rather in the art of self-disguise and the ways of self-deception. The genre of the love poem, which, as the title indicates, is also present in "Prufrock" in order to improve the likelihood of understanding, calls the attention of the reader back to those times that were not, as we allegedly are, lost in subjectivism. In the case of the poem, a salon, as an "objectifying" factor in its own right, might in fact be imagined as a place of events. It turns out, however, that such communicative crutches as a salon are like retreats into a background with no real connection to what is going on.

In "Prufrock," the advantages of poetic speech with respect to the topic of the poem make themselves felt very quickly. Even if one does not subscribe to the notion of poetic speech as a deviation from ordinary speech, poetic techniques produce effects of deviation that in their turn soften or undermine the distinctions private/public and intimate/social (or banal). The text begins with a shift in perception—in fact, an "alienation" of perception—that throws a curtain of reservation over all the subsequent perceptions, be they ordinary or self-evident. The famous image of an evening stretched out like a patient anaesthetized on a table, the half-deserted streets and the cheap hotels, and again the streets, boring and yet mysterious, imposing themselves on perception—all of these urge a highly questionable external situation. This situation imperiously demands an explanation, which, however, declares itself to be superfluous at the very moment at which the question is asked: "To lead you to an overwhelming question . . . / Oh do not ask, 'What is it?' / Let us go and make our visit."[19]

Consequently, the text, in this state of its speaker's irresolution, jumps into the party-room(s) without further ado. The image of women walking to and fro is banal, but it rhymes with Michelangelo, thus suggesting a cultural level that the walking women cannot live up to (13–14). On the positive side, it liberates perception, setting it free for a renewed, stronger, but also more strongly trivialized enigma: the yellow fog surrounds the house like an envelope—and falls asleep (13–14).

At the party, nobody is pressed for time. Interaction can quickly lead to closer contacts but may also drag on laboriously or be terminated from one moment to the next. The event of one person turning suddenly away from another is notorious; reasons may be given or not. (The sociologist Niklas Luhmann concealed motivations for his flight from talk by saying, "I must circulate.") Normally, in such a case, the conversation falls apart into two monologues. The following section of the poem reveals the consciousness of Prufrock, who is tortured by the dilemma that he has plenty of time for the realization of his plans (within twelve lines, time is mentioned eight times) but does not know what his plans ought to be. The party, then, must deal with those (in)communicative situations, altogether very frequent in modernity, in which the personal and thematic prerequisites for a well-structured dynamics of conversation, including the necessary knowledge, are missing. They cannot be acquired even if there is plenty of time. Prufrock must acknowledge that the disturbance of perception spreads quickly to interaction and that it corrodes self-confident action even though time for calm reflection is available. Rhyme contributes its own share toward dissolving visions of interaction into chronic hesitation, until, with the prospect of tea and toast, any vision dries up ("Time for you and time for me, / And time for a hundred indecisions, / And for hundred visions and revisions, / Before the taking of a toast and tea" [31–34]). The women walking to and fro continue to speak of Michelangelo. They appear unfit, on account of this fixation, for more flexible forms of talk and interaction; the cultural topic of Michelangelo, stubbornly pursued, does not absorb the risks of communication but rather increases them. As a consequence, Prufrock's consciousness, forced to abandon the desire for contact, is flooded by anxieties; since interaction is blocked, the mind turns against itself. The immediate product of self-observation, however, is anxiety about being observed by others (see 87: "In short, I was afraid"). Such fearful anxiety suggests that the focus of these observing others is on Prufrock's weak points: as he thinks, a bald spot on his head and his thin arms and legs (37–44).

In this way, Prufrock seems to have arrived quickly at a zero point of interaction and communication. The prospects offered by the party in regard to these are drowned in the vicious circle of a disproportion between time and thought, of anxieties fueling insecure self-observation, of self-observation imagining unfavorable observations by others, and of the latter two intensifying the fear of being stigmatized for one's alleged weak points. But like the Olympic Games in 1972 in Munich according to president of the International Olympic Committee Avery Brundage ("The Games must go on") or the silly but ubiquitous injunction that the show must go on, party communication and interaction must also go on. The remainder of Eliot's text is therefore filled with Prufrock's continuously renewed and failing efforts to find a point somewhere from which he can reinvent and perhaps stabilize himself through comparisons and stylizations. For Prufrock, however, the party does not offer any basis starting from which comparisons and stylizations might make sense. Since he does not relate to the party at all, projecting himself into a plethora of roles offered by mythology, literature, and history does not yield realistic possibilities but rather unreal hallucinations or mere quotations. They culminate in an empty image of the universe (45–46: "Do I dare / Disturb the universe?"). He briefly considers himself as in parallel with Hamlet but then immediately gives up that idea; the role of Polonius, the "attendant Lord" stumbling in complete ignorance through the realities of power, or perhaps the part of the fool(but this is another self-deception), appear to fit better (113–120). Ultimately, such efforts to reconstitute relations with the party are restricted to hairstyle and the way of wearing one's trousers (121–124). But even in such cases of trivial reality the imaginary as a dreaming of oneself into hallucinations takes over. The decision to wear a certain type of trousers on the beach loses itself in dreams about mermaids; human voices seem to wake him up once more, but drowning is inevitable (125–132).

It is easier to fathom Prufrock's lack of substance and belonging, his deprivation of relatability, if one compares his situation to the similar one of a passenger losing himself in dreams of oceanic depth in a poem by Heinrich Heine. Heine's traveler, looking over the rail of his ship, starts dreaming of long-desired cultures, including an ideal mermaid. Losing himself more and more in his dream, especially its erotic aspects, he is in danger of falling over the rail into the sea. But he is pulled back by the captain, who, "annoyed but laughing," asks him, "Doctor, have you taken leave of your senses?"[20] A boat trip, especially a cruise, though no symposium or a direct successor, certainly bears some of its traits. The captain, annoyed but laughing, represents a reality that, employing rules, imposes cohesion among the passengers, a cohesion endangered by the doctor. But the latter, like any passenger on a pleasure trip, can also take some liberties, which is why the captain can laugh about his risky behavior. The captain condenses two types of reality (stable overall rules vs. situational dynamics or interactive variability) into one, types that form part of the framework for the symposium introduced at the beginning of this book.[21]

By contrast, the court society in *Hamlet*, which Prufrock refers to, was no longer capable of embodying this double potential. The way it appears in the play, it has been "de-auraticized" into a power machine that, although programmed like a machine, does not offer either its stability or its dynamic drive. Its characteristic behavioral mode in the poem is described as anxious observation, but it might as well be called by its real name: spying upon others. Prufrock in particular cannot tolerate that. In Shakespeare, too, the tension between the two proves unmanageable, which is why there is nothing sympotic about *Hamlet*. Instead, we get what may be the first images of terror, both brutal physically and more subtle psychologically, in English literature.

This was a crucial problem for Eliot. At first glance, it is hard to see where guarantees for both types of reality might still come from. In Eliot's second important text concerned with the role of the party (*The Cocktail Party* [1950]), we meet, as we also do in Virginia Woolf's *Mrs. Dalloway*, the psychiatrist as a new element in literature. The psychiatrist has the difficult task of saving both ordinary reality claims and the more interesting opportunities for the subtler forms of in-between. Eliot's play draws attention to the singular position of the psychiatrist at the very beginning and without any explanation. He shows up as an unknown and apparently also uninvited figure in possession of information from which the others are excluded. He seems to promise a cure for the fundamental structural defect of the party, which consists in the unexplained and unexcused absence of the female host. This is a first piece of evidence for what the psychiatrist will go into later at some length: the inability of people to organize their relations in satisfactory ways. They do not know enough about their own deficits, nor can they legitimize their authority to act in certain ways. Inexorably, and step by step, the psychiatrist uncovers those deficits in the hosts' and guests' constructions of human relations: the hosts are confronted with divorce; moreover, the husband is involved in an "illegitimate" relationship that does not satisfy either of the partners. To make matters worse, Peter Quilpe, a guest, believes that he has recognized an existentially important reality ("My first experience of reality") in Celia Coplestone, Edward Chamberlayne's lover (a relationship Quilpe does not know about).[22] Celia, in her turn, thinks she can keep her relationship with Quilpe on a casual level. Meanwhile, Quilpe is also involved with Lavinia Chamberlayne.

The most conspicuous feature of the dialogues among the group is the impulse, independent of topic and relevant knowledge about it, to be right at all costs. At the same time, people do not seem especially interested in what they are talking about or in what being right might involve. Since they are still capable of mild forms of humor, conversation could also be seen as a parody of itself. Neither in serious nor in humorous form, however, do conversations even come close to, much less challenge, the interests and the levels of competence of the psychiatrist. His contributions to conversation are restricted for quite a while to rejections of the topics chosen by the others.

It seems obvious that, in such constellations, a need for talk between two people would only arise, with or without the psychiatrist, outside the party. The party betrays a defect revealed by most successors to the symposium more clearly: in spite of its potential forms, from intimate to distanced, the institution of the party lacks range. As soon as it ceases to provide a reliable framework for conversation, strong conversational disparities make themselves felt. The behavior of the psychiatrist changes drastically once he is alone with Edward Chamberlayne and tells him clearly that he should be glad if Lavinia did not come back to him. The topic in question—let us call it the "deconstruction" of conventional emotional investments and projections in the modern world after the end of sentimentality—injects a considerable analytical rigor into the "comedy."[23] The psychiatrist, still unidentified, does not mince words: the loss of Lavinia will entail losses in Chamberlayne's own personality as well as a salutary humiliation. Edward will shrink, he is told, to a "set / Of obsolete responses."[24] Edward immediately sends Peter Quilpe through an analogous process of disillusionment ("You would have found that she was another woman / And that you were another man. I congratulate you / On a timely escape."[25]).

Confronted with failures in human self-organization and interaction, the psychiatrist can claim a superior albeit limited professional knowledge that is enriched with older forms and practices going back into archaic levels of cultures. This includes the function of the guardian angel (it turns out that there are three: the psychiatrist himself, Julia, and Alex[26]), together with a certain degree of ritualization that brings the party closer to a religious drinking rite ("the libation"). It also includes an important function of the party: crossing its own boundaries, precisely because these are so visible and superficial, to suggest a deeper dimension where we are bound together and overcoming their superficial relational discrepancies. Consequently, asserting a religious dimension of marriage and existence is a standard element in interpretations of the play. In the end, therefore, another party takes place that promises to be a full success after the psychosocial maladies of the participants have been healed. This result, however, remains ambivalent at best, as is more than hinted at in the question as to what the success of a party consists in.[27] In Virginia Woolf's *Mrs. Dalloway*, the question will make itself felt painfully at the end of the novel.

Of central importance for the play and its historical significance is, of course, the psychiatrist. In addition to his special and professional knowledge, he must be able to muster considerable rhetorical abilities and in practice refute the manifold assertions concerning the alleged decay of older rhetorical systems. He is expected to admit only that we haven't yet found an adequate language for all of the inner states and events of modern people. More important, the psychiatrist stands for the sympotic potential of the party—if only people were able to throw off egocentric or socially conventional modes of thought and feeling and adopt sociable ones such as those, extolled by Simmel, for instance. To a large extent, the play, propelled onward by the psychiatrist, is set in the framework of a party trying to transcend itself toward a symposium. The judgment as to whether the psychiatrist Harcourt-Reilly practices family therapy or arrogates religious functions to himself is of secondary importance, because the range and the dimensions of his language and his codes, even if professional in origin, cannot be controlled fully on the professional level. Since the characters have difficulties finding names for their woes, they tend, once they believe they have found something, to stick desperately to these findings. The psychiatrist faces the task of demoting dogmatized findings to provisional conventions, which is especially difficult with those terms that have to do with ego identity and so-called personal or intimate feelings that very often block or come in the way of interaction.

Accordingly, for instance, Harcourt-Reilly informs Celia that his primary function consists in telling them that the nature of their illness is not as interesting as they had imagined. It is highly instructive that a Cambridge professor of Greek in Doris Lessing's novel *Briefing for a Descent into Hell* (1971) puts such teachings into practice. Apparently, the professor thinks there have been psychocultural shifts that make it difficult for human beings to utter the word "we" as easily as the word "I." It follows that we tend to take personally anything that seems to touch or concern us even remotely. Distancing himself from this habit is easy for the professor because he has gone through the hell of amnesia (implying a loss of self) and because the ancient Greeks, his professional specialty, did not ascribe feelings and events to a personal center that we seem to have become used to. For the professor, even the feeling of personal responsibility has to be handled with care.[28]

Eliot's characters, by contrast, fall victim, without any protective preparation, to situations that strike them as existentially threatening dead ends. Lavinia feels herself as "completely prostrated"; Edward sees himself in the clutches of a "death of the spirit," an illness worse than extreme physical pain. The psychiatrist gives both of them a dressing-down, calling them "self-deceivers" taking "infinite pains, exhausting their energy, yet never quite successful"—Edward thinking himself incapable of loving another person, Lavinia, by analogy, torn apart by the conviction that no man can love her. Celia's lesson takes the form of an insight into the life of a couple:

> Two people who know they do not understand each other,
> Breeding children whom they do not understand
> And who will never understand them . . .
> . . . .
> It is a good life. Though you will not know how good
> Till you come to the end. But you will want nothing else,
> And the other life will be only like a book
> You have read once, and lost. In a world of lunacy,
> Violence, stupidity, greed . . . it is a good life.[29]

A good life, certainly. But, moreover, a cheap version of overheated so-called personal-emotional needs. If one is able to leave these behind, then one can see that the psychotheological architecture of the psychiatrist is made up of at least two further goals that challenge the person to the brink of self-abandonment. Celia describes her vision as a "craving for something I cannot find."[30] It is at such moments that the transcendence of the party toward the symposium is rudely stopped. The psychiatrist gives up the role of symposiarch he might have played in pulling her toward a life-threatening expedition into the unknown. It is "a terrifying journey"[31] indeed, which will end with her death by crucifixion during her work on behalf of the natives of Kinkanja. (Colonialism is certainly a large issue here and has been discussed intensely.)

In other respects as well, the psychiatrist leaves the sympotic promise in the lurch. Has anything changed in the lives of the ordinary characters whose mismanagement of relations has triggered the intervention of Harcourt-Reilly? Most interpretations (at least the "traditional" ones) take a line sanctioned by Eliot: "the pompous Edward and the frigid Lavinia ... accept their humiliation, they take their medicine, and in the end they are cured" (240). The renewal of a married life seemingly at the end of its tether follows the much-repeated teachings of a good Christian marriage. We may hesitate to join in because it is difficult to decide whether the marriage in its new shape has to offer more than the dubious niceties of male compliments and female household duties.[32]

This type of interpretive question, including the more modern ones concerning such issues as colonialism, does not bear upon the party as a sympotic institution. For that purpose, it is much more important to come to terms with the role of the three guardian angels (Harcourt-Reilly, Julia, and Alex). Why does the play need the three of them in order to bring about a reorientation of the other characters? Nevill Coghill, for instance, in the commentary to his edition of the play, devotes fifteen pages to the guardians without asking himself what might qualify Julia and Alex for a job that Harcourt-Reilly could take on single-handedly. Guiding and redirecting the lives of the characters could be left to him alone. It would clearly be silly to write up a list of qualifications for a guardian angel, but the criticism, frequently made against all three of them, of an arrogance presuming interventions into the (not only spiritual) fate of their *protégés*, was predictable and unavoidable.[33] Even in the case of Harcourt-Reilly, it is often hard to distinguish between a full range of competence and limited dogmatism.

The evaluation of figures such as Julia and Alex taking over a few amusing parts of the dialogue, or else, like Alex, representing a speciously benevolent version of nineteenth-century colonialism and imperialism but otherwise remaining redundant and well-nigh useless, must then be made from the outside. If Eliot had intended to present a system of guardianship by increasing the "staff" handling it, then this ambition failed: there are no observable achievements with which Julia and Alex could be credited. If doubts concerning them have once taken hold, then the psychiatrist is not immune to reservations either. Where and how did his often-rude interference achieve anything of note? With Celia, his influence was certainly strong but also deadly; Chamberlayne wanted to have his wife back anyway and to give up Celia; Peter Quilpe has matured all by himself through his activities as a filmmaker in California. It is difficult to see what kind of cognitive, perhaps even evolutionary, advance the profession of the psychiatrist might represent. His warnings against overestimating human relations, later taken up by Doris Lessing in *Briefing for a Descent into Hell*, amount to a stifling of the sympotic impulse that, in the case of the party, is in principle there. It is not relations that must be questioned but the investments of feelings and values thought essential for each partner with which they are burdened. Harcourt-Reilly's proposal of a contrast program—namely, the total existential individual commitment that Celia is supposed to exchange for social banality—is hiding the deadly risks involved in it. The psychiatrist, it would appear, has not found his place in a shifting cognitive and historical landscape. This comes from Eliot's refusal to let psychology and psychiatry push aside philosophy and theology and with them a Christian concept of the soul.[34] In Virginia Woolf's *Mrs. Dalloway*, though an earlier text, the psychiatrist's profession, even when dealing with the traumatic devastations of World War I, has already been completely normalized.

The difficulties of the psychiatrist's existential project suggest that the psychosocial substance of the party, its cohesive range and possibly deeper significance of interaction, depend heavily on external conditions. It follows that Canetti, quoted above in regard to the English party, was not completely wrong when he asserted that decisions of belonging to the relevant circles and in-groups are always taken before the event. In comparison to the old Athenian symposium, as well as to some extent to the French salon and, as we will see, the US-American party, the selection is predetermined. One cannot negotiate one's way into acceptance. The class system is flexible at a different point: in its recruitment procedures, not in later interaction. The relation between society and sociability is always leaning toward society. Sociability happens in social circles amusing themselves, which is why Eliot, the seriousness of its themes and problems notwithstanding, called his play a comedy. We would need a lengthy debate in order to decide to what extent class and comic entertainment can be considered the main ingredients of the English theater after Shakespeare—and possibly in Shakespeare himself.

This form of a sociability largely determined by social interests may remain relatively stable for a long time. Forms of power both outside and inside the plays as well as other genres converge, as do structures of feeling or the lack of them. Or perhaps we should say, it is not having or not having strong feelings that is in question but rather the ways of showing or hiding strong feelings. The reputation and examples of understatement are legendary, yet however well-oiled the mixtures of power and sociability may be, they cannot completely prevent shocks. Shocks of the sociopolitical kind can be intercepted well enough by the gentry, the land-owning nobility that has been called the backbone of English society; restricted to an urban milieu, however, the ruling class would become victims of nervousness and other forms of neurasthenia much more quickly. Personal shocks are a different matter. An instructive, if not perfectly appropriate, example is offered by Lord Peter Wimsey, who has been introduced above. Wimsey is the second son—always the more difficult—of a duke and the amateur detective in the novels of Dorothy L. Sayers. In a letter also mentioned above and printed in several of the novels, his French-English uncle Paul Austin Delagardie, reporting on Wimsey's development, draws special attention to Wimsey's nightmares as a child, intensified later by drumfire and being buried alive in the war, which resulted in a nervous breakdown. Delagardie's education of Wimsey transforms the energy of these traumas into a heightened sensibility and intelligence, but he is unable to keep the nightmares completely at bay. In any case, equipped in this way, Wimsey succeeds in extricating his older brother from an accusation of murder and to repeat that feat for the writer Harriet Vane, who becomes his wife.

This example demonstrates clearly that members of the upper class can find themselves in psychologically deep waters. Sociologically, they can even endanger the class structure if the costs of their manifold hobby horses, their behavioral oddities, become too high. But this is an old problem of the English aristocracy, so let us point out its stabilizing effects. Because the younger children of an aristocratic family normally must try to compensate for their disadvantage of birth through increased economic activities of their own, the combination of aristocratic descent and such activities has contributed and continues to contribute to the stability of the overall system through increased flexibility.

For this reason, we should not attach too much importance to the relatively mild shock caused by the death of a lower-class man in the life of a young upper-class girl, which occurs in Katherine Mansfield's short story "The Garden Party" (1922). It is true that even the smallest disturbance of highly banal activities and procedures or else the matter-of-factness with which craftspeople perform their duties can trigger panic-like disruptions in the minds of children, but they can also make them respectfully aware that class distinctions, "these absurd class distinctions," may pale in the face of calm competence.[35] In Mansfield's story, the adults try to ignore and push away the sudden and unexplained death of their neighbor ("Not in the garden?"[36]). The young daughter of the host, who has not yet gone through sufficient training in desensitization, would like to cancel the party altogether, but she is informed by her mother about what we today would call a lack of emotional extension ("People like that don't expect sacrifices from us"[37]). The party becomes a big success. Later, however, her husband returns to the "beastly accident" and the six children of the man who was killed, and their aristocratic daughter hits upon the idea of distributing the food left over from the party among the "poor." This intention ends up in a scene of total lack of communication,[38] but to be sure, class-bound communication will resume its ways.

While Mansfield's short story does not present or suggest a great drama, it is not without hints that would argue for a psychological calculus of the human emotional costs involved in class distinctions. The implications for various significant levels of existence that are illuminated in Virginia Woolf's *Mrs. Dalloway* (1925) are far more radical.[39] The novel does not deny Eliot's positions in *The Cocktail Party* altogether, but the interest of the oligarchy in sociopolitical power comes to the fore to such a degree that solutions for the totality of society are not to be found. Mrs. Dalloway is driven by a nervous unrest and insecurity because, understandably, she is unsure if her party that same evening will be a success or not. Her nervousness is also due to the partial fictitiousness of the institution of the party, which in itself cannot claim actual relevance anymore. Success or failure are just cover-up terms for the participation or absence, respectively, of powerful and prestigious guests, especially in this case the prime minister. Yet even the presence of the prime minister would not be a sufficient guarantee of the party's success, because he does not look like a prime minister. Thus he nullifies the important relation between visual perception and symbolic suggestiveness that is indispensable for the formation of an image of identity and leadership in English society (261–262). On the periphery of the interest in power, we witness the growth of normally hidden problems of life, for which the party provides the occasion and the trigger but cannot claim any communicative value of its own.

The pivotal point of the changes that Virginia Woolf has made in comparison to Eliot's *Cocktail Party* is anchored in the figure of the psychiatrist. *Mrs. Dalloway* appeared more than twenty years *before* Eliot's play. But it develops a distinctly more modern—that is, more problematic—version of that figure whose topicality is still strongly urged today by new symptoms in images of illness, especially of the posttraumatic kind. Eliot's Sir Henry Harcourt-Reilly is the master of an anthropology reaching up into religious domains, an anthropology whose adequacy he can plausibly assert; his range of competence does not allow for any doubt that it covers both the extension and the intensity of psychic disturbances. This is no longer true for Sir William Bradshaw in Woolf's novel, who styles himself as "the ghostly helper, the priest of science," but proves his competence first and foremost by demanding steep honoraria (142–143). He, the son of a shop owner, has worked his way up to the top (one of the typical dynamic structural elements of English society). Now, however, he is chiefly busy nailing the general practitioners and other layers of the medical profession down to their lowly place in the medical hierarchy ("It took half his time to undo their blunders" [144–145]). The comprehensive approach of Harcourt-Reilly has here shrunk to a scaled-down version: "Sir William said he never spoke of 'madness'; he called it not having a sense of proportion" (146).

For his part, Bradshaw's sense of proportion has turned into a highly desirable general metaphor for all domains of life and activity (149–151). It is obvious, however, that World War I has wreaked havoc on such a conviction. (For Eliot, apparently, two world wars were not enough to convince him that the "waste land" of twentieth-century culture could not be restored to a pristine condition.) It is an outsider, Peter Walsh, who, having worked for a long time in India, is struck by the changes in English life. He also notes, however, that these changes do not have much impact on the important question of how a party is organized. This is why, in his opinion, English snobbism—an insistence on status difference without a "real" basis—has turned into an archaism—an archaism, however, with an ongoing social function (108–109). What is worse is that the lack of relation between Bradshaw's sense of proportion, which still thrives albeit precariously on the basis of the antique, medieval, even Shakespearean "degree" and an idea of essential human features, brings catastrophe to those exposed to it: Septimus Warren Smith, traumatized (like Wimsey in the Sayers text) by drumfire, being buried alive, and seeing dead comrades everywhere, went to war believing in a Shakespearean picture of humans as humane. The war warped this picture into its opposite, also derived from Shakespeare. Following Hamlet, Smith invests both his positive and his negative anthropology with Shakespearean imagery and as a consequence is driven to accuse himself of crimes against human nature merely because he took part in the war. Worse, he cannot even describe what kind of crime he might have committed. Confronted with the conflicting fatality of Shakespearean imagery, Bradshaw's sense of proportion shrinks to a trivial idealization of social normalcy. He tries to counter Smith's threat to kill himself with a prescription of tranquility and rest that he will be receive in the sanatorium. This does not stop but rather accelerates Smith's suicide.

It seems hardly possible to imagine a more extreme degree of incomprehension between these central persons. We do not know, of course, whether anyone or anything can help a victim of war like Smith, but we may take it for granted that in this case a routine forty-five-minute treatment by way of a schematic and rigid list of questions will not initiate a process of healing. Matters get worse because Lucrezia, Smith's wife, is also unable to find a language by which to communicate with Bradshaw, who, in his turn, has nothing to offer in response to her expectations of help, which, to put it mildly, are by no means unusual (149, 226). To make matters more difficult, Woolf uses a different representational technique in order to intensify the force of the contrast between the psychiatrist and his patient. In most cases, we see things from the perspective of a single consciousness. The combined criticism of proportion and conversion (i.e., conversion as a central element of Christianity), however, is cut off from the perspective of one person, assuming instead the character of an objectified, almost Old Testament–like wrath not couched in Christian or denominational terms (esp. 151). We are also plunged into a massive criticism of psychiatry with (dis)qualifications such as "this exacting science" that "has to do with what, after all, we know nothing about—the nervous system, the human brain" (149), a science, that is, which demands a lot but does not offer precise values in return.

Within such horizons, a double deconstruction of persons and the party appears inevitable. If a person shows up in the consciousness of another person (and this is practically the only way in which we see them), the status of that person is almost automatically damaged by the reservations and qualifications of the representing consciousness. Such reservations and qualifications may relate to professional dissatisfaction (even in the case of Mr. Dalloway, who will not obtain a strongly desired cabinet post) or failure (as in the case of Peter Walsh, who is not successful in either India or London). They may have to do with illness, with obvious aging or other conspicuous and disadvantageous changes, especially of the physical kind, or with other factors; in the first ten pages of the novel, almost all of these aspects are mentioned. Striking changes of the positive sort, on the other hand, are far less important. This does not lead to a dissolution of personality or even amount to a thoroughly negative view of people, but the consciousness perspective transforms most characters in the novel into a center of oscillations of striking, problematic features. It is only in rare cases that these oscillations can be condensed into the impressive maximum of a life curve. In even rarer cases, such condensation reveals the mystical core of a person. Mrs. Dalloway, for instance, sees Lady Rosseter, her erstwhile girlfriend Sally Seton, with whom, many years ago, she may have found herself on the way to an unconsummated lesbian relationship. Clarissa suddenly remembers the scene of a stroll with Sally and others. Both stop at the place of a stone urn; Sally takes a flower and kisses Clarissa on the lips. "Then came the most exquisite moment of her whole life. . . . The whole world might have turned upside down!" (52; see 48–52). But nothing in that scene has really remained as a possession for life; instead, soon afterward, by way of contrast, Peter Walsh is introduced as "the elderly man in the hall" (59). He, too, thinks he sees that Clarissa has aged (60) and confesses to her (whom he had wanted to marry in former times) that he wants to marry a young Indian woman who is still married. Then he breaks into tears (66–69).

Clarissa's parties as evening events for the London upper class take place regularly, yet to call them events in sociability in Simmel's sense is not possible. They do not transform crude social categories into moments of a more intense life, nor do we witness, in the garb of sociability, superior forms of political renegotiation. People visit the parties mainly in order to engage in personal espionage, that is to say, in order to find out, hopefully, that others have aged more quickly than they themselves—a common feature as well in Proust's commentaries on the salon.

This kind of party, then, degenerates into a sympotically empty formula. Its framework is paradigmatically sympotic because it clears the social space and makes it available for nonstandard and original possibilities. But nobody seems to take advantage of the communicative potential and changes of context that the framework makes possible. In principle, the party appears to fortify the liberal strand of modern social life; in practice, it is the difficulty of controlling liberalism and thus running unforeseeable risks and embarrassments that makes people hold back.

In an institution of personal espionage, sociability disappears; it reappears as an organized form of *envy*. It looks, indeed, as if there is, in that respect, a gap in the sociologist Helmut Schoeck's theory of envy. Schoeck has demonstrated the ubiquity of open and hidden forms of envy, but he does not really comment on envy's organized encoding and its effects.[40] One reason for this omission is the neglect of Thorstein Veblen's concept of "conspicuous consumption"[41] and a tacit preference for US-American conditions.[42] Strictly speaking, the forms of conspicuously, demonstratively organized and institutionalized consumerism seem to challenge and call forth comparisons with envy. The part of envy in conspicuous consumption can be downplayed only if the criterion of belonging is exhausted by the acceptance of conspicuous consumption. A society organized around that concept does not need any of the forms of sociability we have been concerned with so far, because its cohesion is immediately visible in conspicuous consumption and in the national ideology "from rags to riches." Whoever can show the signs of rise and consumption and fulfill a few symbolic demands belongs.

Parties and the Postsympotic Turn

We may walk into a trap if we expect a party either to promote affectively and socially productive relations or at least to facilitate the initiation of relations. In his song "Wonderful Tonight," Eric Clapton has hinted at that trap in a musically indirect but also directly touching way. A man and a woman want to attend a party. Having completed preparations in terms of makeup and clothes, she wants to hear how she looks. In their collection of predictable communicative moves the answer must be: "Yes, you look wonderful tonight." Her question whether he feels well must have the corresponding answer: "Yes, I feel wonderful tonight." The man is talking himself into feeling well because he thinks he can see the love in her eyes. The correct answer, however, is given by his body and his head: "And I've got an aching head." Since he mentions that explicitly, the headache must be severe or else be a pretext for not going to the party at all. After the party, she takes him to bed. He feels obliged to offer at least some commentary both on the party and on his partner and opts for the weakest version—a repetition of what he said before the party: "You were wonderful tonight."

Obviously, no speech act is in this case to be taken literally. The communicative possibilities of the party, from intimate to distanced, have been transformed into boundaries and limitations, with the tacit injunction that they are not to be talked about because they would be mired almost automatically in suspicions of insincerity. Boundaries and suspicions in the context of the relationship of a couple, unstable in any case, add up to the classic syndrome of psychosomatic stress. This must be avoided, if possible, in forms that do not create additional stress. This is why psychotherapists such as Paul Watzlawick and others have come to recommend terms and techniques like metacommunication—that is, an emphasis more on relationships than on affective content which is difficult to identify anyway. During the party, in particular, as Heinz Bude has said with appropriate irony, one must be able to signal that one might give away confidential information, fully knowing that one is running the risk of blurring the difference between confidentiality and rumor. Small talk should be practiced in such a way that undesirable conversationalists are encouraged to leave rather than go on with a talk.[43] Here, another difficult but significant aspect, hitherto neglected, comes into play. The sympotic forms dealt with or mentioned above presuppose the mutual acquaintance of the participants or at least a substantial number of them. At a party, personal acquaintance is always possible, but it is not necessary. At a party for which personal acquaintance is of minor importance, the participants move in or into a culture in which personal relations with transpersonal repercussions are not particularly important. Where personal acquaintance is important, on the other hand, we tend to find ourselves not so much in one of the innumerable so-called networks that are the fashion today but rather in a culture of cultivated transitions to which access is of course blocked at some point. (The networks today are professionally oriented only.) Europeans might think of a country such as Austria or Italy.

These are somewhat complicated matters. In order to get at least the beginning of a grip on them, we will have to assess the specific modernity of cultures. Decades ago, Ralf Dahrendorf drew up a rough balance of the relation between dominant social structures of a country and its characteristic modes of thought. It is easy to see that theology belongs originally to European feudal society in the same way that philosophy has its privileged place in the transition to modernity; sociology clearly fits best into industrial societies. Such connections can be further narrowed down: not only theology but also philosophy (especially philosophies of certain kinds) shows more affinities with Europe, and especially northern Europe, than other areas of the world. The German philosopher Hegel had already devoted some interesting thoughts to such distributions. Since the Industrial Revolution has spread its effects over practically the entire world, one would expect sociology to have followed suit, but it appears likely that both the validity and popularity of sociological modes of thought have had their strongest impact in the United States. Arnold Gehlen (the representative of philosophical anthropology already introduced in Chapter 3) has formulated this idea more incisively than Dahrendorf: "This is because sociology is in all countries, and especially in America [i.e., the United States], the place for rational and that means scientific self-assurance not only of bourgeois, but also of post-bourgeois society."[44] European astonishment at the changeability of what Europeans used to consider as natural givens contrasts with the matter-of-factness with which the basic category of competition propels change. This is no wonder: the United States has presented itself from the outset as the country of movers and shakers and therefore had to develop behavioral norms that made sure the competition inherent to that self-image did not get out of hand. Again, Europeans in their turn are tempted to interpret these norms as euphemistically veiled individual demands hiding their brutality; this view is then extended to the contractual nature of many social relationships and to the many expressions with which the unpleasant face of naked competition is somewhat embellished ("keep smiling," "fair play," "getting along with each other"). In a book titled *The American Character*, published back in 1944 but reprinted many times, British writer, historian, and political scientist D. W. Brogan (1900–1974) thought he could identify an "American Impulse," which is supposed to consist in everybody introducing themselves to everybody and everybody to everybody else, thus including everybody in the group of social intercourse. The completeness of contacts in a given group is then tantamount to their indifference. The automatic self-presentation may result in comic scenes, such as the one about the late US president Richard M. Nixon, who during a party at the White House introduced himself to all the groups and people in attendance ("Hello, I'm Richard Nixon"), not noticing that his wife Pat was in one of the groups. She answered: "Yes, dear, I know, I'm Pat." (It goes without saying that the anecdote was related by British biographers.)[45] Europeans are often tempted to mock this kind of behavior, sometimes also to imitate it with an effort.[46] It would be better to look upon it as a small element of a cultural model that does not need a sympotic or sociable mediation between the individual and social dimensions because in public individual features always show up in their social form. The social transformation of the individual manifests itself, again to the surprise of many Europeans, in a higher degree of ritualization. Sports and academic events are good examples; in sports events in particular, the ritualized part seems to become independent of the event that called it forth in the first place.

Let us assume that the party, including the US-American variety, developed its dominating shape between 1920 and 1940. This was also the period when the mass media and the service industry embarked on their victorious march and, especially in regard to the other-directed person, was targeted by David Riesman, Nathan Glazer, and Reuel Denney in *The Lonely Crowd* (1950), the first sociological world bestseller. Around this same time, George Herbert Mead elevated the other-directed person into the philosophically and sociologically basic model of human identity formation, while also revealing its basic defect. Models of human behavior are never sufficiently well defined not to need an interpretation by language, significant symbols, and more. "Taking the role of the other" (one of Mead's most famous formulas) is a process in constant danger of failure. Riesman and his collaborators assume that other-directed people orient themselves, especially insofar as their leisure, entertainment, and consumption behavior is involved, along the lines of others. But these authors also insist that other-directed people are troubled by anxieties that they can barely shake off: above all, the anxiety that they cannot satisfy the ritualized pressure for conformity. Riesman and his colleagues do not foreground the question of cohesion, yet it is and remains their virtual center. In a discussion with his friend C. Wright Mills concerning Mills's concept of a power elite, the cohesion and assertive power of modern groups have come under general suspicion.[47]

Given such premises, the party can indeed be elevated to the status of a paradigmatic but pseudo- or postsympotic and predominantly US-American institution. It avoids the ambiguities of the European type, in which participants always run the risk of sinning too much on the side of intimate or small talk. But it also avoids the factually exclusive and preordained selections of the English type of party that are hidden in the cloaks of politeness. The US type of party holds communication in a middle distance, thus leaving open the possibility of later interaction in all directions. Such variety of communicative directions is also prepared for by student parties: generally, the ritual and interactive potential of sororities and fraternities in colleges and universities by far surpasses their original European models. Whether we accept or reject the thesis of the priority of the English or the US-American form of the party, in both cases a postsympotic cultural model has imposed itself in which the role and the range of conversation is reduced. Both illustrate the shift in cultural geography articulated by the German Anglicist Herbert Schöffler: "We are standing in the Anglo-Saxon day of world history, whether we welcome or curse the sun of this day."[48]

With the end of World War II, Europeans had an opportunity to welcome or curse a US-American sun. At first glance, the US-American party together with a Riesman type of other-directed people might not seem all that attractive. But it holds a remarkable aesthetic potential: the combination of problems such as symbolic interpretation, insecurity, leisure, and the implications of consumerism demands literary or filmic treatment. Its first vivid literary version comes early with F. Scott Fitzgerald's *The Great Gatsby* (1925); it ultimately explodes with *American Psycho* (1991) by Brett Easton Ellis. "Gatsby parties" became social models and still are: catering companies now offer Gatsby events based on the films starring Robert Redford (1974) and Leonardo DiCaprio (2013), although film versions go back as far as a lost silent movie made in 1926.

It will suffice to look at a few superficial features of the text in order to understand the justification for treating the weekly parties given by Jay Gatsby (i.e., strictly speaking, James Gatz) as a psychoculturally central paradigm. The objection, seemingly plausible, that the sole purpose of the parties is to entertain the rich does not hold water. Gatsby and his butler do take care of any need, however expensive, of the guests, who may come back at any time, even if uninvited, provided they were invited before. Gatsby's methods, however, of not taking *too much* care of his guests are even more remarkable: these include measuring out well-calculated doses of attention and inattention that, sooner or later, will induce the behavior desired by Gatsby in the guest. On a smaller scale, the guests may deploy the same technique; thus Gatsby's parties become models of modernity. There are no certainties but a large number of guests, who can—indeed must—choose forms of contact most convenient to them, and in case of an error, they must be able to block further contact quickly.

This kind of modernity is not welcomed by everybody, since it may easily harm older models—that is, forms of sensibility bound up with an acute sense of individuality. In the narrator, Nick Carraway, the awareness of modernity in human relations is limited, eclipsed by old-fashioned romantic ideas. He cannot handle the large number of unknown guests ("Dressed up in white flannels I went over to his lawn a little after seven and wandered around rather ill-at-ease among swirls and eddies of people I didn't know"[49]). He uses romantic clichés to describe his experience in New York ("I liked to walk up Fifth Avenue and pick out romantic women from the crowd and imagine that in a few minutes I was going to enter into their lives, and no one would ever know or disapprove. Sometimes, in my mind, I followed them to their apartments on the corners of hidden streets, and they turned and smiled back at me before they faded through a door into warm darkness. At the enchanted metropolitan twilight I felt a haunting loneliness sometimes, and felt it in others" [62]).

Jordan Baker, a sportswoman (today she would be called a professional golfer), describes the "Gatsby party" model of modernity succinctly: "'Anyhow he gives large parties,' said Jordan, changing the subject with an urbane distaste for the concrete. 'And I like large parties. They're so intimate. At small parties there isn't any privacy'" (54). This is not a paradox; Jordan has understood perfectly the logic of the modern initiation of human relations, which takes the anonymity of large numbers and, with it, a relative lack of presuppositions and conditions in initiating contacts for granted. But it also presupposes the possibility of ending a contact immediately in case of dislike. Jordan, for one, is capable of giving up her affectively unclear relationship with Nick on the spur of the moment and without complaint: "When I had finished she told me without comment that she was engaged to another man. . . . 'Nevertheless you did throw me over,' said Jordan suddenly. 'You threw me over on the telephone. I don't give a damn about you now but it was a new experience for me and I felt a little dizzy for a while'" (189; see 62–63). Compared to this directness, Nick's wavering self-characterization, allied with vague suspicions against Jordan, carries a touch of dishonesty in a man who proclaims himself to be a last specimen of honesty ("At first I was flattered to go places with her because she was a golf champion and every one knew her name. Then it was something more. I wasn't actually in love, but I felt a sort of tender curiosity. The bored haughty face that she turned to the world concealed something—most affectations conceal something eventually" [63]). When Jordan is suspected of having "corrected" the position of a golf ball "by hand," a scandal threatens, but it collapses when a caddie retracts his testimony and a witness admits that he might also have seen something else (63). Under such conditions, Nick's self-diagnosis does not sound very convincing: "I am one of the few honest people that I have ever known" (65). Nor does Nick present himself as a tolerant man when he dismisses Jordan as "incurably dishonest." To make matters worse, he adds that dishonesty in women is not so important (64).

Of course, Nick's problematic attitudes, if ignored, would not change Gatsby's parties back into a sympotic form. There are other deficiencies, at the same time both trivial and basic, that tend to undermine their sympotic potential. Although the criticism, albeit indirect, of consumer society sounds trivial, perhaps it is not. Consumer society includes the mythology of the American Dream, which in Gatsby appears to have become a reality. His main assets in that regard are money and luxury goods, with which the development of the affective maturity and subtlety necessary in regard to the value, material and otherwise, from affective to spiritual, of these objects cannot keep up. The novel observes and focuses on such discrepancies mainly on the level of disturbed and unsatisfactory relations with people and objects: consumer society feeds desires that it does not fulfill. Allen Tate, who described this structure of deception with unequaled precision during and for that very period, saw the resistance of art as the only way out. Art must preserve humane forms of life that threaten to disappear in the "'democracy' of appetites, drives, and stimulus-and-response," "in a mechanical society in which we were to be conditioned for the realization of a *bourgeois* paradise of gadgets and for the consumption, not of the fruits of the earth, but of commodities."[50] Gatsby shows that high-class luxury goods such as expensive shirts and cars, because of their bodily affinities, may come close to acquiring the status of transitional objects, in D. W. Winnicott's sense, that they may impart the sensation of being part of the human body and its experience of movement but only with the restriction of an "almost": as soon as affective turbulence is tormenting the person, the aesthetics of luxury goods starts to pale and crumble. Gatsby stages childish maneuvers in order to see his great love, Daisy, again. The promise of being "possessed by intense life" is not redeemed—quite the contrary: the dispute with Daisy's husband, Tom Buchanan, a nationally known former football star, turns out to be as silly as Gatsby's maneuvering, now with both men fighting for signs of Daisy's love (Fitzgerald, *Great Gatsby*, chap. 5). Jordan Baker exacerbates the problem by passing on the information that Gatsby had bought his palace only to be near Daisy; in order to meet her, he needs Nick's mediating services. As a personality, Gatsby is partly saved by his charismatic smile, which, however, does not commit him to anything (1); calling him a "son of God," on the other hand, awards him an undeserved greatness (2). The "son of God" metaphor falls to pieces anyway because it is incompatible with his fits of crude sensuality (3). Some quotations are in order here:

> He smiled understandingly—much more than understandingly. It was one of those rare smiles with a quality of eternal reassurance in it, that you may come across four or five times in life. It faced—or seemed to face—the whole external world for an instant, and then concentrated on YOU with an irresistible prejudice in your favor. It understood you just so far as you wanted to be understood, believed in you as you would like to believe in yourself and assured you that it had precisely the impression of you that, at your best, you hoped to convey. Precisely at that point it vanished. (53)

> The truth was that Jay Gatsby, of West Egg, Long Island, sprang from his Platonic conception of himself. He was a son of God—a phrase which, if it means anything, means just that—and he must be about His Father's Business, the service of a vast, vulgar and meretricious beauty. (105)

> His heart beat faster and faster as Daisy's white face came up to his own. He knew that when he kissed this girl, and forever wed his unutterable visions to her perishable breath, his mind would never romp again like the mind of God. (109)

In different ways, Tate's diagnosis catches up with all the characters. Nick Carraway, narrator and investment broker, is unable to establish enjoyable relations with either his profession or other people. As narrator but not as someone involved in the action properly speaking, he serves well because he observes from a middle distance and has limited tolerance, and because he is careful not to judge quickly ("Reserving judgments is a matter of infinite hope" [3; see 4]). This may also be the reason for his prudence in handling the dubious and possibly criminal background of Gatsby and his partners' business transactions: he hints at problems but does not pursue them. (Fitzgerald is opening here the wide field of "white-collar crime," which in and around the late 1930s began to make its way into sociology and criminology. Issues relating to this will come up in Chapter 10.) He does not perceive that anything is amiss when an astonished guest tells him that the books on Gatsby's shelves are genuine and that therefore the book as a cultural icon is on the wane (50). The fact that hardly any party guest or business partner attends Gatsby's funeral does not trouble him very much. He is not aware that sports has become business. For him, physical and mental changes in Tom Buchanan, the wealthy former football star, are regrettable but merely personal matters: Buchanan's body and soul, he thinks, have hardened, with the soul replacing its former subtle structure with arrogance and the body replacing its former strong and elastic performance with sheer power ("It was a body capable of enormous leverage—a cruel body" [9]).

In a traditional sense, Gatsby may be the main character of the novel. In Daisy Buchanan's case, older affective structures clash in a much more telling and dramatic way with modern times, which have no use for them. Daisy is repeatedly shaken by "turbulent emotions" (19), motherly feelings for her little daughter, for instance. On the other hand, she knows that she has seen and experienced everything, that she must be called "sophisticated" (20). In such self-descriptions, the narrator can discover only forms of insincerity (21); he does not see the suffering that springs from a lack of synchronization between older emotions, wherever they might come from, and the demands of affective muffling in the present, a synchronization that Jordan Baker seems to have successfully "installed" in her inner life.

In the background of the party and the beauty of its makeup, then, psychosocial discrepancies loom large: the discrepancy between a personal inner world and the situation to which it is not attuned anymore; the tensions between people who can neither harmonize their qualities, however acquired, within themselves nor coordinate them with those of their partners in interaction; and finally, the deficiencies in orientation, the lack of certainty in regard to the world out there, which floods people with an unending stream of what is neutrally called complexity. The party is a form of sociability, but it neither mobilizes energies of solidarity among people nor does it connect them better with the world at large. Party life is deceptive insofar as it may suggest that an acquaintance with some people and perhaps some elements of their world amounts to a knowledge of "the" world. While giving and attending parties is a habit that will stay, in terms of sympotic forms it is comparable to what in the world of cars and elsewhere would be called a model to be discontinued. Though of relatively recent origin, it has aged quickly. It is a collection—US-American, English, continental European, to say nothing of Asian varieties—of sympotic forms that, because of various built-in barriers, fulfill their original, their "anthropological," functions as described by Burckhardt and Simmel only rarely.

In some respects, Gatsby was successful, more or less, in taming or making invisible those of his emotions that could not be smoothly coordinated with the world. ("He knew women early and since they spoiled him, he became contemptuous of them, of young virgins because they were ignorant, of the others because they were hysterical about things which in his overwhelming self-absorption he took for granted. But his heart was in a constant, turbulent riot. The most grotesque and fantastic conceits haunted him in his bed at night" (105–106). If one can trust the narrator, Gatsby pays for that with "his unutterable depression" (117). Daisy cannot tame, that is, dissimulate, inner turbulence as well as Gatsby. She tries to escape into theatrical scenes that she herself can hardly take seriously. She and Gatsby would fit together well were it not for the opposed styles with which they try to control discrepancies. The final reflections of the narrator, who tries to figure out whether the text presents a "story of the West" (because all the main characters are westerners [188]) that is just taking place in the East, have, as usual, little to do with the real issues.

In its main characters, *The Great Gatsby* illustrates a central thesis of modern systems theory: an individual person finds themselves on the periphery of modern social systems, not at all in their midst. A person must not imagine that they can directly interfere in the processes of these systems, whether it is a question of law, of the economy, of politics, of education, or even of religion. Fitzgerald, it is true, casts a veil over this situation, because his characters often seem to have their way within the domains in which they operate. Gatsby and his associates are experts, for instance, in exploiting the weaker parts of economic and legal norms; with their success, they seem to make a difference. We do not see, however, to which kind of competence that success is due.

Bret Easton Ellis and *American Psycho* (1991) have pushed ideas of the individual making a difference into the growing collection of social illusions. The profession exercised by a person has become as indifferent a matter as questions of individual emotional evaluation. In contrast to these, the "personnel" of *American Psycho* have established a logic of the party in which prestigious consumer goods have completely replaced individual qualities. In former times, conservatives would have included such developments in the decay of the human substance. It is perhaps still possible to cultivate such language when one is confronted with the real, the radical other side of top luxury brands of all kinds. This other side consists in a sadism that, in order to remain satisfactory, must be intensified all the time. This, in turn, is necessary, because, as human relations with luxury goods in terms of affective value become more and more difficult, Bateman substitutes the use of increased sadism. Ellis uncovers the risks of the luxury-goods drug much more clearly than Fitzgerald. The novel describes the qualities of the new quite precisely but presents them without any emotional participation or involvement of the person who is supposed to enjoy that luxury. The prestige of expensive merchandise from Armani to Zegna can be taken for granted, but to flaunt them in the context of a small-group party hardly impresses anybody, nor does it satisfy Bateman (the protagonist) himself. The presentation resembles a monotonous litany; an emotional tension of some kind, which is necessary if people are to be interested, is totally absent.[51] For Bateman, the party just prepares the transition to his sadistic séances afterward. The party in Ellis abolishes the swings of the pendulum between the poles of society and sociability that already, with Gatsby, took place only in appearance. Society is left to itself, depriving sociability of any significance beyond self-referential pleasure. Now, however, pleasure means sadistic pleasure; pleasurable variation becomes difficult very quickly.

In regard to the aspects discussed so far (type of party, communication, "dialectics" of self-referential pleasure), *American Psycho*, in spite of the excess of events, does not really go beyond *The Great Gatsby*. With the cruel body of Tom Buchanan (not really explained by Fitzgerald), for instance, the earlier text, in terms of the problem involved, comes close to the sadism of *American Psycho*. The later novel separates itself from the earlier one by its distinct relation to a crucial but often neglected element in cultural theory and history. First, the intensified combination of horror and sadism of Patrick Bateman—the name alludes of course to the notorious shower scene in Hitchcock's movie *Psycho*—sometimes strikes Bateman himself. In such situations, he cannot cope with the sheer amount and horror of his crimes and feels compelled to confess them to his friends, although they do not take him seriously. Similarly, his lawyer assumes that another confession of a particularly horrible murder is a joke. When Bateman returns to the apartment of a friend whom, among others, he has murdered, he finds that the apartment is freshly painted with no trace of the murders left and is being offered for sale. Apparently, the police do not investigate.

Second, the lack of investigative interest on the part of the police hides another serious problem. Modern nation-states, especially those called welfare states (in dictatorships this is to be taken for granted), are often no longer able and eventually no longer interested in guaranteeing the security and order for which their citizens pay taxes and adopt orderly behavior themselves. Certainly, older forms of state and society were still farther removed from such mutualities, but it is only in modern societies that the principal law concerning the dynamics of civilization formulated by Peter Sloterdijk has developed its full force. Sloterdijk maintains that the sum of energies liberated in the process of civilization is always higher than the potential of cohesive forces. In light of the present analysis, the twenty-five corollaries following from Sloterdijk's main law must be supplemented by one more: in such societies, more crimes are committed than those societies would care to uncover and punish.[52] Deficits in the state control of social life must be taken for granted in those forms of society prior to the eighteenth and nineteenth centuries (in some cases also later) in which the law was administered locally. But these societies did not fall prey to the modern ideology and practice of control; rather, there is a higher probability that sympotic institutions were able to build up forms of solidarity that the state could neither catch up with nor replace. Such cohesive forces may have thrived on interactively reinforced emotions, on agonistic conditions, or on factors in between, but they bring about relations that allow for a common local and regional view of problems, weaknesses, and liabilities. What is more, they facilitate consensus about what can be seen as such at all. It seems to me that such "intermediate forms" are enjoying something of a comeback in present times; modern societies certainly are in command of a vocabulary and (e.g.) scientific terminologies for problem description. But the problem with problem-solving tools is not that there are too few but that there are too many. A unified and binding problem *identification* is difficult to achieve in this way. Rather, Opus Dei bishop Aringarosa in Dan Brown's *The Da Vinci Code* (2003) was correct in formulating as the fatal consequence of the generalized party as a communicative model: "Church doctrine has degenerated into party talk."[53] The bishop was talking about church doctrine, but his words would seem to apply to the relevance and urgency of any topic as an element of problematic culture. For him, the basic law of communication theory (it is impossible not to communicate) is valid at all times—that is, also during party time—but there no higher cultural or personal level can be enforced. There is a stock of possible themes that are ready for quick use in concrete communicative processes. "We call this stock of themes *culture*, and, if explicitly preserved for communicative purposes, we call it *semantics*."[54] If "we" do that, however, from the point of view of the party, we may easily witness the decline of communication into talkativeness and prattle.

Unintentionally, in a party perspective, systems theory also reveals what Luc Boltanski has called a basic contradiction of modern states and societies in regard to their relation to reality, insofar as reality must be located primarily in differences, inequalities, and subdivisions that "tear apart the texture of the nation," and in regard to their relation to "the impossibility, in the era of capitalism, to protect the nation by impregnable boundaries."[55] This may sound overly dramatic and saddle the party with a burden of proof it cannot carry. But, on the one hand, most modern societies are still seen emphatically as nations; the development of capitalism, on the other hand, confronts them with the ruin of traditional communities[56] for which the party acts as a surrogate. The party, however, is the emblem of dwindling binding powers, not a cure for it; we cannot expect the party to develop new binding powers or renew the older ones. Modern societies are not necessarily compelled to develop or renew such powers, nor can they simply digest the erosion of the social dimension of pleasure that the important thinkers of the eighteenth century had still more or less taken for granted. For Hume, sympathy was the central principle of interaction guiding and organizing the structure of the other emotions. Nineteenth-century capitalism was instructive in that it victimized large parts of the population; it was also instructive in that it pushed the growth of other forms of—admittedly problematic—emotion such as dramatic sentimentality. To some extent, the impact of losses must be cushioned or made good.

This situation means that the problem of this book will now require another turn of the screw. First, we must examine forms of compensation for the partial loss of sociable complexity. Since the beginning of the twentieth century these forms have consisted mainly in the break-up of complexity into idealistic, visionary, or utopian social projects, on the one hand, and into disillusioned, cynical versions, on the other hand. In forcing or relying on compensation packages, modern societies enter a theoretical and practical dead end, which, however, has hardly prevented anyone from going on with this activity. Joseph Conrad named the country—Russia—in which the break-up of complexity into opposed orientations took an almost archetypal form. In parallel developments, also duly noted by Conrad, terrorism enters the political scene. Autocracy was for Conrad *the* obvious form of rule for Russia ("the land of spectral ideas and disembodied aspirations"). It does not really matter whether, in dating cynicism, we follow Sloterdijk or not; Conrad's description, which will be taken up below, is practically identical with Sloterdijk's initial characterization. Philosophy confesses, thus spake Sloterdijk, that the great themes were pretexts and half-truths. These beautiful flights of thought—God, the universe, theory, practice, subject, object, body, spirit, meaning, nothingness—these are not what we have been looking for. These are nouns for young people, for outsiders, clerics, and sociologists.[57] But Conrad's Russia demonstrates that the clash of idealistic conceptual agony and real catastrophes that produces cynicism occurs in a distinctly more dramatic form than Sloterdijk's formula would lead us to believe. Boltanski,[58] for one, has drawn attention to the infernal variation of the complementary contrast idealism/negativism in Hitler and Goebbels.

Second, we must pay attention to changed forms of compensation for the failure of state, public, and more or less public agencies of control. Here we turn to the curves of a movement, running in opposite directions, of reality defined and lost by the state as described, for instance, by Habermas. In early modern times, the mythic images of the state as Leviathan or Behemoth—that is, of an omnipotence embodied in the sovereign or the absolutistic ruler—tend to lose their hold on the imagination. (This did not, of course, prevent them from making a comeback much later.) This development is conspicuous in theories of the state from Hobbes to Locke. While state omnipotence does not disappear, it has to use, apart from the direct exercise of power, more indirect and, because of indirectness, more efficient procedures described by Foucault and others in his wake as the control techniques of biopolitics, normalization of various kinds (using statistics for instance), the mixture of welfare and control, the use of the law and today of big data, emotive formulas, and more. In such forms of "modernization," fascist variations of a return to myths amount to no more than catastrophic relapses into old habits. The national varieties of securing rule—in England the compromise between the Crown and a Parliament dominated by the upper class, in France an administration fully partaking of the splendor of elite universities,[59] in Germany a conglomerate of agencies, institutions, and lobbies—often contribute heavily to makeshift forms of order as well. Boltanski's brief description of the French situation is exemplary: "The administration is the only *dispositif* which remains above the milieus and the political parties and is capable therefore of embodying the state and of ensuring its continuous existence."[60]

For those nations that have gone through the processes of modernization, the ongoing existence of the state may only rarely be in question. And yet there are always serious sources of instability that add a question mark to any simple assertion of stability; apocalyptic scenarios continue to be written. In federal nations, the experience and renewed threat of secession are well known and cannot always be dismissed as simplistic and hysterical hallucinations. Quite generally, in many instances both past and present, another form of compensation for the lack of communicative binding forces or other deficits in state organization and administration have become active by staying in the background. Both representatives and critics have had recourse to secret societies in order to correct what they consider as abuses or worse of the state or to keep outside enemies—real, imagined, or invented—at bay. Secret societies must, of course, operate under cover. Existing laws often lose some of their validity for them; they withdraw difficult problems from public attention or debate. Such moves encourage conspiracy theories that are dismissed by their opponents as fantasies or stereotypes.[61]

It would be dishonest to behave as if this merry-go-round of denouncing fantasies as always the fantasies of the other did not create difficulties for the present volume. Secret societies, to say nothing of secret services (see below), must have their own techniques for managing relevant information about themselves. There is, however, a third way out that is conventional but less risky. We will use a symptomatology (a rigorous selection) of the modern detective novel together with other evidence less difficult to access (e.g., Opus Dei) in order to illuminate the state of sociability in the postsympotic world. Since reevaluating the detective novel obviously means dealing with what is today the dominant literary (some would say subliterary) genre, it is therefore best to undertake it with guidance from authorities in several relevant fields. I have chosen Umberto Eco and Luc Boltanski, both of whom have declared the detective novel to be a philosophical genre because, according to Boltanski, it takes the relation of state and reality as an occasion to soar up into metaphysical heights in order to elucidate the unusual neighborhood of metaphysics and banality. This ascent entitles the detective novel to claim the status of a model of aesthetic productivity in nonsympotic times. It can also claim this status because it connects the policeman and the private detective—that is, degrees of the private and public domain—in their secret and open dimensions and because it provides various outcomes to the competition between what is legal or illegal. The detective novel, then, sticks to a limited visibility of what is legal while at the same time embodying the attractions of what is illegal.

The type of experience provided by the symposium, sensually pleasurable and intellectually superior, is not banished from the world of the detective novel. In the twentieth and twenty-first centuries, pleasure does not so easily embody the social and intellectual dimensions with which the literature of the centuries before had equipped it. Forms and possibilities of pleasure have multiplied in inflationary ways, in the process of which, as I have said repeatedly, pleasure has become self-referential. It is not interested in "constructive" relations with society, politics, or even culture. If it is interested in politics, it is politics in the sense of promoting its recognition and legitimacy at large, not in the sense of Simmel's cultivated sociability or the interactional correlates of Hume's eighteenth-century sympathy as the core area of human nature.[62] Boltanski, for instance, attributes a "negative anthropology" to Georges Simenon's Commissaire Maigret: people basically know only two passions, sexuality and money, which often work together in motivating crimes. They are mentioned as motifs but do not occur as fully developed motivations or as contextually narrated modalities of experience in either the criminals or Maigret.[63]

Or rather, they rarely occur in full-blown shape. Modern self-referentiality has also come to mold the dominant forms of pleasure in Richard Sennett's *The Fall of Public Man* (1977), his well-known book on the decline of public life and the tyranny of intimacy. Sennett attributes to secular city culture and modern capitalism, that scapegoat of many writings on modern life, a pressure of privatization that in the end destroys the quality of experience. In the nineteenth century, eroticism must still take a number of social demands into account: any erotic relation is enmeshed in the nets of already existing families, especially parents and other social relations of the protagonists. It is difficult to assert that much in regard to twentieth-century "affairs," These affairs activate the basic narcissistic energies (Sennett) of the persons involved, which in turn penetrate all other interactions. Producing social bonds falls prey very easily to the impact of big cities and big money.

PART 3
Sympotic Relics
Secrets and Literature

CHAPTER 8

Securing Power and Auxiliary Evidence

THE FOLLOWING THREE CHAPTERS might appear to be remote from the topic of the symposium, but we need them in order to sketch and document drastic social and political changes, especially in nineteenth-century Europe, and to emphasize the need for new controls of so-called reality. In the midst of these changes, something like the resurrection, the reemergence, of the symposium (or at least of parts of it) on the alternative horizons of social cohesion and social anomie (laws are still in force but are not enforced anymore) takes place. It is only in this context that the reemergence can be argued intelligibly. Even the manifold resources of modern states, the efficiency, at least in principle, of governmental and administrative techniques, cannot prevent occasional disturbances of order. Each form of government and rule has weak areas and soft spots that must be dealt with in however makeshift ways if vital processes of the state are at stake. The means by which such areas and spots are supposed to be eliminated or neutralized can take the most heterogeneous forms.

Secrets and Confession

Since the Middle Ages, secret societies and associations have come into being, claiming—only in secret documents and negotiations, of course—to have the ability to remedy the wrongs and shortcomings of rule and to replace a defective order by a better one. Dangers from the outside, threatening to damage or annihilate a state, must be neutralized or outwitted by secret services, whose history, as far as we can tell, dates back much farther than the history of secret societies. Wolfgang Krieger, a well-known German historian of secret services, thinks they date back as far as the times of the pharaohs of ancient Egypt; a recent volume on secret services, *Die Macht der Geheimdienste. Agenten, Spione und Spitzel vom Mittelalter bis zum Cyberwar* (2020), tries to prove their antiquity with wordplay (espionage as the oldest profession in the world) but then immediately corrects itself: only from the times of the Renaissance onward did ruling noblemen send out secret diplomats in order to spy on enemies and competitors. Eventually, in the nineteenth and twentieth centuries, the size and complexity of international conflicts required secret services of a correspondingly enormous size. In earlier times, spies restricted their activities to information useful for a battle, for instance, as substantiated in Shakespeare with regard to even much earlier times. In Shakespeare's own times, the fate of a whole country or at least a ruling dynasty might be jeopardized by negligence in matters of espionage. Internal and external Catholic foes presented a serious threat to the stability of England and the rule of Elizabeth I; even Shakespeare himself and his family were suspected of Catholic conspiracy. The need for a clever organizer of espionage and counterespionage became imperative, and Sir Francis Walsingham took over, with a network of agents that extended over more than half of Europe.[1]

The work of secret services is conservative: it is normally geared toward making the rule of the powers that be more secure by aiding in the defense against foreign enemies and in the regulation of interior conflicts, as well as by "optimizing" the financing of the two preceding tasks.[2] Secret societies, by contrast, aiming at the improvement of state institutions, may take a conservative or a progressive or even a revolutionary attitude. Whatever their attitude or intention may be, it is apt to raise the suspicions of and lead to observation by secret services or other state agencies. Since the beginning of the twentieth century, at the latest, securing rule against threats of disturbance from the inside as well as the outside and against crime have probably become of equal importance, which means that secret services and the various forms of police must be counted among the elementary realities of modern life. They may interfere with people's lives at any time, the mere threat of which is enough to include them in people's calculus of reality, influencing their thoughts, feelings, and behavior. Even so, most people cannot but be ignorant of the operational realities of these institutions, for which reason we need narratives, imaginatively enriched, in order to provide checks and balances on these institutions in the minds of people who might easily turn into the objects of their investigations.

It is mainly the detective novel and its relatives (and film, of course) that provide us with such imaginary versions. Therefore, I again assert that detective novels and spy novels have registered changes in consciousness and to some extent in social structure very precisely and treated them in ways that in quite a few instances deserve the label of great literature. Since the beginning of the twentieth century, literature, very broadly speaking, may be divided into two groups with competing orientations. For the first group, often called modernist, reality falls apart into a multiplicity of fictions. The second group, which I shall call analytical-historical, is still committed to explorations of what might be called operational realism, despite an awareness of fiction and fictitiousness and an ironic view of older forms of realism. It is committed to the operationally relevant mechanisms that decide whether, for the time being, something can and will be called real. Sometimes both orientations play their respective roles in the total work of an author. The conflicts in Hermann Broch's trilogy *The Sleepwalkers* unfold in three novels devoted to historical and epistemological intricacies. Joseph Conrad's works seem to reverse their orientation midway between the modernist variety in earlier works and the analytical-historical emphasis in later ones (see also Chapter 9), a move that could almost be declared a relapse into old European debates concerned, for instance, with individualism and a "communal view of human life and responsibility."[3]

As a goal, the communal view has been formulated quite often; as an interactively important and practical reality, its prospects have shrunk considerably. Its implementation presupposes sympotic resources, especially bodily grounded interaction, together with opportunities for debate ranging all the way from philosophical to intimate topics. Looking at widely practiced forms of debate—political, academic, and otherwise—one might entertain mixed feelings about both their enjoyment and their usefulness. Interviews, another bodily and, by extension, media-grounded genre, do not inspire great expectations either. An opposed but very intriguing level of commonality has been opened up by crowds in soccer stadiums, recently analyzed by Hans Ulrich Gumbrecht: "Alone with our bodies, we belong to a mass and become a part of a *relationship* with other bodies which for a while has nothing to do with common interests, solidarity or with consensus."[4] While in the crowd, bodies may become (like) a mystical body, but it is more than difficult to see how the mystical body, unless for some moments only, could ever be linked up with the problem orientation suggested by communal terms such as "common interests" or "solidarity." This difficulty is certainly one of the reasons why secret societies allot large spaces to precisely choreographed communal sympotic rituals. For their members, this eases the psychological burden of keeping secrets because it makes talking about them more difficult. Secret sociability reinforces feelings of belonging. It allows first for the simulation, then for the testing, of new and utopian figures of interaction. Interactive sociability protects secrecy and prefigures new forms of behavior and social order.

In state-historical and -organizational respects, secret services and secret societies, as well as secret activities among the criminal police, are united by the need for enabling nation-states to cope with and neutralize governmental and administrative as well as legal defects. These tasks must be performed under the sign of secrecy because open debate breeds disunity. Again it was Georg Simmel who wrote perhaps the most interesting analyses of this, although it must remain undetermined how secrets and secrecy relate to the concept of sociability. Simmel's approach can be made even more productive by a psychoanalytical contribution from the Japanese psychoanalyst Takeo Doi. Simmel's sociability maintains a balance between variable distances of communication; it foregrounds, however, its chances for intimacy and even existential import. The secret, by contrast, is charged instead with massive functions in the domains of cultural history and sociology: "The secret in this sense, that is the hiding, by positive or negative means, of realities, is one of the greatest achievements of mankind; compared to the childish situation in which any movement of the mind is immediately spoken out, in which any enterprise is immediately accessible to each and any look, the secret achieves an immense extension of life, because many of its contents cannot surface at all if pulled into full publicity." The secret offers the possibility of "a second world beside the visible one, and the latter is strongly influenced by the former."[5]

Such formulations may still betray existential concerns. But in what follows, Simmel turns more decidedly to the secret societies that can spring up at any time. It immediately becomes apparent, however, that this question must be dealt with in a much fuller historical perspective. Secret societies come into existence especially in those times—and they are destined to do so—in which, like the eighteenth century, that is, the Enlightenment, new contents of life want to break the resistance of existing powers, trying to impose themselves. More generally: "The secret society, by preference, comes into existence as the correlate of despotism and police restriction, as defensive and offensive protection against the violent pressure of central powers."[6] This can happen on all levels (politics, church, school classes, family) We must add that secret societies flare up as a response to obvious shortcomings or the total failure of the official political power in creating forms of order that are necessary. (Even revolutionaries need and want some order.) In the twentieth/twenty-first century, obviously, this has often been the case. No one needs to know how "real" such failures are or precisely when something must be done. Nor is it necessary to distinguish cogently between reforms one can postpone and those that must be tackled on the spot; here, the overkill of the mass media comes into its own.

Takeo Doi has named the nineteenth century as the primary European period for the downgrading, indeed the tabooing, of the secret. In his *Das Wesen des Christentums* (The essence of Christianity [1841]), Ludwig Feuerbach, for instance, talks about all kinds of secrets in this religion. In doing so, however, he wants precisely to show that these secrets can be explained (away) by ordinary human reasoning. Doi holds that all older cultures have elevated the secret—that is, the habit of keeping secret essential human qualities hard to put into ordinary language or innermost personal "possessions" into core elements of their notions of a human being.[7] The task of preserving such secrets is handed over to the "mask," a facial expression (a problematic term) that disguises and hides the inner state of a person. Doi shares this high respect for the mask with a few Western thinkers (there are not many) such as Nietzsche and the Helmuth Plessner of *Grenzen der Gemeinschaft* (The limits of community; see the third section of Chapter 1). With the concept of mask, Nietzsche wanted to disempower the cheap demands for sincerity, honesty, and authenticity of the then-current moral norms and was broken by the effort.[8] Freud believed that with the interpretation of dreams he had found the key to open up the innermost secrets of the individual human soul, but he overlooked the fact that the soul, in order to feel well, needs secrets. He could not see that the ideal state of the inner life is reached when it is at peace with its secrets.[9]

Like most psychoanalytical conceptions, Doi's approach aims at a general, not just historical, insight. Plessner, too, as we have seen, asserts the right to wear a mask to be a natural part of human beings, who must protect themselves and their inner life from being ridiculed, hurt, or exposed to broad daylight. But the publication date of this short book (1924) indicates that the text also reacts against and resists the partly confused demands for authenticity in what might be called a utopian period during the Weimar Republic. The refusals to bow to such demands also became the hallmark of Helmut Lethen's famous book *Verhaltenslehren der Kälte. Lebensversuche zwischen den Kriegen* (Behavioral doctrines of coldness: Trying to live between the wars [1994]). In advanced modern societies, in which the communicative type of the symposium does not obtain anymore, secrets, used by the state and individuals in their own special ways, function like a sociopsychological compromise. Secrets help the state to extend the range of its rule; they enable individuals to refine techniques of dodging or evading forms of both private and state control, although individuals reach a problematic extreme when efforts at dodging or evading lead to inner exile.

Adopting a "functional" perspective may also help to defuse what might otherwise find itself in a specious opposition to the secret—namely, the confession. This concept targets the manifold forms of the pressure to confess what is going on inside a person. In Europe, the pressure took on institutional shape, with medieval monks having to observe their inner stirrings and communicate them to their superiors. It then spread over secular domains, infiltrating literature in subtly differentiated forms that, for literary scholarship, have become indispensable tools for textual analysis, particularly of narrative texts. Hyunseon Lee has shown how drastic and fulsome the compulsion to confess ultimately has become in the show trials and self-accusations staged with particular zeal in Communist regimes.[10] For a while, it has the effect of torture, but in due course, interiorizing the pressure over time can transform into a personal narcissistic need articulating itself best in sophisticated literature. The confession then barely refers to sins or crimes but is used as the primary tool of individuals striving to render themselves intelligible to themselves, needing to assure themselves about themselves. Modern subjects are pushed into self-positionings; they develop a sufficient awareness of themselves by comprehending their individuality as well as communicating its essence. This might be the point where the principle of systems theory—that is, the impossibility of not communicating—reaches its highest intensity. In regard to the confession, this principle must just be recast into the more active form of wanting to communicate. Erving Goffman's classic *The Presentation of Self in Everyday Life* (1959) offers a late, sociologically tinged approach among culturally extended processes of mediatization that, since Mme. de La Fayette's *Princesse de Clèves* (1678), have become indispensable for literature too. The center of that mediatization has come to be occupied by the different forms of the I-novel, its masked presence in other genres, and also the soliloquy in drama. As soon as the compulsion to confess has been interiorized, decisions concerning forms and strategies must be found or invented. The following assertion sounds risky, but it must be made: large parts of Western literature since the *Princesse de Clèves* have been produced, in open or covert ways, under the sign of the confession, of the intensity of looking at oneself and at one's literary, later multimedia, exteriorization. Meanwhile, a high price has to be paid for this in talk shows and similar formats. Staging confession for the sake of individual profile retroactively damages the nineteenth-century idea(l) of a strong personality living in and on special and especially impressive qualities.[11] Originating in the nineteenth century, this conception takes the place of the idea of the natural human being—that is, of a more or less normative anthropology with a constant repertory of characteristics. Balzac was the writer whose novels drove the strong personality to epic and demonic excess. In the strong personality, the importance of secrets and confession appears to be erased, but this, again, is just an appearance forced by the self-staging of the seemingly autonomous power of the strong personality. The socially as well as psychologically basic function of confession as the flip side of the secret remains unimpaired. The detective novel exploits this configuration through an asymmetric organization of its narratives, devoting many pages to the attraction of secrets and condensing confession into the intensity of epiphany-like short scenes.

This asymmetry is the main source of aesthetic productivity in the detective novel. Cutting down solution and confession to short passages at the end and, conversely, stretching the role of secrets and mysteries to the utmost, the detective novel emphasizes and wallows in an atmosphere of threat and fatality. The denser this atmosphere can be made, the more habitual realities are entitled to a comeback. The frequent monotony of the processes between crime and solution does not matter, because investigative success in the conflict of superbrains represented by police, detective, and criminal rekindles trust in the stability of reality, however trivial, which has been shaken by crime in the first place. Luc Boltanski has written a long book on these connected matters:

> The detective novel and the spy novel offer characters which resemble types even more than in the society novel. Likewise, they create a reality even more banal than in the society novels. But this banalization forms the basis for the impression of acute crisis, of a crime in the process of happening which for a while we cannot ascribe to anything or anyone and which demonstrates how insecure that reality is, how little reality this reality can bear.[12]

The banalization of reality in the detective novel is bought with the instability of both reality and banality. What makes us really tremble, Umberto Eco has said, is the "metaphysical shudder" evoked by the detective novel, which, for Eco too, turns that type of novel into the most metaphysical and philosophical one. For Boltanski, the metaphysical dimension arises in the special tension (suspense) of that type of novel, which in its turn springs from the intense questioning of the reality of reality.[13] Perhaps the popularity—indeed, the inflation—of detective series on TV is, apart from many other reasons, due to the power of rhythmic intensification that the serial character makes possible. (Unfortunately, it also makes possible the opposite.)

There are further reasons for Eco's and Boltanski's metaphysical shudder, which have to do, for instance, with the specific shudder due to cruelly dismembered bodies of murder victims. In a text, film, or TV series, the body is not really present, but its narrative or filmic/TV presentation may bring it into quasi-physical contact with the reader or viewer. In the detective film and TV series, therefore, scenes in autopsy rooms and forensic medicine have come to play an important role, sometimes consisting in a mysterious clarity evoked, for example, in Carlo Emilio Gadda's *That Awful Mess on the Via Merulana* by the dismembered, not simply dead, body of a woman:

> A deep, a terribly red cut had cruelly opened her throat . . . frayed at both edges, as if cutting had restarted again and again—terrible. . . . The neck was covered in sticky blood and, in front, the blouse and the sleeve: the hand, painted with a ghost-like black-red color, like a color by Faiti or by Cengio. . . . In the hand, like insults, the scratches: as if this dirty bastard had found his pleasure in applying these decorations to her, this murderer, this monster.[14]

There are many such passages in this and other novels. They add to the impression that "it is not the analysis of motivation, causes, reasons which is at stake. Rather, the detective (the author, the reader) abandons his task of enlightenment." He gets involved with "the intensity of an immediate action of bodies, of a movement of the senses irreducible to anything else," with a communication of bodies, inaccessible to causes and morality.[15]

Finally, the metaphysics of banality is alloyed and strengthened with an often latent but somehow noticeable political dimension. The detective novel, and perhaps even more so, the spy novel disturb the functioning of the law with which the modern state, whatever its primary self-definition may be, appears or pretends to guarantee the inviolability of its citizens and their property.[16] In the end, however, the astute detective, that hero of ingenuity as he has been called, assures us, in solving the case, that the metaphysical shudder is not much more than a veil thrown over the reality of which he is in command and in which readers, after a period of uncertainty, can feel at home again. With the precarious "reconciliation" of metaphysics and banality at the crossroads of the imaginary and political import we are in the presence of the most efficient replacement of the sympotic.

Within the framework of the history of textualizations, the violent crime, especially the one called murder, has exerted a "fatal attraction" in most cultures and most periods. Parts of what, in the manner of the Oedipus drama, is officially classified as tragedy might as well be viewed or read as a murderous criminal drama. Dorothy L. Sayers, among many others, has read more or less all of Greek tragedy as the form of detective story appropriate for the period. In that context, the *Poetics* of Aristotle offers recipes, still valid today, of how to make true events more probable—that is, more interesting and gripping—by enriching them with invented additions. Furthermore, it is hard to ignore that since the eighteenth century, and particularly since the nineteenth century, criminal acts and criminological matters have not only infiltrated texts classified in traditional genres but have also developed into textual genres themselves. I suspect this is due to the problem that the program, initiated or extended in these centuries, to civilize people and teach them (better) manners, or rather to humanize them properly, has been compelled more and more often to call on the police in order to stop violations. For the psychocultural treatment and management of such cases, narrative texts can claim a certain priority; the events we tend to call crimes often need plausible narratives in which, if possible at all, contours and deep structures of an act gain better visibility. In *A Maggot* (the text is set in the eighteenth century), John Fowles has sketched in exemplary fashion the movements of a pendulum between the narrated histories of suspects and the steps of police work leading up to cross-examination. Although T. S. Eliot, who cannot be said to have particularly preferred the detective novel, did not describe the best nineteenth-century novels as thrillers, he did at least say they were thrilling.

In the preceding paragraphs, I have merely thrown around some hints but not pursued a systematic argument. Another such hint supporting the Eco and Boltanski theory about a metaphysics of banality would consist in pointing out the indignation that broke out in 2012, the year of the Brothers Grimm jubilee in Germany, when many people asked questions about the relation between fairy tales and real criminal cases. They asked even more urgent questions about the degree to which Wilhelm Grimm in particular simply erased crimes mentioned in his sources in order to soften the uncanny energies and (in)human potentials feeding the original texts. It is not only criminologists who agree that the fascination of imagined delinquency, from fairy tales to films, is enormous and that the mixture of imagined and real delinquency, improbabilities or downright errors in invention notwithstanding, must not be underestimated.

This is still not the last word on the matter. The trio of sociability, social power, and aesthetic productivity focused upon in the beginning of this book is now coming back with a vengeance. In what follows, we will see that these elements of social and cultural binding energies are no longer coupled with each other and cannot be joined together to form a coherent concept of reality. Modern societies, especially those taking pride in calling themselves welfare states, may appeal to such energies in their government propaganda, but we know only too well that in pluralistic societies the half-life of such programs is radically limited. Thus, detective fiction, film, and TV series are like psychocultural insurance companies that pay for the larger cases of social damage. As we will see, they produce ever more extreme feelings of insecurity but suggest at the same time that we can still afford them.

Thus, we could say that modern literature moves in the foggy environment of a concept of reality that forces people to acknowledge that they encounter realities as forms of resistance;[17] texts present people who must and will account for success or failure in such meetings. The individuality of such meetings is built up in situations of reality resistance that provoke confessions of experience, of success (rare) or failure (much more common). Even through the communication and confession of experience, however, situations do not gain full transparency. In some cases, circumstances may successfully impose themselves as indubitable realities, but normally we (including the characters in such texts) cannot rely on regularities even if they seem to penetrate and determine circumstances and situations.[18] Yet this is mainly the type of reality to be found in detective literature. The detective novel, thriving upon confessions, does not adopt the form of confession prevailing in nondetective fiction but concentrates on the shakiness of what, with quite some justification, we hold to be real. Looking for the motivation of a crime provides essential help in that enterprise, but it does not normally tell us much about the individuality of persons and situations involved.

Secret Societies and Violence

Today we cannot deny that individuals are struggling in (or perhaps enjoying) a swamp of confessional activities and of processes of their mediatization. There is hardly any limit to the psychological as well as the media expansion of confession. This expansion seems to be contradicted by the continuation, revitalization, or new founding of institutionalized forms of secret practices. The contradiction is only apparent; rather, we are dealing with a complementary relationship. The domineering gesture of media confession makes us easily forget that the notions of reality we seem to have acquired on our own and that therefore seem to bear the stamp of authenticity are anything but reliable and sufficient. Important domains of what, at some point, must be understood as real, perhaps even the possibility of understanding oneself in any comprehensive fashion, do not bow to individual conviction. The confrontation of conviction with complexity has meanwhile provoked unpleasant questions touching the levels and relevance of individual competence in domains such as science, the economy, and politics. Looking for realities, most of us, as Dante's metaphor had it long ago, are wandering around in a dark forest.

At this point, secret societies come into the picture again. Analysis is tempting but beset with traps: it encourages the fabrication of conspiracy theories, often of the most abstruse kind. On the other hand, the analysis of secret societies, if possible at all, can sharpen our awareness that the important events in negotiations of the real can hardly be those singled out by the mass media or by official statements day by day. Since their secret character must be protected, one can only try to formulate a rough logic of these societies. Secret societies recruit members by offering them superior perspectives on society and human beings that are rarely, if ever, found in real life. Transcending common sense and the partial rationalities of the economy, science, and politics, Freemasons, for instance, claim that their society and plans are based on what is common to all good people. Their secret—and this is indeed consistent in terms of conceptual logic—does not reside primarily in their doctrines but in the rituals that are supposed to prepare for the practical application of the doctrine. Even in the case of the "most disreputable criminal gangs," Simmel thinks, the enumeration of formulas, habits, and rituals takes up considerable space.[19] The center of initiation is in the rituals—and not only that: "Rather, the complete content of the masonic anthropology can be acquired by participating in the initiation rites."[20] If the emphasis of many secret societies is on their rituals, then we can conclude that they carry on sympotic traditions. In other instances, where the power of the central state repeatedly shows limitations and where the state claims to be a democratic one, it is difficult to enhance that power in legal ways, in which case secret organizations prove helpful. Normally, however, they do not cultivate sympotic forms, because their tasks lack the loftiness of the goals of good people. One need not think only in terms of extremely "nasty," terroristic organizations such as the Gestapo: as we will see in the third section of Chapter 10, the texts by Stieg Larsson set in highly democratic Sweden will provide enough food for thought.

At least two consequences follow from this. Ritual practices will hardly exude literary inspiration, since ritual does not normally mobilize much narrative tension. More important, while the political application of, for instance, masonic doctrine (wherever it might be extracted from) may appear to be imperative, most practical political efforts in that direction have failed. Freemasons have occasionally tried in vain to ally themselves with the Illuminati, a secret group politically active for a short while, especially in Bavaria.[21] Seen in their totality, such efforts have turned out to be chaotic. In the eighteenth century, the Freemasons supported the monarchy in Prussia; in France, they helped to bring the monarchy under the guillotine. In twentieth-century Italy, whatever the precise assignment of responsibilities, a good part of political power was transferred to the secret lodge P2 (Propaganda Due), tightly linked with government officials.[22] It is therefore anything but clear whether Lorenz Jäger's effort to grant a more sublime total motivation to the Freemasons can be called successful. Jäger, a well-known biographer of Adorno and Heidegger, for instance, follows Carl Schmitt, Reinhart Koselleck, and Michel de Certeau, for whom the Freemasons filled the empty space that had opened up with the preservation of the façades, which remained standing, but not the dogmatic and spiritual content of religion in the period of absolutism, as religious institutions were undermined by the state and its interests. The Freemasons jumped in, posing as representatives of the civil, the liberal, and replacing religion with morality, the general human form, as it were, of these institutions.

Further difficulties with secret societies, especially those of the ritualistic type such as the Freemasons, are preprogrammed. Since in most cases they cannot really be kept secret, projects to improve humanity and optimize forms of political rule will elicit contradictions at best, or in worse cases, the immediate intervention of the authorities. Even Simmel uses the well-worn proverb that a secret is a secret no more where two persons know about it.[23] If none of these possibilities materializes, it is hard to avoid the suspicion that the secret society has pledged allegiance to the ruling powers. Better outcomes seem to have emerged only in a case such as that of Thomas Jefferson in the United States, where a political conception based on masonic ideas could be imprinted on virgin political territory.

Political risks for masonic conceptions begin right away with the seemingly harmless claim to promote the common good of all mankind. In the ranks of the Freemasons there have often been representatives of what in former times would have been called the political center or middle—that is, representatives of an attitude in which official government positions and masonic principles did not clash. But the society did not always pay sufficient attention to the ways in which broadly acceptable attitudes, especially when also relatable to Enlightenment ideas, could drift into the deep waters of politics. Underestimating these risks led to a remarkable helplessness on the part of the Freemasons in regard to those secret societies, such as the Carbonari and many others in the nineteenth century, that definitely pursued political goals.[24] Freemasons, then, would best qualify as "an esoteric community without ideology." The clearest example of a kind of neutral presence of their ideas in a political context is offered by the US independence movement and its documents, which, to repeat, was possible because of the absence of prior and comparable political structures and the attack on faraway and obsolete political systems that, within a very short time, had come under fire in Europe themselves.[25] Where, however, political energies have completely vanished or are submerged by the rituals, secret societies such as the Freemasons come to resemble the operatic images that Mozart presented in his *Magic Flute*. Mozart's genius, in contrast to societies bound by rituals, enabled him to compose a different kind of music as well. His "Maurerische Trauermusik" (masonic funeral music) bathes the ideals of the Freemasons in a nobly restrained and solemn atmosphere that facilitates its interiorization without language. It is, of course, impossible to "read" any social commitment into this music—Mozart's music, like music in general, does not really "speak" of such commitments.

In contrast to the Freemasons, the Illuminati projected a rational scheme of policies and politics. Its main thrust was aimed at staff policies; they wanted to control the apparatus of government. The risk, also in contrast to the Freemasons, was obvious: such an intention could hardly be kept secret. It was only to be expected that, as they were trying to undermine the staff structure, they were persecuted relentlessly. No other secret society, Fabian has said,[26] saw itself surrounded by so many enemies. Its founder, the Ingolstadt professor Johann Adam Weishaupt (1748–1830), and its later but also important member Baron Adolph von Knigge (1752–1796) are early examples of what later would be called networking, certainly a highly problematic transformation of sympotic elements. Knigge resigned in 1784 because he could no longer stand Weishaupt's mania for control. Former members gave insider information to state authorities, and in 1784, the Illuminati became a thing of the past. The fate of the Illuminati has remained instructive. In clearer forms than in the case of the Freemasons, it does not merely embody the connection or the lack thereof between secret ritualized sociability and sociopolitical power but also the modern problem of a drying-up of aesthetic, including psychological, productivity in important domains of reality.

Among early secret societies, the Order of the Knights Templar (1118–1312) demands special attention, in spite of—or perhaps because of—its enigmatic end and the legends and rumors that adorn its period of greatness. In its combination of archaism (religious faith with absolute personal obedience) and the avant-garde (modern organization of financial and military power), it reveals a modernity in the construction, direction, and control of the real in exemplary ways. According to Fabian's story, fanatical preachers such as Saint Bernard of Clairvaux, aided and abetted by the pope, recognized that the Crusades would be crowned by success only if conducted by elite military troops. Aside from their military abilities, these troops had to swear unconditional personal obedience to the pope. This exclusive mental and emotional devotion produced a "strange mixture of a warrior and of a saint," of religion and war, of monastic asceticism and military excess, of weapons and their symbolism (also exploited in later times in rituals of dedication and consecration). In their joint effect, these elements exerted a singular spiritual attraction that rematerialized in the form of generous financial support by various donors; the donors, in their turn, could be sure that they had secured the saving of their souls. This extraordinary flow of money necessitated special financial techniques and media. Merchants, for instance, who needed protection by the Templars, could deposit money in one of their branches and, using receipts and bills of exchange, dispose of that money in other branches. Secret signs on such papers, as on modern notes, would protect them against forgeries.[27]

Consequently, in times when emperor and pope were fighting, with ambiguous results, for secular and spiritual hegemony, the Templars' unique combination of religious exclusiveness, military prowess, and financial power presents itself as the most advanced model for producing, defining, and controlling the meaning of situational reality. In comparison to this achievement, the riddle of their ruin and other mysteries lose importance. Fabian adduces the case of the French king Philippe le Bel, who, plagued by debts, is supposed to have organized the overpowering of the Templars and the show trials to which they were subjected. Lawrence Durrell, who, in *Monsieur, or The Prince of Darkness* (1974), has a character report on his professional historian's main work, *The Secret of the Templars*, seems to lean toward a thesis like Fabian's; he also plays with the accusation of heresy and the psychological pattern of greed and arrogance producing more greed and arrogance. Durrell's historian is made to speculate on whether sexual deviation might have finished off the Templars. What seems clear is that the elimination of the Templars succeeded only because Philippe le Bel was in a position to organize a perfectly concerted action that prevented the Templars from mobilizing their entire army.

The Templars, then, embody one modern model of how to produce dynamic realities that, owing to financial and military resources, are also able to convey a strong sense of stability. Although we cannot really know or say anything conclusive about that, such a model must have included quite a few sympotic elements—otherwise, the mental and emotional coherence of the group would scarcely be conceivable. Philippe, in his turn and also in his dealings with the pope, can claim responsibility for a second modern model that, like the first, is still partly relevant today, involving the adaptation of Machiavellian techniques. Philippe's rule creates the impression of modernity precisely because he did in fact implement modernization of the systems of justice and administration, but also and particularly because he handled and preshaped archaic violence and its selective application as a tool for modernity. For such purposes, the concepts of reality cultivated in modern philosophical and literary studies are not suitable: they do not take the criteria of the situational management of adequacy and of the resources available for it, which determine who can seize the power to define the temporary validity of the real, sufficiently into account.

A short digression may help to further clarify this issue. The assertions of Durrell's historian in the above-mentioned novel are quite compatible with those in the historiographical literature on the Templars, as well as being equally incompatible with the way in which modern literature would handle the issue.[28] The characterization by a novelist in Durrell's later novel *Livia* (1978) is, strictly speaking, superfluous or even illegitimate, since it is made in the same medium used to downgrade itself. But it is also important—Durrell is searching all the time, although in a very skeptical mood, for unexhausted possibilities of literary writing. Even the fascinating problem of the Templars, however, does not yield them:

> Europe was fast reaching the end of the genito-urinary phase in its literature—and he recognised the approaching impotence it signalled. Soon sex as a subject would be ventilated completely. "Even the act is dying," he allowed Sutcliffe [the novelist reinvented by the novelist in the novel] to note, "and will soon become as charmless as badminton. For a little while the cinema may conserve it as a token act—as involuntary as a sneeze or a hiccough: a token rape, while the indifferent victim gnaws an apple."[29]

Even so, the European novelist continues to be tormented by the impenetrable secrets and brutal overthrow of the Templars around 1300. Modern literary procedures do not seem to be able to lay hold of their military and financial achievements such as the invention of the bill of exchange. Historians can at least try and plunder the archives in order to make up lists of possibilities. They are not expected to transform such possibilities into a gripping story; novelists are.

In the wake of their success, the Templars may have ascribed considerable amounts of power to themselves, but they did not challenge the supremacy of king and pope. In Europe, particularly in Italy, however, the distribution of power between a top level of government, a secret society, and socially effective power became explosive in the nineteenth century. At that time, the well-known socioeconomic miseries of the nineteenth century drove many people into the criminal underground and the founding of criminal secret societies. The origins of such societies may be located in the remote past, but the crucial shifts took place in the nineteenth century. This is true for the model of the Mafia (Sicily) and more emphatically for the model of the Camorra (Naples and environs).

In Italy, above all, the emergence of a new nation-state runs into the tough resistance of feudal or quasi-absolutist structures. Whoever must pay the bills of suffering and repressive exploitation—normally the lower classes or the downright poor—these structures are still in some kind of working order and try to continue in their old ways. The conclusive judgment of John Dickie on the origins of the Mafia cements the supposition that these origins are intimately linked to the birth of an Italian state that cannot be trusted.[30] Roberto Saviano holds responsible the centuries-old inability of politics to solve the serious problems of the Mezzogiorno, especially in the domains of work, living space, privileges, functions, and tasks of the state.[31]

In parts, Saviano's book reads like a horror novel or a novel of suspense. Conversely, one may argue that a novelist who chooses such topics should have some closeness of experience in regard to his object, although such closeness would be fraught with life-threatening dangers. It goes without saying that criminal secret societies such as the Mafia and the Camorra cultivate forms of sociability; without them, it would be much more difficult to achieve the necessary affective cohesion even of criminal gangs. Sociability is reinforced by ideology, for example, questions of honor, or less euphemistically and more realistically, by the Mafia commandment of *omertà* (silence, probably derived from the Italian word *umiltà* and/or from the Sicilian word *umirtà*, both for "humility"). But it goes equally without saying that this sociability, even if affectively cushioned, may change into brutal violence at any moment. In the worst case, rituals of sociability are staged to hide preparations for an attack on internal competitors or external foes.

If, finally, we want to obtain an estimate of the power of Mafia-like organizations to produce and control realities, we are confronted with the assumption, hardly risky anymore, that there has been and will continue to be multiple failures of the state institutions of feudal society, then of constitutional and parliamentary monarchies, and finally, of democracy. This failure runs through the books by Dickie and Saviano as a common thread. Initially, Garibaldi's achievements in unifying Italy were treated as heroic and legendary feats, but soon their image began to oscillate between dream and nightmare because they also triggered violent turbulence between Sicily and the Kingdom of Italy. Garibaldi's expedition prompted a further revolt that caused the Bourbons' rule of Sicily to rapidly crumble. But with the integration of 2.4 million Sicilians into the new nation-state, the revolt also led to "epidemics of conspiracies, hold-ups, murders, and the settling of old accounts." In the alliances between republican revolutionaries and semicriminal gangs, there lurked the "grimace of anarchy." Nobility and church wanted the Bourbons back; local politicians fought each other with murder and kidnapping; ultimately, the new nation-state imposed martial law on Sicily.[32] Between 1860 and 1870 the confrontation between gangs and martial law kept repeating itself, illustrating the resistance against the wild mixture of foreign rulers under which the Sicilians (to some extent even its aristocracy) had been suffering for centuries. This same confrontation also widened the range of activities of the gangs and other criminal associations: the real estate and building industries turned, both literally and metaphorically, into their domain. The modern state, on the other hand, specifically Italy, did not and does not really impose or enforce its monopoly on violence, thus encouraging the formation of an "industry of violence" on the other side.[33]

Moreover, the Mafia and Camorra do not simply portray themselves as adversaries of the state but assume the role of a state within the state. At times, allied with other secret societies such as the Freemasons or the notorious lodge P2 mentioned above that includes government officials, they arrogate the status of the true state to themselves: "From 1876 onwards the Mafia became an integral component of the Italian system of government."[34] The viewpoint of a member of Camorra is even more telling: for him, there is no state/counterstate paradigm but only a territory on which business is conducted, with or without the state.[35]

Distinctions between the law and even justice, on the one hand, and market, power, and violence, on the other, may be blurred or erode, but they do not disappear. Concepts such as law or justice may be exposed as being naïve illusions, and we may not be able to define them clearly; many normative concepts (like those for values) have become free-floating. Nevertheless, they still carry charges of energy of such strength, mobilizing motivation and action, that one must reckon with them. The extent to which drives and motivations can be flattened into a simple mixture of money and violence also depends on the complexities of commitment, courage, and competence that the state as an opponent cares to invest in the fight against crime. There is no single picture; fighting against crime is a different matter in different countries. In the fascist period, the Italian state, led by the "iron prefect" Cesare Mori, seemed capable of pushing the Mafia into a corner. This is not as surprising as it may sound: the legal deficiencies of that state and especially its police granted a "freedom" of action to the police that is rarely possible in ordinary democracies. Mori also enlarged the scope of legal aggression considerably.[36]

These times have passed. The Camorra is probably accurate in characterizing its organization, its form of business and violence, as a system that surpasses all other forms of business in terms of opening new businesses and profitability, having, for instance, become the world's top weapons dealer.[37] What this means for the rest of Italy has been described by Alessandro Silj as a "permanent coup d'état," using the term in order to mark the extraordinary life span of key political structures of power and their alliance with criminal secret societies.[38] It would be silly, of course, to hold the failure of the state responsible for the emergence of criminal instead of sympotic societies; states fail elsewhere, too, although the geography of failure would be an interesting topic. At least the Mafia, Camorra, and their ilk are stigmatized, or rather have stigmatized themselves, by using the most horrible forms of violence. We would deceive ourselves, however, were we to assume that violent crime, as well as crime without obvious violence such as financial manipulation, can still be used to distinguish legitimate (state) from illegitimate power; rather, we have to admit that violence has made its way as an unavoidable ingredient into the political and economic realities of the later twentieth and the twenty-first centuries. In 1981, the political scientist Karl Dietrich Bracher devoted a book to the question as to how unavoidable and indeed necessary violence has become, in which he collected a dense sequence of developments whose import is unmistakable.[39] To account for this, we might make an arbitrary beginning with theories about the counterviolence directed against the state in more recent political utopian texts. There is also the right to resist, and in fact its necessity, directed not only against a rule of blatant arbitrariness such as the Hitler dictatorship in Germany, which could easily be transformed into a justification of violence (14). In many cases, the relationship between human rights and political constitution has remained ambiguous (chap. 2). The decisive opportunities by which the use of violence has increased its power to produce and control realities have accrued to it through the weakness of democracy, visible above all as a "vacuum of power" (85 and chaps. 4 and 5).

Independent of concrete conditions of power, the vacuum may be concealed in an ideological weakness—namely, that behind the catchword of democracy and its institutions there may be lurking the most heterogeneous ideas and plans to implement not only the people's rule but forms of rule totally opposed to each other, from a constitutional state committed to freedom to a totalitarian dictatorship (51). Right from the beginning, ideological weakness and a cult of action (see 51) seem to undermine the reasons that may be put forward in order to legitimize political projects. Mixing up behavior in conflicts with behavior in situations of violence becomes commonplace. For Bracher, the year 1917 marks the beginning of an age of ideologies, in which so-called international relations are sucked up and redefined by the moods and general ideologies of different countries (127). Dangers of war and war-mongering begin to increase tremendously, also because, in an age of intellectual indifference, reasons for them can always be found. The leap from ideological instability to a readiness for war is made still easier because war no longer has to be declared; it has become informal, as it were. The example for this has been set by the United States: troops have been sent into theaters of war in over two hundred cases (including the Korean and the Vietnam wars), in only five of which did Congress formally declare war.[40]

Dogma and Elasticity: Opus Dei and the Negotiation of Reality

Descriptions and arguments in the preceding chapter may have struck some readers as diversions from our intended goal. They belong, however, to the topic of the production and control of realities in which sympotic configurations and potentials are either able to thrive or are doomed to extinction. Configurations and potentials are exposed to power formations of all kinds, often damaged in their turn and in various ways not always remote from political delinquency. Very generally, the upshot of arguments pursued in very different, indeed heterogeneous, domains of reality is that the constructive (one might also say, humane) connection between social (sociopolitical) and sociable dimensions has been severed. I have reserved a section of its own for the Catholic order Opus Dei because it is the master of the production and control of a reality in which that connection still seems to work. It also seems capable of holding ideology and violence, so destructive of social-sociable complexes, at a comfortable distance—and, incidentally, the order played a well-concealed role in the German elections of 2021.

Reality control requires techniques of definition and pressure. Employing such techniques has become difficult for religious orders nowadays because they do not have access to military options. In my opinion, Opus Dei demonstrates the successful use of such techniques better than other religious communities. In principle, it would also be possible to pursue such analyses using larger associations such as Scientology, the Mormons, or others; in fact, Daniel J. Boorstin has compared the Mormons to the early American Puritans, a religious denomination derived from Calvinism whose members made it into one of the most economically successful groups in the world.[41] For these larger associations, however, repeated violent flare-ups due to internal dogmatic and organizational competition have increased the difficulty of acquiring reliable information. Moreover, literature on the Mormons (e.g., Conan Doyle's *A Study in Scarlet* [1887]), as well as on Scientology, is minimally protected against polemical one-sidedness.

For quite some time, not only violence but also legal doctrines concerning how to interpret texts and laws have provided evidence for how far the logic of laws and judgments can be stretched. Connecting the virtuosity of norm interpretation and techniques of power; of serving the parent institution, the Catholic Church; and of invisibilizing the interests of the order, nonviolence, and the "energetic" guidance of members—all of these have apparently been mastered to a rare degree by Opus Dei, a religious order founded in 1928 by the Spanish priest Josemaría Escrivá (1902–1975). The organization maintains its status behind a veil without really concealing it. It knows how to employ various strategies of discretion, depending on the situation and on what object of interest is being negotiated; members do not talk about their membership unless directly challenged. The contrast with the Jesuits is evident. Most of the important writings of the founder and his successors are publicly accessible. The *Statutes* of 1982 prohibit secret activities, and yet, time and again, some members succeed in conquering new religious "markets" that appear to remain closed to ordinary priests. The feeling that there must be more to it than meets the eye is hard to dispel. It is difficult to find a descriptive paraphrase for what Opus Dei might be. Calling it a secret brotherhood[42] is obviously wrong because the order admits women. "In principle," their status is on a par with that of men; in terms of numbers, their membership amounts to 55 percent,[43] although the precise meaning of equal status is, like many other things, quite another matter. Any question of some significance allows for several opinions and counteropinions; there are witnesses and counterwitnesses for everything. There seems to be one undisputed article of faith: private revelations—that is, evidence irrefutable in principle but also unverifiable—are supposed to have driven Escrivá to found Opus Dei as well as its female department in 1930. There is also the common opinion that Opus Dei fared very well during Franco's rule in Spain and the Pinochet dictatorship in Chile: "the membership's center of gravity is clearly on the right."[44] In many respects (dogmatic, religious, and social policies) Opus Dei is perhaps best, albeit somewhat vaguely, characterized as traditionalistic.[45]

Further questions concerning the rituals and practices of the organization may be asked. Self-flagellation has drawn a lot of fire; Dan Brown, in his novel *The Da Vinci Code* (2003), condemned it strenuously. For others, the role of women in everyday life and religious rituals continues to be dubious. One must assume that this criticism is at least partly justified, because much of it comes from (former) "numerarios," those full members pledged to celibacy and chastity "who make Opus Dei their immediate family"[46] and work for Opus Dei but may also pursue professional activities of their own. Again: Criticism and apology, however well-argued they might seem, do not suggest the amount of neutrality necessary for taking them at face value. Such criticism of criticism is certainly necessary for Dan Brown's novel, which portrays the order, Fabian thinks,[47] as a kind of unacknowledged gang of murderers.

Judgmental oscillation is certainly a consequence of the skillful and elastic handling of situational definitions of the real on the part of Opus Dei. But how does a Catholic organization obedient to the pope transform itself from being the embodiment of an older reality concept (the representation and interpretation of dogma) into being the representative of procedures that both represent dogma and do justice to contemporary demands for situational adequacy? There is no doubt that church dogmas provide blueprints for action, but there is also, more or less latently, an ingeniously constructed central norm that can change dogma into a very flexible instrument. This norm, which may look quite orthodox at first glance, widens considerably the scope for shaping and fixing the goals of specific enterprises. Allen has described it in the following way: "The core idea of Opus Dei, as presented by Escrivá, is the sanctification of ordinary work, meaning that one can find God through the practice of law, engineering or medicine, by picking up the garbage or by delivering the mail, if one brings to that work the proper Christian spirit."[48] Put differently: "At its core, the message of Opus Dei is that the redemption of the world will come in large part through laywomen and men sanctifying their daily work, transforming secularity from within."[49]

The use of the nice catchphrase "sanctification of everyday and professional work" may lead us to overlook the impossibility of determining with any degree of precision what the right Christian spirit might consist in. The phrase may refer to a full and perfectionist devotion to professional standards, or it may warn about a conflict between a Christian perspective and everyday professionalism. In other words, concepts such as sanctification make it seem as if there is a norm to follow, but in point of fact they leave open the concrete form of practice and make it available for all kinds of variation: the dogmatic norm acts as a framework, the situation as its filling.

To a large extent, the various criticisms of Opus Dei have ignored this central problem. They have forgotten the historical model that originated in a totally different religious environment. Calvinist Protestantism had particularly thought through the motivations and consequences of the sanctification of professional work. Calvinism was obsessed with the notion of profession as a "calling" ordained by God. Although a great deal of criticism was leveled against that mode of thought and its "psychology" by Max Weber, some crucial intuitions in his *The Protestant Ethic and the Spirit of Capitalism* (German original 1904/5) may still be quoted with impunity. Weber was justified in asserting that Catholicism lacks the "psych(olog)-ic(al) boni [rewards]" that Protestant Calvinism had placed on *industria*— that is, on the full-hearted, workaholic-like devotion to professional work. Opus Dei decisively dealt with this lack: "The God of Calvinism did not want his followers to do single good works. He wanted their adherence to the idea of the holiness of work transformed into a system." Here, we can replace Calvinism by Opus Dei; both have exploited the implications of this devotion to the worldly domain in the shape of work: "The sanctification of life thus could almost assume the character of a business."[50]

The sanctification of life and work, seemingly a normative given, is thus attenuated into a supplier of impulses without clear boundaries. It neither wants nor is able to slow down or prevent the degeneration of Christian values into secular—particularly economic and financial—transactions. If the values belonging officially to the Christian tradition keep maintaining the appearance of orthodoxy, economic and financial activities basically operate without rules that could put an end to them at some problematic point. Their sanctification leads inevitably into the perfection of professional efficiency. What else, indeed, could it consist in? A similar inevitability must be claimed for the acquisition and increase of social power for the organization and, in a larger sense, for the church. Here, Dan Brown is right and wrong at the same time. A victory in the conflict with the Prieuré de Sion, frequently called the successors of the Templars, would enlarge the power of Opus Dei tremendously.[51] It is, in fact, a question of power. The assumption (circulating in Brown, whoever may hold it) that power will be won mainly through such conflicts is wrong; rather, winning and increasing power is engineered as the extension, masked by the sanctification of work, of a multiplicity of relevant positions of power.

Although members of the organization can freely choose their professions, it is expected that they will indeed undertake some profession (a good one, hopefully). The expectation that by choosing and sanctifying professional work members would also qualify more easily for positions of leadership is formulated explicitly in the *Statutes* and in Escrivá's *El camino* (The way). If one looks for examples particularly suited for sharpening the profile of sanctified work, one may encounter an uncommon specialty: Opus Dei members are not only busy with the sanctification of work and the acquisition of a leading position; the organization is also engaged in a most intensive manner with optimizing the *preparations* for obtaining positions that are as good as possible—that is, as good as possible in terms of the acquisition of wealth. Here we find the mechanism of producing, defining, and controlling reality at work again: a seemingly normative framework leaves open many possibilities, if perhaps not all. Their commitment to this is evinced most clearly with educational institutions, to which the order likes to offer "doctrinal and spiritual guidance."[52] Although details remain secret, in its both veiled and efficient participation in educational institutions, particularly elite economic schools, up to 2005 Opus Dei had captured leading positions in 15 universities with about eighty thousand students, 7 hospitals with more than one thousand medical doctors, 11 schools of economics, 36 primary and secondary schools, 97 schools for job training, and 166 student residences, as well as somewhat looser associations with an equal number of other educational institutions.[53] These institutions are located in that ambiguous space between what might look like an idealistic sponsoring of educational organizations, including for the underprivileged, and platforms for the potential extension of power.

The group activities of members will provoke, almost unavoidably, analogous judgments. Unsurprisingly, religious ceremonies predominate. Leisure activities, on the other hand, are a different matter; it is a moot point whether they deserve to be called sociable at all. While the term may seem to be correct, there is a lurking suspicion that it may not apply at all to organizations such as Opus Dei. Strict regulation of rituals was one of the hallmarks of the symposium in ancient Greece. We might surmise that with Opus Dei, compulsory ritualization portraying religious content overrides the pleasure its performance can in principle provide. As long as ritualization runs along smoothly, compulsory aspects and dogmatic priorities may remain latent; once frictions or accidents arise, however, this will certainly change. But how? The problem is that ordinary observation is not possible, because the status of a situation is always controlled by the members who are in charge. We can only suspect that Simmel's playful and aesthetic energies of existence do not stand much of a chance in what one must call supervised situations. This suspicion gains additional plausibility in view of the fact that Opus Dei does not seem to be aesthetically productive or inspiring. Dan Brown's *Da Vinci Code* is a melodrama, a melodramatic thriller at best; it does not offer vistas of complex situations involving consciousness, theory, and the world at large.

It is possible, though, that organizations such as Opus Dei have not yet received their adequate textual or visual treatment. One can imagine assemblages of religious norms achieving precisely what they are officially supposed to prevent—in this case, coming to the best possible terms with a sinful world instead of clarifying the difference between a sinful and a Christian life. Certainly, the norms carry a considerable load of normativity, but they also reside on the edge of fictitiousness. In their double orientation, they are the crucial instruments by which decisions will be made as to which courses of action are to be taken or rejected. Opus Dei demonstrates that cultural and literary modernity has probably overdone the role of fictions. Hans Vaihinger, in his *Die Philosophie des Als Ob* (Philosophy of "as if" [1911]), a long philosophical book with an astounding international success, appeared to have developed a historical and conceptual logic that seemed to make the totalization of fiction inevitable. Vaihinger was aware that he had fallen into a kind of paradox: that one could act successfully on the basis of wrong, that is, fictitious, assumptions. Opus Dei shows that fictitious assumptions need not be wrong ones: they may be dynamic potentials waiting for their "realization" in one way or another. In principle, everything may be or become a fiction, but many things may also be pushed into the opposite direction and turn into provisional realities. That is why, I imagine, practices or rituals of sociability can also be treated as an important *elementum humanum* by Opus Dei. Its "real" arrangements must be left to the masters of ceremony of the order.

CHAPTER 9

The Paradigm of Isolation and Its Consequences
Joseph Conrad

THE POSSIBILITIES AND CAPABILITIES for constructing realities by elastic techniques of persuasion and coercion presuppose a very sophisticated mixture of solid organization and shock-absorbing flexibility, of authority and pliability, of obedience and individual initiative—a collection of qualities determining what is seen as real, of characterological repertories encountered only rarely in the world out there. In particular, so-called historical reality and its political version invariably seem to be subjected to a fatal equivalence of apparent oppositions such as idealism and cynicism. If we follow K. D. Bracher's fixing 1917 as the year of birth for an "age of ideologies" (see the end of Chapter 7), then we can find even more reasons to connect idealism and cynicism as central elements of twentieth-century ideologies. The term "idealism" does not refer, of course, to the objective idealism of a hundred years earlier, although this philosophical movement, in its insistence on subjective idealism as at least a transitional stage, may well have ended up in its ideologically degenerate version. Here I use the term "ideological idealism" for a clearly visible excess of positive-ideal values against the empirical evidence available, with cynicism as its opposite.

In this regard, the present chapter is targeting a central twentieth-century problem. The "fabrication of fiction" (Carl Einstein), cultivated or criticized with particular zest in the literary and philosophical sectors of culture, has not exorcised the need, individual and social, for meaning and significance. Quite the contrary: Carl Einstein (1885–1940), for one, a historian of art and a severe critic of the inflation of fiction, had to experience personally the virulence of fiction and the need for more reliable meanings. (Einstein took his own life as an exile in France after the defeat of France in 1940.) Nor has the Opus Dei model of defining, producing, and controlling realities and their meaning been generally adopted; it has not extinguished the sense-making desires, including the ambition of being right, of individuals and larger groups. If this claim sounds acceptable, then the question is: Can we compare the strength of social values (here called ideologies) in orienting behavior in fairly direct ways with the more indirect training due to interaction in sympotic contexts? In this respect, the special significance of a good part of Joseph Conrad's novels resides in his shift of perspective from the *value* of values to the *function* of values in specific situations. Conrad lays bare the implications of a position adopted by Nietzsche, who makes the comparison between two ways of handling values. Aristocratic cultures, in his view, possess a perfect assurance of the function of their regulating unconscious instincts. Their noble morality grows out of itself, because these cultures include, or rather presuppose, a powerful physical presence, a blossoming, rich, exuberant health—in short, everything belonging to strong, free, and cheerful action. This situation changes with the advent of Judeo-Christian religions, when the rebellion of slave morality begins. Values are sought outside instead of inside. In their resentment, the masses think they know better than the nobles and their practices, but their newfound values are absolutely wrong and would be even more abhorrent if implemented. They move up and away into a separate sphere of higher morality that is both dogmatic and insecure.[1]

Age of Ideologies

Quotations and borrowings from Nietzsche are easy to come by and often trite, ready for use for any purpose. Too often they stand in remarkable contrast to what we know about Nietzsche's personality. Even so, they may still have a strong effect on how we see things, and for this reason they provide a plausible connection to Conrad's depictions of problems following from individual isolation. The fates of Conrad's protagonists in *Lord Jim* and *Heart of Darkness* take their course against a background of amorphous masses and dogmatic morality. In the characters' professional contacts with the heterogeneous staff of international shipping and commercial companies, the justification of actions and the adequacy of opinions is constantly challenged.[2] The potential for insecurity and isolation accumulates under a blanket of more or less accepted notions of duties and values. All of the texts by Conrad discussed here are orchestrated by way of roughly similar causes driving the individual into isolation.

Isolation, to be sure, is a catchword, not a concept. Reading Conrad (born Józef Teodor Nałęcz Konrad Korzeniowski, 1857–1924), however— still a rewarding activity—would be much more difficult without the help of catchwords, whose usefulness comes immediately to the fore with Conrad's biography. The patterns of his life as well as his works stand out prominently from those of his peers. For a long time, Conrad research has tried to make do with terms such as "intermediate position" in order to do justice to his otherness.[3] Can we find better terms in order to grasp Conrad's individual profile and then use them as prompts for the analysis of the characters in his novels as figures of isolation? Biography, often outlawed by literary criticism, does in fact help here. Joseph Conrad came from the tiny Polish minority living around Ukrainian Kyiv (Kiev), which, after the Second Partition of Poland (1793), was handed over to the Russian czarist regime. Even before the rebellion of 1863, his father was arrested and banished; his wife and his son followed him into banishment. From 1796 until the end of World War I, there was no sovereign Polish state. Conrad's mother and father died when he was seven and eleven years old, respectively; an uncle took over his education. Conrad turned to a seafaring career, learning much more about the world than his landlubber literary peers. He advanced to the rank of captain but exercised that function only once. Instead, he contracted malaria, which would trouble him until the end of his life. He began learning English at the age of twenty; in 1889, when he was thirty-two, he started work on his first novel, *Almayer's Folly*. From this point onward, his literary production proceeded at top speed, although without success for a long time. The reading public and most other writers took little notice of him, nor did he know "great" writers such as Virginia Woolf, James Joyce, or D. H. Lawrence. He also ignored Freud—yet he read Proust and Gide.

Values and the Culture of Surface
(Lord Jim, Heart of Darkness, Nostromo)

Before and during Conrad's time, the situation of Poland and of Polish minorities in particular was, to put it bluntly, miserable. Polish self-interpretations, especially those of members of minorities such as Conrad's father, tried to balance this with high claims for a nation-state, even though they were unable to substantiate these claims historically. It is no wonder, therefore, that Conrad's consciousness was filled with, if not dominated by, a central category of nineteenth-century thought: individual and social values must govern and soften the transition from older ("concrete") communities to the abstract forms of a capitalism for which the only concrete forms left were those of nationalism. Conrad the seafarer, on the other hand, also made the acquaintance of "exotic" tribal communities. Whether they embraced similar or completely different values and behavioral programs remained in the dark because the whites did not know their codes. This situation hardened into a challenge of a special kind, often ending with the violent death of the white intruders both in life and in literature.

In any case, the conviction that ideas and behavior must conform to values such as honor, faithfulness, duty, solidarity, and so forth seems to dominate, openly or latently, the consciousness of Conrad's important Western characters. This is not to say that earlier times did not have at their disposal a repertory of similar values—on the contrary: the elaborateness of value systems may have been more sophisticated and explicit in ancient and medieval philosophy. Significantly, however, there is an emphasis on duty in Conrad that would suggest a latent weakening of other values: if one no longer knows how to apply one's values to complex situations in life, one may readily privilege duty because its meaning and application seem to be clear. Since Schiller's criticism (e.g., in *On Grace and Dignity*) of Kant's notion of duty, however, this concept has been burdened with a somber rigidity in the West. Schiller rejects it because for him it is only a less painful form of servitude or bondage; for him, Kant's concept points to a fundamental disturbance in the human relation to law. The genealogy of the concept that Giorgio Agamben has outlined from Aristotle to Heidegger makes this disturbance even more disturbing. Aristotle's doctrine of virtues, Agamben holds, does not go beyond behavioral instructions; it is limited to a theory of the habitual human character. Kant, in his turn, seems to have been so uncertain about what he was doing when he introduced the notion of respect (*Achtung*, the "dispositive" that activates the self-compulsion of moral duty) that he felt compelled to explain this dark feeling in a long footnote in the *Grundlegung zur Metaphysik der Sitten* (Groundwork for the metaphysics of morals [1785]).[4]

Two British thinkers of the eighteenth century resisted this dubious development with a reaffirmation of sociability. I mention them once more in order to insist on the historical urgency of the problem. For David Hume, social usefulness does not simply spring from individual acts of conformity ("to render men tractable, and subdue their natural ferocity and selfishness"). Social action itself ("the social virtues") must be such that people feel aesthetically and affectively interested in it ("The social virtues must, therefore, be allowed, to have a natural beauty and amiableness"). With Edmund Burke, the cohesion of society is best achieved by what he describes as the "mutual compliance, which all men yield to each other, without constraint to themselves, and which is extremely flattering to all."[5] Burke's thoughts are directed toward the "enjoyment" of the embodiments and institutional forms of the state; he expects a "pleasure" that must be offered by institutional embodiments and extensions of love and beauty if the inescapably social existence of humans is meant to have any chance of success. (In the *Reflections on the Revolution in France in a Letter Intended to Have Been Sent to a Gentleman in Paris* we may read accordingly: "To make us love our country, our country ought to be lovely"[6]). The experience of a beauty emanating from an institution long in the making, the respect for and devotion to the people who embody such an institution, are counted by Burke among the strongest forms of pleasure. The experience of the power of a great king resembles the experience of a deity: "If we rejoice, we rejoice with trembling."[7] Social systems must then be organized in such a manner that they meet, as it were, contingent human needs halfway, and they must at least allow for pleasurable interactions with other people.

The social goals of Hume and Burke might appear like calls from a sunken world to us. With Burke especially, this world seems to have withered away to a "world we have lost."[8] His comments on the French Revolution in that regard reinforce this impression but also a somewhat more realistic hope that something might be done about it. Unfortunately the revolution has also brought about "a considerable revolution in their ideas of politeness," that is, in the tasteful and elegant interaction of people.[9]

Hume and Burke should probably be considered to be the last representatives of a mode of thought in which the spirit, if not the structure, of the old symposium is maintained. For Hume, it is true, that kind of sociability does not go completely uncontested: off and on, he needs solitude. But he needs pleasurable society even more in order to protect himself against "this philosophical melancholy and delirium," that is to say, to ward off the delirium in which people may literally lose their mind if they keep ruminating in solitude.[10]

In the nineteenth century—paradoxically (or so it may seem) after the French Revolution, which wanted to improve everything—the concept of social virtues, still very much alive in Hume and Burke, is transformed into social duties. Duties were meant to provide orientation in the face of a new social complexity, which is precisely what they did not achieve, because, as a concept, duty was far too simple to cope with nineteenth-century forms of complexity, to say nothing of the loss of pleasure in interaction (to remedy that, Oscar Wilde had to mount the stage). It also increased behavioral disorientation. Conrad, to whom we now return, presents situations in which the concept of duty is neither refuted nor really applicable, either. His characters are not able to come to terms with the discrepancies implied in the names of Kant, on the one hand (although Kant still cultivated his form of a somewhat dictatorial sociability), and Hume and Burke, on the other. On a boat, for instance, notions of duty cannot be simply thrown overboard, but their precise meaning and situational adequacy are entirely different matters and extremely hard to agree upon. Nor are values in any sense givens. It is practically impossible to use them as instruments of social cohesion; their use and their function are burdened with difficulties to such an extent that many characters in Conrad's novels give up on the idea of applying them altogether. Instead, they replace them, as Marlow does in *Lord Jim*, by a category very easy to handle and applicable to almost any situation somewhat out of the ordinary such as "the inexplicable." They must be accepted just like the waves battering us when we are swimming in rough seas. *Lord Jim* (1900), appropriately ringing in the twentieth century and inspired by an accident with the pilgrim ship *Jeddah* (1880), leaves the reader in the dark. It does not "explain" why Jim, officer on the *Patna* with Mecca pilgrims on board, is one of the first to leave the ship after the collision. He goes on trial and loses his commission, then for some time ekes out a living as a "water clerk." Eventually, he lands on the South Sea island of Patusan, where he climbs up the social ladder to become a kind of magician for the natives. After another instance of neglected duty—or is it just a mistake?—he does nothing to prevent the father of a young native from shooting him to death. Jim has caused the death of the young man because he did not fight pirates, as people were wont to say, with the necessary determination.

The multiplicity of perspectives that the narrator Marlow and his informers have mobilized in order to throw some light into the darkness of Jim's motivations fail completely in their task. They merely project isolated beams of light on Jim, each of them illuminating a new facet of Jim's "strangeness." Jim himself does not seem to be interested at all in what made him jump ship prematurely; he comments on his behavior with the laconic remark: "I had jumped . . . it seems."[11] But the perspective of the human enigma, of the "Inconceivable," the "Irrational," the "inexplicable" (80, 105, 296; see 155 etc.), is also just one among many others that are equally possible (96; see also *Heart of Darkness* and *Nostromo*). Marlow the narrator has fallen in love with it, but that does not help, since he is practically always distant from events and depends on secondhand reports.

In spite and in the face of Marlow's unreliability, one can still try to construct a plausible version of events—more plausible than Marlow's in any case. We can reasonably assume, for instance, that Jim's relation to values such as duty and honor remains superficial: they belong to his vocabulary but do not have any real motivational force. Likewise, he lacks any grip on the reality of his environment, in which case we could speak of a dreamlike aestheticism. After having jumped from the ship, he believes that his honor is tainted and laments repeatedly over the loss of his clean slate and good name (159–160). While this description of his situation sounds convincing, it lacks cogency. The suicide of the very successful Captain Brierly, a member of the "court of inquiry" investigating the *Patna* incident, may make the reader wonder and think of other possibilities. Brierly is one of those cases where certainties and uncertainties of character and motivation are mixed by several narrators in an almost exasperating manner ("it wasn't money, and it wasn't drink, and it wasn't woman [*sic*]" [50]; "there was some reason" [55; cf. 48–59]). The most interesting reason offered is that he thought the inquiry was a mistake because the values that were officially in question—neglect of duty, lack of courage—were no longer valid anyway; that he was bored by it and by life in general (see p. 49, where he is said to have been bored by Jim's case, and p. 59, where he is said not to have been bored; cf. pp. 56–57, where Brierly denies the usefulness of courage and the inquiry). Jim, however, remains passive. Marlow sticks to the myth of the "Inconceivable" and yet goes on to invalidate that myth by introducing the notion of a "true essence of life" and getting more and more lost in speculations about Jim's alleged subtleness and the possessors of his soul (79–80). Marlow does not ask whether the idea of an "Ability in the abstract," introduced on the very first page, does not consist in more than the abilities of a water-clerk. In a reformulation of the myth of the Inscrutable and the like, "Ability in the abstract" might very well refer to flexible modes of action and reaction that people may need in many situations of unforeseeable challenges. The German merchant Stein seems to have that in mind when he calls Jim a "romantic," which for Stein is someone who projects idea(l)s directly onto situations normally far from clear. Stein contrasts Jim's behavior with a concept of life where one is immersed all of the time in an unknown element such as the ocean: like swimming, one must try to stay afloat by moving one's hands and feet and in that way securing the ocean's help (184–185).

It would appear, then, that there are analytical needs in regard to *Lord Jim* that definitely go beyond the horizons opened, as well as often closed again, by the narrative mode of the text. These needs cannot be satisfied within this mode because the limitations of the narrators are obvious. The remedy is not, but there are plenty of hints that the conduct of life cannot simply consist in efforts to follow the apparent dictates of values. The famous short novel *Heart of Darkness* (1902; inspired by the situation in the Congo under Belgian rule) reveals, in its turn, the impossibility of returning to communitarian forms of life and their rituals that might at least remind us of the symposium. The wheels of systemic abstraction in modern life cannot be turned back, not even in cultures where its tribal contours are still visible or partly valid. *Heart of Darkness* is therefore less concerned with a story told from deficient perspectives; rather, it concentrates on the cognitive apparatus supposed to elucidate what really happens. Once more, and more clearly than before, this is Marlow's function. The strangeness of human beings, their "heart of darkness," is not simply asserted but presented as a process in which impressions are formed and changed. Marlow tells us less about Mr. Kurtz, his proper topic, but assembles essential elements of his own individuality. Whatever he narrates is much more relativized by the commentaries of his listeners than in *Lord Jim*. As an "authority" on the Inscrutable, he comes under ironic fire right at the beginning and for a while is allowed to wallow in his orgy of the mysterious.[12]

But he is not in control of perspectives, in four of which Kurtz appears. While the managers of different jungle stations see him as a reformer, they also see him as someone who promotes the exploitation of the jungle for the benefit of his company. A Russian, his constant companion, transforms him into an object of general reverence. Finally, his fiancée believes that she knows him "for real" as a man full of love and goodness. Marlow, however, comes to know him when he is already on the brink of death. He knows (and this is real knowledge) that Kurtz did not die with the name of his fiancée on his lips but with the words "The horror! The horror!" Confronted with contradictory impressions and opinions, Marlow tries to reconstruct the development of Kurtz from the author of a pamphlet about the suppression of savage habits of life up to a short note in which Kurtz seems to demand the extermination of the "brutes." At the same time, Kurtz appears to enjoy being celebrated by the "brutes" as a magician. Marlow must assume that Kurtz's relation to the jungle is much closer than he had surmised, that he must have revitalized the Dionysus cult of the late nineteenth century in his own way. In Europe, communitarian forms of life had disappeared (I still have something to say about possible reasons); in the jungle, Kurtz drives them into an excess that includes cruelty: Kurtz's house is surrounded by heads on stakes.[13] His personal development has become contradictory: he does not get rid of European traditions altogether but pushes the natives into the exploitation of ivory. If he embodies anything, it is the "hollow man" whose specter-like portrait T. S. Eliot had painted in "The Hollow Men."

Concepts coming as close as possible to the matter at hand—Kurtz's form of isolation—may be available in role theory.[14] Neither Kurtz nor Marlow grasps the far-reaching nature of roles in behavior and personality. They are not aware of the stability granted by roles to behavior, nor do they acknowledge their scope, in which instability may arise and contradictions (between humane behavior and competition or cruelty) may thrive. In such cases, the appearance of roles as real (natural, immanent) properties of character is attenuated, although Kurtz apparently does not become aware of that. Caught between the reality claim and the attenuation of its illusory substance, Kurtz glides into a pathological and chronic "role stress." The "role relation"[15]—that is, the relation between the person playing a role and the role itself—is too tight. Even when contradictions become glaring—for instance, between his early role as reformer and his later role as a cruel jungle magician—he does not distance himself from either. He cannot handle the loss of what the contradictory roles demand and take away from his personality, at least in the form of energy. Although role discrepancy does not per se destroy the possibility of sympotic opportunities, it takes a lot of careful management to prevent that.

Limiting their import, one could say that Jim's and Kurtz's isolation and their deaths are the products and results of exceptional situations. One could also downgrade to exotic special cases the ability in the abstract to keep one's head above water and Stein's philosophy of life and its metaphoric doctrine of how to do that. One could try to argue that the tight organization of life in ordinary society at least partly takes care of the abstract openness and metaphoric flailing about in water. This hope, however, gets short shrift right from the beginning of *Nostromo* (1904). Conrad uses and changes a simple narrative procedure: the role of (formally) omniscient narrator is largely transferred to Captain Mitchell—a simple soul, the reader might be tempted to say—who knows, that is to say, has heard something about everything. Mitchell adheres to a fairly naïve belief in progress and follows the code of behavior inherent in the duties of his post without complaint. He sees through the elements of illusion that have slipped into the code but counts them among those saving illusions which protect against destructive skepticism. This attitude enables him to comprehend the history of the Latin American country of Costaguana (its factual counterpart may have been Colombia) as a sequence of meaningful events. Such an opinion is not, of course, absurd: the interests of different groups of people (mine owners, the population, rebels and their leader, dock workers, and others) in both the silver and the silver mine of the western province of Sulaco, often called "material interests"[16] can be seen as the organizing principles of the sociopolitical, capitalist, and even religious realities of the country.

But it is precisely these realities that produce an uncoordinated and nontransparent complexity full of contradictions. In the midst of this confusion, the rebels lose the silver treasure that they need. Above all, the main actors in the effort to save the treasure, the journalist Decoud and the boss of the dock workers, the Capataz de Cargadores called Nostromo, lose their lives. Decoud, apparently unable to bear the solitude in which he finds himself, commits suicide; Nostromo is erroneously shot to death by the father of his bride. Here, the problem is not role strain but the normalcy of sociopolitical conditions, always somewhat confused but also to some extent ordered by identifiable structures, that throws individuals into a state of chaotic and catastrophic isolation. The loneliness of Decoud, but also the superior manipulations of Nostromo, the unilateral actions of Sotillo, the leader of the rebels, and the megalomania of Montero, the separatist general (322–325), are merely four of the conventional forms of isolation (but see also, on an entirely different level, the marriage between Mrs. Gould and Mr. Gould, the owner of the mine) out of an unmanageable multitude of possibilities. The events that follow cannot be controlled because their determining factors reach into both the past and the future. In contrast to people, events cannot be isolated; they do not have origins and ends, at least not perceptible ones. The more Captain Mitchell digs into his memory (or merely talks about events), for instance, the more his narrative is subject to overlaps and ramifications ("Captain Joseph Mitchell prided himself on his profound knowledge of men and things in the country—*cosas de Costaguana*," 22; he was "really very communicative under his air of pompous reserve," 24; see 48, 269–290, etc.). In no case is an existing situation identical with the motivations or intentions of individuals or reducible to them.

The discrepancy between events and individual timetables is not always clearly indicated: events seem to resemble the place allotted to them in the narrative and there are probabilities into which they seem to fit for a while. Nor is it possible to explain the events centered around the silver as the result of an anthropologically grounded greed. While greed certainly exists, quite a few of the characters remain untouched by it. Moreover, greed meets the same fate as the other human drives (or what appear as such): it is counterproductive and adds to rather than reducing confusion. Sotillo, for instance, believes that the merchant Hirsch knows where the silver is hidden; he interrogates and tortures him. In a final gesture of revolt, Hirsch spits in Sotillo's face, and in a fit of fury Sotillo shoots him (370), thus depriving himself of the last chance to learn the whereabouts of the silver.

Apart from Captain Mitchell, the role of narrator—perhaps one should say, the provider of narrative perspective—remains fairly unclear. That is why we do not learn to whom or what source some sort of rhetorically conspicuous summary of the world of this novel should be attributed: "The cruel futility of things stood unveiled in the levity and suffering of that incorrigible people.... Unlike Decoud, Charles Gould could not play lightly a part in a tragic farce" (302). In any case, even the combination of personal integrity and political idealism does not save the figures from isolation. Old Garibaldino Viola keeps cultivating his youthful spirit of liberty; Don José Avellanos fights for the ideal of national righteousness. Their confessions of transpersonal commitments carry a certain value because they are guaranteed by personal sincerity and unselfishness, but to hold these ideals not only rigorously but rigidly is tantamount to blindness. Viola feels himself to be above the conflicts of the present, although he took part in the battles of Garibaldi only as a cook. His ideal is shown in a comic light when he remains sitting, in a dreamlike state, with his old rifle in front of a portrait of Garibaldi, but it turns deadly when Viola thinks he is defending the honor of his family and, in doing so, erroneously kills Nostromo.

Only a few of the characters are able to escape the double bind of confusion and isolation; Mrs. Gould and Dr. Monygham, for example, pay the price of passivity for being exceptions. Nostromo enjoys the transpersonal quality of an excellent reputation, believed to be professionally excellent, reliable, and incorruptible. Thus he accepts Mr. Gould's mission to transport the silver, together with Decoud, to the safety offered by a small island. But the silver transforms him into its prisoner like the others: he sneaks onto the island repeatedly in order to take the silver away piece by piece. And on one of his expeditions, he is shot by Viola.

The (Self-)Destruction of Communities
(*The Secret Agent, Under Western Eyes*)

The perspectives that I have employed up to this point—they are, of course, not the only possible ones—belong to Conrad's early and middle career as a writer. The works from that period aim at the extension and cementing of individual isolation, an isolation accompanied by the gradual or full destruction of psychosocially satisfactory forms of community. The logic of such perspectives contains the further possibility of—indeed, the demand for—looking at social disintegration from a primarily social rather than personal viewpoint. If it is the case, as parts of modern sociological systems theory assert, that persons find themselves in a peripheral position with respect to social systems, then the decay of social structures may well be an independent process of its own. Narratives and speculations of the latter kind abound in Conrad's later work, especially the two successive novels *The Secret Agent* (1907) and *Under Western Eyes* (1911). Prevalent attitudes in these texts are of either the idealistic or the cynical kind. In a somewhat laborious way, one could say that Conrad also offers (a contribution to) a genealogy of these attitudes. Very generally, the eighteenth century would then be the inaugural period of idealistic modes of thought in the *secret societies*; the nineteenth century, on the other hand, would be the period of a cynicism breaking through the walls of sentimentalism, a breakthrough engineered by the cynical institutional turn in the *secret services*. At the beginning of the twentieth century, all of them are in full swing and in various degrees of mixture (with Bracher's year 1917 as the general beginning of an age of ideologies). In the eighteenth century, the advanced thought of the Enlightenment, propelled by political stagnation, creates the scope for idealistic projects. In the nineteenth century, nationalism and similar dogmatic restrictions of thought provoke cynical disillusionment in those who know better. Nationalisms remain virulent and ideologies are rampant in the twentieth century. It seems obvious that the minimal compulsion for the past century must have consisted in the modernization of the military and, more especially, of secret services and espionage.

Our discussion will begin with the later novel, in which the political belatedness of the despotic czarist regime is compounded by the belatedness of social and civil institutions and further exacerbated by the confrontation of feudal conditions with a revolutionary idealism that in Russia goes by the name of nihilism. For Western Europe, this was an extraordinary situation—if proof were needed, it could be found in the fact that Oscar Wilde, rather than joking about it, wanted to start his career as a playwright with a serious drama about the nihilists and their failing conspiracies (*Vera; or, the Nihilists* [1883]; withdrawn one week after the premiere).

Conrad was aware, as indicated by the title, of the likelihood of distorting Western prejudice. His narrator, a language teacher in Geneva, the center of exiled Russians, admits to "my European remoteness."[17] Inevitably, observation and narration must take place from some kind of distance. This also means that both East and West find themselves in an experimental situation ("It is unthinkable that any young Englishman should find himself in Razumov's situation" [25]). Razumov, a student intent on embarking on a profitable career, is caught in the problems arising out of the murder of a prominent statesman (7; an allusion to the murder of the minister of the interior Viatscheslav Konstantinovitch Plevne in 1904). For the narrator, the fate of the minister provides an example of "the moral corruption of an oppressed society where the noblest aspirations of humanity, the desire of freedom, an ardent patriotism, the love of justice, the sense of pity, and even the fidelity of simple minds are prostituted to the lusts of hate and fear, the inseparable companions of an uneasy despotism" (7). This catalogue foreshadows the contradictions in the order of values that, in the characterization of Russia as the "land of spectral ideas and disembodied aspirations" (34), as the country of absent group solidarity and free-floating ideologies, will ultimately be deprived of any foundation. Many "brave minds" are therefore yearning for autocracy (34). The hallmark of both Russian autocracy and of revolt, however, is cynicism: nobody really believes in what they hold up as an ideal. Consequently, the narrator does not see his primary task as the telling of a story but exposing "the moral conditions ruling over a large portion of this earth's surface" (67; see 163). In such a climate of opinion, Razumov begins to think about his own treason in regard to his revolutionary co-student Haldin, who had asked him for help in his flight after the murder (93–94). Razumov commits another act of treason later, after having emigrated to Geneva, by telling Haldin's mother and sister, also in Geneva, lies that are hard to expose or refute.

The relationship between Razumov and Natalia, Haldin's sister, might be a sincere one, since they need each other erotically (347–348). But the treason that cost Haldin his life cannot be talked about—the knowledge would ruin any relationship. On the political side, values are destroyed by the rhetorical grandiloquence in the speeches and unending discussions of the self-styled but powerless revolutionary emigrants. The entire range of visions, utopias, and revolutionary, even feminist, mysticism (95, 104, 131) is cut off from any connection with possibilities of action. The discussion between Razumov and the professional woman revolutionary ("woman revolutionist," 246, 249, 273; "the true spirit of destructive revolution," 261), Sophia Antonovna (238–281), resembles a conversation between ghosts, as it proceeds on the basis of totally erroneous assumptions. The apparently concrete revolutionary schedule looks hopeless, even if set up by professional terrorists (19, 330). The image of the schedule, including the self-image of the revolutionaries, is disastrous. Madame de S——, whose salon is visited by the Geneva revolutionaries, looks upon them as a disorderly crowd of "members of committees, secret emissaries, vulgar and unmannerly fugitive professors, rough students, ex-cobblers with apostolic faces, consumptive and ragged enthusiasts, Hebrew youths, common fellows of all sorts . . .—fanatics, pedants, proletarians all" (218–219). Razumov is beaten up and crippled for life by revolutionary hooligans after his role as a traitor in the Haldin case has eventually become known in Geneva (368–370). Conrad's diagnosis shrinks to the conventional cliché of Russians loving to listen to themselves talking (4, 228). Wherever possible, the revolutionaries retire into a petty bourgeois, at best charitable, life (378, 381).

History has proved Conrad partly wrong. About ten years after the novel appeared and while Conrad was still alive, a revolution of global importance took place in Russia. At the time of publication, World War I could not be foreseen, but judging from the novel it could not have been ruled out, either. In its most important aspects, however, Conrad's diagnosis has remained correct. At the beginning of the twentieth century, the state could no longer pose as representing ethical values or the totality of what is called a people or a nation, nor were there any other communitarian forms of life that could take its place, because all the candidates were discredited by the ideological aggressiveness they needed in order to justify their positions. Apologists of the state were cynics; their adversaries—that is, mostly revolutionary groups of various sizes—were most commonly dubious idealists. The example, in *Under Western Eyes*, of autocratic despotism in czarist Russia may be an extreme one. The history of fascism in the first half of the twentieth century shows, however, that moderate or radical versions of this transformation of the state into an illegitimate apparatus of compulsion and the degeneration of its opponents into speechifying losers had to be reckoned with forthwith. In 1910, Leo Tolstoy died, the last champion of the theory and practice of communitarian life-forms with more than local repercussions.

Even before then, in *The Secret Agent* (1907), Conrad had shifted his perspective toward an unflattering portrait of Western states. With England as his prime example, the noblest task of the state had turned into the protection of the property of the rich and ruling classes. (Incidentally, the classic portrait of *The Man of Property* by John Galsworthy came out at almost the same time, in 1906.) In Conrad, those who underestimate the complexity of the task are now called idealists:

> Protection is the first necessity of opulence and luxury. They had to be protected; and their horses, carriages, houses, servants had to be protected; and the source of their wealth had to be protected in the heart of the city and the heart of the country; the whole social order favourable to their hygienic idleness had to be protected against the shallow enviousness of unhygienic labour."[18]

More clearly than in *Under Western Eyes*, Conrad draws attention to a significant parallel: the interior protective function of the state by the extension of the authority of the police force must be optimized by espionage or state terrorism against foreign countries as potential enemies. England—as seen by the German embassy (Germany having recently advanced to the position of England's main enemy)—must be taught modernity by the international community (as we would cynically say today) in that crucial regard, since this old-fashioned country still believes in the ideal of individual freedom ("England lags. This country is absurd with its sentimental regard for individual liberty. . . . England must be brought into line" [33]). In order to force England to adopt more radical measures, the secret agent Adolf Verloc, paid by the Germans, is ordered to organize terroristic acts against English institutions. Verloc must talk with the first secretary of the embassy about suitable subjects—that is, about the greatest publicity to be obtained by certain acts (such as blowing up the National Gallery [34–37]). The Germans, of course, overestimate the risks of individual freedom for England; they ignore its function for securing the hegemony of the upper classes in the sense quoted above.

After this beginning, the main activity of the terrorist espionage group consists in its self-dismantling. Verloc thinks about the character of the revolutionaries among them and recognizes in them merely the enemies of discipline and fatigue: "There are natures, too, to whose sense of justice the price exacted looms up monstrously enormous, odious, oppressive, worrying, humiliating, extortionate, intolerable. Those are the fanatics. The remaining portion of social rebels is accounted for by vanity, the mother of all noble and vile illusions, the companion of poets, reformers, charlatans, prophets, and incendiaries" (51–52). In the eddies of opinions and programs constantly relativizing each other, one motif keeps recurring and becomes a consistently held radical position: the state and its organs and terrorism are interchangeable. "The terrorist and the policeman come both from the same basket. Revolution, legality—countermoves in the same game" (64). There is talk about "unexpected lines of continuity" between conspirators and police (76). Theft is reexamined as a "form of human industry, perverse indeed, but still an industry exercised in an industrious world" (81). Motivation is the same as with "normal" work, except that the risks are higher (82). State institutions are exposed to the permanent pressure of public opinion, "that strange emotional phenomenon" (88). Chapters 6, 7, and 10 are devoted primarily to the exploration of such equivalences. Discussions concerning questions of procedure take place between Chief Inspector Heat and the assistant commissioner of police, on the one hand, and between the assistant commissioner and a "great personage" (114), Sir Ethelred by name but otherwise remaining unknown, on the other. Sir Ethelred is probably a kind of gray eminence: Heat's talks with him and Verloc reveal not only forms of collaboration and secret agreements between the police (Inspector Heat) and "terrorists" such as Verloc but also an enormously modern awareness of how "facts'" can be manufactured ("facility to fabricate the very facts themselves" [117]). The reader is also confronted with the existence of what is called "authorized scoundrelism" (118) in the text. Obviously, the skills of contemporary politicians in this respect are lagging far behind.

Conrad's text does not really question a sort of superior validity normally bestowed upon state legitimacy. This does not, however, grant an analogously superior legitimacy to single actions and the measures of state agencies. Groups of whatever kind do not conform to other criteria that might support and stabilize their cohesion either; individuals and groups must gauge the risks of their enterprises in each single case, risks that they run in regard to public opinion or agencies of judgment or potentials of solidarity. Legitimacy, even legality, is not pregiven but is formulated after the event. In the opinion of the first secretary, terrorist acts obey an imperative formulated long before in Thomas de Quincey's *On Murder Considered as One of the Fine Arts* (1827; cf. also Oscar Wilde's "Pen, Pencil and Poison"): they must be as impressive as possible. The assassination or an attempted one of a crowned head or a president does not satisfy this demand anymore. A bomb in the National Gallery "would make some noise," But art is not enough of a fetish to create a sensation. The bombing of Greenwich, the center of global timelines, would be better (35–37).

Verloc, too, repeatedly miscalculates the risks. The mentally handicapped brother of his wife is supposed to set off a bomb with a special delaying mechanism. But he activates that mechanism prematurely when he stumbles over the root of a tree and is killed himself (172). Inspector Heat lets Verloc go because his story would not be believed anyway (173). The two representatives of government, the assistant commissioner (with Sir Ethelred's blessing) and the first secretary, agree on a version of events acceptable to both (180–186). Verloc miscalculates a last time: he is stabbed by his wife after he tells her about the death of her brother in rather unfeeling words. She flees with the revolutionary Ossipon, who, however, is afraid of being stabbed by her himself; he cheats her out of her money, thus driving her to suicide.

The novel is constructed along events that undermine binary value structures and hierarchies of legitimacy. Other or new types of order are not visible: older forms of group formation do not stand a chance against the interests of modern states. Each individual or group must calculate the risks of their doings themselves. An emblematic embodiment of the situation is provided by the chemist of the revolutionary group ("the Professor"). He builds the bomb but is running around with a bomb himself that he could set off in twenty seconds in case he is arrested. Nothing happens, but something might happen at any time; readers are kept on tenterhooks. Chain reactions of unexpected events tend to take on the character of grotesqueries.

Isolation does not mean that society would consist of isolated individuals and fall into anomie. By and large, life follows its routines: forms of order can be recognized; people behave more or less according to roles and scenarios. Even so, schedules of events are thwarted all the time; they may trigger other events remarkable by the nontransparent complexity that they imply. In such cases, many people react with predetermined and fixed opinions. The main problem is not complexity as such but the lack of elasticity in reactions to it. It is the way in which Verloc tells his wife about the death of her brother, not the fact as such, that drives her to stab him and pushes her on the path toward her own death.

Conrad has reduced the social chances of sociable groups in two main respects. Where they still exist, in the pristine integrity of "exotic" spaces, as it might appear, one can foresee that the culture clash with the West will dissolve their essential bonds (*Lord Jim, Heart of Darkness*). In Western societies, by contrast—that is, in contexts of overpowering modernization on all fronts—sociable communities will be either marginalized or disempowered as merely imaginary, "romantic" projects or stifled by ever-ready forms of ideological criticism (*The Secret Agent, Under Western Eyes*). It would appear that utopias are the only form in which political and economic blueprints for the future may be sketched. They are not under the pressure of immediate implementation because, utopia also meaning no man's land, they may be under no pressure whatsoever. Moreover, their social and scientific ambiguities have been recognized for a long time. We should be aware that most of the phalansteries (sometimes called utopias, sometimes colonies) founded in the nineteenth century in the wake of Charles Fourier were shut down only a year after their foundation. We should also be aware, however, that attempts have been renewed time and again, that cultural studies has always hesitated to qualify Fourier's projects as (merely) utopian, that perhaps a need for such forms of life should not simply be written off. It appears that the colony of Condé-sur-Vesgre, an Île-de-France village of about 1,200 inhabitants, has survived from 1832 till today in changing forms.

CHAPTER 10

Beyond the Sympotic
Aesthetic Productivity and Sociable Bonding in the Detective Novel

AT THIS POINT, another provisional stocktaking of the results to be claimed for the analyses so far is necessary. The classical symposium in ancient Athens followed numerous rules, although these rules should not be misunderstood as the expression of some theoretical or normative anthropology. Yet an anthropological framework is implied, because the symposium presents the relative rather than full totality of an interactive and communicative, often-playful mobilization of bodily, emotional, and intellectual energies in smaller groups. One must accept that such an anthropology does not satisfy all the demands and conditions of philosophical anthropology (see the second section of Chapter 3), but its historical range as an inspirational model is considerable. The results of a fuller and final confrontation between implicit and philosophical anthropology will be reviewed in the final chapter of this book.

It is also clear that the historical range of this inspirational model cannot be extended indefinitely. While impulses and elements do live on in manifold postsympotic institutions, it appears that their inspirational power is brought to a halt with the party. Earlier institutions such as the salon and the club seem to have had limitations; the impact of class, at least in part, reduced their socially cohesive strength. This does not mean, however, that the societies in question faced anarchy, a social catastrophe that struck fear in the heart of Matthew Arnold in his essay *Culture and Anarchy* (1869). For Arnold, public welfare and social or, more generally, human well-being are endangered by the segregation of the main classes (the proletarian "Populace," the culturally and morally impoverished "Philistines," and the aristocratic "Barbarians"). Unfortunately, Arnold's therapy loses itself in cloudy metaphors ("sweetness and light") and vague compromises (such as the combination of Hellenism and Hebraism); apparently the role of the empire in regard to social cohesion did not trouble him. But it seems clear that, while ideologically the empire may have exerted a cohesive force, its empirical, down-to-earth problems (such as crime) posed different challenges. The

Sherlock Holmes stories by Arthur Conan Doyle, including and surrounded by a lot of "scientific" literature, function as forms of ambivalent analysis and, at the same time, as involuntary studies in prejudice. In the late twentieth and early twenty-first centuries, the problem has returned in the form of migration and refugees.

More generally, we must take for granted that the inspirational range of the symposium is limited. The main reasons are to be sought, if need be, in structural social changes in nation-states. We need not decide which descriptive model is best suited for identifying the changes: Habermas's *Structural Change of the Public Sphere* or Sennett's decay of public life and the tyranny of intimacy, or more concretely, the different forms of power remaining with the nation-state and the organization of security needs. In every case, the empirical complexity is such that the explanatory power of any hypothesis is—more or less obviously—limited; One cannot follow either Habermas or Sennett in every single case. Sennett appears to be at his best in the analysis of exemplary cases. As noted above, the decay of an interactive public life can be demonstrated in the rise of the department store. Sennett also describes and explains in subtle terms how the magnificence of the Opéra Garnier in Paris has destroyed the spatial potentiality for sociability: the Opéra building and its interior richness are there in order to be admired, independent of what happens inside in musical terms and forms of hospitality. Also impressive is his further thesis that Richard Wagner, much as he opposed this type of narcotic theater, worked to produce the same effect with his Bayreuth ambience of almost silent restraint.[1]

For my part, I try to understand these and other developments as surrogate forms of possible experience in the face of the growing inaccessibility to individuals of urban, industrial, and—in a different sense—media realities. For individuals, the experience of such massive realities remains inadequate and unsatisfactory. These realities must be redesigned, aestheticized in some way, so as to make possible their largely illusory experience—an experience that must remain so because their production is directed by partial interests and pressure groups.[2] In order to invest them with intelligibility of some kind, they are translated into emotive language and domestic familiarities. According to Sennett, this psychological transformation of social reality is unsuccessful because these realities cannot be sufficiently understood—to say nothing of controlled—in terms of psychologically motivated needs, although efforts in this direction continue. Sennett fears that human beings may be deprived of their civilized achievements and abilities because their real needs and the offerings of the media, for example, never tally. Consequently, frustrations are built up that are reinterpreted as the right to behave in whatever way one prefers. In such situations, conservatives (like Matthew Arnold), in their turn, tend to see the barbarians at the gate. Being civilized, however, should mean (according to Sennett, Plessner, and others) the exact opposite—well-meaning efforts to spare other people the burdens of one's own contingent individuality. This would entail that people, with respect to their inner life, build up a repertory of behavior in which their own impulses can be treated flexibly. And it would mean, with respect to outside contacts, that one wear a (metaphorical) mask most of the time, since the mask does not prevent sociability but provides it with an essential scope, at least partly freeing people from the inequalities of their living conditions and emotional dispositions.[3]

There is, it is true, an ambivalence to the mask that makes it easier to perceive and understand the resistance against it, resulting from the possible closeness, for modern periods, between humane sympotic and criminal behavior. In dissimulating individuality, the mask also conceals possible criminal intentions; as soon as that possibility has worked its way into the minds of people, everybody overreacts. Danger seems to lurk everywhere: conflicts about women who hide their faces for religious reasons in cultures where this is not normally done are only the most glaring cases. Distinctions between forms of sociability and secret societies are harder to draw. It was the purpose of Chapter 8 to sketch the potential for conflicts between the state and secrecy, with collateral damage to sociability. Being forced to wear a mask (in the literal sense) during the Covid pandemic has certainly made people hesitate even more.

Triviality and Metaphysics in the Detective Novel

The most important theater of war in which such conflicts take very concrete shapes is supplied by detective novels and films. It is not surprising, then, that these novels and films also offer glimpses, however rudimentary, of new sympotic relevance. They offer redress for radical disturbances of our senses of the real, performing this task by acting as a psychologically rare mixture of suspense (i.e., excitement) and tranquilizer.[4]

First, then, we must remind ourselves of what has been said about the detective novel in the wake of Boltanski and Eco. This genre intensifies feelings of insecurity arising from inevitable violations of an order that most of us cherish, notwithstanding our knowledge that this order is in many cases merely imaginary. The more enigmatic such disturbances appear, the more the detective must possess special qualities, especially in logical reasoning or the semiotic deciphering of circumstantial evidence.[5] The enigma is particularly disturbing if it impacts realities of a trivial kind that would normally appear to be immune to it, and it may grow still worse if the presumed qualities of the detective can barely be distinguished from enigmatic deviancy itself. Generally, it is the triviality of the disturbance, or rather the disturbance of the trivial, combined with the threshold experience of murder that may produce, in Boltanski's and Eco's terms, a metaphysical shudder.[6] As to the threshold or boundary situation and its experience of death, authors of detective novels might invoke the support of Karl Jaspers, for whom death together with doubt and wonderment, both also very much present in detective literature, belong to the origins of philosophy.

This leads me to the proposition that metaphysical shuddering together with the tension between gray and trivial realities and boundary situations trigger an involvement of the reader's consciousness that marginalizes the apparent radical isolation of the criminal and the detective, but also, against the hopes connected with my main argument, the importance of sociability. For the time being, this cannot be helped. Indeed, the emphasis on the lack of sociability in a club established for the sake of sociability—namely, in Dorothy L. Sayers's *The Unpleasantness at the Bellona Club* (1928; discussed in Chapter 6)—is almost comic in its insistence. The club is credited with the atmosphere of a mortuary or "the privacy of the confessional"[7]—which is, it should be noted, not a strong argument for the absence of sociability, since the class relations of such a club do indeed demand this muted form.

To clear away a final obstacle to the evaluation of detective literature, I should admit that novels, films, and TV shows in that genre are not, of course, immune to a significant problem of any media product. With the basic situation remaining more or less the same, how do writers invent interesting, gripping, or innovative variations? It appears that one can write in one of two main ways in order to prevent the metaphysical scheme from becoming monotonous and at the same time to keep anxieties about the fragility of a well-ordered everyday life under control. In the first way, the "objective" way, one can enrich crime as well as everyday realities with forms of horror of all kinds. In the reader's tortured mind, these will cry imperiously for solutions as immediate as possible. Such solutions are normally provided, and the procedure may then repeat itself several times.

There are writers who are masters in measuring out the appropriate doses of the procedure. Their genre is the so-called psychothriller. Horror offers the metaphysical and psychological advantage of coupling external realities and the psyche directly. It can leave the environment partly un(der)determined and, precisely because of that, is able to draw the psyche into its orbit. Since terrible injuries and dismemberments are part of this arsenal, the powerful effect of an ingredient integrated not that long ago is still further enhanced: the visual presence and psychological impact of autopsies and coroners—in short, of forensic medicine. Since women pioneers such as Patricia Cornwell and Kathy Reichs, often combining the literary role and the real job, have moved into this territory, detective novels without forensic medicine have practically become inconceivable.

In the second way of writing, we have to confront a problem described, in his aesthetics, by Georg Lukács, as the "disanthropomorphizing" effect of science, especially in its modern forms. In this way, science exacerbates the threatening and enigmatic character of the world—but only transitorily, for a while, after which it normally takes over its "enlightenment" function again. Lukács maintains that the antihumanist work of science embarked on a contradictory ascent. In the slave economy of antiquity, it barely had a chance because that economy set narrow boundaries to any potential competitor. This would also provide a late explanation for the fact that a relatively small part of the population—an oligarchy in fact— and its rituals such as the symposium, could hold on to political power for quite a long time.[8] Generally, also in regard to Lukács, we may quarrel over whether the way that religions buy trust in the world with trust in the other world is better than science or whether belief in the other world offers a sufficient number of certainties. In any case, there are plenty of people for whom reconciling the secrets of reality with the standards of science is preferable to the doubling of secrets in those of the world and those of the other world.

Psychological thrillers have kept propelling the complementary and contrasting aspects of horror and "scientific" enlightenment to ever new heights. The power of such couplings has to some extent forced "normal" detective novels to pay a toll to them. By feeding at least the idea that horror can be imagined in the context of ordinary realities, detective literature crosses the boundaries that were still respected in discussions about a "pleasurable form of horror" in the eighteenth century and on up to Georges Simenon.[9] Ultimately, this literature is looking for and then exploring narrative procedures that replace the weak relics of interactive culture with a tranquilizing world picture that reconciles terrifying and horrible events with Enlightenment perspectives. Its main focus, however, is no longer a possible ordering of the world but rather control of unusual situations, in extreme cases those of anomie. Such cases, mentioned above, involve social situations in which the laws are still valid but cannot be enforced. Psychological thrillers, by contrast, strive, within the shakiness of trivial realities, to push the extremes of possible, psychologically challenging events to the utmost, according to the notion that what can be imagined can become real. Even forms of very unpleasant horror are enjoyed by a large number of readers, but I very much doubt this trend will continue to assert itself for very long: maximum effects, once normalized, tend to lose their efficacy quickly. In some recent examples, maximally sadistic effects are slowed down with narrative assurances of conventional but intact worlds of feeling.[10]

In the course of its history, detective literature has not infrequently made use of scientific results, and its detectives have likewise behaved as if they were applying scientific methods and procedures. This makes sense: common sense is rarely enough for solving extraordinary problems. Contemporary more-radical versions of the pair of opposites horror and enlightenment, however, call for ongoing reevaluation of the cognitive resources of those who handle enigmatic cases. In particular, normal procedures are incapable of coping with crimes committed by criminals in command of cognitive as well as technological and scientific superiority. Metaphysical shudder as well as uncertainties and anxieties about the reliability of everyday reality may be provoked with special intensity in cases where the criminals seem to surpass the police in terms of intelligence—that is, a mixture of logic, knowledge, and equipment—or where detectives such as Sherlock Holmes appear to contribute to social disorder themselves, by taking drugs, for instance; in quite a few countries, we are told, this has become normal. Sherlock Holmes was also the first detective whose cases were treated not so much as conflicts between police and criminal but as personal duels between superintelligent adversaries. In such cases, despite narrative conventions and expectations (with the happy ending in the shape of a solved case), the result may be unclear for an alarmingly long time; in fact, the duel between Holmes and Professor Moriarty, that "Napoleon of Crime," ends in a draw that is deadly for both (Conan Doyle's later revocation can be ignored), an ending that is particularly troubling because it casts a shadow on Holmes, whom readers would normally perceive as the apogee of detective intelligence. Moriarty, of course, is an expert mathematician—that is, a master of the science that combines all the abilities best suitable for crime. Thus the remainder of Chapter 10 will be devoted to the question of whether anxieties about the fragility of the real, augmented by expert criminal professionalism and the absence of traditional sympotic-interactive reassurance, might call forth, against all the odds, new sympotic potentials.

Maigret, Imagination, and the Symposium of Clochards

Beginning our search for such potentials, we must first note some significant deviations from the most common forms of detective literature. Georges Simenon's Commissaire Maigret, for instance, can claim an extraordinarily high percentage of solved cases, although we have no idea which of his abilities might be responsible for it. Readers who pay close attention will note that there is a mixed intelligence at work with Maigret, an intelligence combining an exceptionally precise awareness of whether a situation is or is not criminal and a similarly precise attention to the non-everyday significance of everyday details. This kind of "epistemology" can be easily overlooked because Maigret flattens its profile in casual remarks and observations and in questions that are clearly formulated, on the one hand, yet, on the other hand, unclear in regard to the target they aim at, that is to say, the situations they are supposed to elucidate. Maigret's interrogation technique of concrete abstraction drives suspects into a corner: the questions are easy to understand as far as their ordinary meaning is concerned but difficult in regard to the purpose for which they have been asked. Maigret can deploy these questions because he can imagine possible crime scenarios behind the questions much better than his colleagues or the suspects. Apparently, the ability to conceive of or imagine such scenarios is much more important than their logic, which, after all, functions only on the basis of a situation to which it is supposed to apply—otherwise it is suspended in thin air. Experience in police work also plays a role in Maigret's success, although it is not really foregrounded. In imaginative complexes, social motives, including those of solidarity, can more easily find their place than in detective reasoning, which is based only on logic and scientific evidence, crucially important as these are. The imagination, if we may use this very broad term, is connected to complexes of ideas floating around in the mind, ideas no longer very common but occasionally decisive. For our purposes here, this is where Simenon's Maigret novels take on their cultural importance.

Such positionings do not invalidate the characterization of the classical detective, whether police or private, as a hero of acuity (*Scharfsinnsheld* [Ulrich Schulz-Buschhaus]) or as an advanced semiotician (myself); in any case, that characterization must be seen in context.[11] The detective's acuity of mind is fully activated only when the detective can imagine a situation in which the crime can be embedded. It would not be wrong to attribute a high degree of empathy to crime situations imagined by Maigret. In *Maigret à Vichy* (1967), they turn out to be especially plausible, probably because Maigret and his wife stay at a health resort: relaxation and leisure help in the unfolding of imaginative activity. A short summary of the story might look like this: Two sisters have been successfully exploiting an industrialist for years with the claim that he has fathered a son with one of them (his mistress) and that he must pay for the son's education. The industrialist pays without complaint for a son who does not exist and whom, consequently, he has never seen. It is only when he does not see any picture or other piece of evidence of the so-called son in the house of the "mother" that he demands proof of his existence, and during a quarrel he inadvertently kills her. Maigret tracks him down and tries to imagine his situation:

> He imagined him, using each occasion.... For him, the murderer of Hélène Lange had stopped being a vague entity. He began to take form, to acquire a personality.... For Maigret, for example, the young woman in purple was not simply the victim of murder, nor was she a person who had led this or that kind of existence. He began to know her and made an effort, almost without knowing it, to deepen this knowledge.[12]

During cross-examination, Maigret hardly needs to make an effort in order to make Pélardeau confess. He rather feels pity for him ("Poor man!" [*Maigret à Vichy*, 175]), because he has adopted, without noticing it, the role of the victim of the two women so easily. Even when he confronts Pélardeau with the facts, he refuses to accept them because he cannot believe in the monstrous badness of people (176–182, 186). For Maigret, therefore, Pélardeau is not a man who should be punished. When Maigret's wife asks him how many years Pélardeau will probably have to spend behind bars, he answers, "I hope he will be acquitted" (189).

In general, Maigret's combination of imagination and logic does not belong to the repertory of human cognitive (including affective) achievements. Taking another step, we can see signs for its role as a thematic symptom; again, we will be dealing with rather brief remarks in which I will offer a psychosocial diagnosis of a specific present. In the novel *Maigret et la vieille dame* (1950), we find passages that we can read as critical analyses of dominant social groups. The world of the upper bourgeoisie appears to be unperturbed: their servants are still wearing their yellow-striped vests and the maids have donned their old lace caps (*Maigret et la vieille dame*, 93). People and things can be clearly interpreted, although they have perhaps become a little remote and convey a slight impression of having turned "anonymous, impersonal." This reality, to a large extent held together by the mutual acceptance of classes, though changing and sometimes confused (124), appears fairly stable. For the time being, the rich bourgeoisie can aspire to push into irrelevance the differences between them and the aristocracy. Théo Besson, for instance, originally a rich bourgeois who has largely squandered his fortune in aristocratic mimicry, simply refuses to abandon that lifestyle: "Maigret had just discovered whom Théo tried so hard to resemble: It was the Duke of Windsor" (119; cf. 115). In such cases, social decline becomes a real possibility. Above all, since official class and de facto lifestyle no longer always correspond, both the aristocracy and the bourgeoisie are threatened by a total matter-of-fact coldness of human relations that is hitherto unknown. Arlette Sudre, wife of a petty bourgeois dentist who has nonetheless experienced the life of the upper bourgeoisie with her parents and her Besson brothers, practices an utterly unfeeling form of sexual promiscuity. Even Maigret is totally embarrassed when she offers him the "services" in question with complete directness; he needs quite some time to recover from the mere offer (81–86).

Under more ordinary circumstances, Maigret is not easily impressed by unusual forms of behavior. Within the slow and gradual destabilization of class society, characters and forms of behavior emerge that remind him, from a great distance as it were, of an older type of humane group solidarity. In the background, contours of the old symposium are vaguely visible, although the members and the group they belong to—namely, the clochards—have changed drastically: clochards are officially the lowest, the most powerless, members of society and not the uppermost and most powerful social group in France. Clochards show up frequently in Simenon's work, for instance in *Maigret et l'homme tout seul* (Maigret and the solitary man [1971]), which seems to be the only instance, however, in which one of them is the target of murder. It is also, I expect, only rarely that clochards are credited with an "ideal state of being," a "higher human perfection" than the average citizen. Yet it is an event—an exceptional event, to be sure—that brings us back into a sympotic center.[13]

In *Maigret et le clochard*, a former doctor (still called "docteur" by his fellow clochards) barely survives a murderous attack: Flemish boatmen pull him out of the Seine just in time. Activating her Alsatian relatives, Maigret's wife finds out that the victim must be a willful nonconformist doctor whose marriage had failed for reasons of incompatibility between the partners: his wife, having come by an inheritance, wanted to rise in society, giving parties (!) and receptions for that purpose, whereas the doctor wanted to follow the example of the famous humanitarian jungle doctor Albert Schweitzer, who established a hospital in Lambarene, Gabon. This would-be follower, however, was expelled because of his insubordination; returning Paris, he entered upon a "career" as a clochard. In the course of his investigation, Maigret comes to concentrate increasingly on one of the two supposed rescuers of the doctor. The latter had observed the boatman when he killed the father of his future bride (who would never have accepted him as son-in-law)—the man, in a drunken condition, having fallen into the water. The boatman, knowing or suspecting that he had been observed, wanted to eliminate the witness but again felt he was being observed and could do nothing but pretend that he was rescuing and pulling the doctor out of the water. Maigret needs only the testimony of the doctor in order to prove that.

The doctor, just coming out of a coma, uses tacit signals in order to make Maigret understand that his assumption is correct. But he stubbornly refuses to confirm it in language, even though he is able to do so. Obviously, social and legal normalcy has for him become a matter of complete indifference. Solidarity of and with the underprivileged, on the other hand, has become so important to him that he does not want to help file an accusation against the boatman; the doctor neither judges nor condemns. And it is now Maigret who follows him: "They had understood each other and Maigret smiled when he remembered that sort of complicity which had been established suddenly between them, under the Marie bridge" (*Maigret et le clochard*, 191).

The complicity between Maigret and the clochard(s) is tied to situations and occasions, not structurally fixed. Under "normal" circumstances, Maigret, like most people, would like to see wrongdoers punished, but in this novel there are frequent hints suggesting a substantial amount of sympathy for the life experiment of the doctor (*toubib*) and its connection with the more emphatic implications of clochard existence.

As a result, the novel delineates a structural potential in which Simenon comes close to an old demand of the US-American sociologist C. Wright Mills. The demand, which, as far as I can see, has become a reality only in very few cases, touches upon the necessity of a "sociological imagination." Mills appears to be in considerable agreement with the remarks on literature made at the beginning of this book when he says that literature, as well as sociology in its own way, should not dodge the task of working out imaginative shapes of what may count as historically real and its relevance for "the inner life and the external career of a variety of individuals"—in short, to establish intimate links between history and representative biographies. Confronted with the task of competing with an extremely dynamic historical reality and equally malleable political "facts" adduced in biographies, literary and sociological discourses both keep maneuvering on the edge of failure.[14]

With his style, Simenon accepts this challenge, but not by pouring, in a well-known literary fashion, a plethora of linguistic variations on his crime situations. Rather, he adopts a method of linguistic scarcity, strewing short suggestive remarks here and there. Thus, apart from the final remarks on complicity, there are just a few hints concerning not only a possible solidarity of the lower classes, but even solidarity between different classes: "There is, between these people there, more solidarity than between those who live normally in houses" (*Maigret et le clochard*, 121). Maigret's wife, "who had spent her life in order and decency" and could not believe that one could exchange the life of a doctor for that of a clochard, is told that he, Maigret, might understand the *toubib* who, he thinks, has been disappointed everywhere (91). Her further criticism, telling him that he spoke as if he had known the doctor all his life, is parried with the admission that this is partly so—"the human problem" resembles itself everywhere (117); at least, he claims, he is getting to know him better step by step (119–120). The Flemish boatman, too, suspected of murder and attempted murder (117), who is organizing his defense with considerable brusqueness, is pulled into the orbit of the "human problem" when Maigret develops a gripping and insistent image of the motivation for and course of the crime—that is, when he presents him with an imaginatively and empirically saturated version of the events (141, 163, 172).

Exploiting the vague term "imagination" epistemologically in no way indicates a return to the use of the term as a kind of royal way to the essence of being in Neoplatonism and Romanticism. With Maigret, the imagination maintains a close relation with what the experience of the detective accepts as probable facts. This is why even the idea of solidarity between different classes gains in probability, although it may not yet have turned into empirical reality. The objection that society in the time of the old Athens symposium was in fact a class society has no bearing, because structural alternatives did not belong to the repertory of possible thoughts or realities at that time. Moreover, the community of clochards and its rituals (which Simenon does not go into) can be taken only as a point of departure, in C. Wright Mills's sense, for thinking about probabilities and a direction of change in French class society for which such change does belong to the repertory of possible thoughts and realities—a possibility already seen to be emerging at the end of the discussion of salons in this book. There is quite some irony in this unlikely coupling of Proust and Simenon, insofar as a model for changes in class structure might owe some of its inspiration to the clochards. But nobody knows what is possible or not: in April 2021, French president Emmanuel Macron announced, in what was hailed as a revolutionary step, the dissolution of the École nationale d'administration, often referred to as the symbol of French inequality. This represents a drastic change in the state administration in France (as it seems) that only some years ago, as we have seen, Luc Boltanski declared to be the only embodiment of the state.

To the theses brought to bear in my argument on Simenon and only a small number of his texts, one might object that I am here elevating a few utopian motifs of minor importance into the last refuge of the symposium. This objection cannot be simply overruled, but it can be significantly weakened if one looks at similar, more systematically organized connotational spaces in the writings of G. K. Chesterton. I mention this because of the imaginative but also very empirically oriented epistemological drift in both writers. (Simenon, of course, does not share the religious element in Chesterton, but there are hints of the latter's socioeconomic ideas.) I also mention this because Chesterton, together with Hilaire Belloc, has shown that this epistemology can be enriched by remarkable socioeconomic elements that have enjoyed a brief existence at least as so-called distributism. The term refers to the search for a third way beyond capitalism and socialism, with a commitment to smaller forms of capitalism, a better distribution of the means of production, and more institutions of mutuality. Such ideas may belong to the "gallery of foolishness" that Hegel had identified earlier in his lectures on the history of philosophy, or they may have been overrun by the forms of big capitalism that they were intended to overcome. Such a fate is probably waiting for all projects devoted to a communitarian spirit that are not backed by strong institutional support. For their critics, they resemble, as does the unanimism of Jules Romains, either old dreams of Christian brotherhood or totalitarian mass regimes. Simenon, in his turn, does not offer institutional guarantees for his sparse hints concerning social alternatives. Although his image of society is conservative, it is an open, not a dogmatic, conservatism; it does not exclude soft spots and tacit possibilities.

Stieg Larsson and the Republic of Hackers

Using the example of Sweden (Stieg Larsson, 1954–2004) and the context of Austrian and German police work (Andreas Gruber, born in 1968), two authors have demonstrated the speed with which soft spots and tacit possibilities may acquire a realistic profile that, in its turn, can pose challenges to state power. An analysis of their textual models would appear to be urgent. In the Larsson texts, there is a direct confrontation between a shifting concept of crime and the modern welfare state in its Swedish—its most elaborate—form; Gruber presents speculative images of advanced police work and its implications. In both cases constellations are built up that may be interpreted as remote but emerging and modernized analogies of the idea of the symposium.

Whereas Simenon's French class society is only marginally perturbed, Larsson presents the bill for the much higher costs of the Swedish welfare state. If in Simenon's case the reader can still feel that French class society is also embedded in older life-forms and their partly sympotic rituals, Larsson reveals the paradoxes of democratic solidarity, a solidarity partly imposed, partly also dismantling itself and changing into its opposite. Larsson's text occasionally refers to Sweden as a dictatorship.[15] If there is anything to that, it casts an oblique light on sociological research concerning social cohesion, research that is obviously very different from C. Wright Mills's sociological imagination. Be that as it may, Sweden ranks very high on the index of successful social cohesion as documented in the Bertelsmann Foundation Social Cohesion Radar, according to which Sweden ranks fourth within a group of thirty-four Western states, surpassed only by its Scandinavian neighbors. Countries such as Germany, France, and Great Britain are left far behind, to say nothing of Italy, where social cohesion is weak. Decisions in this ranking were made primarily on the basis of income and the state of liberal democracy but also on well-being and "life satisfaction 'at present.'"[16]

Clearly, there is a conflict between Larsson's image of Sweden (or my image of Larsson's image) and social cohesion sociology, which concerns the criteria of democracy and life satisfaction. The difficulties of establishing data, of concept formation, and of empirical validation, especially with respect to the latter criterion, are well known. Using one of the big contemporary sociological theories would not defuse the conflict. Happy people, however diagnosed; dissatisfied ones; those profiting from or victimized by structural change—all would probably belong to the new middle class established by Andreas Reckwitz.[17] Perhaps we should pass over the conflict and grant some justification to both Larsson's image of Sweden and social cohesion sociology from time to time. The time index "at present" seems to hint at such a possibility, as does the somewhat vague reference to "post-materialist orientations." One significant gap, however, remains in this piece of comparative sociology. The essay by Delhey et al. fails to ask questions about the conditions of important and, as far as life opportunities and risks of existence are concerned, not only important but possibly crucial institutions. In Larsson's trilogy, psychiatry is moved to the center of attention; according to the putatively well-researched novel *1793* by Niklas Natt och Dag (2019), precursors of the social control exercised by psychiatry in Sweden date back as far as the eighteenth century.

Within the framework of modern democracies, the Swedish model can be described, without further proof, as the most elaborate welfare state to date. (Some would like to claim the beginnings of social security in Sweden for as early as the sixteenth century; whether one would be inclined to grant that claim after reading *1793* and its sequel *1794*, both of them, according to their author, thoroughly researched and dealing with the end of a very barbarous eighteenth century, must remain undecided here.) In any case, democracies do not automatically weaken or destroy the anchoring of existence in pleasurable group activities. In Larsson, though, a tendency toward the dissolution of solidarities is unmistakable: existential guarantees for individuals are shifting from group anchoring to abstract rights. Larsson may have overdone this tendency when he or his narrator (an irrelevant distinction here, since only the mention of the motif is in question) asserts that Swedish democracy is based essentially on one freedom, the freedom of opinion, which can be enjoyed by all Swedes, from "the most primitive Nazi to the stone-throwing anarchist" (*Vergebung*, 343). The problem here is that the exercise of such a freedom does not merely involve the utterance of a conviction; rather, the utterance is loaded with high amounts of affective charge. This is true, in various proportions, for all the "gifts" the welfare state has bestowed and keeps bestowing on its members, such as the contributions of the state to medical and unemployment insurance; as everyone knows, most of those who are happy or lucky enough to receive these "gifts" must also add their own contributions to them. No matter how client friendly the system of taxes and contributions may be, there is no honest way in which one can escape the interpretation that such contributions are an unpleasant burden or duty. This interpretation, in turn, is at odds with the feeling that basically the state might as well pay for everything—expectations that election campaigns nourish as much as possible.

Having to make regular and substantial contributions to a system of insurance that becomes more and more expensive while at the same time regarding them as a legitimate claim will, in the long run, reduce affective satisfaction and instead, more often than not, produce chronic dissatisfaction in the recipients of such state "favors." Neither freedom of speech nor financial claims, psychologically stored in narcissistic phrases such as "I am entitled to it," know any built-in limits; they can be expanded indefinitely. In combination with affective routine, they lead to the corrosion of efficient institutions that could provide some sort of socially relevant interactive pleasure or an experience of solidarity. It is noteworthy that the first volume of Larsson's trilogy mentions such groups (although these have already become ambivalent), including youth groups with manifold interests and Bible study groups (*Verblendung*, 277, 370, 374, 679), although, early on, nationalist Nazi groups are also mentioned (112–113, 214; see also 64). Above all, however, most of the first volume focuses on the interpenetrations of a family and its business empire. Although the protagonist of all three volumes, the journalist Mikael Blomkvist, charged by the family patriarch with searching for a member of the family who disappeared decades ago, brings to light a horrendous amount of perverse and mass murderous behavior as well as the threat of ruin for the business empire, the family member, once tracked down, returns and joins the board of directors. Firm and family continue to exist, despite several skeletons in the closet, in unstable and uneasy solidarity, at least in the shape of common business interests.

By contrast, the second volume is devoted almost exclusively to the fate of Lisbeth Salander, a computer wizard and expert hacker, described as extremely individualistic and indeed as asocial. Social institutions such as the legal system, psychiatry, churches, sects, and last but not least the family are held responsible, more or less directly, for Salander's lack of both social and sociable abilities (*Verdammnis*, 70, 379, 504). Her family in particular has disintegrated into adversaries locked in mortal combat against each other (709–728, 734–751).

The third volume widens Salander's asocial individualism (here used merely as a rough descriptive term) into an overall picture not of a Hobbes-like fight of everybody against everybody else but of groups fighting other groups. In due course, these fights absorb and exhaust the reserves of solidarity of all group members. No group is sufficiently homogeneous and therefore capable of developing the abilities and peculiarities of its members in notably different ways. Such developments are sometimes more useful to competitors than to the group itself—for example, in the case of organizations such as the media and the police (and its subgroups), as well as for political and even criminal formations. No group—more generally, no area of social reality—is able to offer activities that would, in Feldenkrais's sense, provide pleasure, that is to say the sensation, manifesting itself also bodily, of an action that one likes to perform and is able to do easily (see the first section of Chapter 1).

Such development follows from a fatal structural dynamic of democracy: the more a sociopolitical system grants rights and favors to all of its members, the faster rights and favors are transformed into seemingly self-evident claims for all individuals to make. Once this transformation has become a mental habit, individuals have no difficulty in identifying anything they wish for as potentially a claim and by extension a general right. This transformational chain from favor to claim to general right is particularly characteristic of advanced welfare states such as Sweden. The transformational chain, moreover, continues: individuals not only transform favors into claims and rights but anticipate and invent claims as rights. These inventions may be derived from natural law, from basic human rights, or from other parts of the legal system. In the framework of such processes, it is not the form of communication—that is, the situational adequacy of communicative steps taken—that is decisive; rather, it is the content, defined as justified and relevant, that carries the day. If this is not accepted by the powers that be, demonstrations must drive them into compliance.

In this way, the process of creating law is inverted. Its beginning is not marked by political conception and debate but by arbitrary opinions pitted against each other. Conceptual and behavioral dogma—that is, dogmatic opinion and demonstration—tend to arrogate priority to themselves. There is a direct pathway from opinion to demonstration, or worse, aggression. Whether justified or not (and who has the authority today to decide that?), the contents of opinions posing as justified claims know no limits. Traditional values have no chance against them—even Blomkvist, contradicting his own professional ethos, agrees to "the most macabre hush-up maneuver he has ever heard of" (*Verblendung*, 605).

If claims and opinions clash with existing laws, the outcome of the ensuing conflict is very uncertain, because the legal system, in the course of the permanent interpretation and reinterpretation of laws, has itself been drawn into the maelstrom of such developments. There is hardly any decision of high-ranking courts that is not pulled into the vortex of a series of dogmatic disputes. Larsson offers the example of perversions, whose definitions are stretched to such an extent throughout the three volumes that they can be applied only to extreme forms such as the most brutal and sexually tinged sadism. This is the case with Lisbeth's second guardian, a lawyer called Bjurman, as well as with the CEO of the family business mentioned above, the sadistic mass murderer Martin Vanger, who has built his own torture chamber (518–540). The concept is essentially absolute, because plausibilizing notions such as motivation do not seem to apply. (Private torture chambers seem to have become very popular in thrillers and should perhaps be investigated more closely.) Vanger argues coolly, vis-à-vis Blomkvist, that his crimes are merely "socially not acceptable," that they are directed mainly against "the conventions of society" (529). and he is prepared to discuss "the moral and intellectual aspects of my doings all night long" with Blomkvist (534).

A Seemingly Apologetic Remark in Between
It would be a mistake to assume that the theses advanced in the preceding few pages were meant as representations of conservative, right-wing, or reactionary positions. Rather, they are meant to be descriptions of a systemic logic, as probable realizations of a potential ambivalence in a double sense—namely, the combination of social-structural and intellectual

achievements of modern times. Of particular importance within the domain of intellectual achievements we would normally include the ideas of personal liberty and rights, which had been accepted as "inalienable" after extended conflicts within diverse anciens régimes. They became ambivalent—indeed, they had to become ambivalent—because they were thrown into the marketplace of ideas without any instructions for use, in particular, without any rules for temporarily halting their application in nontransparent situations.[18] It would be silly to think that one might discover such instructions in the programs of right-wing political groups. Both right- and left-wing groups, depending on country, may have enlarged their political territories for the time being, but their worldviews are far too simple to live up to the ambivalent dynamics of modernity.

On a smaller scale, Larsson's trilogy concentrates on drawing exemplary portraits of characteristic tensions and mutual (de)formations of persons and groups. Groups such as the Vanger family with its business interests, but also smaller- and middle-sized groups such as the investigative magazine *Millennium*, must manage—and indeed, manage fairly well—along the lines of both internal sociable relations and external social functions. With *Millennium*, it is particularly the self-imposed task of critical enlightenment that takes care of the affective saturation of most activities for most employees. Group cohesion is such that affective saturation together with investigative enlightenment is able to surmount difficult periods such as Blomkvist's absence owing to a prison term and his research for the Vanger family, or during the editor's, Erica Berger's, absence when for a short time she takes over a big daily newspaper. But *Millennium* is the only organization that can rejoice in the face of such a fate. The magazine broadens its basis of existence by turning into a life-form: in its offices employees may eat, drink, sleep, and more. Central as Blomkvist may be for all group functions there, his absences do not create interactive or more general communicative difficulties. His research (finding Harriet, the niece of the Vanger family and business patriarch) strengthens *Millennium* because the patriarch supports the magazine financially.

The relationship of any single person with a group, especially with their main group, can still be heightened into almost arbitrary emotional intensities or at least into protestations of such; it can also be used and incorporated as material for identification. An instructive example and late climax is supplied by the "drama" that flares up on the occasion of Erica Berger's abandoning *Millennium*, her "baby," for a new commitment that will be quickly canceled anyway. But the high emotional charge of many scenes cannot dispel the impression that there are no real binding forces between two or more people. The gap between protestation and real arbitrariness widens still more when sexual relations are in question (Larsson, *Vergebung*, 518, 525, 619, 640, etc.). Larsson's pedantic precision while keeping the accounts in that regard does not invest this domain of experience with an aura of intimacy but rather puts it away into the cool distance of a mechanical process.

The psychiatrist Teleborian holds that many "sociopaths" (697) are running around in Sweden. Although he is presented as a leading representative in his field, he must be seen very critically. If there is anything to his assertion, however, it will be relevant, more or less, for other countries as well; the number of mass-murderous attacks with firearms speaks all too clearly. Teleborian's opinion is even more relevant if one understands "sociopath" not as a clinical term but as an indicator of a mostly latent but easily triggered potential for violent behavior. This thesis reflects the way in which the complex of state and science perceives highly problematic social developments—namely, as threats to the orderly functioning of the state. The problem is exacerbated by the difficulty of formulating and implementing efficient responses to the threat. These can no longer consist merely in an increase in the severity of penalties: "sociopaths" could or would react to such measures with an escalation of violence.

Sociopaths enjoy a further advantage inasmuch as they can identify their enemy with relative ease; the state does not often have that chance. The fight against sociopaths, terrorists, and similar foes must therefore consist in measures planned and executed by experts who, if possible, are not known to the sociopath. An essential part of reality insofar as it is related to action, especially in the very long third volume (850 pages), is thus shifted to the formation of secret societies, whose existence, of course, is not officially acknowledged. A special logic of existence can be claimed by a secret organization within the security police: this paradoxical paragon of secrecy is so secret that neither its status (a section of "counterespionage"? [428]; "a secret operational department" [429]) nor its budget nor of course the civil identity of its members can be proven. The group itself pretends to be called, very appropriately, "Section for Special Analysis" (463). There are dark hints in the text that the group was involved, in one way or another, in the murder of (the real) Prime Minister Olof Palme (435), who, it is hinted, might have worked for the KGB (473). Larsson speculates about other historical prime ministers (Fälldin, Carlsson, Bildt III [431]). Their colleague in the fictional present, one of Palme's predecessors; the minister of justice; the head of the Office for the Protection of the Constitution; and a female collaborator (who, predictably despite being forbidden officially, strikes up a sexual relation with Blomkvist)—all of them have to be forced into doing their duty and shedding some light on the darkness of secrecy (432–440, 477–484, 507, 537, etc.). These difficulties are compounded by different levels of secrecy being accessible to different people and by the Section for Special Analysis, which tries to suppress belated effects: it appears that a crisis of state could still break out at any time, triggered by the ongoing activities of the former Soviet secret service man Zalatschenko, who had changed sides.

Zalatschenko is Lisbeth's father. With him and his factotum Ronald Niedermann, monster-like and insensitive to pain and in fact her half brother, Lisbeth finds herself in a permanent and violent conflict, which ends only when she is able to kill Niedermann and the former head of the very secret society shoots Zalatschenko. Andreas Gruber (see the next chapter) introduces a "Section d'intervention," which acts in France and on a very high professional level as an unofficial connection between criminal police, the secret service, antiterror groups, and economic-industrial espionage.[19] In Larsson, state power is troubled in several respects by Lisbeth. She herself does not have a clean slate (among other things, she has amassed, using illegal computer tricks, a huge fortune). But with the help of her lawyer (Blomkvist's sister), she uncovers the corruption jointly perpetrated by psychiatry and the legal system with such panache that the lawsuit against her is dropped.

This is not the end of Lisbeth's important contribution to the problem referred to here as symposium. In a conventional sense, she might be seen as the prototypical incarnation of the asocial person. The second volume, it would seem, illustrates in impressive detail her journey into an asocial or antisocial existence. We are following a character who does not conform to even minimal demands of consideration for others. At the same time, she embodies the resurrection of a single sympotic element better than any other figure in the book. While this sounds like a paradox, it is not. The strength of secret societies is in the interests of the state, but it is not built up in an abstract space: it takes place within personal networks. Binding forces in such networks may range from personal sympathies, joint activities, and exercises to ideological convictions. Swedish Nazi groups as well as national-socialist associations in general demonstrate, in the history of the early twentieth-century Europe, the excessive growth and finally a certain autonomy of the ideological dimension—that is, the destruction of sympotic impulses that may have been included at an earlier point. Larsson makes this very clear from the outset (*Verblendung*, 111–113, 214; for other political-ideological groups, see 64, 80). In the religious sphere, ideological convictions are transformed into enthusiasm or rapture (370); in secular groups analogies may appear in the shape of ethic reformulations (110, 605). The third volume concentrates on political scenarios (*Vergebung*, 112–113, 343–344, 431–433, etc.) that the general state prosecutor thinks will produce the most exciting investigations in Swedish history (675).

On the other hand, the icy asocial crusts of Lisbeth's personality are apparently melting to a large extent in the community of ingenious computer hackers. Her rigidity is replaced in part by groups with names clearly alluding to symposia of yore ("Mad Round Table," 381; "The Knights," 553). The groups add up to a "Hacker Republic," a "very exclusive club" open only to "the best of the best," an elite troop for which any military commander would have paid enormous sums (378). Online we read about a member of the club with whom Lisbeth works: "Plague was an intelligent, socially competent citizen. In reality, he was a highly overweight and socially dysfunctional early pensioner" (380). The Hacker Republic, the exclusive "club" working with the most advanced and secret computer technologies, is an answer to the secret organizations of the state working with older technologies such as firearms. This does not mean that the hackers can rely on perfect professionalism only—on the contrary; one could say that the further professionalism progresses, the more such groups will stand in need of Old European values and attitudes such as trust. The mechanisms for recruiting hackers must remain in the dark; no examinations or guidelines for recruitment exist. Members must assume that, professionally, other hackers are as excellent as they are, and they must feel sure than any effort at deception and fraud will be detected sooner or later. This might be called *negative trust*: it is a bet on equal competence, not on the immanent value of a person, but whatever we call it, it is of paramount importance. There would seem to be a crucial difference in comparison to the old symposium in that for the Republic of Hackers, physical presence is not a necessity for their forms of cooperation, but there are residual elements in the cooperation between Lisbeth and Plague that suggest that feeling comfortable with the other person might be a prerequisite for and in the Republic.

The role of trust as a necessary advance on expectations to be redeemed may occasionally check the dissolution of behavioral standards and their replacement by arbitrary claims. State institutions, too, must provide some space for such checks. Corruption, Larsson seems to say, has become ubiquitous; it cannot be stopped because the problem of controlling the controllers cannot be solved. In Larsson's trilogy, it is the Office for the Protection of the Constitution in whose members the terrifying feeling of state weakness calls forth the equally old-fashioned conviction that older methods might be more successful; yet this is true only in some cases. The remnants of the very secret society hire killers in order to get Blomkvist out of way, because he sits like a spider at the center of an informal personal network running crossways through all kinds of official institutions. But Blomkvist's contemporary network proves stronger, if only just barely (670–688).

Jacob Burckhardt thought that, in regard to classical Athens, we are unable to answer the question as to whether families were organized into *phratries*, the latter in their turn into *phylae*, and these again into *tribes*. But Burckhardt was also sure that he knew that in regard to outside relations, the *poleis* were dominated by hate and cruelty, by the idea of completely destroying external enemies.[20] In Sparta, losers could only choose between all kinds of slavery, destruction, and exile.[21] This conviction would suggest or indeed justify the assumption that "pathologies" belong to the evolution of societies. Apparently, in that development one is dealing not so much with specific problems but with intensities of problems, which are manageable as long as they do not turn into structural problems. If and how such transitions take place depends also on observers and on the ways in which observations are fed into the machinery and policies of the media. For modern societies, such a remark concerning the well-nigh immediate "mediatization" of anything that might be called an event offers nothing more than a tiresome triviality. The image of modern societies in Larsson's texts oscillates in a somewhat indeterminate fashion between the excitement of scandal discovery (especially in the magazine *Millennium*) and the routine of news fabrication, in which journalists are less interested than in fights with their colleagues.

In Athens, tragedy and comedy, and even more the symposium, assumed different perspectives of second-order observation. At the same time, the symposium stands out as a social and sociable institution in which matters of concern for a commonwealth between community and society were treated by way of intense and pleasurable interactivity. The possibility of such a simultaneous double orientation has become largely a matter of the past. Larsson's texts are suggestive because the formation of politically relevant sociable structures—namely, the Republic of Hackers— is shown to be possible even in highly advanced technological environments.

Andreas Gruber: The Detective as Genius and the Symposium in the Head

In the previous chapter, Sweden was taken as the paradigm of a modern (democratic) state. That form of the state is, of course, very different from the ancient *polis*, frequently if controversially defined as an urban state of citizens. In the modern state, the interaction of the citizens is replaced by state and national interests (such as territorial ones) of various kinds. The functional place of the symposium is now occupied, in Larsson's picture, mainly by informal personal networks, bolstered by trust and a high degree of professionalism. According to Henrik Vanger, the patriarch of the Vanger family business, even companies must and can build up such or similar structures:

> I have always tried to be a man of honor, even as a capitalist and as the boss of a company. . . . I have never played political games. I have never had difficulties in negotiations with the trade unions. I was concerned about ethics. I was responsible for a decent life of several thousand people; I took care of my employees.[22]

Looking at the modern state, we must get used to the idea, if we haven't already, that parts of the power of the state have changed owners: some of the networks, especially the technologically oriented ones, are, to quote George Orwell's *Animal Farm*, more equal than others. Their power, that is, may be subtler, but it reaches farther than the arm of the state. This is also one of the reasons why the function of sympotic elements has changed. If the symposium of old Athens can be understood as improving the internal stabilization of a *polis* constantly beleaguered by both external and internal forms of fate and contingency, the Republic of Hackers increases the risks of malfunction in modern nation-states and beyond. This is not inevitable: its probability also depends, in Larsson's text at any rate, on the extent to which the laws adopted by states try to regulate behavior in overly rigid ways. Increased rigidity entails decreased possibilities of control. Lisbeth Salander is also able to dupe the state because she thinks she has discredited its representatives of the law, whom she takes to be the primary exploiters and profiteers of only partly legal manipulative potentials that compel her to assume the role of victim. This argument touches upon an important motif in US-American political philosophy and sociology: thinkers such as Robert Paul Wolff, Barrington Moore Jr., and Herbert Marcuse were worried about the possibilities of the state's exercising control in the guise of tolerance ("repressive tolerance" [Marcuse]) or through the paradoxes of liberalism. Moore has published instructive contributions on trajectories from agrarian societies to modern industrial ones. Marcuse's concept of repressive tolerance points out that many forms of tolerance granted by the state are rather exercises in conformity in an oppressive climate of ill-understood total consumption. In *The Poverty of Liberalism* (1969), Wolff demonstrates how liberalism may easily end in the ridiculous idea of the sanctity of each and any individual impulse ("sanctity of idiosyncrasy"), but he has also rehabilitated forms of anarchism as the self-affirmation of the individual against claims of excessive power by the state (*In Defense of Anarchism* [1970]). In Wolff, both the criticism of liberalism and the rehabilitation of limited forms of anarchism are related to each other in an indissoluble contradiction, one that seems to characterize Lisbeth Salander aptly. It could also serve as the point of departure for an analysis of the Republic of Hackers: the sociable part of the new symposium is condensed in trust as a form of intimacy; its social component must be negotiated between transgression (Wolff's limited forms of anarchism) and moderate conformity (the hackers, after all, are not simply criminals).

Such conceptions, especially those of Wolff, vaguely foreshadowing new sympotic contours also serve to characterize the initial situations in a series of thrillers by the Austrian author Andreas Gruber (b. 1968) as a logical continuation of the scenarios in Larsson. It is true that, at first, the claims made here for the symposium, already sorely tried in the case of Larsson, may totally collapse in the novels of Gruber. In a pentalogy of thrillers, Gruber sends the Dutch detective, profiler, and instructor Maarten S. Sneijder to the front to solve advanced and complex crimes. Sneijder resembles an enhanced version of Sherlock Holmes: Sneijder has an almost unbelievable 100 percent success rate in solving cases (sometimes only 97 percent in blurbs). He can also boast of a 100 percent lack of any communicative and interactive or common-interest orientation; he practices autarchy as a form of self-sufficiency that does not shun the most violent conflicts with colleagues and superiors (of which there are anyway very few). Sneijder not only avoids sociable events but eschews any form of communication unless it has to do with his occasional function of instructor at the Federal Bureau of Investigation (Bundeskriminalamt) in Wiesbaden. He lives entirely by himself in a house that is almost inaccessible to anyone else. In difficult cases, information and instructions for his collaborators are given in the form of orders; there is no other talk. Gruber presents a milder version of Sneijder, mainly in insurance cases, with the private detective Peter Hogart. Hogart stands between Simenon's Maigret and Sneijder, as it were: what counts for him are, above all, "a sharp eye, some higher intelligence and empathy for the psyche of a criminal."[23]

Detective novels and thrillers can be criticized for many things; that they are replete with mythically stylized and therefore "unrealistic" characters who move on the edge of self-parody is probably the most important criticism, especially because defects in characterization entail other shortcomings. And in recent times, horror effects almost certainly have been overdone. All of these defects, however, can still serve very well as cultural indices. There are predecessors for Sneijder's refusal to talk to people or be together with them, as well as for his self-nomination as the genius of detectives, and not only in detectives such as Sherlock Holmes and a host of others. First, we must remind ourselves of—let us call it—Proust's assumption, according to which high intelligence may diminish or destroy sociable capabilities; Paul Valéry coined its classic formula in *Monsieur Teste*: "Stupidity is not my forte" (*La bêtise n'est pas mon fort*). In many of the famous fictional detectives, sociable inclinations tend to disappear completely. At the same time, the memory of the symposium returns in virtual form, as a symposium in the head, as it were.[24]

A large field of significance opens up when one puts this motif in context. Schopenhauer, for instance, in his prefaces sought conversations with his contemporaries, but only in order to tell them that he did *not* intend to enter into conversations or other forms of contact with them. Alfred Estermann has studied the way in which a conversation, hardly begun, ends with insults directed at possible addressees or philosophical adversaries.[25] Moreover, Schopenhauer's practice in his prefaces is not only very methodical but is embedded in a context of some significance in the history of ideas. In his biography of Schopenhauer, Rüdiger Safranski details its essential elements. The story begins at the end of the eighteenth century; a sociable, wine-drinking group comprising Hegel, Hölderlin, and Schelling is sitting together. The occasion is a serious one: they are thinking about how to create a new mythology for the times, which stand in dire need of it, or so they assume. No such mythology can be found in the texts of tradition; they will have to find it in their own heads. "Later, the protocol of this cheerful meeting was called the oldest program for a system of German idealism."[26] The ego would like to become part of the world, to "walk into greatness" in the company of the Romantics (194–195), but it distances itself from the moral assumption of ego power that Fichte had wanted to implant in the younger generation. For a while, the ambition is taken to reside in the aesthetic self-enjoyment of the "world-creative ego" (196). For Novalis, the archetype of the German Romantic poet (here Feldenkrais would come in again), the ego must first free itself from its enmity with the body: if human beings acquire a "certain and precise feeling for their body," then they will also be able to acquire true knowledge about their soul, the world, life, death, and the world of the spirit. The body promises the concreteness of knowledge, but unfortunately there is either too much or too little trust in the body and the ego. The ego may easily overreach itelf; it must find something firm. Only Fichte remains what he was: the moral ego in its massive seriousness (199; see also 198–199).

This ego posits itself in philosophical thought; it is formed and connects to others practically and most pleasurably in the sociable togetherness of small groups. To me, it seems emblematic of the situation that this togetherness, although present in the original group of Hegel, Hölderlin, and Schelling, did not last long—their egos parted company; their lives, doctrines (Hegel and Schelling), and textual orientation (mainly poetry with Hölderlin) went in different directions. The very idea of sociable closeness and philosophical thought, which might have provided the foundation for a new form of symposia, fell apart. In regard to both the communicative range of philosophical thought and adequate sociable forms, Schopenhauer, too, is shipwrecked. His philosophy posits an embodied but anonymous will as the unstable ground of human beings; therefore, sociability is practicable only as "a distant behaviour" (qtd. in English by Safranski, 291) as the art of pretending to go along with and participate in truth as the art of self-denial and resignation (290).

Western philosophy had been looking for an Archimedean standpoint to assure the certainty of being, thinking for a long time that it could be had by somehow participating in being. The tremendous changes in the world at the end of the eighteenth century, however, had caused such certainty to fall apart. The philosopher as an observer now believed he could construe stable, or at least unified, worlds using what seemed for a while to be the tremendous powers of the mind combined, for instance, with the experiential knowledge of the sciences. Schopenhauer, to give him his due, still had an inkling as to what participation in being might mean. There is the famous story that takes place in a hothouse in Dresden, where he was lost in contemplation of the physiognomy of the plants "speaking" to him. Even the sceptic Arnold Gehlen praises Schopenhauer's "intuition of the living organic form" in this case: "Whoever, in contemplating an animal, a leaf, was gripped by a nameless astonishment that something like this exists has understood one of the prime and original experiences of Schopenhauer."[27] The intuitive grasp of the beauty of a plant and its functionality is difficult; But even if it were possible, we could not apply such modes of understanding to grasping a person and their individuality or to the group behavior of people; it cannot be transferred to the intuitive grasp of an individual person or to the ways in which an individual behaves in a group (see also Safranski, *Schopenhauer*, 438). Ludwig Feuerbach (1804–1872) was probably the last thinker who, in his own kind of strange emotional anthropology, thought he could elevate the senses of the body into the "organ of the absolute" and a community of people into the reality of freedom and infinity—in contrast to "solitude," which he understood as limitation (Safranski, 450).

Meanwhile, such ways to being and to the being of other persons have been barred. The second-best possibility for reopening paths, however indirect, that lead to other persons, in order to construct at least images of community, lies in the self-optimization of thought. In other words, consciousness must look for and cultivate the intimate acquaintance of what it experiences as the best thoughts in terms of insights about itself and others. This experience expands into its form of (mental) sociability. Alexander Pope's "What oft was *Thought,* but ne'er so well *Exprest*" (*Essay on Criticism* [1711], line 298), a recommendation of average enlightenment, is not enough here. Pope delivers verses of highly quotable wisdom for literary colleagues and more generally for a "good society" and their circles of sociability. Schopenhauer's sociability of consciousness, sometimes also called "thinking for oneself" (*Selbstdenken*), is quite a different matter. He practices this in the long years in Frankfurt, mainly during the three morning hours he spends writing and rejecting the abundant possibilities of conventional sociability during a long lunch in a restaurant called Englischer Hof (English Court). The person thinking in solitude (*der geistvolle Mensch*) is like a small world unto themselves. Indeed, Schopenhauer has unpleasant things to say about "ordinary" sociability ("All crooks are sociable," he says in the first volume of *Parerga und Paralipomena*, chapter "Paränesen und Maximen.") But even for Schopenhauer, the matter does not rest there. While the preference for solitude is emphatic and undisputed, in the volume just mentioned, its value depends to some extent on age: solitude is easier for older people. Moreover, not everyone can claim to possess one of the very best minds; for lesser minds, sociability is like people warming up each other. The space Schopenhauer grants, again in the first volume of *Parerga und Paralipomena*, to the discussion of the status of a person in society ("Von Dem, was Einer vorstellt") according to rank, honor, and fame is much more copious than the space devoted to what somebody is or possesses. Entering the world at birth, we find ourselves already in a community of parents and often siblings. We need society, but we participate in it while remaining basically alone. Safranski (497) quotes the advice to import one's solitude into society, that is, into circles of sociability.

Similarly, the detective Sneijder chooses the most difficult crimes as the circle of sociability for his mind. Analogous to Schopenhauer, his claims for his philosophy of crime and the possibility of solving crimes are lofty; for the rest, he is alone. The basis of a common approach to thought and to thought about crime is condensed into one sentence: "Western religions rely on redemption by somebody else (some Messiah), Asian religions rely on self-redemption."[28] Max Scheler would have agreed. Redemption in Indian thought is self-redemption in the act of knowledge. Again according to Scheler, there is no savior with the attributes of God but only a teacher of wisdom who shows the way.[29] In the present context, this is not merely a fundamental difference between abstract worldviews but also between the top levels of professionalism. Sabine Nemec is the only colleague with whom collaboration seems possible for Sneijder, and it does in fact begin. Sneijder thinks she is adequately qualified according to his standards, but even she takes Sneijder's description of the religious difference as one befitting an egocentric.[30] She is mistaken. Self-redemption in the sense of Zen Buddhism starts by freeing the mind from the dross of everyday trivialities; it then catalyzes the process of the continuous self-optimization of the detective's mind. Quite in line with this, Sneijder begins one of his rare self-introductions with the professional stylization of the cognitive situation of Simenon's Maigret. Maigret had claimed to be able to imagine and therefore to solve a crime. Sneijder maintains that he practices a "method of visionary seeing" that he uses, in an elaboration and further development of another colleague's method of cross-examination, in order to descend into the "maw of hell." According to his method, he identifies with the criminals, connects to their minds, and learns about "things which nobody should see." The "art" of the detective, then, does not consist in feeling pity for the victims but in understanding why the crime provides extreme excitement for its perpetrator. "You have to enter the mind of the murderer and learn how to love evil."[31] The ultimate climax of this argument occurs in the novel *Todesmärchen* with the deadly duel between Sneijder and his son Piet van Loon, whose life has driven him into an extraordinary criminal career. He is different from other murderers for the same reason that distinguishes his father from other detectives: "He studies his environment and the people with whom he has to do very precisely. It is uncanny. He feels his way into them, knows what they think and knows how to manipulate them."[32] The more a colleague such as Sabine Nemec is capable of plunging into the seas of such ideas, the more Sneijder's behavior toward her takes on sociable traits. In its shortest form, the central insight goes: "The closer you come to madness, the better you understand reality."[33]

The connection between theoretical aspects of consciousness with sympotic and professional matters in detective work has a long history. We may recall the roles of music and drugs in the Sherlock Holmes stories. We find an almost exact parallel in Sneijder, who smokes marijuana all the time (in order, he says, to keep his headaches at bay); he drinks vanilla tea by the liter and practices acupuncture on himself. Music has, of course, belonged to the basic sympotic and cultural equipment of humanity for centuries. Since the eighteenth century, this achievement has often sunk into a latency just below the cultural surface, but it can be reactivated at any time. With an emphasis on the form of a crime—that is to say, the precise and aesthetically conspicuous elaborateness of its perceptible structure, implying a certain distancing of average humanity—both the criminal and the great, sensitive detective may come close to artists and their claims for the cultural level of their work. In Gruber, murders are committed that follow the patterns and motifs of fairy tales or insist on the pictorially careful exhibition of the victims. In such cases, the reasoning of criminals and investigators is organized as an extended self-mirroring. By dint of his professional perfection, Sneijder turns into the myth of a specialized but objective spirit and into a basic figure of the virtual symposium—in other words, into a basic figure of today's subjectivity as the mental form of sociable solipsism. The more the consciousness of the detective operates along the lines of logic and imagination, the more it leaves everyday modes of thought behind. This is also the gist of Proust's assumption, already quoted several times, according to which high intelligence reduces the need for social contact. This form is highly sociable and reduced at the same time. It is not based on real—that is, bodily or materially grounded—elements that our concept of reality normally demands. That the virtual symposium in the mind may be far more real than the other kind was noted by Paul Valéry in a very succinct and telling way, when in the year of his death, 1945, he said that his "cahier perpétuel" (the exercise books in which, each day for long hours in the early morning for decades, he had been jotting down "his" ideas) were his "Eckermann."[34] Today all social forms are incorporated and restaged by markets, mechanisms, and media. Valéry's practice of the imaginary, by contrast, foreshadows the contours of what Hamlet called "a consummation devoutly to be wished."

Hamlet is a crime story. And there is another Shakespearean crime story in which the image of the mind as a quasi-symposium in the self-production of thought shows up for the first time. After Richard II, in the play of the same title, has been deposed by Henry IV and is held captive, waiting for his execution, he starts observing the workings of his mind:

> My brain I'll prove the female to my soul, / My soul the father, and these two beget / A generation of still-breeding thoughts, / And these same thoughts people this little world, / In humours like the people of this world; / For no thought is contented. The better sort, / As thoughts of things divine, are intermix'd / With scruples, and do set the word itself / Against the word . . . / Thoughts tending to ambition, they do plot / Unlikely wonders."[35]

CHAPTER 11

Consequences and Conclusion(s)
The Anthropological-Institutional Trap and the Resurrection of Literature

(RE)TURNING TO SHAKESPEARE must signal at least a partial step toward a rehabilitation of literature that was exposed to some skepticism in the beginning of this book. In Shakespeare, the self-production of thought, the symposium in the head, takes place as a continuous movement between literal and metaphorical dimensions. It is spurred on by an unbounded imagination. In the texts by both Simenon and Gruber, the literal-metaphorical process has to share its constitutive textual role with logic and information. In this triple orientation, the texts seem to be able to escape what I shall call the anthropological-institutional trap. This is the conflict between what philosophical anthropology above all has to say about the essential properties of human beings and the impact of institutions, including larger economic, social, and even national organizations of human life. In the perspective of institutions and larger organizations, the practice of the "original" symposium has become impossible, mainly because, in human evolution, bodily grounded communication and interaction have lost substantial parts of their previous status. The texts by Simenon and Gruber have replaced them with a sociable solipsism, that is, a symposium in the head. Literature as a symposium in the head has its greatest chances in forms of rearrangement of imagination, logic, and information. There is no need to insist upon the necessity that such rearrangements be distinguished by complex elasticity rather than rigid simplicity.

Societies and Survival

This demand for elastic rearrangements of imagination, logic, and information entails a second one. The question of cohesion in the case of larger or even very large associations such as nations has already been mentioned several times. Since this book cultivates a certain preference for literary representations of sympotic configurations in which the units of investigation are smaller, it must be understood that judgments concerning larger structures can be impressionistic at best. Today it would appear that such structures (such as nations) stumble back and forth between global pressures and their own remaining but diminished capacities for self-determination. Their destiny need not automatically decide on the development of smaller associations such as sports clubs or very small ones such as dog breeders and choral societies. Depending on circumstances and conditions such as mutual personal acquaintances, definitions of goals, activities, and the like may secure survival for a comparatively long time. Although it is mentioned in Aldous Huxley's *Brave New World*,[1] the joke according to which it is not the philosophers but the fretsaw workers and the stamp collectors who make up the backbone of society need not be taken literally, although such jokes may contain a grain of truth.

Alehouse politics and politicizing swagger or politicizing gestures practiced in small associations or by groups of regulars in pubs do not establish any real contact with the political dimension properly speaking, even if politics meanwhile may occasionally have become similar to political swagger. In many cases, politics may have lost its own systemic structure and become the prisoner of lobbies and special interests of various kinds. It was precisely the task of the old symposium to maintain possibilities of relation between all kinds of existential dimensions, from communicative stagings of the body to those with a real or only apparent lack of bodily involvement such as politics or philosophy. The evaluation of potential successors, some of which have been analyzed here, allows us to assume that, notwithstanding the assertions in Chapter 1, modern societies have preserved comparable and related forms but have drastically cut down on the range of human involvement. This by itself does not amount to much because, in spite of manifold connections, the cohesion of societies must be distinguished from their continuance and survival: both may but need not be correlated. Depending on circumstances, identical guarantees of survival such as military strength may produce highly divergent effects. While the Roman Empire lasted for about a thousand years, Hitler's Thousand Year Reich barely made it to twelve years; the life span of the Athens of antiquity was somewhere in between. The example of the British Empire shows that structural weaknesses endangering national or parts of social existence may be barely visible and yet have their effects. At regular intervals there is talk about specific national illnesses, supposedly referring to some particularly dangerous shortcoming. There has been talk, for instance, about an "English disease" (allegedly consisting in militant trade unions, traditional management linked to those privileged by the social structure, and in general sticking to the wrong traditions). Such alleged diseases, people think, may push a country to the brink of disaster. At the same time, such thinking cannot but sound arbitrary. This also holds for converse assumptions concerning the beneficial or detrimental effects of expenses reduced in one socioeconomic field for the advantage and advance of other fields. Sometimes apparent miracles happen, but we cannot rely on their arrival.[2]

And yet we can suppose that internal cohesion, preferably brought about in a way at least comparable to the Athens symposium, improves the chances of survival considerably. Even under Roman rule (from 146 BC onward), Athens maintained the relative integrity of its culture, which attracted foreigners, especially the Romans themselves, in great numbers. If we include its cultural longevity, the survival value of Athens as a model can be set at about one thousand years.

Implicit Anthropology and the Symposium: The End of an Affair

The cultural longevity of Athens should warn us not to underestimate the long-lasting vitality of the symposium. Its anthropological ground, as I am not tired of repeating, is not anchored in any static basis; rather, it is the result of a plurality of interactive and communicative as well as playful investments of bodily (including sensual) and spiritual sources of vitality in the context of smaller to medium-sized groups. The symposium enhances pleasurable vital tensions in ritualistically regulated ways; equipped in such ways, the symposium deserves the title of an implicit anthropology with its performance relatively unimpaired by systemic social constraints. Historically, the guiding thesis of the present volume is that, in Europe at least till the end of the eighteenth century, various selected elements of the symposium have been kept alive and assembled into widely different models. Dr. Johnson in England and Diderot in France were two famous symposiarchs, comparable though not identical in what they had to handle as productive sociable units. From the nineteenth century onward, social disparities having to do with a polemical deterioration of class distinctions in the face of so-called democratic movements, have made nonsense of that implicit anthropology. The virulence of class distinctions does not tolerate the idea of a common humanity, which consequently emigrates into a type of emotionalized, intellectually often limited novel. Taking England as an example, I follow David Cannadine's views in *Class in Britain*, for whom the eighteenth century had "class without class struggle" (the title of his second chapter). But the nineteenth century did not only entertain various models of class, with notions of hierarchy being preferred: "the significant difference was that these visions of society were now more consciously and contentiously politicized than before, at least until the 1840s." Cannadine adduces "the seismic shocks" of the French Revolution, the Agricultural and Industrial Revolutions, and population growth as the driving forces behind this hardening of class distinctions. It is also visible in the polemical terminology used by Matthew Arnold in *Culture and Anarchy* ("populace," "philistines," "barbarians").[3]

In some ways, Arnold's polemical terminology (especially the terms "populace" for the common people and "barbarians" for the aristocracy) is reminiscent of the Middle Ages, when elements of sympotic culture were overrun by barbarian forces. Here, the carriers of culture—namely, the aristocracy and the various courts—were busy fighting for territorial gains and intradynastic positions of power. While there certainly were sympotic elements of all kinds, behavior, despite an abundance of ritualizations, was more precisely characterized by anarchic brutality. There are telling descriptions in Arno Borst's *Lebensformen im Mittelalter* (Life-forms in the Middle Ages)—see his chapter on human beings and communities.[4] "All people stand at the edge of death; their games with each other hardly know any social rules at all. Between sophisticated psychological calculus and brutal slaughter there is hardly any distance." The ideas about human beings cultivated by kings and bishops "converge in the contempt of Christian and humane behavior according to norms. . . . The Christian church and the Frankish empire invoke old prescriptions, the Ten Commandments and the loyalty of family and men, but their rank . . . must be daily fought for."[5] The risks of existence did not only stem from biological and geographic conditions that small groups had to master but also from the fights for and between larger associations—that is, from questions of rule and hierarchy. Where human beings stand against each other eye to eye, there is no continuity in behavior, only a pure present.[6]

Philosophical Anthropology and the Idea of the Full Human Being

It is possible to see erosions of the sympotic idea and practice in the Renaissance, too. Habermas has singled out the change from social differentiation in terms of close or extended family relations to increasingly centralized forms of power in the development of nation-states. In the latter, the growth of classes defined primarily in socioeconomic terms diminished the importance of families and their ways of sociability.[7] In earlier parts of this book (see the third section of Chapter 1 and the second section of Chapter 3), I have justified my extended use of German philosophical anthropology historically. The catastrophic outcome of World War I for Germany appeared to compel German philosophy early on and with greater urgency than elsewhere to reexamine the range of human potential. This had not been so difficult to fathom before then, because the traditional low speed of change in assumptions about or definitions of what a human "essence" might consist in did not seem to call for radical revisions. There had been, of course, the rumblings of challenge issued by the various so-called revolutions (French, industrial, agricultural; see Cannadine above). But these could not come close to the experience of the loss of masses of human lives in the war. Moreover, the millions of people killed as never before in an industrialized war demanded an explanation of mass destruction as a human or social failure. While philosophical anthropology remained anthropology in the sense of Max Scheler's *The Human Place in the Cosmos*, other thinkers such as Gehlen ultimately undermined their own original approach by stressing the role of institutions. Still others, as we have seen in the case of Plessner, came to privilege the beneficially humanizing function of masks, that is to say, a general restraint in the management of human impulses and therefore an emphasis on sociability. Philosophical anthropology therefore was and has remained a highly instructive example of theoretical initiatives that were analytically and descriptively very productive and yet maneuvered, more often than not, on the brink of self-refutation.

It is safe to say, therefore, that it was this mode of thought that, while trying to revise the canon of the human, had to acknowledge that such a canon was no longer possible. This also came to mean that a mode of thought that, according to some of its representatives, came to insist on the constitutive role of institutions had failed to do justice to their dynamism. Theories that seemed destined to supply us with conceptual options for a theory of the symposium or its possible successors locked themselves out of this enterprise.

Thus it happened that the unifying impulse of philosophical anthropology broke apart. Scheler still could talk about the "wholeness" of the human being. Gehlen, in his turn, while confirming the validity of large parts of Scheler's anthropology, wiped Scheler's foundations off the anthropological map. He criticized the vagueness of Scheler's cornerstone, hidden somewhere in the religious domain and eradicated Scheler's central human category, spirit, because the latter had set it up as a principle opposed to life.[8]

Most of Scheler's other views, Gehlen thought, could claim a far stronger persuasive power ("Scheler," 248), although its full scope was not apparent because Scheler could not have known about the most recent advances in biological behavioral research (concerned with the importance of instinctual reduction).

Gehlen was touching here upon a dilemma of his own as well as of (philosophical) anthropology in general. Kant had provided a basic model with his *Anthropology from a Pragmatic Point of View*—suggestions and instructions for a better knowledge of human nature and the ways of the world, also of an empirical kind, of the world and human beings. But this model was no longer enough, because now the findings of "positive" sciences such as biology had to be taken into account. As soon as the anthropologist uses information supplied by these disciplines (today, for instance, neurobiology), the question of dubious dependency arises. Nobody can assimilate and appreciate all the scientific information that might be relevant, nor can it be welded into a unified picture. Gehlen initially believed that there could be a "total theory" (*Gesamttheorie*) presenting a magnificent picture of the suffering and Promethean human ("Ein Bild vom Menschen" [1941], 50–62, 248), but the total theory was soon cut down to a "complete system" or "complete scientific approach" and then further reduced to "models" or model pictures as experiments in fragmentation ("Zur Systematik der Anthropologie" [1942], 65–112). Constructing a system is already difficult enough: human beings as "unspecialized beings," equipped with nothing but a brain representing infinite plasticity, must cope with a progressive "indirectness of behavior" and a gap between drives, desires, and interests, on the one hand, and actions, on the other. The full human being is receding into thin air (63–112, 69, 85, 87, 96, 101).

In regard to our topic, it follows that heterogeneous and changing sociocultural conditions will force people to develop different "materializations" of their infinite plasticity. While this does not necessarily throw the idea of the symposium and its analogies into havoc, it definitely does not make their institutionalization any easier. More or less centralized modern nations, to say nothing of older and authoritarian ones, depending on or enforcing disciplined behavior, do not tolerate each and any transformation of desires and impulses into action. In Gehlen's view, drives, desires, and impulses that do not find external objects of satisfaction will continue as phantasms and, at best, ideas "in the sphere of inner worlds" (111). This would support my thesis concerning the symposium in the head and may also serve as part of an explanation for the high value we have come to place on the imagination.

According to this perspective, the crucial problem of the present volume can be reformulated in the following way. If, as the years 2020, 2021, and 2022 (so far) have amply demonstrated, the outer world and in particular its political dimension becomes restrictive or repressive, then the sphere of complex or diffuse, possibly also aggressively tinged, inner worlds will widen. Communication, motivational arrangements, and action will then become more than usually ambiguous and multidimensional, carrying more than the ordinary number of mental reservations. Certainly, dialogues in antiquity practiced indirectness and ambiguity; people knew, especially with the weakening of myths, that action might be subject to more than unilinear motivation. But the dominion of multiple motivations in that time appears to have been more limited than in ours.

In his later essays, Gehlen seems to have taken into account such perspectives. He dismantles the idea of the wholeness of human beings that he himself had promoted ("Der gegenwärtige Stand der anthropologischen Forschung" [1951], 122); there are only "fragmentary results" (125) that must give us an idea of how pluralistic and indeed anarchic human tendencies are ("Der Mensch im Lichte der modernen Anthropologie" [1952], 128). The "history of anthropology" ("Zur Geschichte der Anthropologie" [1957], 143–164) would strongly argue for close ties between the "fluidity of our drives, the activity of the imagination, the manifold and colorful external circumstances"—in short, the "fantastic vegetation of our inner world and the diversity of institutions, the astounding, contradictory abundance of customs" (161).

The Sphere of the Inner World and the Anthropological-Institutional Trap

At this point, at least since the eighteenth century, the anthropological-institutional trap looms large. Since Gehlen himself speaks of a contradictory abundance of customs and institutions, we may and must ask how close—and free of contradictions of their own—ties between the "fluidity of our drives, the activity of the imagination, the manifold and colorful external circumstances"—in short, the "fantastic vegetation of our inner world and the diversity of institutions, the astounding, contradictory abundance of customs" are supposed to be. Human beings are not sure of their instincts, but they are full of energy; the risks following from this situation must somehow be controlled. For Gehlen, this task rests plainly with social institutions, but he neglects to tell us how the institutions of customs, of the law, of the rules of living together, of family, work, and state must themselves be ordered, how their historical development must be assessed if they are to regulate anarchic drives in the best possible ways. The main thing for him seems to be that they simply exist; he says nothing about the degree(s) to which they can legitimately claim the obedience of the individual. Human beings spend their energy fighting against nature, against other people, against their own inner world—possibly, in the end, against the culture they themselves have created ("Ein anthropologisches Modell" [1968], 215). About this, Gehlen is very eloquent, but he keeps silent about whether, how, and under what institutional conditions we may also enjoy our energies. We do not learn anything about the driving forces that are or should be responsible for changes that are necessary in the institutions themselves.

By contrast, the analyses of this book support the premise that it matters less whether institutions spare us the trouble of making risky decisions from one situation to the next than whether they allow us to spend energies in pleasurable ways and to what extent they make this possible. Eighteenth-century thinkers such as David Hume and Edmund Burke knew, as we have seen, that societies must permit the development of experiences and behavioral patterns that are at least comparable to pleasure if they want to secure their own long-term acceptance.[9] Where this happens, we find ourselves in sociable institutions, the archetypal paradigm of which is here taken to be the symposium in ancient Athens.

In Chapter 3, I quoted Arno Borst on the Middle Ages, whose descriptions allow us to assume that autocratic, dictatorial, authoritarian, or repressive forms of rule—unsurprisingly—are not interested in either the theory or the reasonable practice of pleasure—unless that practice in some way takes the form of *panem et circenses*. At this point, looking at the complex of pleasure and the efficiency of rule, a comparison between utopian texts such as George Orwell's *Nineteen Eighty-Four* and Aldous Huxley's *Brave New World* may be rewarding: the relatively brutal and joyless methods in the former seem to be less effective than the sophisticated and pleasurable techniques in the latter. In the Middle Ages, the combination of ritual and the immediacy of behavior in Borst's sense may have pushed the question of bodily, socially, and intellectually communicative experience into the background anyway.

Soon after the Middle Ages if not earlier, a regulation of bodily behavior set in that changed culture considerably. Rudolf zur Lippe, for one, has analyzed what he calls the subjection of nature in the case of human beings; he describes, for instance, postmedieval new dances as forcing movement into antibodily rhythms.[10] While this does not ring in the end of sociability, it indicates a degree and direction of artificial ritualization that marks the beginning of state intervention in the organization of pleasure. This becomes plain with the increase in institutions of control and organizational techniques (government cabinets, police, the secret service, standing and regular armies) on the part of the state and is conspicuous in the inflationary production of ideas about reform or revolution, mostly though not exclusively on the part of secret societies. As soon as state institutions betray signs of weakness in the implementation of control, Mafia-like organizations take over; disempowering or eradicating undesirably soft, often democratic forms of communicative action by eliminating the body as such—that is, murder. For this reason, the present volume has had to offer at least a few rough sketches on the psychocultural and political functions of the secret and its extensions (see Chapter 8).

Both sides, the state and its secret or open critics, had and have to establish priorities; these have to do with the securing of rule, on the one hand, and with social reform and possibly revolution, on the other. These priorities do not quench the desire for sociability, which under the hard conditions of life remains unbroken and may even increase. At the same time, however, sociability may become dubious, because it is undermined by what Gehlen calls the transfer of phantasms and ideas into the sphere of the inner world. There may be a shift of pleasurable entertainment into the reading of literature and in many cases into the fascination of fantasy worlds. But there is also the drawback of its reverse: the vital impoverishment of solitary reading and of the "beautiful souls" formed by reading as much as possible, whose misery is described by Goethe in *Wilhelm Meister.* Not to make too much of it, but the procedure in a representative volume on literary culture and social (sociable?) life in Germany from 1789 to 1806, *Literarische Kultur und gesellschaftliches Leben in Deutschland 1789–1806* (1988), shows this duality to still be rampant. The volume mentions that Jean Paul met the Countess Schlabrendorff in the Berlin salons but does not say a word more on the cultural significance of Jean Paul's relationship with salons. Yet it is a well-known fact that Jean Paul, in many respects an extraordinary man, was overwhelmed by the enthusiasm, especially from the female side, that welcomed him in the salons. The enthusiasm soon died away as a result of his often unusual behavior; his much-admired texts did not save him because, while admired, they were also held to be very difficult.[11] The volume just mentioned does not go into these ambiguities but devotes itself to the analysis of the pleasure—perhaps one should say the lust—of reading, "one of the most seductive of pleasures," attracting the reader with such intensity that one cannot tear oneself away and neglects one's social duties.[12] In the context of the present volume, this situation must instead be evaluated as a *literary transformation of culture* springing up powerfully as sympotic pleasures become more difficult to handle. In German literature, Jean Paul is one of the strongest examples in this regard: he is the lone wolf (though in principle very sociable) whose texts abound with sociable situations. Literature is interesting because it analyzes the sympotic shortcomings in the culture at large to which it partly owes its own existence. Goethe's novel *Wilhelm Meister* can be seen as a cost-benefit analysis of pleasure, especially as far as the arts contribute to the "cultural apparatus for producing joy";[13] Karl Philipp Moritz's novel *Anton Reiser* is even more thorough in this respect. Sociability does not die out, but its radius of activities and spectrum of experience are narrowed down. Political discussions alert the secret police; dimensions of erotic or generally human and world experience tend to suffer from scientific, philosophical, or moral neutralization. Klaus Vieweg, for instance, has traced the effects of the Carlsbad Decrees (1819) on the very interesting life of sociability in Berlin and especially in regard to Hegel—Hegel, on whose negotiations between philosophy and sociability but also on whose cognitive incompatibility of the two one could write an entire book.[14]

The growing incompatibility of discourses, in their turn, and the disparate directions the development of professions seemed to take in the nineteenth century eliminated the communicative advantages the French salons in particular had enjoyed up until then. After World War I, this could be felt as a liberation, which in the German Weimar Republic it was indeed, in all respects. Today's media are still exploiting that unique situation; the success of the TV series *Babylon Berlin* (from 2017 onward) is ample proof of this psychocultural liberation, including forms of sociability hitherto unknown. The liberation effect, together with its opportunities for sociability beyond old boundaries, is also remarkable because of its depiction of class structure. In point of fact and not only in Germany, class *structures* lost a great deal of importance with the breakdown of the old regimes after the war. Within the tendencies of political chaos, however, class *distinctions* could be retranslated into rigid and polemical *ideologies*. In Europe after World War I, in any case, the frequency of fascist dictatorships, with dire consequences for sociability, provides ample evidence for that. Meanwhile, the feeling that any opinion can be ideologically and fanatically charged has ultimately propelled the party into first place as the basic and most popular type of sociability simply because it is easiest to escape from any unpleasant situation there. Even so, such situations—merely talking to the wrong person, for instance—are not exactly rare, and thus the party has declined into a somewhat boring commodity. Its rhythm of establishing, intensifying, and abandoning contact outweighs a large part of the initial attraction. The twenty-first century has therefore begun to look for alternative forms. In some of them (e.g., Burning Man), whether intentionally or not, selective borrowings from the symposium are obvious. Yet one crucial aspect, the transition of sociability into social or political relevance (relations between the economy and the environment, climate, migration, etc.), though intended by many, is difficult to perceive, at least for the time being.

There are no simple remedies for such deficiencies. But it is, or has become, a truism that it is not a lack of solutions but probably the style and "culture" of debate about solutions that is at fault. In German, there is the treacherous term for a culture of quarreling (*Streitkultur*), a culture that is believed to be lacking. But insofar as it is a culture of pitting opinion against opinion, we do not need it—a culture of elastic negotiations seems much more desirable, although it is also much more unfashionable. Borrowings for such a style or culture could again be made from the classical symposium—at least if we trust the descriptions of Jacob Burckhardt. (That additional ancient Greek styles, cultures, and techniques of gaining knowledge might be very useful as well cannot be discussed here.)

And there is a second possibility foreshadowed at this point, where the classical symposium appears to have reached the end of its tether and totally different options, such as the symposium in the head, seem to emerge. Mainly, it is a question of the reemergence of what is often somewhat too glibly called literature, a field of discourse occasionally treated harshly in this book. More precisely, I want to ask whether a slight shift in the components we can expect to be present and active in literature might not increase the effectiveness of literary discourse, components inspired by the detective novel and the symposium in the head: logic, information, and imagination. Their relative importance enjoys more variations than what we normally identify as literary elements. Let it be said that although in regard to the imagination there is a comparative freedom, there is no autonomy. By contrast, we encounter a telling historical example in Samuel Taylor Coleridge's effort to give their due to all components in his work. (There are, of course many more such examples, especially in those cases, including many forms of Romanticism, in which we habitually take the autonomy of the imagination for granted.) Finally, I propose to connect the conceptual trio with an older theory of productive metaphor that was sketched, without great effect, it seems, about a hundred years ago.

The Symposium in the Head and the Role of Literature

The classical symposium is a thing of the past, and with it, though some time later, disappeared the idea that, for the purpose of social cohesion, it might be replaced with convincing motivational equivalents such as shared values or solidarity—not to mention charity. The conviction that people, in times of need, would hold back their sacred egotism has vanished; we cannot even be sure that an effort to move in such a direction would be worthwhile today. Not only has the "international community," so much invoked, become a fiction or always been one; in the meantime, even the nation has turned into a merely imagined idea. Smaller units, presumed to be unities, will follow. The sociologist Helmut Schelsky, in the wake of World War II, stated peremptorily that many traditionally sacred concepts, ideas, and notions had been deprived of their former solidity, their substantial and experienced reality. The place of experience in the family, the city, or the countryside, in professional companies and enterprises or in workers' unions, has been usurped by thinking in terms of programs, doctrines, generalizable articles of belief—in short (again), of ideologies. Many sociological diagnoses have, in terms of their factual content, simply become wrong.[15]

We need not discuss here to what extent this diagnosis is still correct or if it has to be extended to other areas of experience. In many domains the increased distance between discourse and experience can hardly be disputed. The notion of experience itself as something to be directly ascribed to a person has been relativized in many ways and sacrificed to the incessant bombardment of the media. In any case, all of these trends might rehabilitate a field of discourse in which, since the eighteenth century, strong waves of a derealization of its own have asserted themselves. Theory quickly followed suit and exploited these trends for a general definition of (large parts of) the field as fictional.[16] There were rare exceptions, such as the philosopher Odo

Marquard, notorious for his cultivation of paradox, who preferred to see art as antifiction. Equally rare were voices that disputed the autonomy of the aesthetic imagination. As a consequence, the strangest inventions were often welcomed with a quasi-religious fervor. More important, that kind of welcome was not only culturally but also economically institutionalized in the media and the universities as a source of jobs.

There is no doubt that societies need discourse spaces for the exploration, the probing, of possibilities; but the probing should remain a probing—that is, an examination of the relative and probable worth of the possibilities. While we may grant the imagination priority for literature (i.e., for what we have come to regard as such), it is legitimate to ask, in fact to demand, that logic and information (knowledge) not be expelled from it completely. This may be happening anyway, because the gap between novels in the broad sense and detective novels, for instance, has been diminishing over time. Theory, also of course in parodistic form, has strengthened its presence in belles lettres. Theoretically, we might note the surprising closeness of thinkers as different as C. Wright Mills and Theodor W. Adorno in this regard: Adorno would like to see an "exact imagination" at work in literature, Mills a "sociological imagination" that might as well be called "anthropological."[17]

In order to inject some urgency into such demands, I will finally have recourse to both a textual and a theoretical model. The textual model has already been nominated: it is embodied by the passage from Shakespeare's *Richard II* quoted above. Shakespeare demonstrates how the basic linguistic process of metaphorization lends a dynamic plasticity to unknown realities (here the very activity of consciousness itself) that can compete with the self-experience and self-observation of consciousness at any time. It does not falsify them; rather, it confirms the assertion of Melvin Konner, according to which the language of the Elizabethans came in many respects closer to the phenomena than scientific terminologies today. The "'humour' metaphor of the Elizabethans is intrinsically closer to the truth as we understand it than was the 'drive' metaphor of the early twentieth century." Contrary to drive theory, the nervous system is not a hydraulic system. We might also profitably look into old research such as Rosamund Tuve's on the logical functions of imagery in Elizabethan and metaphysical poetry and her point of departure that one function of imagery "has been especially in the foreground: the accurate conveying of the sensuous qualities of experience." We owe a contemporary example, no less telling, to the philosopher of law and criminal law Klaus Lüderssen, who maintained that criminology could advance a good deal if it put more trust in studies of the deep structures of criminal cases as depicted in literature. Science and politics should be careful and not simply impose their models on objects such as crime. Conversely, we need not celebrate the products of a totally liberated imagination as unprecedented discoveries.[18]

The passage from Shakespeare makes the structure of the metaphoric process explicit. In that capacity, such structure does not depend on the historical problem involved, that is, the deposition of a king. Decomposing the dynamics of language without giving up its coherence, it draws attention to the back and forth of trust and distrust and the provisional nature of literal and metaphorical levels. The transition between these two "populations" of consciousness seems to be, in Shakespeare, both irrefutably powerful and threatened by taking on too much: There is the fading of the merely metaphoric into literal familiarity and the conquest of new realities in the creativity of metaphors later becoming literal again with their new meaning. Fritz Mauthner, on whose model of the metaphoric process I am relying here, sees any Shakespeare analyst as therefore involved in "an unpleasant and pedantic business" of disentangling the mixture of often highly emphatic images. But he also thinks that in spite of Shakespeare's "contaminations" the distance between the power of suggested reality in his images and those of other writers ("Even Schiller") remains considerable.[19]

In Shakespeare, imaginative energies roll over the images moving back and forth between provisionally literal and metaphoric dimensions. Mauthner's theory of a dynamic of language between metaphoric creativity, literalization, and renewed metaphoric expansion can be used as a rudimentary theory of discourse genres between imagination, logic, and information. In any field, new contents initially conquered metaphorically may be stabilized and then tend to turn into symbols. One of the questions for historical interpretation in such cases is the extent to which they can become "objects of faith." In philosophy, Plato and Schopenhauer might be called "thought poets" (*Denkdichter*)[20]—one of them because, in spite of the logic of his arguments, he revels in metaphors, the other because he tries to think as visually concretely as possible. In general, the history of philosophy, actively advanced by movements such as nominalism, tends to appear as a history of the "self-decomposition of the metaphoric."[21] We need not accept Mauthner's classifications at their face value, but even today, they exercise considerable attraction; their power of discourse distinction is far from being exhausted.

In that sense, the achievements of philosophy in the conquest of new territories in the tension between literal, metaphoric, and conceptual levels (the latter as a kind of regulated compromise between the other two) remain undisputed. A greater productivity of Mauthner's approach must, however, be claimed for literature. In the centuries since the Renaissance, literature has profited greatly from the bad reputation acquired by the control of the imaginary. (Let us say that the concept of the imaginary came into fashion when one had to admit that one did not know anymore what the imagination was.) The effort to control the imaginary seemingly became the hallmark of times in which the church and the state, no longer identical with society, saw themselves as the guardians of essential realities; they defined these realities, and more particularly, defined those institutions that were destined to "educate and socialize the public."[22] Liberal movements of various kinds, fighting for the extension of civil rights, for instance, enlarged the scope of the predominantly literary imagination in the process. This enlargement was transformed and transformed itself into a quasi-autonomous process sanctioned by theory. The joy of securing an area of apparent freedom made people forget reservations such as the one by Nelson Goodman: that while we accept many things, we do not accept everything, not even in the realm of the liberal or radical imagination.

While the "dialectical" process from literal to metaphorical levels followed by renewed turns of the screw that Mauthner goes through may be largely self-referential, it also stands in need of some self-control by what I have been calling, very broadly, logic and information. For that purpose, symposia in the writer's head must take place. There are few writers in whom, like Shakespeare, the unfolding of an almost permanent imagistic power conveys the logically buttressed yet seemingly literal accuracy of sensuous experience. In any case, Rosamund Tuve describes the logical effect emerging in the very act of becoming metaphor as a function of Elizabethan and metaphysical imagery. Such arguments do not refute Christian Enzensberger's criticism that a type of literature wallowing in fantastic spaces is often overrated. Gehlen's judgment concerning literary writers endowed with an acuity of thought that one would like to recommend to and see in philosophers can still be underwritten with confidence. For the time being, the question remains whether Andreas Gruber's "profiler" Sneijder and his symposium in the head presents a realistic promise with operational validity in the so-called real world, or whether he is just another figure of the fantastic.

Notes

Introduction

1. Huxley, *Brave New World Revisited*, 33 (Jefferson), 40 (mass media). Before I go on, a somewhat tricky terminological matter must be clarified. In principle, the correct term for the ancient Athens drinking custom responsible for the writing of this book is *symposion*. This term is indeed still used in quite a few modern and contemporary works on the institution, especially but not exclusively in German classical philology. The prime example in the English-speaking world is Oswyn Murray, the greatest living authority on the topic, with whom I have had extremely valuable contacts (see his 2018 book *The Symposion: Drinking Greek Style*). But Murray has also written standard articles on the problem in which he uses *symposium* without further ado, saying for instance that Plato invented the prose genre of the symposium. In any case, and for whichever reasons, *symposium* has become the standard term for most of the English-speaking world, especially in the United States of America, denoting both the ancient Athens drinking ritual and its modern transformations. It appears that even Dr. Johnson in eighteenth-century England had already switched to that form of the word. (This did not prevent Sir Walter Scott from reverting to *symposion* a bit later.) Since my book is not primarily a study of the original symposion but uses it for further investigations, this word history and its present-day situation with its digital aspects must be taken into account. Except where absolutely necessary, as in the titles of books, I therefore use *symposium* throughout my text. Unfortunately, for reasons of linguistic competence or rather the lack thereof, I can only mention but not discuss an interesting article in Russian by Oleg Zerapin and Olga Shapiro, "Symposion and Symposium as the Modes of the Text Culture," *Epistemology & the Philosophy of Science* 52, no. 2 (2017): 168–183. As far as I can tell, the article, although discussing for instance the sixteenth-century French salon, does not really move into my fields of investigation.

In this context of language problems, I should add that all translations in this book from languages other than English are my own.

2. See Sloterdijk, *Selbstversuch*, 134. For a compromise position, see Borgmann, *Holding On to Reality*.
3. Giddens, *Consequences of Modernity*, 10.
4. Mills, *Sociological Imagination*, 239.
5. Mills, 18–19, 139.
6. https://brocku.ca/MeadProject/Mead/pubs/Mead_1916.html.
7. Gumbrecht, *Production of Presence*.

8. Murray, *Symposion*, 33.
9. See Ackroyd, *Plato Papers*, 25.
10. See Broch, "Das Weltbild des Romans," 105; Iser, *Act of Reading*, 68–85; Rusch and Schmidt, *Das Voraussetzungssystem Georg Trakls*, 323–326.

Chapter 1

1. Burckhardt says that the symposium is the basis for a large part of the "happiness of life" (*Lebensglück*) and of being entirely "fascinated and absorbed" (*die Leute hinreißt*) wherever there is free Hellenic ground (that is not the case with the Spartans and their *syssition*). See Burckhardt, *Griechische Kulturgeschichte*, 774. There are many other passages characterizing the importance of the symposium (e.g., 823–827, with explanatory remarks on Plato's dialogue of that name).
2. See Honneth, *Anerkennung*.
3. www.edge.org; *Süddeutsche Zeitung*, no. 63, 3/15/19, culture page.
4. Wikipedia.
5. *Der Spiegel*, 2/17/2020, www.spiegel.de.
6. See Luhmann, *Soziale Systeme*, 60–61, 222–223, 249–250, and *Social Systems*, chaps. 1, 4, 5. See also Münch, *Globale Dynamik*, 64; see esp. preface, introduction, and chap. 1.
7. Habermas, *Legitimationsprobleme im Spätkapitalismus*.
8. Habermas, 23.
9. Habermas, 27.
10. Burckhardt, *Griechische Kulturgeschichte*, 171–194.
11. Burckhardt, 194.
12. Burckhardt, 173; see also 171–177.
13. Burckhardt, 175.
14. Feldenkrais, *Das starke Selbst*, 55. See also chap. 15 ("Physiology and the Order of Society"). Generally, see also Feldenkrais, *Bewußtheit* and *Entdeckung*.
15. Feldenkrais, *Entdeckung*, 109, 144.
16. Feldenkrais, *Selbst*, 88, 125, 155.
17. Feldenkrais, *Bewußtheit*, 80–81.
18. Some time back, the precise version of a theory like that was hotly debated. In spite of differences, I do think one can speak of a common tendency of opinion in scholars as different as E. R. Dodds in England (*The Greeks and the Irrational*, first published 1951), Bruno Snell in Germany (*The Discovery of Mind*, German original 1946), and most controversial, Julian Jaynes in the United States (*The Origin of Consciousness in the Breakdown of the Bicameral Mind*, 1976).
19. Murray, *Symposion*, 268–270; Murray, 283.
20. Feldenkrais, *Bewußtheit*, 118.
21. Huxley, *Devils of Loudun*, 313–324.
22. Burckhardt, *Griechische Kulturgeschichte*, 55, 171–175, 424.
23. Luhmann, *Soziale Systeme*, 60–61. Parenthetical text references are to page numbers in this edition.
24. See Stichweh, "Die moderne Universität," 346.

25. For Gehlen, see, e.g., the long first part ("Institutionen") of *Urmensch und Spätkultur*. Despite its length, we find no information in this part on how institutions must change if they are to remain acceptable.
26. Luhmann, *Soziale Systeme*, 589.
27. Bertschi, *Im Dazwischen von Individuum und Gesellschaft*. For what follows, see also Simmel, *Grundfragen der Soziologie*, chap. 3 ("Die Geselligkeit" [Sociability]), the revised version of his introductory lecture in Frankfurt. Parenthetical text references are to page numbers in this edition.
28. Sloterdijk, *Sphären*, 362–363.
29. Murray, *Symposion*, esp. pt. 3.
30. Email to the author, August 28, 2018.
31. See also Murray, *Symposion*, 397.
32. Murray, 405 (following Pauline Schmitt Pantel).
33. Simmel, *Grundfragen der Soziologie*, 54.
34. Simmel, 54–55.
35. Simmel, 59–64.
36. See Tönnies, *Studien*. Parenthetical text references are to page numbers in the German edition. In English-language editions of Tönnies's main work(s), the terminology varies.
37. See Delhey et al., "Social Cohesion," 426–455.
38. See Delhey et al., 444, 447.
39. Landsberg, *Wesen und Bedeutung*, 21n1.
40. Gehlen, *Urmensch und Spätkultur*, 128, 161; Plessner, *Grenzen der Gemeinschaft*, 7–133.
41. Burckhardt, *Griechische Kulturgeschichte*, 49.
42. Murray, *Symposion*, 21, 258.
43. Murray, 11.
44. Burckhardt, *Griechische Kulturgeschichte*, 49.
45. Murray, *Symposion*, 13.
46. Murray 19; see 26 on the "elasticity of the concept of kinship."
47. Burckhardt, *Griechische Kulturgeschichte*, 775, 825.
48. Burckhardt, 777, 823, 904–905; see Murray, *Symposion*, 140–142, 150.
49. Burckhardt, *Griechische Kulturgeschichte*, 824; italics in original.
50. Burckhardt, 825; Murray, *Symposion*, 22, 27.
51. See Murray, 47, 107–131, with corresponding as well as pictorial evidence. Concerning lyric poetry and the symposium, see the rich materials in Cazzato, Obbink, and Prodi, *Cup of Song*. For a comparative study of sympotic forms in ancient Greece, see Köster, "Trink- und Mahlgemeinschaften," 48–49. So far as I can see as a nonspecialist, the neglect of Burckhardt in studies of ancient Greece seems to go too far. Murray is an exception: he has published on Burckhardt (I thank him for sending me many of his essays). But even a Swiss countryman, Peter von der Mühll, does not mention Burckhardt in an essay from 1926, "Das griechische Symposion," in spite of identical theses. See Wyss, *Ausgewählte kleine Schriften*, 483–505. Thanks go to Friedrich Uehlein making this book available.

52. Murray, *Symposion*, 173–180.
53. Murray, 187, 197–198.
54. Burckhardt, *Griechische Kulturgeschichte*, 61.
55. Burckhardt, 110.
56. Wecowski, *Greek Aristocratic Banquet*, 77.
57. Wecowski, *Greek Aristocratic Banquet*, 79. See p. 20 for the concept of elite.
58. Wecowski, 23, 24, 34–35.
59. Hobden, *The Symposion*, 157–194. For comparative materials, see also Gagarin, *Oxford Encyclopedia of Ancient Rome and Greece*, s.v. "symposium"; and Hornblower and Spawforth, *Oxford Classical Dictionary*, s.v. "symposium literature" (article is by Murray).
60. Claessens, *Gruppen und Gruppenverbände*, 22. For Aristotle, see Flashar, *Die Philosophie der Antike*, 351 (chap. 2 on Aristotle is by Flashar). For the following, see also Sloterdijk, *Neue Zeilen und Tage*, 106, 110; and Eibl-Eibesfeldt, *Und grün des Lebens*, 346; see also 377n35.
61. Eibl-Eibesfeldt, 346.
62. Weber, *Wirtschaft und Gesellschaft*, 2nd half-vol., chap. 9.1, §3, 548.
63. Nietzsche, *Nachgelassene Fragmente*, 618, see also 617–618; Burckhardt, *Griechische Kulturgeschichte*, 775.
64. Burckhardt, 823.
65. Burckhardt, 774: Clearing away the débris of dinner; distribution of wreaths; offering, together with wine, of a donation; beginning drinking and conversation.
66. Gurewitsch, *Das Weltbild des mittelalterlichen Menschen*, 251; see also 288. For interesting variations, see also Vössing, *Mensa Regia*.
67. For an English-language edition, see Athenaeus, *The Deipnosophists*. The beginning of the first book has information about the scholarly participants. For scholarly opinions concerning the importance of the book, see the German edition translated, edited, and with commentary by Ursula and Kurt Treu: Athenaios von Naukratis, *Das Gelehrtenmahl*, 432. Thanks go to Jo Ludwig for alerting me to this book.
68. Seel, *Die platonische Akademie*. Important references to the academy are to be found in Schmitz, *Die Ideenlehre des Aristoteles*, §84: "Platons Stellung in der Akademie," 369–370, 373; and Landsberg, *Wesen und Bedeutung*, 21. Landsberg wrote this slim volume, an important study that has been almost totally neglected, as a doctoral dissertation in 1922 under Max Scheler in Cologne. Landsberg (1901–1944) came from a Jewish family and became an important philosopher in the 1920s and 1930s; after several internments in France, he died in the concentration camp at Sachsenhausen.
69. Flashar, "Aristoteles," in *Die Philosophie der Antike*, 234. See Nestle, *Die Sokratiker*, 49–50, 54. I am grateful to Friedrich Uehlein for pointing out this book to me.
70. Landsberg, *Wesen und Bedeutung*, 17, 28.
71. Seel, *Die platonische Akademie*, 13–19.

72. Landsberg, *Wesen und Bedeutung*, 19. Parenthetical text references are to page numbers in this edition.
73. Flashar, *Die Philosophie der Antike*, 283–284. Parenthetical text references are to page numbers in this edition.
74. For postulated common traits, see Schmitt, *Modernity and Plato*, 78.
75. Seel, *Die platonische Akademie*, 11–12.
76. For a harsh interpretation along such lines, see Serres, *Rome*, esp. 49, 57, 59, 61, 64.
77. See Hornblower and Spawforth, *Oxford Classical Dictionary*, s.v. "Rome (history)."
78. See Schwindt, *Thaumatographia*.

Chapter 2
1. Le Goff, *Die Intellektuellen im Mittelalter*, 73.
2. Le Goff, 137.
3. See Bumke, *Höfische Kultur*, 1:64–67.
4. Sprandel, *Gesellschaft und Literatur*, 158.
5. Huizinga, *Herbst des Mittelalters*, 16, 19, 21.
6. Lau, *Teutschland*, 143–144.
7. Bumke, *Höfische Kultur*, 1:13; see 12–14.
8. O. Borst, *Alltagsleben im Mittelalter*, 296.
9. For *vreude*, see O. Borst, 41; and Bumke, *Höfische Kultur*, 2:712, 752.
10. Bumke, 1:102–106, 121.
11. Sprandel, *Gesellschaft und Literatur*, 11, 134.
12. Bumke, *Höfische Kultur*, 2:681; see also 679–680.
13. Bumke, 2:728, 740–748.
14. See also Bumke, 2:692.
15. Sprandel, *Gesellschaft und Literatur*, 136.
16. Sprandel, 136.
17. Huizinga, *Herbst des Mittelalters*, 99.
18. Huizinga (see 148–153).
19. Gotthard, *Das Alte Reich*, 30. See also Lau, *Teutschland*, 137–138.
20. Gotthard, *Das Alte Reich*, 69.
21. Huizinga, *Herbst des Mittelalters*, 463.
22. Huizinga, 415.
23. A. Borst, *Lebensformen im Mittelalter*, 89; see also 88–90, 93–97.
24. A. Borst, 334–335.
25. A. Borst, 554.
26. A. Borst, 559.
27. Flasch, *Aufklärung im Mittelalter?*, 7, 25–26, 30. Thanks again to Jo Ludwig, who drew my attention to this important book.
28. Sayers, *Gaudy Night*, 413. Parenthetical text references are to page numbers in this edition.
29. See Schelsky, *Einsamkeit und Freiheit*.

30. Quoted in Ellwein, *Die deutsche Universität*, 25.
31. Sayers, *Gaudy Night*, 427; for academic self-criticism, see also 191, 220.
32. Sayers, 429–430.
33. Gehlen, *Urmensch und Spätkultur*, 211.
34. See Ferruolo, *The Origins of the University*, 25–26; see esp. the chapter on "The Satirists," 93–130.
35. Le Goff, *Die Intellektuellen im Mittelalter*, 155.
36. Flasch, *Aufklärung im Mittelalter?*, 75.
37. Le Goff, *Die Intellektuellen im Mittelalter*, 170–171.

Chapter 3
1. Whitehead, *Science and the Modern World*, 19, 22, 28–30.
2. See Gadamer, *Truth and Method*; Adorno, "Notiz über Geisteswissenschaft und Bildung," 55–56; and Hartmann, *Das Problem des geistigen Seins*, 521n1, 31. See also the second section of this chapter, on the humanities and philosophical anthropology. For the United States, one might think of the early work of Susan Sontag such as *Against Interpretation*.
3. Heinrich, "Zur Geistlosigkeit der Universität heute," 10, 15; Rothacker, *Logik und Systematik der Geisteswissenschaften*, 3–4, 137.
4. See Mattenklott, "Geisteswissenschaften," 1074, 1077, 1080; Simon, "Zukunft und Selbstverständnis," 209–230; and Koschorke, "Wissenschaftsbetrieb als Wissenschaftsvernichtung," 142–157.
5. Friedrich Schleiermacher, "Versuch einer Theorie des geselligen Betragens" (1799), qtd. in Altenhofer, "Geselliges Betragen," 180. Parenthetical text references are to page numbers in this edition.
6. See Kaube, *Hegels Welt*, 418–422.
7. Altenhofer, "Geselliges Betragen," 187.
8. Kaube, *Hegels Welt*, 422.
9. Doderer, *Die Dämonen*, 203–204.
10. Lämmert, "Das Studium der Humanwissenschaften," 21–38, 26–27, 37.
11. See J. G. Fichte's "Deduzierter Plan einer zu Berlin zu errichtenden höhern Lehranstalt," in the volume edited by Ernst Müller, *Gelegentliche Gedanken über Universitäten* (i.e., writings of several authors between 1802 and 1810, among others Fichte, Hegel, W. v. Humboldt, Schleiermacher): the university teacher as "scientific artist," 74, the "strict boundary between science and nonscience," 84. The texts by Wilhelm von Humboldt discussed below are also in this volume.
12. Müller, 103.
13. Müller, 101.
14. Müller, 271.
15. "Über die Innere und äußere Organisation der höheren wissenschaftlichen Anstalten in Berlin" (On the internal and external organization of the higher scientific institutions in Berlin), in Müller, 274.
16. See Vieweg, *Hegel*, 454–469.
17. Humboldt, in Müller, *Gelegentliche Gedanken über Universitäten*, 275.

18. Quoted in Halsey, *Decline of Donnish Dominion*, 126. Parenthetical text references are to page numbers in this edition.

19. I am quoting from and summing up Schlaffer, *Poesie und Wissen*, 225. Schlaffer's treatment of the topic "philology and life-form" is extensive. The references to Dilthey are to the *Gesammelte Schriften* (26 vols.). For recent secondary literature on Dilthey, see Damböck and Lessing, *Dilthey als Wissenschaftsphilosoph*, esp. the first essay by Helmut Johach, "Tatsachen, Normen und Werte in Diltheys Theorie der Geistes- und Sozialwissenschaften," 1–40, who also quotes the longer passage cited here below. Johach also has intriguing passages on the main motivation of Dilthey's philosophy of the sciences and humanities—namely, its relation to social questions and the dualism of facts and values (30–36). For Simmel's tragedy of culture, see his "Der Begriff und die Tragödie der Kultur."

20. Dilthey, *Gesammelte Schriften*, 18:19.

21. Dilthey, 5:31.

22. Dilthey, 5:317.

23. Gehlen, *Wirklicher und unwirklicher Geist*, 113–381, 133. Parenthetical text references are to page numbers in this edition.

24. See Fischer, *Philosophische Anthropologie*, 23–25, 29.

25. See Plessner, *Grenzen der Gemeinschaft*, 5:7–133. Concerning the organization of "social zones" with experts and philosophers, see Fischer, *Philosophische Anthropologie*, 37–38. See also contemporary descriptions of philosophizing everywhere and the sympotic "interpenetrations" with cultural life in Cologne in Fischer, 38–39).

26. Details in Fischer, 223–225.

27. Singer, *Der Beobachter im Gehirn*, 133–134.

28. Gehlen, *Urmensch und Spätkultur*, 114–115. In *Moral und Hypermoral*, Gehlen alludes very clearly and affirmatively to his Habilitationsschrift (97).

29. See Gehlen, *Urmensch und Spätkultur*, 8, 60.

30. See Scheler, *Schriften zur Anthropologie*, editor's introduction, 8–9. For what follows, see Scheler, *Von der Ganzheit des Menschen*.

31. Hartmann, *Das Problem des geistigen Seins*. Parenthetical text references are to page numbers in this edition. See Gehlen, "Rückblick auf die Anthropologie Max Schelers," 248, 258, in connection with the extensive review of the first edition of Hartmann's book (1933) by Plessner.

32. Plessner, "Geistiges Sein," 86. Parenthetical text references are to page numbers in this edition.

Chapter 4

1. See Claessens, *Das Konkrete und das Abstrakte. Soziologische Skizzen zur Anthropologie*; and Saks, *Jury Verdicts*.

2. Tenbruck, "Fragmente zur bürgerlichen Kultur," 13–19.

3. See, e.g., Schulte Beerbühl, "Zwischen Selbstmord und Neuanfang, 107–128. See also Cueni, *Das große Spiel*; and Vogl, *Specter of Capital*.

4. The story is not entirely clear. For what looks like a reliable and prudent version, see DeMaria, *Life of Samuel Johnson*, 234–235.

5. Fussell, *Samuel Johnson and the Life of Writing*, 7, 17. See also Lipking, *Samuel Johnson*, 38. Grub Street, which became a proverbial name, was a street populated by hungry booksellers and hack writers, renamed Milton Street in 1830 and still existing in part in London.

6. See the standard work by Bollenbeck, *Bildung und Kultur*. The subtitle—"Splendor and Misery of a German Interpretational Scheme"—says it all.

7. Old but still informative in these respects is Stang, *Theory of the Novel in England*, esp. pts. 1 and 2.

8. There are innumerable anecdotes about Dr. Johnson in that regard; Walter Jackson Bate has printed three of them on one page. See Bate, *Samuel Johnson*, 35. See also Lipking, *Samuel Johnson*, 175, on "inexperienced and impressionable readers"; and Boswell, *Life of Samuel Johnson, LL.D.*, 35, 226. For judgments similar to Johnson's on the novel, see T. M. Knox's brilliant translation of Hegel's *Aesthetics*, 1:592–593.

9. See Lipking, *Samuel Johnson*, 45; and the second section of Chap. 3 above.

10. Lipking, 186–189.

11. B. Fabian, *Die englische Literatur*, 2:225.

12. B. Fabian, 1:443. See also the difficulties of delimiting the boundary between "novels and other narrative prose" and "prose," esp. 530–543. For similar difficulties, see the chapter "From the Restoration to Preromanticism" by Johann N. Schmidt in Seeber, *Englische Literaturgeschichte*, 161–230.

13. See B. Fabian, *Die englische Literatur*, 2:227.

14. DeMaria, *Life of Samuel Johnson*, 233. For the other details concerning Johnson's sympotic talents and activities, see pp. 141–144.

15. DeMaria, xi, 271.

16. DeMaria, 308–309.

17. See Bruyn, *Das Leben des Jean Paul Friedrich Richter*, 67; see also 162. For the Jean Paul texts mentioned, see *Die unsichtbare Loge*, in *Werke in zwölf Bänden*, 1:16–17, and "Jean Pauls Briefe und bevorstehender Lebenslauf," in *Werke in zwölf Bänden*, 8:968, 999.

18. See the chapter on the "self-taught" ("autodidact") Jean Paul in classical Weimar in Mieth, *Literarische Kultur und gesellschaftliches Leben*, 198–214.

19. Leslie Stephen, qtd. in Lipking, *Samuel Johnson*, 301.

20. Lipking, 301.

21. See Lipking, 14–15; and DeMaria, *Life of Samuel Johnson*, 180–181.

22. See Kluxen, *Geschichte Englands*, 424, 439, 440, 442, 448, 467. See also Chap. 6 of the present volume.

23. See Habermas, *Structural Transformation of the Public Sphere*, pt. 3, §8.

24. Trevelyan, *Geschichte Englands*, 2:573–574.

25. Kluxen, *Geschichte Englands*, 448–449, and generally 436–456.

26. Lipking, *Samuel Johnson*, 188.

27. Hegel, *Phänomenologie des Geistes*, 294.

28. Hegel, 294; Lukács's epilogue, 451–587, 507; Gumbrecht, *"Prosa der Welt."* Thanks to Hans Ulrich Gumbrecht for letting me see this important book early on.

29. See the sigh of Paul Vernière (*Diderot*, VII): "Who will name the professions of Diderot, all of them?"

30. In that regard, two lines of interpretation do not contradict each other: Albrecht, "Die Geburt der Gesellschaft," 21–36, 31; and Vernière: "Diderot stayed away from the salons for a long time, limiting himself to the sordid environment of a popular quarter" (*Diderot*, VII).

31. See Diderot, *Œuvres romanesques*, XVI. Bénac has the singular *antiroman* because at this point he is referring only to *Jacques le fataliste*; but see p. XIV on *Le neveu*. I leave aside the question whether the latter should be called a dialogue and not a narrative text.

32. Diderot, X.

33. See Albrecht, *Zivilisation und Gesellschaft*, 33 (chap. E, "Die französische Salonkultur," 33–100). Parenthetical text references are to page numbers in this edition.

Chapter 5

1. Proust, *Recherche*, 1:517. All Proust quotations from the *Recherche* are taken from Marcel Proust, *À la recherche du temps perdu*, 3 vols. (Paris: Éditions Gallimard, 1954). Parenthetical text references are to volume and page numbers in this edition.

2. See Schulz-Buschhaus, "Gemeinplatz und Salonkonversation," 4.

3. See Schulz-Buschhaus, 7–9.

4. For more details, though still of only speculative import, see Zeldin, *Ambition, Love and Politics*, chaps. 1 ("The Pretensions of the Bourgeoisie") and 4 ("The Rich"); for "style de vie," see p. 15. See also Boltanski, *Rätsel und Komplotte*, 66–67. Boltanski will play a more conspicuous role later in the chapters on the detective novel.

5. Boltanski, 66–67n90.

6. Zeldin, *Ambition, Love and Politics*, 45, esp. 383.

7. Luhmann, *Soziale Systeme*, 224.

8. For ruminations on power and the ways to acquire, use, hide, and lose it, see Greene and Elffers, *Power*; for reputation, see p. 15.

Chapter 6

1. Schwanitz, *Englische Kulturgeschichte*, 1:9.

2. John of Gaunt in Shakespeare, *Richard II*, 2.1.40–42.

3. Quoted in Briggs, *Social History of England*, 133.

4. Briggs, 142, 144.

5. Plumb, *Growth of Political Stability*, 69. Bernhard Fabian consequently called the "Glorious Revolution" a "conservative" revolution. See his chapter on the Restoration and the eighteenth century in B. Fabian, *Die englische Literatur*, 1:97.

6. Plumb, *Growth of Political Stability*, 83, 86.

7. Plumb, 174.
8. Plumb, 187.
9. Boltanski, *Rätsel und Komplotte*, 66.
10. Plumb, *Growth of Political Stability*, 66.
11. Kluxen, *Geschichte Englands*, 74.
12. Kluxen, 75, 76, 77.
13. See Easthope, *Englishness and National Culture*, 81–82.
14. For these opposed estimates, see Aster, *Geschichte der Philosophie*; and Borkenau, *Der Übergang vom feudalen zum bürgerlichen Weltbild*, 446.
15. Hobsbawm, *Age of Revolution*, 29.
16. B. Fabian, *Die englische Literatur*, 1:119.
17. See Enzensberger, *Viktorianische Lyrik*, or also, on Enzensberger's aesthetics, *Literatur und Interesse*. For Hobsbawm, see his *Age of Revolution*.
18. Enzensberger, *Literatur und Interesse*, 2:106.
19. Quoted in Enzensberger, 2:106.
20. Enzensberger, 2:131–132.
21. Experts have no difficulty distinguishing these upper-class clubs from a host of other associations, many of them also called clubs. I am following Leonhardt, *77 mal England*, 291–295; Leonhardt assumes that distinctions are basically easy to make.
22. Leonhardt, 295.
23. Sayers, *Unpleasantness*, 5–6, 9, 28, 34, 86 ("intolerable nuisance," "thoroughly unpleasant"), 161–162, 179. For Wimsey's inner complexity, visible only in rare cases, and for his "biography," see the letter of his uncle Paul Austin Delagardie (printed in several Wimsey novels), here pp. 246–252. Sayers, whose family on her mother's side belonged to the gentry, knew the mechanisms of class from her own experience.
24. Sayers, 239.
25. Sayers, 240.
26. Treiber, "Partygänger," 111–112.
27. B. Fabian, *Die englische Literatur*, 1:101.
28. See Sennett, *Fall of Public Man*, 73–86, 141–149.
29. Sennett, 216–217.
30. See https://oxfordandcambridgeclub.co.uk/visitors/planning-your-visit/.
31. See *Whig Club instituted in May, 1784*. Page viii and the following pages show that admission in groups of one hundred had already begun in May 1787.

Chapter 7

1. See Sennett, *Fall of Public Man*, 217.
2. See, e.g., Ungern-Sternberg, "Politische Bankette." There is a lot of research on this topic.
3. Sennett, *Fall of Public Man*, 218.
4. See Habermas, *Structural Transformation*, 162–164.
5. Sennett, *Fall of Public Man*, chap. 5, 89–105.

6. Habermas, 198.
7. Habermas, 191.
8. Habermas, 165.
9. See Alt, *Schiller*, 1:567–570.
10. Alt, 147–148.
11. Alt, 151.
12. Alt, 157–158.
13. For Schelsky, see the final chapter of *Einsamkeit und Freiheit* on consequences and conclusion(s). See also Habermas, *Structural Transformation*, 157.
14. But see Leonhardt, *77 mal England*, chap. 64 ("What Keeps the Commonwealth Together?").
15. I am following Christopher Clark, *Sleepwalkers*, chap. 12 ("Last Days"), esp. 527–536 ("There Must Be Some Misunderstanding") concerning the outbreak of World War I.
16. For a relatively sophisticated version operating without the demand for moral rigor and absolute sincerity, see Plack, *Ohne Lüge leben*.
17. Sloterdijk, *Selbstversuch*, 125.
18. See Canetti, *Party in the Blitz*.
19. Eliot, *Prufrock*, 10–12. Parenthetical text references are to line numbers in this edition.
20. Heine, "Seegespenst," in *Die Nordsee*, last line.
21. The powerful effects of the ocean on the imagination have been historically confirmed by Adamowsky, *Mysterious Science of the Sea*, in impressive ways.
22. Eliot, *Cocktail Party*, p. 50, line 585.
23. Eliot, act 1, scene 1.
24. Eliot, p. 36, lines 338–339.
25. Eliot, p. 50, lines 580–582.
26. See end of act 2, pp. 146–147, lines 791–805.
27. Eliot, p. 179, lines 541–542.
28. See Lessing, *Briefing*, 109, 206–209.
29. Eliot, *Cocktail Party*, act 2, p. 137, lines 650–658.
30. Eliot, p. 136, line 633.
31. Eliot, p. 139, line 689.
32. Eliot, pp. 148–152, lines 180–181.
33. I am arguing here both for and against Coghill, p. 259.
34. See, e.g., Lackey, *Modernist God State*, 111–120.
35. Mansfield, "Garden Party," 3.
36. Mansfield, 8.
37. Mansfield, 9.
38. Mansfield, 12–13.
39. Woolf, *Mrs. Dalloway*. Parenthetical text references are to page numbers in this edition.
40. Schoeck, *Der Neid*.
41. Schoeck, 246.

42. See below; Schoeck taught in the United States for several years.
43. Bude, "Soziologie der Party," 5–6. Thanks to Ethel Matala de Mazza for drawing my attention to this article.
44. Dahrendorf, *Gesellschaft und Freiheit*, 13; Gehlen, "Genese der Modernität, 31–46, 32.
45. Summers, *Arrogance of Power*, 37.
46. Dahrendorf, *Gesellschaft und Freiheit*, 284.
47. See the 1961 preface in the edition used here, xxix–lxi. The German sociologist Helmut Schelsky has remarked correctly that the German translation of the main title should instead read "The Anxious Crowd" ("Die ängstliche Masse"). As an aside, I should further add that pressures of conformity do not of course prevent the formation of classes or castes, because these can always be interpreted as the success of those working harder and so forth than the others. See, e.g., Baltzell, *Philadelphia Gentlemen*, and *Protestant Establishment*, with new editions up to the present.
48. Quoted in Finkenstaedt, *Kleine Geschichte*, 3, 126.
49. Fitzgerald, *Great Gatsby*, 46. Quotations follow the free eBook version available at Planet Books.com; parenthetical text references are to page numbers in this edition.
50. Quoted in Weimann, "New Criticism," 81–82.
51. See the many observations in Devereux, *Angst und Methode*, e.g., 41, 126, 134, 163.
52. See Sloterdijk, *Polyloquien*, 9–13.
53. Brown, *Sakrileg*, 557.
54. Luhmann, *Soziale Systeme*, 224.
55. Boltanski, *Rätsel und Komplotte*, 72.
56. Boltanski, 257.
57. See Sloterdijk, *Kritik der zynischen Vernunft*, 1:7. For Conrad, see Conrad, *Secret Agent*, 64, and *Under Western Eyes*, 7, 19, 35, 64, 67, 95.
58. Boltanski, *Rätsel und Komplotte*, 253.
59. Boltanski, 66–67.
60. Boltanski, 67.
61. See, e.g., Meyer, *Das konspirologische Denken*.
62. See the eminent—indeed, other-referentially tailored—role of enjoyment even in Rousseau that Helmut Pfeiffer has analyzed: "Le plaisir de la jouissance," 15–45; for Hume, see 35. In the same volume, see my essay on Burke: "Burke und die Implikationen des Vergnügens," 237–250, esp. 247–248 on "social enjoyment."
63. Boltanski, *Rätsel und Komplotte*, 190–193.

Chapter 8

1. See Klußmann and Schnurr, *Die Macht der Geheimdienste*, here the editors' preface, 11–14; for Walsingham, see Borger, "Lieber zu viel Furcht," 25–34.
2. See Krieger, *Geschichte der Geheimdienste*, 14.

3. See Jeremy Hawthorn, introduction to Conrad, *Under Western Eyes*, xxi.
4. Gumbrecht, *Crowds*, 25.
5. Simmel, *Soziologie*, chap. 5 ("Das Geheimnis und die geheime Gesellschaft"), 272. For the psychoanalytic version, see Doi, *Anatomy of Self*, 108–109.
6. Simmel, *Soziologie*, 283.
7. Doi, *Anatomy of Self*, 109.
8. Doi, 112.
9. Doi, 113, 114.
10. Lee, *Geständniszwang und "Wahrheit des Charakters."*
11. See Sennett, *Fall of Public Man*, 150–161.
12. Boltanski, *Rätsel und Komplotte*, 42. See also Eco's short *Nachschrift zum Namen der Rose*.
13. Boltanski, *Rätsel und Komplotte*, 51.
14. Gadda, *That Awful Mess on the Via Merulana*, 74–75.
15. Gendolla and Pfeiffer, "Der gesellschaftliche Kommunikationsdruck," 295.
16. Boltanski, *Rätsel und Komplotte*, 52.
17. I am alluding to a famous 1964 essay by Hans Blumenberg setting up a typology of such concepts. See Blumenberg, "Wirklichkeitsbegriff und Möglichkeit."
18. Boltanski, *Rätsel und Komplotte*, 36–37.
19. Simmel, "Geheimnis," 289, 291.
20. Reinalter, "Einleitung," 14.
21. Reinalter, 11.
22. See, e.g., F. Fabian, *Geheimbünde in Geschichte und Gegenwart*, 139, 178.
23. Simmel, "Geheimnis," 283.
24. For this point, see Reinalter, "Einleitung," 18–19, and "Die ersten politischen Geheimbünde im 19. Jahrhundert," 178.
25. See Reinalter, *Freimaurerei, Politik und Gesellschaft*, 77. Freemasons were barely engaged in the German "culture wars" (*Kulturkampf*) of the nineteenth century either (160). Incidentally, Reinalter distinguishes four types of enlightenment societies: (1) academies and reading societies, (2) patriotic societies and societies for the benefit of the public, (3) secret societies, and (4) popular and scholarly societies that later developed into the politically active Jacobin clubs (68). Here we are interested only in type 3. For further national differences in freemasonry, see also Reinalter, *Freimaurer und Geheimbünde*. Dieter A. Binder construes a closed system of masonic thought where everything is defined, regulated, and without alternatives or options, an effort that will probably not be crowned by success (Binder, *Die Freimaurer*, 135–137). His effort has not prevented others from accusing Freemasons of revolutionary activities of all kinds, of anti-Semitism, and so forth. Binder calls that, perhaps somewhat too violently, the "confused look from the outside" (86–116).
26. F. Fabian, *Geheimbünde in Geschichte und Gegenwart*, 145, 149.
27. F. Fabian, 23, 26–27, 29.
28. Durrell, *Monsieur*, 236–246. These passages do not play any role in the events narrated in the novel.

29. Durrell, *Livia*, 174. For the search in the specific context of what is called the "Avignon Quintet," see, e.g., the third novel by Durrell, *Constance*, 122–123. See also Durrell, *Monsieur*, 240–243.
30. Dickie, *Cosa Nostra*, 61.
31. Saviano, *Gomorrha*, 286.
32. Dickie, *Cosa Nostra*, 48–49.
33. Dickie, 81, 83.
34. Dickie, 96. See also Dickie's second chapter, "The Mafia Is Entering the Italian System: 1876–1890," and the warning that "one will never be able to overcome Cosa Nostra if one does not understand that it is a shadow state, a political formation which sometimes fights the institutions of the legal state, sometimes infiltrates them and sometimes uses them as home base" (353).
35. Saviano, *Gomorrha*, 244.
36. Dickie, *Cosa Nostra*, 219–224, 231–239.
37. Saviano, *Gomorrha*, 63, 65, 70–71, 208–209, 232–237.
38. Silj, *Verbrechen, Politik, Demokratie*, 151.
39. Bracher, *Geschichte und Gewalt*, 15. Parenthetical text references are to page numbers in this edition.
40. See Goetsch, "Kriegsbotschaften amerikanischer Präsidenten," 75.
41. See Boorstin, *The Americans*, 62–65, 447–448.
42. Fabian, *Geheimbünde in Geschichte und Gegenwart*, 69.
43. See, generally and for details, the important book on which I have mainly relied, Allen, *Opus Dei*, 180. Concerning the role of discretion and secrecy, see pp. 134–161; concerning "confidential" writings, see pp. 154–157. Similar on the whole are the judgments in Peter and Deubner, *Opus Dei*.
44. Allen, *Opus Dei*, 110.
45. Allen, 7.
46. Allen, 24.
47. Fabian, *Geheimbünde in Geschichte und Gegenwart*, 69.
48. Allen, *Opus Dei*, 3.
49. Allen, 5.
50. Weber, *Die protestantische Ethik*, 57, 106, 113.
51. Brown, *Sakrileg*, 79.
52. Allen, *Opus Dei*, 33–34.
53. See Allen, 33–37.

Chapter 9

1. Nietzsche, *Zur Genealogie der Moral*, 5:266–273 (nos. 1.7–1.11).
2. We may remember that Nicolai Hartmann thought it was possible to distinguish between the genuine and the counterfeit like mere opinions in the domain of the objective spirit. See the second section of Chap. 3.
3. For an early survey amounting to that "intermediate position," see Schunck, *Joseph Conrad*. See, e.g., "loneliness and alienation," "isolation" of socially ostracized characters, "transitional position," "position between romanticism and

realism," "side by side of modern and Victorian features," side by side of "romantic, Victorian and existentialist-modern features," "intermediate position," 8, 19, 24, 31, 68–69. Schunck already found such classifications too dominating by far; he thought there should be fewer of them with less far-reaching claims. His solution: Protean Conrad, as a thinker and writer, was marked by an individual stature that was more than the sum of currents in the history of thought and literature (68).

4. See Giorgio Agamben's commentary on Kant's metaphysics of morals in his *Opus Dei*, 156, 180; see also 160, 170–171, 179, 183.

5. For Hume and Burke, see Hume, *Enquiries concerning Human Understanding*, 214; and Burke, *On the Sublime and Beautiful*, 43–44.

6. Burke, 214.

7. Burke, 58.

8. See Laslett, *The World We Have Lost*—a famous book that in its chaps. 1, 2, and 3 touches on the themes treated here. See Burke, *On the Revolution in France*, 213, the litany of "It is gone."

9. Burke, 207.

10. Hume, *Treatise of Human Nature*, 269.

11. Conrad, *Lord Jim*, 96. Parenthetical text references are to page numbers in this edition.

12. Conrad, *Heart of Darkness*, 8–10, 50–51.

13. See Conrad, *Lord Jim*, 82–83.

14. One of the most "enlightening" books on this topic is still Dreitzel, *Die gesellschaftlichen Leiden*. But see also Clark, *Sleepwalkers*, 360, for historically manifest forms of "role strain" shortly before World War I.

15. Dreitzel, *Die gesellschaftlichen Leiden*, 102.

16. See Conrad, *Nostromo*, 81. Parenthetical text references are to page numbers in this edition.

17. Conrad, *Under Western Eyes*, 336; see p. 25: "the different conditions of Western thought." For *The Secret Agent*, I have used the Penguin Modern Classics edition (1963). Parenthetical text references are to page numbers in these editions.

18. Conrad, *Secret Agent*, 20; see p. 22: "his mission in life being the protection of the social mechanism"; p. 42: "All idealization makes life poorer. To beautify it is to take away its character of complexity—is to destroy it."

Chapter 10

1. See Sennett, *Fall of Public Man*, 207.

2. Christopher Clark does not answer the question posed by himself, "Did the power to shape foreign policy lie beyond the chancelleries and ministries in the world of the lobby group and political print?," with a simple yes but recognizes a new "fluidity of power" (*Sleepwalkers*, 226, 239; see 226–239).

3. See Sennett, *Fall of Public Man*, 263–266.

4. In an earlier book, I have described this type of individuality as a hysterical one. See Pfeiffer, *From Chaos to Catastrophe?*, 1–2.

5. For more detailed arguments, see my essay "Mentalität und Medium."

6. For the "flat-footed" course of reality, see the Italian detective novel by Fruttero and Lucentini, *Die Sonntagsfrau*, 194.
7. Sayers, *Unpleasantness*, 5, 34.
8. Lukács, *Ästhetik*, 1:77–84.
9. See Zelle, *Angenehmes Grauen*.
10. See, e.g., the relation between the Interpol agent Emilia Ness and the Frankfurt detective Mikka Kessler or the suggestion of a merely interrupted ordinary family happiness in Mark Roderick, *Post Mortem*.
11. See Schulz-Buschhaus, *Formen und Ideologien*; and my essay "Mentalität und Medium."
12. Simenon, *Maigret à Vichy*, 125, 129, 146. Citations to Simenon's Maigret novels are from the following editions: *Maigret à Vichy* (Paris: Presses de la Cité, 1968); *Maigret et la vieille dame* (Paris: Presses de la Cité, 1951); *Maigret et le clochard* (Paris: Presses de la Cité, n.d.); parenthetical text references are to page numbers in these editions.
13. Quoted in Simenon, *Simenon auf der Couch*, 17.
14. Mills, *Sociological Imagination*, 5–6, 16–18. See also 67, 72, and the afterword by Todd Gitlin, 236.
15. Larsson, *Vergebung*, 431; see also 431–434. This is the last volume of a trilogy of about 2,300 pages, the other volumes being *Verblendung* and *Verdammnis*. Parenthetical text references are to titles and page numbers in these editions.
16. "Social Cohesion," 442, 443–444. See also Delhey et al., *Social Cohesion Radar*. The authors of this work are identical with the authors of the essay Delhey et al., "Social Cohesion and Its Correlates."
17. See, e.g., Reckwitz, *Die Gesellschaft der Singularitäten*.
18. Wahl, in *Die Modernisierungsfalle*, has presented an early and very instructive study to that effect. The elements of the trap consist in a universalistic picture of human beings with subjects claiming autonomy and dignity and believing in general progress, as well as in the idea of the individualized love marriage and its promise of happiness.
19. Gruber, *Die Knochennadel*, 180; see also 166, 179. In France, there is in fact a "Section d'intervention rapide," with, however, a lower degree of secrecy—unless we are again deceived.
20. Burckhardt, *Griechische Kulturgeschichte*, 52, 55.
21. Burckhardt, 63.
22. Larsson, *Verblendung*, 110.
23. Gruber, *Die Knochennadel*, 35; see 21.
24. Here, as always in my text, "virtual" is to be understood as in analogy with the virtuality of computers and the internet.
25. Estermann, *Arthur Schopenhauer*, chap. 3 ("Mein Zeitalter und ich sind fremd aneinander vorbeigegangen"), 73–187.
26. Safranski, *Schopenhauer*, 194. Parenthetical text references are to page numbers in this edition.
27. Gehlen qtd. in Haffmanns, *Über Arthur Schopenhauer*, 272.

28. Gruber, *Todesfrist*, 192.
29. Scheler, *Von der Ganzheit*, 76.
30. Gruber, *Todesfrist*, 192.
31. Gruber, *Todesurteil*, 315.
32. Gruber, *Todesmärchen*, 223. For Piet van Loon's life story with the crushing of his testicles as a macabre climax, see 243, 372–373, 376, 526.
33. Gruber, *Todesmal*, 441. At the time of writing, this was the last novel in the Sneijder series. The story develops around a number of murdered babies in a nunnery.
34. Valéry, *Œuvres*, 1:70.
35. Shakespeare, *Richard II*, 5.5.6–19.

Chapter 11
1. Huxley, *Brave New World*, 16.
2. A plurality of scenarios are conceivable and have achieved real status. See the rich materials in Kennedy, *Rise and Fall of the Great Powers*, for instance the comparison between England, France, and Germany after 1945 (423–428).
3. See Cannadine, *Class in Britain*, 58. See also 59, 63 ("hierarchical revival"), and 65 (impact of empire reinforcing a hierarchical view of the world), as well as later subchapters on "the politics of class propounded" and "denied." For Arnold, see also the first section of Chap. 10.
4. A. Borst, *Lebensformen*; see p. 242 (on the impulsiveness of living with each other). Similar descriptions and theses can be found in Borst's namesake and colleague Otto Borst's *Alltagsleben*, chap. 11, 389, 391, 397, 408.
5. A. Borst, 232, 234.
6. See A. Borst, 234, 241.
7. This criterion is mentioned, for instance, by Habermas in a review of Gehlen's *Moral und Hypermoral* in Habermas, *Philosophisch-politische Profile*, 112.
8. See Scheler's *Von der Ganzheit*. See also Gehlen, "Rückblick," 247–248. All essays by Gehlen quoted in this chapter are to be found in this same volume, *Gesamtausgabe*, vol. 4: *Philosophische Anthropologie und Handlungslehre*; parenthetical text references are to titles and page numbers. Gehlen's criticism of Scheler occurs in practically all of the essays devoted to the state and status of philosophical anthropology.
9. See my essay "Burke und die Implikationen des Vergnügens," 237–250, and the chapter "The Paradox of Liberty and Authority" in my *From Chaos to Catastrophe?*
10. See Lippe, *Naturbeherrschung am Menschen*, esp. vol. 1, pt. 2, on the change in dance rhythms, and vol. 2, pt. 2, on the "geometrisation" of human beings in the period of absolutism.
11. Mieth, *Literarische Kultur*, 199. For Jean Paul, see also Chap. 4. For the lone wolf thesis, see esp. Bruyn, *Das Leben des Jean Paul Friedrich Richter*, 162.
12. Mieth, *Literarische Kultur*, 284–285.
13. Max Horkheimer, qtd. in Daniel, *Hoftheater* (Stuttgart: Klett-Cotta, 1995).

14. Vieweg, *Hegel*, 454–464.

15. Schelsky, "Der Realitätsverlust," 395, 397.

16. People stick to this distinction, although it is either too simple or too complex to allow for any consistent version. Both tendencies occur in Kendall L. Walton's monumental and extraordinarily detailed *Mimesis as Make-Believe*. In his chap. 2.2, he starts "from scratch" by presenting the "by no means univocal" and "murky" "fundamental, if rough, differentiation between novels, stories, fables and fairy tales on the one hand and biographies, histories, textbooks, instruction manuals and newspaper articles on the other" (73). This chapter ends with the insight that its moral "is scarcely profound, but . . . is absolutely essential. Notions of works of fiction akin to ours, in the library and bookstore spirit, are in many discussions intertwined irresponsibly with fiction-reality contrasts, with chaotic results. Understanding fiction in terms of make-believe keeps these distinctions appropriately distinct" (75). Yet Walton goes on immediately to obscure the make-believe hypothesis: there is the admitted vagueness of functions of fiction (myths as nonfiction for the Greeks but fiction for us [91]; and legend and myth "may be as good as history" [97]). There is the nagging problem of what kind of understanding a fictional text in particular may promote, a difficulty made worse by Walton's using the German term *Verstehen* also in regard to "nonfiction novels" or "factual fictions" (93–94), and so on. I confess that I do not understand how Walton's "solution" of defining fictional as being fictional in readers' games (e.g., p. 356 in chap. 9 on "Verbal Representations") makes things easier or clearer.

17. For Adorno, see Müller-Doohm, *Adorno*, 210; see also Mills, *Sociological Imagination*, 18–19, 67, 72, 139, 236.

18. Konner, *The Tangled Wing*, 103 (the 2nd ed. 2002 left that thesis intact); Tuve, *Elizabethan and Metaphysical Imagery*, 3 (see, e.g., p. 12 and all of pt. 2 on the logical functions of imagery); Lüderssen, "Der Text ist klüger als der Autor." See also the first essay in the same volume, "Literatur—gesteigerte Realität?"

19. Mauthner, *Beiträge*, 2:502–503.

20. Mauthner, 2:469, 474, 478.

21. Mauthner, 2:473–474.

22. For these and other aspects of this context, see, e.g., Costa Lima, *Control of the Imaginary*. I am quoting from the "Afterword" by Jochen Schulte-Sasse, 208; see also 210 on the contempt for the novel on the part of various eighteenth-century writers, reminiscent of Dr. Johnson and Diderot and their role in this book (Chap. 4) and including Heidegger in the twentieth century. Schulte-Sasse also criticizes the neglect, in many modern theories of literature, of the possibly compensatory function of literature. Costa Lima, in his turn, opens the debate with a quote from Nelson Goodman's *Ways of Worldmaking* (21) according to which "a broad mind" (i.e., a mind ready to accept all kinds of "imaginative realities") is no substitute for hard work."

Bibliography

Ackroyd, Peter. *The Plato Papers: A Prophesy*. New York: Anchor Books, 2000.
Adamowsky, Natascha. *The Mysterious Science of the Sea, 1775–1943*. London: Pickering & Chatto, 2015.
Adorno, Theodor W. "Notiz über Geisteswissenschaft und Bildung." In *Eingriffe. Neun kritische Modelle*, 54–58. Frankfurt am Main: Suhrkamp, 1963.
Agamben, Giorgio. *Opus Dei. Archäologie des Amts*. Berlin: S. Fischer, 2012.
Albrecht, Clemens. "Die Geburt der Gesellschaft aus den Salons. Deutungsmuster bürgerlicher Kultur in Frankreich." In *Die bürgerliche Kultur und ihre Avantgarden*, 21–36. Würzburg: Ergon Verlag, 2004.
———. *Zivilisation und Gesellschaft. Bürgerliche Kultur in Frankreich*. Munich: Wilhelm Fink, 1995.
Allen, John L., Jr. *Opus Dei. The Truth about Its Rituals, Secrets and Power*. London: Penguin, 2005.
Alt, Peter-André. *Schiller. Leben—Werk—Zeit*. 2 vols. Munich: C. H. Beck, 2000.
Altenhofer, Norbert. "Geselliges Betragen—Kunst—Auslegung. Anmerkungen zu Peter Szondis Schleiermacher-Interpretation und zur Frage einer materialen Hermeneutik." In *Studien zur Entwicklung einer materialen Hermeneutik*, edited by Ulrich Nassen, 165–211. Munich: Wilhelm Fink, 1979.
Arnold, Matthew. *Culture and Anarchy*. 1869. Edited by John Dover Wilson. Cambridge: Cambridge University Press, 1981.
Aster, Ernst von. *Geschichte der Philosophie*. 14th ed. Stuttgart: Alfred Kröner, 1963.
Athenaeus. *The Deipnosophists*. English translation by Charles Burton Gulick. 7 vols. London: Heinemann; New York: G. P. Putnam's Sons; Cambridge, MA: Harvard University Press, 1927–1941.
Athenaios von Naukratis. *Das Gelehrtenmahl*. Translated, edited, and with commentary by Ursula und Kurt Treu. Leipzig: Dieterich'sche Verlagsbuchhandlung, 1985.
Baltzell, E. Digby. *Philadelphia Gentlemen: The Making of a National Upper Class*. New York: Free Press, 1966.
———. *The Protestant Establishment: Aristocracy and Caste in America*. New York: Random House, 1964.
Bate, Walter Jackson. *Samuel Johnson*. London: Chatto & Windus, 1978.

Bertschi, Stefan. *Im Dazwischen von Individuum und Gesellschaft. Topologie eines blinden Flecks der Soziologie.* Bielefeld: transcript, 2010.
Binder, Dieter A. *Die Freimaurer. Geschichte, Mythos und Symbole.* 4th ed. Wiesbaden: marix, 2019.
Blumenberg, Hans. "Wirklichkeitsbegriff und Möglichkeit des Romans." In *Nachahmung und Illusion*, edited by Hans Robert Jauß, 2nd ed., 9–27. Munich: Wilhelm Fink, 1969.
Bollenbeck, Georg. *Bildung und Kultur. Glanz und Elend eines deutschen Deutungsmusters.* 2nd ed. Frankfurt am Main: Insel Verlag, 1994.
———. *Eine Geschichte der Kulturkritik von Rousseau bis Günther Anders.* Munich: C. H. Beck, 2007.
Boltanski, Luc. *Rätsel und Komplotte: Kriminalliteratur, Paranoia, moderne Gesellschaft.* Berlin: Suhrkamp, 2013.
Boorstin, Daniel J. *The Americans: The National Experience.* New York: Vintage Books, 1965.
Borger, Sebastian. "Lieber zu viel Furcht als zu wenig. Francis Walsingham, Gründer des englischen Geheimdienstes, kämpfte gegen katholische Verschwörer." In *Die Macht der Geheimdienste. Agenten, Spione und Spitzel vom Mittelalter bis zum Cyberwar*, edited by Uwe Klußmann and Eva-Maria Schnurr, 25–34. Munich: Deutsche Verlagsanstalt, 2020.
Borgmann, Albert. *Holding On to Reality: The Nature of Information at the Turn of the Millennium.* Chicago: University of Chicago Press, 1999.
Borkenau, Franz. *Der Übergang vom feudalen zum bürgerlichen Weltbild. Studien zur Geschichte der Philosophie der Manufakturperiode.* 1934. Darmstadt: Wissenschaftliche Buchgesellschaft, 1980.
Borst, Arno. *Lebensformen im Mittelalter.* Frankfurt am Main: Ullstein, 1973.
Borst, Otto. *Alltagsleben im Mittelalter.* Frankfurt am Main: Insel, 1983.
Boswell, James. *The Life of Samuel Johnson, LL.D.* Ware, UK: Wordsworth Editions, 1999.
Bracher, Karl Dietrich. *Geschichte und Gewalt. Zur Politik im 20. Jahrhundert.* Berlin: Quadriga, 1981.
Briggs, Asa. *A Social History of England.* Harmondsworth, UK: Penguin Books, 1985.
Broch, Hermann. "Das Weltbild des Romans." In *Kommentierte Werkausgabe*, edited by Paul Michael Lützeler, vol. 9, pt. 2, 89–118. Frankfurt am Main: Suhrkamp, 1975.
Brown, Dan. *Sakrileg.* Bergisch Gladbach: Gustav Lübbe Verlag, 2004.
Bruyn, Günter de. *Das Leben des Jean Paul Friedrich Richter. Eine Biographie.* 7th ed. Frankfurt am Main: Fischer Taschenbuch Verlag, 2011.
Bude, Heinz. "Soziologie der Party." *Zeitschrift für Ideengeschichte* 9, no. 4 (2015): 5–11.
Bumke, Joachim. *Höfische Kultur. Literatur und Gesellschaft im hohen Mittelalter.* 2 vols. Munich: Deutscher Taschenbuch Verlag, 1986.

Burckhardt, Jacob. *Das Geschichtswerk*, vol. 2: *Griechische Kulturgeschichte*. Frankfurt am Main: Zweitausendeins, n.d.
Burke, Edmund. *On Taste, On the Sublime and Beautiful, Reflections on the French Revolution, A Letter to a Noble Lord*. Edited by Charles W. Eliot. Harvard Classics. New York: P. F. Collier, 1937.
Canetti, Elias. *Party in the Blitz: The English Years*. New York: New Directions, 2005.
Cannadine, David. *Class in Britain*. London: Penguin Books, 2000.
Cazzato, Vanessa, Dirk Obbink, and Enrico Emanuele Prodi, eds. *The Cup of Song: Studies on Poetry and the Symposion*. Oxford: Oxford University Press, 2016.
Claessens, Dieter. *Das Konkrete und das Abstrakte. Soziologische Skizzen zur Anthropologie*. Frankfurt am Main: Suhrkamp, 1980.
———. *Gruppen und Gruppenverbände. Systematische Einführung in die Folgen von Vergesellschaftung*. Darmstadt: Wissenschaftliche Buchgesellschaft, 1977.
Clark, Christopher. *The Sleepwalkers: How Europe Went to War in 1914*. London: Penguin Books, 2013.
Conrad, Joseph. *Heart of Darkness*. 1902. Harmondsworth, UK: Penguin, 1973.
———. *Lord Jim*. 1900. Edited by Robert B. Heilman. New York: Holt, Rinehart and Winston, 1957.
———. *Nostromo*. 1904. Harmondsworth, UK: Penguin, 1963.
———. *The Secret Agent: A Simple Tale*. 1907. Harmondsworth, UK: Penguin, 1963.
———. *Under Western Eyes*. 1912. Edited by Jeremy Hawthorn. Oxford: Oxford University Press, 1983.
Costa Lima, Luiz. *Control of the Imaginary: Reason and Imagination in Modern Times*. Minneapolis: University of Minnesota Press, 1988.
Cueni, Claude. *Das große Spiel*. 2nd ed. Munich: Wilhelm Heyne, 2008.
Dahrendorf, Ralf. *Gesellschaft und Freiheit. Zur soziologischen Analyse der Gegenwart*. Munich: Piper, 1961.
Damböck, Christian, and Hans Ulrich Lessing, eds. *Dilthey als Wissenschaftsphilosoph*. Freiburg: Karl Alber, 2016.
Daniel, Ute. *Hoftheater. Zur Geschichte des Theaters und der Höfe im 18. und 19. Jahrhundert*. Stuttgart: Klett-Cotta, 1995.
Delhey, Jan, et al. "Social Cohesion and Its Correlates: A Comparison of Western and Asian Societies." *Comparative Sociology* 17, nos. 3–4 (2018): 426–455.
———. *Social Cohesion Radar: An International Comparison of Social Cohesion*. Gütersloh: Bertelsmann Stiftung, 2013.
DeMaria, Robert, Jr. *The Life of Samuel Johnson*. Cambridge, MA: Basil Blackwell, 1994.
Devereux, Georges. *Angst und Methode in den Verhaltenswissenschaften*. Frankfurt am Main: Suhrkamp, 1984.

Dickie, John. *Cosa Nostra. Die Geschichte der Mafia.* Frankfurt am Main: S. Fischer, 2007.
Diderot, Denis. *Œuvres esthétiques.* Edited by Paul Vernière. Paris: Éditions Garnier Frères, 1968.
———. *Œuvres romanesques.* Edited by Henri Bénac. Paris: Éditions Garnier Frères, 1962.
Dilthey, Wilhelm. *Gesammelte Schriften.* 26 vols. Göttingen: Vandenhoeck & Ruprecht, 1913–2005.
Dodds, E. R. *The Greeks and the Irrational.* Berkeley: University of California Press, 1962.
Doderer, Heimito von. *Die Dämonen.* 1956. Munich: Deutscher Taschenbuch Verlag, 1985.
Doi, Takeo. *The Anatomy of Self: The Individual versus Society.* Tokyo: Kodansha International, 1985.
Dreitzel, Hans Peter. *Die gesellschaftlichen Leiden und das Leiden an der Gesellschaft. Vorstudien zu einer Pathologie des Rollenverhaltens.* 2nd ed. Munich: Deutscher Taschenbuch Verlag, 1972.
Durrell, Lawrence. *Constance, or Solitary Practices.* London: Faber & Faber, 1982.
———. *Livia, or Buried Alive.* London: Faber & Faber, 1978.
———. *Monsieur, or The Prince of Darkness.* London: Faber & Faber, 1974.
Easthope, Antony. *Englishness and National Culture.* London: Routledge, 1999.
Eco, Umberto. *Nachschrift zum "Namen der Rose."* Munich: Carl Hanser, 1984.
Eibl-Eibesfeldt, Irenäus. *Und grün des Lebens goldner Baum. Erfahrungen eines Naturforschers.* Cologne: Kiepenheuer & Witsch, 1992.
Eliot, Thomas Stearns. *The Cocktail Party.* Edited by Nevill Coghill. London: Faber & Faber, 1974.
———. "The Love Song of J. Alfred Prufrock." In *Collected Poems 1909–1962*, 13–17. London: Faber & Faber, 1974.
Ellwein, Thomas. *Die deutsche Universität. Vom Mittelalter bis zur Gegenwart.* Wiesbaden: Fourier Verlag, 1997.
Enzensberger, Christian. *Literatur und Interesse. Eine politische Ästhetik mit zwei Beispielen aus der englischen Literatur.* 2 vols. Munich: Carl Hanser, 1977.
———. *Viktorianische Lyrik. Tennyson und Swinburne in der Geschichte der Entfremdung.* Munich: Carl Hanser, 1969.
Estermann, Alfred. *Arthur Schopenhauer. Szenen aus der Umgebung der Philosophie.* Frankfurt am Main: Insel, 2000.
Fabian, Bernhard, ed. *Die englische Literatur.* 2 vols. Munich: Deutscher Taschenbuch Verlag, 1991.
Fabian, Frank. *Geheimbünde in Geschichte und Gegenwart.* Suhl: Wirtschaftsverlag / Mittelstands-Akademie, 2016.
Feldenkrais, Moshé. *Bewußtheit und Bewegung. Der aufrechte Gang.* Frankfurt am Main: Suhrkamp, 1978.

———. *Das starke Selbst. Anleitung zur Spontaneität.* Frankfurt am Main: Insel, 1989.
———. *Die Entdeckung des Selbstverständlichen.* Frankfurt am Main: Suhrkamp, 1987.
Ferruolo, Stephen C. *The Origins of the University: The Schools of Paris and Their Critics, 1100–1215.* Stanford, CA: Stanford University Press, 1985.
Finkenstaedt, Thomas. *Kleine Geschichte der Anglistik in Deutschland. Eine Einführung.* Darmstadt: Wissenschaftliche Buchgesellschaft, 1983.
Fischer, Joachim. *Philosophische Anthropologie. Eine Denkrichtung des 20. Jahrhunderts.* Freiburg: Karl Alber, 2008.
Fitzgerald, F. Scott. *The Great Gatsby.* Free eBook at Planet Books.com, n.d.
Flasch, Kurt. *Aufklärung im Mittelalter? Die Verurteilung von 1277.* Mainz: Dieterich, 1989.
Flashar, Hellmut, ed. *Die Philosophie der Antike,* vol. 3: *Ältere Akademie—Aristoteles—Peripatos.* Basel: Schwabe, 1983.
Fruttero, Carlo, and Franco Lucentini. *Die Sonntagsfrau.* Munich: Goldmann, 1994.
Fussell, Paul. *Samuel Johnson and the Life of Writing.* London: Chatto & Windus, 1972.
Gadamer, Hans-Georg. *Truth and Method.* 1960. Translation rev. by Joel Weinsheimer and Donald G. Marshall. London: Bloomsbury, 2013.
Gadda, Carlo Emiliano. *Die gräßliche Bescherung in der Via Merulana.* Munich: Piper 1986. Translated as *That Awful Mess on the Via Merulana* by William Weaver. New York: NYRB Classics, 2007.
Gagarin, Michael, ed. *The Oxford Encyclopedia of Ancient Rome and Greece.* Oxford: Oxford University Press, 2010.
Gehlen, Arnold. "Genese der Modernität—Soziologie." In *Aspekte der Modernität,* edited by Hans Steffen, 31–46. Göttingen: Vandenhoeck & Ruprecht, 1965.
———. *Moral und Hypermoral. Eine pluralistische Ethik.* 3rd ed. Frankfurt am Main: Athenäum, 1973.
———. "Rückblick auf die Anthropologie Max Schelers." In *Gesamtausgabe,* vol. 4: *Philosophische Anthropologie und Handlungslehre,* edited by Karl-Siegbert Rehberg, 247–258. Frankfurt am Main: Vittorio Klostermann, 1983.
———. *Urmensch und Spätkultur. Philosophische Ergebnisse und Aussagen.* 3rd ed. Frankfurt am Main: Athenaion, 1975.
———. *Wirklicher und unwirklicher Geist.* In *Philosophische Schriften,* vol. 1, edited by Lothar Samson, 113–381. Frankfurt am Main: Vittorio Klostermann, 1931.
Gendolla, Peter, and K. Ludwig Pfeiffer. "Der gesellschaftliche Kommunikationsdruck und sein Anderes. Zur Spezialisierung des Erhabenen im zeitgenössischen 'Kriminalroman.'" In *Paradoxien, Dissonanzen, Zusammenbrüche. Situationen offener Epistemologie,* edited by Hans Ulrich Gumbrecht and K. Ludwig Pfeiffer, 292–315. Frankfurt am Main: Suhrkamp, 1991.

Giddens, Anthony. *The Consequences of Modernity*. Stanford, CA: Stanford University Press, 1990.
Goetsch, Paul. "Kriegsbotschaften amerikanischer Präsidenten seit F. D. Roosevelt." In *Die Rhetorik amerikanischer Präsidenten seit F. D. Roosevelt*, edited by Paul Goetsch and Gerd Hurm, 73–96. Tübingen: Narr Francke Attempto, 1993.
Goffman, Erving. *The Presentation of Self in Everyday Life*. Harmondsworth, UK: Penguin, 1990.
Goodman, Nelson. *Ways of Worldmaking*. Hassocks, UK: Harvester Press, 1978.
Gotthard Axel. *Das Alte Reich 1495–1806*. Darmstadt: Wissenschaftliche Buchgesellschaft, 2003.
Greene, Robert, and Joost Elfers. *Power: The 48 Laws*. London: Profile Books, 1998.
Gruber, Andreas. *Die Knochennadel*. Munich: Goldmann, 2020.
———. *Todesfrist*. 29th ed. Munich: Goldmann, 2015.
———. *Todesmal*. Munich: Goldmann, 2019.
———. *Todesmärchen*. 8th ed. Munich: Goldmann, 2016.
———. *Todesurteil*. 9th ed. Munich: Goldmann, 2014.
Gumbrecht, Hans Ulrich. *Crowds. Das Stadion als Ritual von Intensität*. Frankfurt am Main: Vittorio Klostermann, 2020.
———. *Production of Presence: What Meaning Cannot Convey*. Stanford, CA: Stanford University Press, 2003.
———. *"Prosa der Welt." Denis Diderot und die Peripherie der Aufklärung*. Berlin: Suhrkamp, 2020.
Gurewitsch, Aaron J. *Das Weltbild des mittelalterlichen Menschen*. Dresden: VEB Verlag der Kunst, 1978.
Habermas, Jürgen. *Legitimationsprobleme im Spätkapitalismus*. 3rd ed. Frankfurt am Main: Suhrkamp, 1975.
———. *Philosophisch-politische Profile*. Frankfurt am Main: Suhrkamp, 1987.
———. *The Structural Transformation of the Public Sphere: An Inquiry into a Category of Bourgeois Society*. Translated by Thomas Burger with the assistance of Frederick Lawrence. Cambridge, MA: MIT Press, 1991.
Haffmanns, Gerd, ed. *Über Arthur Schopenhauer*. Zurich: Diogenes, 1997.
Halsey, A. H. *Decline of Donnish Dominion: The British Academic Professions in the Twentieth Century*. Oxford: Clarendon Press, 1995.
Hartmann, Nicolai. *Das Problem des geistigen Seins. Untersuchungen zur Grundlegung der Geschichtsphilosophie und der Geisteswissenschaften*. 2nd ed. Berlin: Walter de Gruyter, 1949.
Hegel, G. W. F. *Aesthetics: Lectures on Fine Art*. Translated by T. M. Knox. 2 vols. Oxford: Clarendon Press, 1975.
———. *Ästhetik*. Edited by Friedrich Bassenge. Frankfurt am Main: Europäische Verlagsanstalt, n.d.
———. *Phänomenologie des Geistes*. Frankfurt am Main: Ullstein, 1979.

Heine, Heinrich. "Seegespenst." In *Werke*, edited by Paul Stapf, 1:258–260. Wiesbaden: R. Löwit, n.d.
Heinrich, Klaus. "Zur Geistlosigkeit der Universität heute." *Das Argument*, no. 173 (1989): 9–19.
Hobden, Fiona. *The Symposion in Ancient Greek Society and Thought*. Cambridge: Cambridge University Press, 2013.
Hobsbawm, E. J. *The Age of Revolution: Europe 1789–1848*. History of Civilization. London: Weidenfeld & Nicolson, 1962; repr. 1975.
Honneth, Axel. *Anerkennung. Eine europäische Ideengeschichte*. Berlin: Suhrkamp, 2018.
Hornblower, Simon, and Antony Spawforth, eds. *Oxford Classical Dictionary*. Oxford: Oxford University Press, 1996.
Huizinga, Johan. *Herbst des Mittelalters. Studien über Lebens- und Geistesformen des 14. und 15. Jahrhunderts in Frankreich und in den Niederlanden*. 11th ed. Stuttgart: Alfred Kröner Verlag, 1975.
Humboldt, Wilhelm von. "Über die Innere und äußere Organisation der höheren wissenschaftlichen Anstalten in Berlin" [On the internal and external organization of the higher scientific institutions in Berlin." In Müller, *Gelegentliche Gedanken über Universitäten*, 273–283.
Hume, David. *Enquiries concerning Human Understanding and concerning the Principles of Morals*. 3rd ed. Edited by P. H. Nidditch. Oxford: Clarendon Press, 1975.
———. *A Treatise of Human Nature*. 2nd ed. Edited by P. H. Nidditch. Oxford: Clarendon Press, 1978.
Huxley, Aldous. *Brave New World*. Harmondsworth, UK: Penguin Modern Classics, 1955.
———. *Brave New World Revisited*. New York: Harper & Row, 1958.
———. *The Devils of Loudun*. 2nd ed. New York: Carroll & Graf, 1996.
Iser, Wolfgang. *The Act of Reading: A Theory of Aesthetic Response*. Baltimore: Johns Hopkins University Press, 1980.
Jäger, Lorenz. *Hinter dem Großen Orient. Freimaurerei und Revolutionsbewegungen*. 3rd ed. Vienna: Karolinger, 2018.
Jaynes, Julian. *The Origin of Consciousness in the Breakdown of the Bicameral Mind*. 1976. Boston: Houghton Mifflin, 2000.
Jean Paul [Johann Paul Friedrich Richter]. *Die unsichtbare Loge*. 2 vols. In *Werke in zwölf Bänden*, ed. Norbert Miller. Munich: Carl Hanser, 1975.
———. "Jean Pauls Briefe und bevorstehender Lebenslauf." In *Werke in zwölf Bänden*, ed. Norbert Miller, vol. 8. Munich: Carl Hanser, 1975.
Johach, Helmut. "Tatsachen, Normen und Werte in Diltheys Theorie der Geistes- und Sozialwissenschaften." In *Dilthey als Wissenschaftsphilosoph*, edited by Christian Damböck and Hans Ulrich Lessing, 1–40. Freiburg: Karl Alber, 2016.
Kaube, Jürgen. *Hegels Welt*. Berlin: Rowohlt, 2020.

Kennedy, Paul. *The Rise and Fall of the Great Powers: Economic Change and Military Conflict from 1500 to 2000*. New York: Vintage Books, 1989.
Klußmann, Uwe, and Eva-Maria Schnurr, eds. *Die Macht der Geheimdienste. Agenten, Spione und Spitzel vom Mittelalter bis zum Cyberwar*. Munich: Deutsche Verlags-Anstalt, 2020.
Kluxen, Kurt. *Geschichte Englands. Von den Anfängen bis zur Gegenwart*. 2nd ed. Stuttgart: Alfred Kröner Verlag, 1976.
Konner, Melvin. *The Tangled Wing: Biological Constraints on the Human Spirit*. New York: Holt, Rinehart & Winston, 2002.
Koschorke, Albrecht. "Wissenschaftsbetrieb als Wissenschaftsvernichtung. Einführung in die Paradoxologie des deutschen Hochschulwesens." In *Universität ohne Zukunft?*, edited by Dorothee Kimmich and Alexander Thumfahrt, 142–157. Frankfurt am Main: Suhrkamp, 2004.
Köster, Anette. "Trink- und Mahlgemeinschaften im archaischen und klassischen Griechenland. Funktionen, Mechanismen, Kontexte." Doctoral diss., Freie Universität Berlin, 2011.
Krieger, Wolfgang. *Geschichte der Geheimdienste. Von den Pharaonen bis zur CIA*. Munich: C. H. Beck, 2009.
Lackey, Michael. *The Modernist God State: A Literary Study of the Nazis' Christian Reich*. New York: Continuum International, 2012.
Lämmert, Eberhard. "Das Studium der Humanwissenschaften im technischen Zeitalter." In *Geisteswissen. Vom wissenschaftspolitischen Problem zur problemorientierten Wissenschaft*, edited by Ernst Müller, K. Ludwig Pfeiffer, and Benno Wagner, 21–38. Frankfurt am Main: VAS, 1991.
Landsberg, Paul Ludwig. *Wesen und Bedeutung der Platonischen Akademie. Eine erkenntnissoziologische Untersuchung*. Bonn: Friedrich Cohen, 1923.
Larsson, Stieg. *Verblendung*. Munich: Wilhelm Heyne, 2006.
———. *Verdammnis*. Munich: Wilhelm Heyne, 2007.
———. *Vergebung*. Munich: Wilhelm Heyne, 2008.
Laslett, Peter. *The World We Have Lost: Further Explored*. 3rd ed. London: Routledge, 2015.
Lau, Thomas. *Teutschland. Eine Spurensuche 1500–1650*. Darmstadt: Wissenschaftliche Buchgesellschaft, 2010.
Lee, Hyunseon. *Geständniszwang und "Wahrheit des Charakters" in der Literatur der DDR. Diskursanalytische Fallstudien*. Stuttgart: J. B. Metzler, 2000.
Le Goff, Jacques. *Die Intellektuellen im Mittelalter*. Stuttgart: Klett-Cotta, 1986.
Leonhardt, Rudolf Walter. *77 mal England. Panorama einer Insel*. Munich: Piper, 1957.
Lessing, Doris. *Briefing for a Descent into Hell*. New York: Bantam Books, 1972.
Lipking, Lawrence. *Samuel Johnson: The Life of an Author*. Cambridge, MA: Harvard University Press, 1998.
Lippe, Rudolf zur. *Naturbeherrschung am Menschen*. 2nd ed. 2 vols. Frankfurt am Main: Syndikat, 1981.

Luhmann, Niklas. *Soziale Systeme. Grundriß einer allgemeinen Theorie*. Frankfurt am Main: Suhrkamp, 1984. Translated as *Social Systems* by John Bednarz with Dirk Baecker. Stanford, CA: Stanford University Press, 1995.
Lukács, Georg. *Ästhetik*. 4 vols. Neuwied: Luchterhand, 1972.
Lüderssen, Klaus. "Der Text ist klüger als der Autor. Kriminologische Bemerkungen zu Theodor Fontanes Erzählung *Unterm Birnbaum*." In *Produktive Spiegelungen. Recht und Kriminalität in der Literatur*, 197–220. Frankfurt am Main: Suhrkamp, 1991.
———."Literatur—gesteigerte Realität?" In *Produktive Spiegelungen. Recht und Kriminalität in der Literatur*, 11–15. Frankfurt am Main: Suhrkamp, 1991.
Mansfield, Katherine. "The Garden Party." In *50 Great Short Stories*, edited by Milton Crane, 1–13. Toronto: Bantam Books, 1952.
Mattenklott, Gert. "Geisteswissenschaften—eine parabolische Geselligkeit." *Merkur* 12 (1989): 1069–1081.
Mauthner, Fritz. *Beiträge zu einer Kritik der Sprache*. 1901–1902; 3rd ed. 1923. 3 vols. Frankfurt am Main: Ullstein, 1982.
Meyer, Kim. *Das konspirologische Denken. Zur gesellschaftlichen Dekonstruktion der Wirklichkeit*. Weilerswist: Velbrück Wissenschaft, 2018.
Mieth, Günter. *Literarische Kultur und gesellschaftliches Leben in Deutschland 1789–1806*. Berlin: Rütten & Loening, 1988.
Mills, C. Wright. *The Sociological Imagination*. Fortieth Anniversary Edition, with a new afterword by Todd Gitlin. New York: Oxford University Press, 2000.
Müller, Ernst, ed. *Gelegentliche Gedanken über Universitäten*. Leipzig: Reclam, 1990.
Müller-Doohm, Stefan. *Adorno. Eine Biographie*. Frankfurt am Main: Suhrkamp, 2003.
Münch, Richard. *Globale Dynamik, lokale Lebenswelten. Der schwierige Weg in die Weltgesellschaft*. Frankfurt am Main: Suhrkamp, 1997.
Murray, Oswyn. *The Symposion: Drinking Greek Style; Essays on Greek Pleasure 1983–2017*. Edited by Vanessa Cazzato. Oxford: Oxford University Press, 2018.
Nestle, Wilhelm. *Die Sokratiker*. Jena: Eugen Diederichs, 1923.
Nietzsche, Friedrich. *Nachgelassene Fragmente 1875–1879*. Vol. 8 of *Kritische Studienausgabe*, edited by Giorgio Colli and Mazzino Montinari. Berlin: Walter de Gruyter, 1988.
———. *Zur Genealogie der Moral*. In *Kritische Studienausgabe*, edited by Giorgio Colli and Mazzino Montinari, 5:245–412. Berlin: Walter de Gruyter, 1988.
Oswald, Hans, ed. *Macht und Recht. Festschrift für Heinrich Popitz zum 65; Geburtstag*. Opladen: Westdeutscher Verlag, 1990.
Peter, Jan, and Thomas Deubner. *Opus Dei. Das "Werk Gottes" zwischen Heiligkeit und Santa Mafia*. Berlin: Argon, 2008.

Pfeiffer, Helmut. "Le plaisir de la jouissance. Selbst- und Fremdreferenz des Genusses." In *Genuss bei Rousseau*, edited by Helmut Pfeiffer, Elisabeth Décultot, and Vanessa de Senarclens, 15–45. Würzburg: Königshausen & Neumann, 2014.
Pfeiffer, K. Ludwig. "Burke und die Implikationen des Vergnügens." In *Genuss bei Rousseau*, edited by Helmut Pfeiffer, Elisabeth Décultot, and Vanessa de Senarclens, 237–250. Würzburg: Königshausen & Neumann, 2014.
———. *From Chaos to Catastrophe? Texts and the Transitionality of the Mind.* Berlin: Walter de Gruyter, 2018.
———. "Mentalität und Medium. Detektivroman, Großstadt oder ein zweiter Weg in die Moderne." *Poetica* 20 (1988) 234–259; repr. in *Der Kriminalroman*, edited by Jochen Vogt, 357–377. Munich: Fink, 1998.
Plack, Arno. *Ohne Lüge leben. Zur Situation des Einzelnen in der Gesellschaft.* Munich: Deutsche Verlags-Anstalt, 1976.
Plessner, Helmuth. "Geistiges Sein. Über ein Buch Nicolai Hartmanns." In *Gesammelte Schriften*, edited by Günter Dux et al., vol. 9: *Schriften zur Philosophie*, 73–95. Frankfurt am Main: Suhrkamp, 1985.
———. *Grenzen der Gemeinschaft. Eine Kritik des sozialen Radikalismus.* 1924. In *Gesammelte Schriften*, edited by Günter Dux et al., vol. 5: *Staat, Kirche, Recht, Geschichte*, 7–133. Frankfurt am Main: Suhrkamp, 1980.
Plumb, J. H. *The Growth of Political Stability in England 1675–1725.* London: Macmillan, 1970.
Proust, Marcel. *À la recherche du temps perdu.* 3 vols. Edited by Pierre Clarac and André Ferré. Paris: Gallimard (Bibliothèque de la Pléiade), 1954.
Reckwitz, Andreas. *Die Gesellschaft der Singularitäten. Zum Strukturwandel der Moderne.* Berlin: Suhrkamp, 2017.
Reinalter, Helmut. "Die ersten politischen Geheimbünde im 19. Jahrhundert: Carbonari, Bund der Geächteten und Bund der Gerechten." In *Freimaurer und Geheimbünde*, 177–187.
———. "Einleitung." In *Freimaurer und Geheimbünde*, 9–20.
———. *Freimaurerei, Politik und Gesellschaft. Die Wirkungsgeschichte des diskreten Bundes.* Wien: Böhlau, 2018.
———, ed. *Freimaurer und Geheimbünde im 19. und 20. Jahrhundert in Mitteleuropa.* Innsbruck: StudienVerlag, 2016.
Riesman, David (with Nathan Glazer and Reuel Denney). *The Lonely Crowd: A Study of the Changing American Character.* Abr. and rev. ed., with an introduction by Richard Sennett. New Haven, CT: Yale University Press, 2020.
Roderick, Mark. *Post Mortem. Tränen aus Blut.* Frankfurt am Main: S. Fischer, 2016.
Rothacker, Erich. *Logik und Systematik der Geisteswissenschaften.* 1927. Munich: Oldenbourg, 1965.
Rusch, Gebhard, and Siegfried J. Schmidt. *Das Voraussetzungssystem Georg Trakls.* Braunschweig: Vieweg, 1983.

Safranski, Rüdiger. *Schopenhauer und die wilden Jahre der Philosophie. Eine Biographie.* 1987. Darmstadt: Wissenschaftliche Buchgesellschaft, 2010.
Saks, Michael J. *Jury Verdicts: The Role of Group Size and Social Decision Rule.* Lexington, MA: D. C. Heath, 1977.
Saviano, Roberto. *Gomorrha. Reise in das Reich der Camorra.* Translated by Friederike Hausmann and Rita Seuß. Munich: Deutscher Taschenbuch Verlag, 2019.
Sayers, Dorothy L. *Gaudy Night.* London: Hodder & Stoughton, 1970.
———. *The Unpleasantness at the Bellona Club.* London: Hodder & Stoughton, 1968.
Scheler, Max. *Schriften zur Anthropologie.* Edited by Martin Arndt. Stuttgart: Reclam, 1994.
———. *Von der Ganzheit des Menschen.* Edited by Martin S. Frings. Bonn: Bouvier, 1991.
Schelsky, Helmut. "Der Realitätsverlust der modernen Gesellschaft." 1954. In *Auf der Suche nach Wirklichkeit. Gesammelte Aufsätze zur Soziologie der Bundesrepublik.* Munich: Goldmann, 1979.
———. *Einsamkeit und Freiheit. Idee und Gestalt der deutschen Universität und ihrer Reformen.* Reinbek bei Hamburg: Rowohlt, 1963.
Schlaffer, Heinz. *Poesie und Wissen. Die Entstehung des ästhetischen Bewußtseins und der philologischen Erkenntnis.* Frankfurt am Main: Suhrkamp, 1990.
Schmidt, Johann N. "From the Restoration to Preromanticism." In Seeber, *Englische Literaturgeschichte*, 161–230.
Schmitt, Arbogast. *Modernity and Plato: Two Types of Rationality.* Rochester, NY: Camden House, 2012.
Schmitz, Hermann. *Die Ideenlehre des Aristoteles*, vol. 2: *Platon und Aristoteles.* Bonn: Bouvier, 1985.
Schoeck, Helmut. *Der Neid. Eine Theorie der Gesellschaft.* 2nd ed. Freiburg: Verlag Karl Alber, 1968. Translated as *Envy: A Theory of Social Behaviour* by Michael Glenny and Betty Ross. Indianapolis: Liberty Fund, 1987.
Schulte Beerbühl, Margrit. "Zwischen Selbstmord und Neuanfang. Das Schicksal von Bankrotteuren im London des 18. Jahrhunderts." In *Pleitiers und Bankrotteure. Geschichte des ökonomischen Scheiterns vom 18. bis zum 20. Jahrhundert*, edited by Ingo Köhler and Roman Rossfeld, 107–128. Frankfurt am Main: Campus, 2012.
Schulz-Buschhaus, Ulrich. *Formen und Ideologien des Kriminalromans. Ein gattungsgeschichtlicher Essay.* Frankfurt am Main: Athenaion, 1975.
———. "Gemeinplatz und Salonkonversation bei Marcel Proust." In *Das Aufsatzwerk*, 1–15. Permalink: http://gams.uni-graz.at/o:usb-06C-349, n.d.
Schunck, Ferdinand. *Joseph Conrad.* Darmstadt: Wissenschaftliche Buchgesellschaft, 1979.
Schwanitz, Dietrich. *Englische Kulturgeschichte.* 2 vols. Tübingen: A. Francke, 1995.

Schwindt, Jürgen Paul. *Thaumatographia oder Zur Kritik der philologischen Vernunft*. Heidelberg: Universitätsverlag Winter, 2016.
Seeber, Hans Ulrich, ed. *Englische Literaturgeschichte*. 5th ed. Stuttgart: J. B. Metzler, 2012.
Seel, Otto. *Die platonische Akademie. Eine Vorlesung und eine Auseinandersetzung*. Stuttgart: Ernst Klett, 1953.
Sennett, Richard. *The Fall of Public Man*. 1977. New York: W. W. Norton, 2017.
Serres, Michel. *Rome: The Book of Foundations*. Stanford, CA: Stanford University Press, 1991.
Shakespeare, William. *King Richard II*. Edited by Peter Ure. London: Methuen, 1966.
Silj, Alessandro. *Verbrechen, Politik, Demokratie in Italien*. Frankfurt am Main: Suhrkamp, 1998.
Simenon, Georges. *Simenon auf der Couch. Fünf Ärzte verhören den Autor sieben Stunden lang*. Zurich: Diogenes, 1985.
———. *Maigret à Vichy*. Paris: Presses de la cité, 1968.
———. *Maigret et la vieille dame*. Paris: Presses de la cité, 1951.
———. *Maigret et le clochard*. Paris: Presses de la cité, n.d.
Simmel, Georg. "Der Begriff und die Tragödie der Kultur." In *Philosophische Kultur*, 2nd ed., 223–253. Leipzig: Alfred Kröner, 1919.
———. *Grundfragen der Soziologie (Individuum und Gesellschaft)*. 1917. 3rd ed. Berlin: Walter de Gruyter, 1970.
———. *Soziologie. Untersuchungen über die Formen der Vergesellschaftung*. Berlin: Duncker & Humblot, 1908.
Simon, Dieter. "Zukunft und Selbstverständnis der Geisteswissenschaften." *Rechtshistorisches Journal* 8 (1990): 209–230.
Singer, Wolf. *Der Beobachter im Gehirn. Essays zur Hirnforschung*. Frankfurt am Main: Suhrkamp, 2002.
Sloterdijk, Peter. *Kritik der zynischen Vernunft*. 2 vols. Frankfurt am Main: Suhrkamp, 1983.
———. *Neue Zeilen und Tage. Notizen 2011–2013*. Berlin: Suhrkamp, 2018.
———. *Polyloquien*. Berlin: Suhrkamp, 2018.
———. *Selbstversuch. Ein Gespräch mit Carlos Oliveira*. Munich: Carl Hanser, 2000.
———. *Sphären. Plurale Sphärologie*, vol. 3: *Schäume*. Frankfurt am Main: Suhrkamp, 2004.
Snell, Bruno. *The Discovery of the Mind*. Translated by T. G. Rosenmeyer. Brooklyn, NY: Angelico Press, 2013. German original: *Die Entdeckung des Geistes. Studien zur Entstehung des europäischen Denkens bei den Griechen*. Hamburg: Claassen, 1946.
Sprandel, Rolf. *Gesellschaft und Literatur im Mittelalter*. Paderborn: Schöningh, 1982.
Stang, Richard. *The Theory of the Novel in England 1850–1870*. New York: Columbia University Press, 1959.

Stichweh, Rudolf. "Die moderne Universität in einer globalen Gesellschaft." In *Die Krise der Universitäten. Leviathan. Zeitschrift für Sozialwissenschaft*, edited by Erhard Stölting and Uwe Schimank, 346–358. Wiesbaden: Westdeutscher Verlag, 2001.
Summers, Anthony (with Robbyn Swan). *The Arrogance of Power: The Secret World of Richard Nixon*. London: Victor Gollancz, 2000.
Tenbruck, Friedrich. "Fragmente zur bürgerlichen Kultur." In *Die bürgerliche Kultur und ihre Avantgarden*, edited by Clemens Albrecht, 13–19. Würzburg: Ergon, 2004.
Tönnies, Ferdinand. *Studien zu Gemeinschaft und Gesellschaft*. Edited by Klaus Lichtblau. Wiesbaden: Springer Fachmedien, 2012.
Treiber, Hubert. "Partygänger, Premierenbesucher und andere kulturelle Wallfahrer bei der Arbeit—Zur Rekonstruktion von Wirklichkeit in und durch Klatschkolumnen." In *Macht und Recht. Festschrift für Heinrich Popitz zum 65. Geburtstag*, edited by Hans Oswald, 95–120. Opladen: Westdeutscher Verlag, 1990.
Trevelyan, George Macaulay. *Geschichte Englands*. 3rd ed. 2 vols. Munich: Leibniz Verlag, 1947.
Tuve, Rosamund. *Elizabethan and Metaphysical Imagery: Renaissance Poetic and Twentieth-Century Critics*. Chicago: University of Chicago Press, 1947.
Ungern-Sternberg, Antje von. "Politische Bankette zur Zeit des Direktoriums." In *Symbolische Politik und politische Zeichensysteme im Zeitalter der französischen Revolutionen (1789–1848)*, edited by Rolf Reichardt, Rüdiger Schmidt, and Hans-Ulrich Thamer, 131–154. Münster: Rhema, 2005.
Vaihinger, Hans. *Die Philosophie des Als Ob*. Leipzig: Felix Meiner, 1911.
Valéry, Paul. *Œuvres*. Edited by Jean Hytier. 2 vols. Paris: Gallimard (Bibliothèque de la Pléiade), 1957–1960.
Vieweg, Klaus. *Hegel. Der Philosoph der Freiheit. Biographie*. Munich: C. H. Beck, 2019.
Vogl, Joseph. *The Specter of Capital*. Stanford, CA: Stanford University Press, 2015.
Vössing, Konrad. *Mensa Regia. Das Bankett beim hellenistischen König und beim römischen Kaiser*. Berlin: Walter de Gruyter, 2004.
Wahl, Klaus. *Die Modernisierungsfalle. Gesellschaft, Selbstbewusstsein und Gewalt*. Frankfurt am Main: Suhrkamp, 1982.
Walton, Kendall L. *Mimesis as Make-Believe: On the Foundations of the Representational Arts*. Cambridge, MA: Harvard University Press, 1990.
Weber, Max. *Die protestantische Ethik und der Geist des Kapitalismus*, 1904/1905. In *Religion und Gesellschaft*, 11–183. Frankfurt am Main: Zweitausendeins, n.d.
———. *Wirtschaft und Gesellschaft. Grundriß der verstehenden Soziologie*. 5th, rev. ed. Edited by Johannes Winckelmann. Tübingen: Mohr, 1980.
Wecowski, Marek. *The Rise of the Greek Aristocratic Banquet*. Oxford: Oxford University Press, 2017.

Weimann, Robert. *"New Criticism" und die Entwicklung bürgerlicher Literaturwissenschaft*. 1962. 2nd ed. Munich: C. H. Beck, n.d.
Whig Club instituted in May, 1784, by John Bellamy. To be composed of gentlemen who solemnly pledge themselves to support the constitution of this country, according to the principles established at the Glorious Revolution. London: J. S. Barr, 1799.
Whitehead, Alfred North. *Science and the Modern World*. 1925. New York: Mentor Books, 1945.
Winnicott, Donald W. *Vom Spiel zur Kreativität*. 16th ed. Stuttgart: Klett-Cotta, 2020.
Wolff, Robert Paul. *In Defense of Anarchism*. New York: Harper & Row, 1970.
———. *The Poverty of Liberalism*. Boston: Beacon Press, 1969.
Wolff, Robert Paul, Barrington Moore Jr., and Herbert Marcuse. *Kritik der reinen Toleranz*. 7th ed. Frankfurt am Main: Suhrkamp, 1970.
Woolf, Virginia. *Mrs. Dalloway*. New York: Harcourt, Brace & World, 1925.
Wyss, Bernhard, ed. *Ausgewählte kleine Schriften von Peter von der Mühll*. Basel: Friedrich Reinhart Verlag, 1976.
Zeldin, Theodore. *France 1848–1945*, vol. 1: *Ambition, Love and Politics*. Oxford: Clarendon Press, 1973.
Zelle, Carsten. *Angenehmes Grauen. Literaturhistorische Beiträge zur Ästhetik des Schreckens im achtzehnten Jahrhundert*. Hamburg: Felix Meiner, 1985.

Index

academy, function of, 36
Ackroyd, Peter, 6–7
Adorno, Theodor W., 54, 242
aesthetic productivity, within detective novel, 163
Aesthetics (Hegel), 55
Agamben, Giorgio, 185
age of ideologies, 183–84
"Age of Johnson," 84–85
agora, 27
À la recherche du temps perdu (Proust), 96, 98–103
Albrecht, Clemens, 93–94
Allen, Woody, 19–20
Altenhofer, Norbert, 56, 57
American Character, The (Brogan), 140–41
American Impulse, 140–41
American Psycho (Ellis), 148–49
analysis, conspiracy theories and, 167
analytical-historical group of literature, 159
anarchism, 223
Animal Farm (Orwell), 222
anthropological-institutional trap, 230, 236–41
Anthropology from a Pragmatic Point of View (Kant), 235
Anton Reiser (Moritz), 239
archaism, 170
Archenholz, Johann Wilhelm von, 86
aristocracy: competition of, 96; conflict within, 42; cultural supremacy of, 103; education of, 44; within Parliament, 108; political power

decline of, 93; salons of, 99, 101; self-representation within, 44
Aristotle: within the academy, 37; arguments of, 37–38; influence of, 36, 52; *Nicomachean Ethics*, 38; philosophy of, 37; *Poetics*, 165; *Politica*, 38; *The Symposium*, 36; viewpoint of, 15, 27; virtue doctrine of, 185
Arnold, Matthew, 101, 200, 233
Art and the Industrial Revolution (Klingender), 95
Athenaios of Naucratis, 33
Athens, 27, 221–22
author, defined, 86
authoritarianism, 61
autopsy, within TV/literature, 164
avant-garde, 170

Babylon Berlin, 239
Bank of England, 88
bankruptcies, 80
banquets, 33, 116–17
Barbarians, 200
behavioral doctrines, 26, 80
Belloc, Hilaire, 211
Bellona Club, 112
Bernard of Clairvaux, 170
Bertschi, Stefan, 20
Bildung, 90
Blackstone, William, 81
blind spot of sociology, 20
blood feud, 42
bodies, within a crowd/as mystical, 159
body therapy theory, 14–15

Boltanski, Luc, 150, 153, 163, 164, 202–3, 211
Boorstin, Daniel J., 177
boredom, warding off, 94
Borst, Arno, 47–49, 233
Borst, Otto, 44
Boswell, James, 85
bourgeois, 96, 101, 118
Bracher, Karl Dietrich, 175, 176, 182
Brave New World (Huxley), 2, 231, 237
Brave New World Revisited (Huxley), 1
Briefing for a Descent into Hell (Lessing), 132
Briggs, Asa, 106–7
British Empire, 231
Broch, Hermann, 7, 159
Brockman, John, 12
Brogan, D. W., 140–41
Brothers Grimm jubilee, 165–66
Brown, Dan, 150, 178, 181
Bude, Heinz, 139
Bumke, Joachim, 43–44
Burckhardt, Jacob, 4, 11, 16, 25, 28, 33, 65, 221
Burke, Edmund, 85, 106, 185–86, 237
Burning Man, 6
Byatt, A. S., 123

Calvinism, 179
Cambridge University, 49, 62
Camorra (Naples and environs), 172, 174, 175
Canetti, Elias, 123–24
Cannadine, David, 232–33
capitalism, 24, 150
Carlsbad Decrees, 239
Carlyle, Thomas, 81
Catholic Church, 177
Chambers, Robert, 81
Charles I, 107
Charles II, 107

Chesterton, G. K., 211
Chile, 177–78
citizens, adaptation of, 79–80
civilized behavior, 202
Claessens, Dieter, 26, 31, 79
Clapton, Eric, 138–39
Clarendon Code, 11
Clarissa, or, The History of a Young Lady (Richardson), 83
Clark, Christopher, 121
class: disruptions within, 18; distinctions within, 11; elastic, 106; evolution within, 18–19; flexibility within, 132; within Germany, 239–40; human emotional costs within, 134; segregation dangers regarding, 200; structure challenges of, 133–34
Class in Britain (Cannadine), 232–33
clochards, symposium of, 206–12
Cocktail Party (Eliot), 135
coffeehouses, limitations of, 113–14
cognitive-conceptual dimension, 37
Coleridge, Samuel Taylor, 241
commitment, model of, 120
communication: forms of, 65; within parties, 122–23, 125, 139, 142, 150; principle of systems theory and, 162; types of, 139
communication theory, sociability and, 117–18
community: experience within, 35–36; forms of, 24; group size within, 32; limitations of, 67, 69; self-destruction of, 193–99; within society, 24–25
confession, 162–66, 167
Conrad, Joseph: background of, 184; *Heart of Darkness*, 183, 187–90; *Lord Jim*, 183, 184–87; *Nostromo*, 190–93; *The Secret Agent*, 193–95, 196; significance of, 183–84; tribal communities and, 184–85; value function and, 183; viewpoint of,

151; *Under Western Eyes*, 195–99; writing style of, 159
consciousness, transition of, 243
consequences of modernity, 2
conspicuous consumption, 43
conspiracy theories, 167
conversation, 94, 118
conviction, complexity and, 167
conviction, in Sparta, 221
Cornwell, Patricia, 204
corruption, 221
counterviolence, 175
couples, bonds within, 22
court administration, 43
court festivals, 43–44
court poet, 45
Covid-19 pandemic, 1–2, 120, 202
creativity, 15
crime, 174, 175, 228
criminology, 243
Crusades, 170
Cueni, Claude, 80
cultural loss, 118
cultural performance, within the symposium, 31
culture: carriers of, 233; defined, 150; of elastic negotiations, 240; literary, 82; literary transformation of, 239; modernity of, 140; of quarreling, 240; tragedy of, 65
Culture and Anarchy (Arnold), 200, 233
culture of surface, 184–93
cynicism, 182

Dag, Niklas Natt och, 213
Dahrendorf, Ralf, 140
the dandy, 120
Das Konkrete und das Abstrakte. (The concrete and the abstract [1980]) (Claessens), 79
Da Vinci Code, The (Brown), 150, 178, 181
debate, forms of, 159

deceptive continuities, 34–40
Defoe, Daniel, 88, 89
Deipnosophistae (Banquet of scholars), 33
DeMaria, Robert, 85
democracy, 29, 215–16
democratic institution, 1
Denney, Reuel, 141
department stores, 201
Descartes, René, 95, 96
detective novel: aesthetic productivity within, 163; banalization of reality within, 163–64; characteristics of, 153, 158, 164–65, 166; characters within, 163; imagination within, 206–12; Maigret within, 206–12; metaphysical dimension of, 164, 202–6; reader perspective regarding, 203–4; scientific methods within, 205; triviality within, 202–6. *See also specific titles*
dialogue, within salons, 97
Dickens, Charles, 7, 110–11
Dickie, John, 173
Dictionary of the English Language (Johnson), 85–86
Diderot, Denis: French salon culture and, 91–92; leadership of, 91; skepticism of, 86; viewpoint of, 93; writings of, 84, 90, 91; writings regarding, 92; writing style of, 93, 95
Dilthey, Wilhelm, 63, 64–65, 70–71
disanthropomorphizing effect of science, 204
Discours de la méthode (Descartes), 95
disembedding, 2
dissatisfaction, 69–70
Doderer, Heimito von, 58
dogma, 176–81
Doi, Takeo, 160, 161
domestic life, 56–57
Donne, John, 50
Doyle, Arthur Conan, 108, 201
Dreyfus affair, 96–97

Drieu la Rochelle, Pierre, 120
drive theory, 242
ducal salon, 100
Durrell, Lawrence, 171, 172
duty, 185, 186
dystopia, 2

Easthope, Antony, 108–9
Eco, Umberto, 153, 163–64, 202–3
efficiency of rule, pleasure and, 237
ego, 225
Eibl-Eibesfeldt, Irenäus, 32
Einstein, Carl, 182
elasticity, 176–81
elastic negotiation, culture of, 240
Eliot, T. S., 90, 124–28, 135, 165, 190
Elizabethans, humour metaphor of, 242
Elizabeth I, 158
Ellis, Bret Easton, 148–49
"Éloge de Richardson," 92
Emerson, Ralph Waldo, 63
emotions, novels and, 79
Encyclopédie, 91, 92
England: influencers within, 89; as motherland of modern democracy, 105; political system within, 88, 105–6, 107, 108; ritual within, 121; self-interpretation within, 121; social competition within, 107; sociological imagination within, 3
English class society, 106
English club: characteristics of, 111; communication within, 113–14; discretion within, 113; exclusiveness within, 116; introduction to, 105; limitations of, 200; member conduct for, 111–12, 114; reading culture within, 116; self-closure within, 112; sociability of, 116; solidarity within, 115
English disease, 231–32
Enlightenment, 193
enlightenment societies, 257n25

envy, sociability as, 138
Enzensberger, Christian, 110, 244
epistemology, 211–12
eroticism, 153–54
erotic motif, 46
erototope, 22
Escrivá, Josemaría, 177, 180
espionage, 158
Essay Concerning Human Understanding (Locke), 108–9
Essay on a Theory of Sociable Behavior (Schleiermacher), 82
Estermann, Alfred, 224
euphrosyne, 15
Europe, 162, 172, 240
exclusiveness, within English clubs, 116
experience, 79, 241

Fabian, Bernhard, 85, 110, 170
faculty, 50–51, 58, 62
Fall of Public Man, The (Sennett), 153
familial intimacy, 118, 119
family, as community of consumers, 119
fantasies, falling prey to, 70
fascism, 195–96
fascists, 120
Feldenkrais, Moshé, 14–15, 16
festivals, 47, 48
feuds, within aristocracy, 42
Feuerbach, Ludwig, 161, 226
Feu follet, Le (Drieu la Rochelle), 120
Fichte, J. G., 60
fiction, 82–83, 86, 173, 182, 204, 262n16. *See also* detective novel; novels; *specific works*
Fischer, Thomas, 12–13
Fitzgerald, F. Scott, 39–40, 142–47
Flashar, Hellmut, 37
Flexner, Abraham, 62
Fontenelle, Bernard Le Bovier de, 96
forensic medicine, 164
forger, 51

Foucault, Michel, 151–52
Fowles, John, 165
France, 89, 104, 116–17, 120
François I, 42
Freemasons, 167, 168, 169–70
French Revolution, 186
Freud, Sigmund, 161
friendship, forms of, 38
full human being, 233–36
Fussell, Paul, 81–82

Gadamer, Hans-Georg, 54
Gadda, Carlo Emilio, 164
Galsworthy, John, 196
gambling, 80
"The Garden Party" (Mansfield), 134
Garibaldi, Giuseppe, 173
Gaudy Night (Sayers), 50, 59
Gehlen, Arnold: *Der Mensch* (Man), 67; *Die Seele im technischen Zeitalter* (Man in the age of technology), 67; *Moral und Hypermoral* (Morality and hypermorality), 67; quote of, 65, 69, 70, 84, 140, 226, 236; *Urmensch und Spätkultur* (Early humans and late culture), 67, 71; viewpoint of, 18, 26, 51, 66, 68, 71, 72, 234–35, 236, 237, 244; writings of, 67, 97
Germany: class structure within, 239–40; community within, 25; concerns within, 3; egoism within, 121; Hitler dictatorship within, 175; literary culture and social life within, 238; *Minnesang* within, 45–46; university characteristics within, 50–51; World War I and, 234
Giddens, Anthony, 2
Gitlin, Todd, 2–3
Glazer, Nathan, 141
globalization, 62
Glorious Revolution, 107, 108
Goethe, Johann Wolfgang von, 238, 239

Goffman, Erving, 162
Goldsmith, Oliver, 85
Goodman, Nelson, 244
Great Britain, globalization within, 62
Great Gatsby, The (Fitzgerald), 39–40, 142–47
Greece, 18, 39
greed, 192
Grenzen der Gemeinschaft (Limits of community) (Plessner), 67
Grimm, Wilhelm, 166
group size, within society, 28–34
group writing, 87
Gruber, Andreas, 212, 219, 222–29, 244
Guermantes salon, 101
Gumbrecht, Hans Ulrich, 5, 159
Gurewitsch, Aaron J., 33

Habermas, Jürgen, 13–14, 88–89, 117, 119, 120, 201
hack writing, 81
Halsey, A. H., 62
Hamlet (Shakespeare), 127, 229
happiness, 11, 16, 17–18, 25, 65, 66, 246n1
Harley, Robert, 89
Hartmann, Nicolai, 54, 67, 68, 72–73, 74
Hawkins, John, 85
Heart of Darkness (Conrad), 183, 187–90
Hegel, Georg Wilhelm Friedrich, 55, 72–73, 90–91, 140, 212, 239
Heinrich, Klaus, 58
Hemingway, Ernest, 20
Hermeneutics and Criticism (Schleiermacher), 82
Hildesheimer, Wolfgang, 7, 96
historical reality, idealism and cynicism effects to, 182
history, repositioning within, 117
Hitler, Adolf, 175, 231
"Hollow Men, The" (Eliot), 190

Holmes, Sherlock, 205–6
Holy Roman Empire (Germany), 46–47
Honneth, Axel, 11
honorary degrees, 81
horror novel, 173, 204
Hoxie, Robert F., 4
Huizinga, Johan, 46, 47
human beings, 15, 237, 238
humanities: artistic-sociable behavior and, 57; challenges to, 70–71; hermeneutic foundation of, 65; knowledge within, 59; methodology and, 54; professionalism and, 58–59; rationality within, 54; science gap with, 53; sociability and, 55; spirit of, 63–75; vulnerabilities of, 63–64
human nature, ancient Greek models of, 16
Human Place in the Cosmos, The (Scheler), 234
Humboldt, Wilhelm von, 50, 60–61
Hume, David, 11, 80, 150, 185, 186, 237
Huxley, Aldous, 1, 2, 16, 231, 237

idealism, 182
ideological idealism, 182
ideologies, age of, 183–84
Iliad (Homer), 15
Illuminati, 168, 169–70
imagination, 206–12, 241, 242, 244
implicit anthropology, 232–33
individualism, 24, 57, 69
individualization, within novel writing, 87
Industrial Revolution, 89, 109, 140
inner world, sphere of, 236–41
institutions, 72, 75, 80
intellectual world, 57
intelligence, excess, 102
interactions, 18, 26, 61, 97, 125
interviews, forms of, 159
intimate sphere, polarization of, 117
intoxication, 16

Iser, Wolfgang, 7
isolation, 183–84, 190, 198
Italy, 121, 172–74

Jäger, Lorenz, 168
James II, 108
Jansenism, 95
Jaspers, Karl, 70, 203
"Jean Paul's Letters and Impending CV" (Paul), 86
Jefferson, Thomas, 1, 169
Jesuits, 95
Johns Hopkins University, 60
Johnson, Boris, 105
Johnson, Samuel: "Age of Johnson," 84–85; biographies of, 85; cultural position of, 85; *Dictionary of the English Language*, 85–86; influence of, 87, 88; Literary Club and, 85, 87; overview of, 81–82; *Rasselas*, 84; viewpoint of, 83, 93; writings of, 84, 90; writing style of, 91
Johnson, William, 1
Judeo-Christian religion, 183
juries, 79

Kant, Immanuel, 185, 235
Kaube, Jürgen, 58
Kettle, Arnold, 110
King Lear (Shakespeare), 43
Klingender, Francis D., 95
Kluxen, Kurt, 90, 108
Knigge, Adolph von, 170
knighthood, 41–42, 46–47
knowledge, 49
Konner, Melvin, 242
Krieger, Wolfgang, 157

La Fayette, Mme. de, 162
Lämmert, Eberhard, 58
Landsberg, Paul Ludwig, 25, 36
language, decomposing dynamics of, 243
Larsson, Stieg, 212–23

Law, John, 80–81
law and justice, 174, 216
leadership, variations of, 41
Lebensformen im Mittelalter (Forms of life in the Middle Ages) (Borst), 48–49, 233
Lee, Hyunseon, 162
legitimacy, state, 197–98
Le Goff, Jacques, 41, 52
Lessing, Doris, 132
Lethen, Helmut, 161
liberalism, 223
liberation effect, 239–40
Licensing Act, 88
Lichtenberg, G. C., 86
linguistic scarcity, 210
Lipking, Lawrence, 87, 90
Lippe, Rudolf zur, 238
Literarische Kultur und gesellschaftliches Leben in Deutschland 1789–1806, 238–39
Literary Club, 85, 87, 88
literary culture, development of, 82
literature: analytical-historical of, 159; for citizens, 80; defined, 85–86; impression of, 66; influence of, 7; knowledge of, 44; modern, reality concept within, 166; modernist group of, 159; purpose of, 44–45; role of, 109–10; as symposium, 230; symposium within, 241–44; unity methods of, 21. *See also specific works*
Livia (Durrell), 172
living common spirit, 74
Locke, John, 108–9
logic of existence, 218
Lonely Crowd, The (Riesman, Glazer, and Denney), 141
Lord Jim (Conrad), 183, 184–87
"Love Song of J. Alfred Prufrock, The" ("Prufrock") (Eliot), 124–28
Lüderssen, Klaus, 243
Luhmann, Niklas, 13, 17, 20, 125

Lukács, Georg, 91, 204
lying, 122
lyric poetry, 45–46

Macaulay, Thomas Babington, 106
Macht der Geheimdienste, Die (Schnurr and Klußman), 157–58
Macron, Emmanuel, 211
Mafia (Sicily), 172, 173, 174
Maggot, A (Fowles), 165
Magic Flute (Mozart), 169
Magna Carta Libertatum, 108
Maigret, Commissaire, 206–12
Maigret à Vichy (Simenon), 207
Maigret et la vieille dame (Simenon), 208
Maigret et le clochard (Simenon), 209, 210
Maigret et l'homme tout seul (Simenon), 208–9
Mann, Thomas, 7
Man of Property, The (Galsworthy), 196
Mansfield, Katherine, 134
Marcuse, Herbert, 223
Marquard, Odo, 241–42
masking, 161, 202
"Maurerische Trauermusik" (Mozart), 169
Mauthner, Fritz, 243
Mead, George Herbert, 3–4, 141
media, 17, 167
melancholy, 66
Menschenunkunde (ignorance of human beings), 86
Merchant of Venice, The (Shakespeare), 110
merchants, 170
metacommunication, 139
metaphorization, 242
metaphysics, within the detective novel, 202–6
metaphysics of banality, 164–65
metics, 27

Middle Ages: banquets within, 33; court festivals within, 43–44; sympotic culture within, 233; university role within, 41, 48–49, 51–52; vreude (pleasure) within, 44
Midnight in Paris, 19–20
Mills, C. Wright, 2–3, 96, 210, 242
Minnesang (Germany), 45–46
modernist group of literature, 159
modernity, 124
modernization, 151–52
modern society, 150
modern state, 222
modern systems theory, 147
monarchy, competitions regarding, 43
money, as passion, 153
monks, confession and, 162
Monsieur, or The Prince of Darkness (Durrell), 171
Monsieur Teste (Valéry), 224
Moore, Barrington, Jr., 223
moralistes, 95
Mori, Cesare, 174
Moritz, Karl Philipp, 239
Mormons, 177
Mozart, Wolfgang Amadeus, 169
Mrs. Dalloway (Woolf), 123, 129–33, 134–38
Münch, Richard, 13
murder, 112, 165, 228
Murray, Oswyn, 5–6, 23, 28, 32, 39, 245n1
music, 228
Musil, Robert, 7
mutual infiltration, of public and private domain, 117

nationalism, 121, 193
national society, 18
natural human being, 163
Nazis, 219–20
negotiation of reality, 176–81
neoteny, 67

nervous system, 242
networking, 170
Newton, Isaac, 96
Nicomachean Ethics (Aristotle), 38
Nietzsche, Friedrich, 36, 52, 161, 183
Nineteen Eighty-Four (Orwell), 237
Nixon, Richard M., 141
Nostromo (Conrad), 190–93
novels: behavioral models within, 80; challenges of, 81, 84; characteristics of, 83; emotions and, 79; length of, 83; opposition against, 82–83; suspicion regarding, 91; usefulness of, 83; viewpoints regarding, 86; writing process of, 87. *See also* detective novel; fiction; *specific works*

objective spirit, 73, 74–75
Odyssey (Homer), 15
Oliver Twist (Dickens), 110
Opéra Garnier (Paris), 201
operational realism, 159
Opus Dei, 176–81
Order of the Knights Templar, 170, 171, 172
Orwell, George, 110, 222, 237
Oxford and Cambridge Club, 115
Oxford Classical Dictionary, 38, 39
Oxford University, 49, 62
Oxford Women's College, 50, 51

painting, 55
Pamela, or, Virtue Rewarded (Richardson), 83
Parerga und Paralipomena (Schopenhauer), 227
Parliament, aristocracy within, 108
party: communication within, 122–23, 125, 139, 142, 150; development of, 141; establishment of, 122; *The Great Gatsby* (Fitzgerald) and, 142–47; interaction within, 125; within literary scene, 122–23; personal acquaintance within, 139;

postsympotic turn and, 138–54; as sociability form, 146–47; as US-American institution, 142
Party in the Blitz (Canetti), 123
Paul, Jean, 84, 86–87, 238–39
personality, characteristics of, 163
personal liberty and rights, 217
personal spirit, 73
perversions, 216
phantasms, 238
Philippe le Bel, 171
Philistines, 200
philology, 64
philosophes, 95
philosophical anthropology, 26, 63–75, 233–36
Philosophie des Als Ob, Die (Philosophy of "as if") (Vaihinger), 181
philosophy, 140, 244
Philosophy of As If (Vaihinger), 122
phonotope, 22
Plato: within the academy, 36; influence of, 51; *Politeia*, 38; Socrates contrasted to, 35; *The Symposium*, 37; as thought poet, 243; viewpoint of, 37
Platonic Academy, 35
Plato Papers, The (Ackroyd), 6–7
pleasure, 153, 237
Plessner, Helmuth, 26, 67, 68, 75, 161
Plumb, J. H., 107, 108, 115
poet, court, 45
Poetics (Aristotle), 165
poetry, 45–46. *See also specific works*
poets, defined, 86
Poland, 184
polarization, 117
polis, 27, 222
Politeia (Plato), 37, 38
Politica (Aristotle), 38
political will, 121
politics, 103, 104, 231–32
Pope, Alexander, 226
Populace, 200

Poverty of Liberalism, The (Wolff), 223
power: competition within, 43; demonstration of, 43; within festivals, 47; knowledge and, 49; within modern society, 150; within modern state, 222; Order of the Knights Templar and, 172; positions of, 180; securing, 152; signs symbolizing, 43; sociability and, 88, 133; within society, 28–34; techniques of, 43; through conflicts, 180; vacuum of, 175–76
power elite, 141
Presentation of Self in Everyday Life, The (Goffman), 162
Prieuré de Sion, 179
Princesse de Clèves (La Fayette), 162
principle of systems theory, 162
private domain, 117, 119
profession, as calling, 179
professionalism, 58–59, 62, 63
professionalization, 81, 93–94
propaganda, national, 120–21, 166
Propaganda Due (P2), 168
Protestant Ethic and the Spirit of Capitalism, The (Weber), 179
Proust, Marcel, 7, 96–104, 120
psychosomatic stress, 139
psychothriller genre, 204–5
public sphere, within private domain, 117
Puritans, 177

quarreling, culture of, 240

Rasselas (Johnson), 84
rationality, methodological generalization of, 53–54
reading, communicative value of, 82
Readings, Bill, 62
reality, 176–81, 182
Reckwitz, Andreas, 213
Reichs, Kathy, 204

Reichshofrat (Holy Roman Empire), 46–47
Reichskammergericht (Holy Roman Empire), 46–47
reinterpretation, 108–9
relatedness, 120
Republic of Hackers, 220–22, 223
Research Institute Social Cohesion, 12–13
Reynolds, Joshua, 85
Richard II (Shakespeare), 229, 242
Richardson, Samuel, 83, 92
Riesman, David, 141
ritualization, 5, 16, 180–81
rituals, of secret societies, 167–68
Robinson Crusoe (Defoe), 84
role relation, 190
Romains, Jules, 212
Romans, 38–39, 40
Rothacker, Erich, 55
"Round Tables of the Present," 12
Russia, 151, 195

Safranski, Rüdiger, 224
salons: aristocratic, 99, 101; bourgeois, 101; characteristics of, 98; competition within, 96; culture within, 94–95, 104; decline of, 117; dialogue within, 97; Diderot within, 91–92; ducal, 100; dynamics within, 94; extension of, 95; Guermantes, 101; hierarchy of, 102; interactions within, 97; limitations of, 113, 200; membership within, 94; nineteenth-century, 96–104; politics within, 103; Proust and, 96–104; role of, 93; sociability within, 93; status within, 98; success of, 100
satire, university, 51–52
Saviano, Roberto, 173
Sayers, Dorothy L., 50, 51, 59, 112, 133, 165, 203
Scheler, Max, 68, 69, 72, 227, 234–35
Schelsky, Helmut, 119, 241

Schiller, Friedrich, 118–19, 185
Schlaffer, Heinz, 64
Schleiermacher, Friedrich, 56–57, 58, 82
Schmidt, Siegfried J., 7
Schmitz, Hermann, 36
Schöffler, Herbert, 142
scholarly disciplines, 60
Schopenhauer, Arthur, 225, 226–27, 243
Schücking, L. L., 118
Schulz-Buschhaus, Ulrich, 97–98
Schwanitz, Dietrich, 105
science, 12, 53, 54, 60, 204
Secret Agent, The (Conrad), 193–95, 196
secrets, 161–62, 169
secret services, 158, 160
secret societies: analysis of, 167; attitude/intention of, 158; communal sympotic rituals of, 159–60; confession and, 157–66; formation of, 160–61; formulas, habits, and rituals within, 167; Freemasons as, 167, 168, 169–70; preprogramming of, 168–69; recruitment tactics of, 167; rituals within, 167–68; secret services *versus*, 158; strength of, 219; techniques of, 152; unity of, 160; violence and, 167–76; writings regarding, 160
Seel, Otto, 34–35, 39
self-closure, 112
self-destruction, of communities, 193–99
self-empowerment, 1
self-flagellation, 178
self-positioning, 162
self-presentation, 140–41
self-recruitment, 30
self-redemption, 227
self-referentiality, 153
self-representation, 47, 74
self-transcendence, 16

semantics, 150
senior common rooms, 63
Sennett, Richard, 113–14, 153, 201–2
service, as art, 57
sexuality, 153
Shakespeare, William: argument regarding, 118–19; characteristics of, 230; espionage and, 158; *Hamlet*, 127, 229; influence of, 106; *King Lear*, 43; *The Merchant of Venice*, 110; *Richard II*, 229, 242
Silj, Alessandro, 175
Simenon, Georges, 153, 206–12
Simmel, Georg, 4, 20–21, 24, 25, 90, 160, 167
sincerity, lying *versus*, 122
Sincerity and Authenticity (Trilling), 122
Singer, Wolf, 69
Sleepwalkers, The (Broch), 159
Sloterdijk, Peter, 22, 31–32, 68, 122
small talk, 139
Smith, Adam, 11
Snapchat, 6
Snow, C. P., 53
sociability: within Athenian symposium, 14; characteristics of, 227; communicative-interactive positioning within, 14–15; defined, 3; of the English club, 116; as envy, 138; group, 92; institutions of, 22–23; literary potential of, 21; modern elements of, 6; overview of, 19–23; particularity control within, 24; power and, 88, 133; practices within, 24; reinforcement of, 173; Simmel's viewpoint regarding, 160; social interests and, 133; socially relevant, erosion of, 82; social repercussion from, 5; society relationship with, 132–33; transition of, 240
sociable behavior, 56, 57
sociable solipsism, 230

social cohesion, 11–12
social differentiation, 11
social evolution, 18
social expansiveness, 85
social institutions, 72
social integration, 13
socialization, 21
social profit, 24
social reality, 201–2
social sphere, 117, 119
social systems, 17
social usefulness, 185
society: certainty of lifeforms within, 21; characteristics of, 21; cohesion within, 28, 185; community order within, 24–25; compensation for loss within, 150–51; discrepancies within, 18; group size within, 28–34; national, 18; overview of, 19–23; power within, 28–34; sociability relationship with, 132–33; state control of, 149; survival and, 230–32; system *versus*, 17
Society for the Humanities at Cornell University, 6
Sociological Imagination, The (Mills), 2–3
sociology, 140
sociopaths, 218
Socrates, 34–35
Sparta, 221
Speakers' Corner, Hyde Park, 113
special interests, solidarity from, 116
Specter of Capital, The (Vogl), 81
sphere of the inner world, 236–41
Spheres (Sloterdijk), 22
spies, 158
spirit, of the humanities, 63–75
spiritual-intellectual mutuality, 73
sports, ritualization within, 141
Sprandel, Rolf, 44, 45
spy novel, 163
state legitimacy, 197–98
states of being, 66

Structural Change of the Public Sphere
(Habermas), 201
suicide, 120
survival, society and, 230–32
Swann, Charles, 97
Sweden, 212–13, 222
symbolically generated media, 17
sympathy, 150
Symposion (Murray), 23
symposium: academy and, 36; accomplishments of, 3, 27; as aristocratic event, 29–30; challenges of, 219; characteristics of, 4–5, 13, 14, 221; communicative potential of, 28; cultural performance within, 31; deceptive continuities within, 34–40; experience within, 153; group size within, 31–34; happiness description of, 11, 16, 17–18, 246n1; implicit anthropology and, 232–33; inspirational range of, 201; institutional complex within, 25; intoxication viewpoint within, 16; introduction of, 69; literature as, 230; member characteristics within, 30; as paradigm, 23–28; reemergence of, 157; ritualization within, 16; rules within, 28, 200; simplicity within, 32–33; talk and interaction within, 15; term use of, 245n1; as transgressive feast, 30; unity within, 14
Symposium, The (Aristotle), 36
Symposium, The (Plato), 37
symposium literature, 31
symptomatology, 152
syssition, 30–31
system, society *versus*, 17
systems theory, 30

table talk, 33
Tacitus, 33
tact, 24
"taking the role of the other," 141

television, detective series on, 164, 166
Tenbruck, Friedrich, 79
That Awful Mess on the Via Merulana (Gadda), 164
theology, within European feudal society, 140
thought poets, 243
Thrales family, 85
Todesmärchen (Gruber), 228
Tönnies, Ferdinand, 24
torture, 162
tragedy, 165
Treiber, Hubert, 113
Trevelyan, G. M., 89
Trilling, Lionel, 122
triviality, within the detective novel, 202–6
troubadour poetry, 46
trust, role of, 221
Truth and Method (Gadamer), 54
Tuve, Rosamund, 242, 244
Two Treatises on Government (Locke), 109

Ulysses (Joyce), 83
Under Western Eyes (Conrad), 195–99
United States, behavioral norms within, 140
unity, 13, 14
universities: deficit within, 59–60; as form of life, 60–61; funding for, 60; growth of, 41; knighthood and, 41–42; knowledge production within, 49; as machines, 48–49; market solution focus of, 63; within the Middle Ages, 41; significance of, 41–42; state interference with, 61; teacher role within, 50
University in Ruins, The (Readings), 62
University of Paris, 51–52
university satire, 51–52
Unpleasantness at the Bellona Club, The (Sayers), 203

upper class, 133–34
urbanism, 118
uterotope, 22

vacuum of power, 175–76
Vaihinger, Hans, 122, 181
Valéry, Paul, 224, 229
value, 183, 184–93
Vanger, Henrik, 222
Veblen, Thorstein, 43
Veldeke, Heinrich von, 45
Verblendung (Larsson), 214–15
Verdammnis (Larsson), 215
Verhaltenslehren der Kälte (Behavioral doctrines of coldness) (Lethen), 161
Vieweg, Klaus, 61, 239
violence, secret societies and, 167–76
Virgin in the Garden (Byatt), 123
Vogl, Joseph, 81
Von der Ganzheit des Menschen (On the wholeness of human beings) (Scheler), 72
vreude (pleasure), 44

Wagner, Richard, 201
Walpole, Robert, 107
Walsingham, Francis, 158
war, 97
Watzlawick, Paul, 139

Weber, Max, 29, 32, 179
Wecowski, Marek, 29
Weimar Republic, 161, 239
Weishaupt, Johann Adam, 170
welfare state, 119, 166, 213, 214
Wesen des Christentums, Das (The essence of Christianity) (Feuerbach), 161
Whig Club, 114–15
White, W. H., 118
Whitehead, Alfred North, 53–54
Wilde, Oscar, 122, 186
Wilhelm Meister (Goethe), 238, 239
William of Orange, 107
Wimsey, Lord Peter, 112
Wolff, Robert Paul, 223
"Wonderful Tonight" (Clapton), 138–39
Woolf, Virginia, 123, 129–33, 134–38
wordplay, 157
workplace, competence within, 58–59
worldviews, development logic within, 13–14
World War I, 66–67, 135, 195, 234
writer, defined, 86

Xenocrates, 35

Zen Buddhism, 227

The authorized representative in the EU for product safety and compliance is:
Mare Nostrum Group
B.V Doelen 72
4831 GR Breda
The Netherlands

www.ingramcontent.com/pod-product-compliance
Lightning Source LLC
Chambersburg PA
CBHW021959220426
43663CB00007B/884